Positive Body Image Workbook

Positive Body Image Workbook

A Clinical and Self-Improvement Guide

Nichole Wood-Barcalow, PhD
Tracy Tylka, PhD
Casey Judge, PhD

CAMBRIDGE
UNIVERSITY PRESS

CAMBRIDGE
UNIVERSITY PRESS

University Printing House, Cambridge CB2 8BS, United Kingdom

One Liberty Plaza, 20th Floor, New York, NY 10006, USA

477 Williamstown Road, Port Melbourne, VIC 3207, Australia

314–321, 3rd Floor, Plot 3, Splendor Forum, Jasola District Centre,
New Delhi – 110025, India

79 Anson Road, #06–04/06, Singapore 079906

Cambridge University Press is part of the University of Cambridge.

It furthers the University's mission by disseminating knowledge in the
pursuit of education, learning, and research at the highest international
levels of excellence.

www.cambridge.org
Information on this title: www.cambridge.org/9781108731645
DOI: 10.1017/9781108758796

Cambridge University Press © 2021

First published 2021
Reprinted 2021

Printed in the United Kingdom by TJ Books Ltd, Padstow Cornwall

A catalogue record for this publication is available from the British Library.

ISBN 978-1-108-73164-5 Paperback

Contents

Foreword

For 33 years I taught abnormal psychology, introductory psychology, and an upper level seminar on eating disorders at a liberal arts college. Most of the students I taught were in the top 10% of their high school classes. Around 75% eventually went on to graduate school and/or professional training in fields such as psychology, medicine, law, the arts, or business.

Typically, the students were very bright, curious, and analytical. We had lively, sometimes boisterous discussions, often with personal examples, of a great many topics. These included language, symbolism, and Freudian psychosexual stages; the pleasures, hilarity, risks, and all too frequent tragedy of alcohol and other drug use; and people we have known—and, in some sad instances, grown up with—who had The Dark Triad of personality characteristics (Furnham, Richards, & Paulhus, 2013): narcissism, subclinical psychopathy, and Machiavellianism. Only one topic, from fall 1980 through spring 2012, unfailingly evoked uncomfortable silence. If your first thought is trauma, think and feel again.

Body image was and remains for most people simultaneously too personal, too interpersonal, and too complex. It is freighted with strong emotions, it is deeply rooted in our past while always lurking in the immediate future, and it is influenced by a network of powerful forces in our cultures. When "body image" became the focus of that social phenomenon we call a "college class," one could almost see and smell the self-consciousness and shame seep into the room, like foul-smelling smoke under a door.

I offer this observation neither as an experienced college professor nor as a body image expert. Standing or sitting with my students in class I experienced it, too. Every time. And right now in memory, as the adult form of a small, physically frail boy growing up in 1950s and 1960s southern California, with big ears, easily irritated skin, and curly hair and long eyelashes that girls envied, right above eyes that necessitated glasses at age 7 . . . a mere 2 years after I really began to need them. In the early 1960s, puberty and acne underway, I and my misery/shame/helplessness prevailed upon my thrifty middleclass parents to give money and time they could ill afford to securing for me what was then called "plastic surgery." At a hospital 50 miles away in Los Angeles the bones in my "hey, there's Dumbo!" ears were rearranged in order to set them back toward my head. This helped for a while, although I wonder how many of my peers noticed, really, when middle school resumed in the fall (see the epigram at the beginning of chapter 22). And a mere 2 years later the Beatles and their "mop top," ear-obscuring hair became an international sensation, and a sexiness ideal for White boys in middle and high school, including those of us with curly hair . . . .

Body image. Body dissatisfaction. Shame. Should. Ought. If only I looked like . . . . A few words, easily processed and elaborated in cool, conceptual form (e.g., actual-ideal disparity) while reading about and in some instances discussing these topics. But where to begin—as a person who wants to be healthier, as a grand/parent determined to resist imposing their past and the culture's stifling present on children, as a counselor or a coach or a physician who wants to be a positive influence—to understand the hot emotionally and morally charged layers of body image? The whole matter is complicated by the fact that the geography of body image reflects an unruly set of influences ranging from genetics, to teasing, to trauma, to gender/sexual identity, to advertising as it represents economic and political forces.

It's hardly sage advice for me to offer you Internet platitudes, such as "Stop. Breathe deeply. Step up, be mindful, and begin somewhere. Love yourself. Embrace health. Be the change you wish to see in the world . . ." But "Read and use the *Positive Body Image Workbook*" is not only sage advice, it is a compassionate, effective, and socially constructive move on my part. In fact, this is a book not only to be read, it calls us to engage with it mindfully, frequently, and in an intentionally recursive way. Whether you are a curious teenager, a frustrated 30-something dieter, or a pediatrician, this book is a unique and rich means of beginning to learn and practice the very skills necessary to improve our own body image, those of people we know and care about, and our societies in general. *And*, ultimately, the *Positive Body Image Workbook* will likely enable you to "love yourself" and "be mindful" and "embrace health" and "be the change you wish to see in the world."

With its focus on skills and learning as they apply to each person, this book is, in the words of Dr. T. Aaron Beck, founder of Cognitive Therapy, person-centered and problem-focused (Beck, Rush, Shaw, & Emery, 1979). In this regard, I call your attention to the chapter that covers one important aspect of positive body image: body acceptance. Chapter 6 of *Positive Body Image Workbook* exemplifies how this book helps each reader as an individual to understand, accept, and overcome without a wasteful, self-critical fight the neurotic dynamics of negative body image, that is, the self-defeating and self-perpetuating vacillation between dysphoria (shame, anxiety, guilt), avoidance, and rumination. The *Positive Body Image Workbook* directly, matter of factly, and compassionately helps the reader to identify nonjudgmentally and then address the many external and internal forces that threaten and sometimes overwhelm body acceptance. This book itself, infused with the wise voices of its authors, is a great foundation, in terms of modeling, advice, knowledge, and support, for beginning to build and participate in what the authors call a Community of Acceptance (see chapter 17).

The methodology of the *Positive Body Image Workbook* is grounded in a flexible form of therapy, teaching, and strategic encouragement that emerged nearly 100 years in the decidedly non-Freudian eclecticism of Alfred Adler (1929). Adler's approach to therapy, education, and indeed social change combined brief lectures, guided discussion, analogies, stories, homework assignments, humor, and careful, multifaceted analysis of cognitions we accept as painful, suffocating truths instead of the mis/guiding, malleable fictions they really are. And yet the *Positive Body Image Workbook* couldn't be more rooted in and guided by current research and evidence-based practices to reducing negative body image while developing a positive body image. I counted explanations, guidance, and exercises, from, in alphabetical order: Acceptance and Commitment Therapy (ACT), Behavior Therapy, Cognitive Therapy, Cognitive Behavior Therapy (CBT), Dialectical Behavior Therapy (DBT), Feminist Therapies, Health at Every Size® principles, Media Literacy, Mindfulness-Based Therapy, Motivational Interviewing, and Stress Inoculation Training. These are integrated by the book's systematic yet flexible approach to helping people make significant changes and by the wisdom of the authors, drawing on their vast experiences in research, clinical work, and self-reflection.

Another truly unique aspect of the *Positive Body Image Workbook* is its layered approach to self-assessment. This feature derives from the authors' expertise, and in some instances their leadership, in the science of tests and measurements for assessing facets of body image. The authors guide the reader in self-assessment—and thus a deeper understanding of important constructs—by making extensive use of valid questionnaires and opened-ended, semi-structured questions. At the simpler levels this connects with the reader's desire to understand multidimensional concepts more fully and how they apply to the self. Here there is guidance for scoring questionnaires and interpreting total scores. However, two truly distinctive features of the *Positive Body Image Workbook* constitute the more complex levels. One is inviting the reader to return to their responses to individual questionnaire items to explore those responses, as well as the productive potential inherent in alternative responses. This sets the stage for the transition to using such in depth self-assessment for goal-setting and for anticipation of both supports and obstacles.

Without either complicating or oversimplifying the task, the *Positive Body Image Workbook* provides, in clear steps, the perspective, the motivation, and the skills necessary for

healthy, sustainable changes toward body positivity within a fuller life. This book literally enables you to practice engaging, instead of avoiding, the dialectic between acceptance of the unchangeable *and* commitment to applying skills for what can be changed—*and* the proverbial wisdom to know the difference. This encouragement is particularly important for approaching one's body image, which may feel intractable. Tracy, Nichole, and Casey are authoritative—knowledgeable and nurturing—throughout this book. They also consistently serve as models for the courage to change. They know the task of transcending the past and the culture (not to mention the self) is daunting. They know there will be experiences of confusion, anxiety, and shame, and they know there will be setbacks. *And* in every chapter they are willing to be there—and for us to join them in the enterprise—with their healthy values and to stay present and mindful, and to take action, all in the presence of anxiety, doubt, and humility.

I was initially a bit reluctant to agree to write a foreword about a "workbook," even though I have known, admired, and drawn upon the work of Tracy and Nichole for over 15 years. After all, I am not a clinician, I was trained to be suspicious of anything that was not a peer-reviewed journal article, and, yes, I've spent too many painful hours either avoiding or ruminating about my own body image issues. *And* as an advocate for the prevention of negative body image and disordered eating, I believe in the prospect and the psychosocial significance of positive body image, *and* I need to practice being courageous. I found, to my delight, that in reading the *Positive Body Image Workbook* I had the privilege of learning much more about negative body image (e.g., self-objectification; chapter 13) and positive body image (e.g., protective filtering; chapter 17). I also had the "life-enhancing" (see chapter 21)—personally, professionally, politically—opportunity to discover in each of the 23 chapters four of the pillars holding up the foundation of positive psychosocial development, of which positive body image is so clearly a major dimension.

The first pillar is *compassion* for the complexity, confusion, and challenges evoked by "working" in any manner, including use of a workbook, on body image. The authors understand, at all levels, that body image is not "just" anything. Rather, it is a fascinating but bewildering network of beliefs, strong feelings, sensations, visual images, auditory echoes, and, to paraphrase Carl Jung (1965), "memories, dreams, and reflections." Moreover, all these important dimensions are embedded in transactions with how we behave and the contexts in which we live. Second, the authors, by virtue of their extensive years of research, clinical work, advocacy, and self-reflection, have the *skills* to provide us with the specific skills we personally need to (a) understand the positive and negative dimensions of body image, and then (b) gently *and* fiercely tackle the challenge of long-term change while embracing the process of discovering what positive body image means to us in the context of our own body agency.

Third, along with compassion, the authors infuse this workbook with the determination, reinforcement, humor, and patience necessary to help people learn through doing that change is a *practice*. This is the rare workbook that is well-researched by world-class experts and well-organized by scientists who are clear thinkers and effective writers. *And* these authors know that to use this workbook effectively, one has to do what one does while engaged in any process of meaningful change—go back and forth, across the chapters, across the exercises, across the years of one's life, across the skills, across the dialectic between acceptance and change. This leads to the final pillar, which is the importance of being guided by experts who are part of a *community* in which they themselves continue to develop personally, professionally, and politically in terms of the power to transform a world that all too often makes positive body image sound preposterous.

I am a psychologist who works in the body image and eating disorders fields. As noted, I am also an advocate for prevention of eating disorders and related conditions, including body dissatisfaction. *And* I am a 70-year-old husband and father whose body image issues stretch sideways and back beyond memory, but well into pain that can be all too fresh. This book has provided me with knowledge, inspiration, self-compassion, skills, and more, including the willingness to learn and practice embodying its important lessons.

– Michael P. Levine, Ph.D., FAED
Goleta, California, 9 March 2020

Adler, A. (1929). *The practice and theory of individual psychology* (Rev. ed.). London: Kegan Paul, Trech, Trubner & Co.

Beck, A. T., Rush, A. J., Shaw, B. F., & Emery, G. (1979). *Cognitive therapy of depression.* New York: Guilford Press.

Furnham, A., Richards, S. C., & Paulhus, D. L. (2013). The Dark Triad of personality: A 10 year review. *Social and Personality Psychology Compass, 7,* 199–216.

Jung, C. G. (1965). *Memories, dreams, reflections* (A. Jaffé, Ed.). New York: Vintage Books.

Acknowledgments

Thank you . . .

Cambridge University Press and the amazing editorial staff for believing in us and joining with us in this exciting collaboration.

Esteemed colleagues for contributing to the field of positive body image, encouraging us to engage in this endeavor, allowing the use of your intellectual property, and offering invaluable feedback to contribute to the success of this workbook.

Cherished clients for your wisdom, courage, trust, and vulnerability. May this workbook be in honor of your struggles and successes.

Dear families, friends, and mentors who walked with us each step of the way with unwavering support and love.

Chapter

1

Introduction to the *Positive Body Image Workbook*

Welcome to the *Positive Body Image Workbook*! In this chapter, we offer an overview of positive body image, introduce ourselves and our work, share what inspired us to write this workbook, and describe how you may use it in your clinical practice (for clinicians[1]) and everyday lives (for clients and readers[2]).

What is Positive Body Image?

This workbook focuses on increasing positive body image and reducing negative body image. Right now, you may be wondering, "Won't reducing negative body image automatically improve positive body image?" In some ways, yes – but not in all ways. Negative body image includes negative feelings and thoughts about our appearance. Positive body image is broader than simply "positive feelings and thoughts about our appearance." Positive body image includes appreciating our bodies in terms of how they function along with appearance. It means loving our bodies for their unique characteristics, which may change across time (e.g., "our scars are beautiful"). Holding a positive body image means that we perceive a wide range of appearances as beautiful, not just the bodies portrayed as attractive in social media, magazines, TV, movies, etc. Positive body image also includes how we "bounce back" from body image threats (or attacks on body image), such as negative comments made about our bodies. Positive body image can be expressed as taking care of our bodies (e.g., self-care), showing the world that we feel positively about and respect our bodies, and mentoring others to hold a positive body image as well. And, as you will see in this workbook, it is so much more.

Some people believe that it is unrealistic to have a positive body image. This skepticism is related to a narrow definition of positive body image: "loving every aspect of the body at all times" without experiencing discomfort or moments of negative body image. We agree that this outcome is unachievable when defined in this way, especially in cultures that value appearance ideals. Furthermore, we acknowledge that we all have moments in which our body image is not what we would like it to be. Our definition of positive body image, in contrast, includes loving and accepting our bodies regardless of appearance and functioning, showing compassion for differences and difficulties, and responding effectively when body image distress occurs. This definition is based on research studies (which we provide in this

workbook) as well as our clinical experience of witnessing clients transform from negative to positive body image.

Who We Are and Our Guiding Beliefs

We are three colleagues and friends who have collaborated on published studies related to body image, intuitive eating, and disordered eating, and have provided services (including psychotherapy and trainings) focused on promoting positive body image. We share similar values (integrity, collaboration, and quality research and clinical work) and a passion to help all those who want to move toward positive body image. We believe that *positive body image is attainable for any and all* who are willing to commit and invest in it.

We each have our Ph.D. in counseling psychology, a discipline that focuses on individual strengths to help build resilience when faced with challenges while also promoting meaningful and fulfilling lives [1]. We draw from positive psychology, the scientific study of human strengths that help people thrive and cultivate what is best within themselves [2]. Incorporating strength-based approaches into clinical treatment enhances outcomes beyond focusing solely on what is wrong [3]. Counseling psychologists honor multiple social identities (e.g., race, gender, class, age, weight, sexual orientation, gender identity, ability, etc.), explore how these social identities interact to shape experiences, and work to dismantle discrimination and stigmatization.

Our professional and personal identities shed light on the perspectives we bring to this workbook. We have had experiences with both privilege and disadvantage throughout our lives which shape our worldviews, and as a result, how we view body image work. We offer some of our guiding beliefs:

- Positive body image is unique from negative body image.
- Positive body image is attainable for all persons of varying social identities.
- It is important to focus on changing *internal experiences of body image* rather than external appearance. The problem with negative body image is not about the actual body itself but rather viewing oneself as deficient or unacceptable. As a result, we do not recommend weight loss goals for body image issues, given that weight and body mass index (BMI)

---

[1] We refer to all professionals who work with clients who have body image concerns as "clinicians" to honor the diversity of professionals in this area (e.g., psychologists, counselors, social workers, dietitians, nurses, psychiatrists, medical doctors, and more).
[2] Those engaged in therapy are referred to as "clients." The term "reader" is for anyone who is interested in using this workbook for self-improvement.

are rather poor indicators of health [4–5]. Instead, we promote self-acceptance and compassion.

- Biological issues and maladaptive behaviors (e.g., chronic dieting, self-induced vomiting, excessive exercise) need to be recognized and addressed in advance of body image work.
- Negative body image is, in part, a byproduct of societies that idealize appearance and that treat individuals differently based on weight and body size, with higher-weight individuals often experiencing weight stigma. We advocate to reduce weight stigma (as well as other types of stigma) at various levels (e.g., societal, individual).
- A weight-inclusive philosophy (supporting the well-being and health of people of all body sizes) is essential for moving toward positive body image.
- Clinicians benefit from exploring how their own body image issues impact themselves and the clients with whom they work.
- Self-care (e.g., consistent nourishment, life-enhancing movement) is the essence of moving toward positive body image and requires intentional effort and practice.

Inspiration, Vision, and Integration

The inspiration for this workbook emerged many years ago while Nichole contemplated how to share with fellow clinicians and clients alike her process of synthesizing research concepts about body image into clinical practice. The vision was to create a workbook solely focused on practical applications to promote positive body image that is grounded in research findings along with clinical insights.

We recognize that communication challenges exist between researchers and clinicians who specialize in positive body image. We believe that researchers benefit from the clinical expertise of clinicians specializing in this area and that clinicians benefit from integrating research findings into clinical practice. As both researchers and clinicians ourselves, we have created this workbook with the goal of increasing communication within the profession as well as making the information available to the general public. For this particular workbook, Tracy drafted the "Theory and Research" sections, and Nichole and Casey drafted the clinical tools ("Talking Points", "Treatment Goals and Objectives", "Applications", and "Assignments").

For the **researcher**: We integrate up-to-date research on positive body image topics from peer-reviewed journals and academic sources in the "Theory and Research" sections. We reference each original source for additional reading. We also offer valid and reliable assessments along with instructions on how to interpret them and apply them within a real-world context for each of the body image topics.

For the **clinician**: We review relevant information about components of positive body image in an easy-to-read format that you can then share with your clients. The "Treatment Planning" sections offer specific talking points that you can include in your sessions as well as goals/objectives that you can tailor for treatment plans.

We include assessments along with instructions and applications for your clients to use at different points of treatment to gauge and demonstrate progress (e.g., clients can witness first-hand their objective change, substantiate gains to third party payors). We intentionally incorporated elements of various treatment modalities so that this workbook would be interesting and applicable to clinicians with different theoretical orientations: Cognitive Behavioral Therapy [6], Dialectical Behavior Therapy [7], Acceptance and Commitment Therapy [8], Emotion-Focused Therapy [9], Compassion-Based Therapy [10], Interpersonal Therapy [11], Exposure Therapy [12], social justice [13], and Motivational Interviewing [14]. The assignments included in each chapter can be reviewed during sessions and/or offered as homework assignments to assist your clients in moving toward positive body image.

Of special note, we devote an entire chapter (Chapter 3 – "Clinician Preparation") focused on how to help clients move toward positive body image within your clinical work. We also offer specific considerations and assignments for you as the clinician to promote introspection into how your personal experiences intersect with that of your clients.

For the **client and general reader**: We offer factual information about positive body image that is based on research and clinical expertise. You can complete the assignments at your own pace based on your needs and interests.

Unique Features of Our Workbook

Our workbook offers these unique features in one source:

- *Accessibility*. An easy-to-use resource for clinicians, clients, and general readers who would like to know more about positive body image and/or wish to improve their body image.
- *Introspection*. Preparation chapters for clients/readers (Chapter 2) and clinicians (Chapter 3) to increase self-awareness. Both of these chapters offer common questions and answers on how to move toward positive body image. For clients/readers, the chapter addresses topics such as motivation, values, strengths, purpose, goals, and more. For clinicians, the chapter focuses on how to prepare both professionally and personally for this work. Assignments specially created for clinicians are included.
- *Education*. Nineteen chapters provide information on different components of positive body image such as embodiment, body appreciation, self-care, intuitive eating, social comparison, body talk, and more.
- *Intervention*. Treatment planning tools, including "Talking Points" along with treatment plan goals and objectives, are included in each chapter to promote effective clinical interventions.
- *Assessment*. Twenty-one reliable and valid assessments with guidelines for interpretation and applications accompany each body image topic.

Table 1.1 Workbook Overview

Section	Portion	Clinicians	Clients	Readers
I. Introductory chapter (Chapter 1) and preparation guides (Chapters 2–3)		Chapter 3: **Clinician Preparation** is specifically designed for the clinician providing interventions for clients/ group of clients with body image issues. This chapter offers suggestions on how clinicians can: (a) help clients move toward a positive body image, and (b) facilitate awareness of their own body image experiences which can impact client interventions. Commonly asked questions along with answers are included as well as specially created assignments to promote increased self-awareness in the clinician. It is recommended that the clinician **review this chapter before proceeding with the rest of the workbook**.	Chapter 2: **Client and Reader Preparation** is specifically designed for the client engaged in body image work with a clinician or for the interested reader who would like to learn about how to move toward positive body image. This chapter includes information on problem identification, how to prepare for body image work, core values, character strengths, purpose, goals, and committed action (and more!). Commonly asked questions along with answers are included as well as specially created assignments to promote increased self-awareness. It is recommended that the client/reader **review this chapter before moving on to other chapters**.	
II. The Journey Toward Positive Body Image (Chapters 4–22)	**Theory and Research**	Each content chapter includes an overview of a particular body image topic complete with up-to-date information from researchers and clinical experts from around the world in one source. A **definition** of the body image topic is offered along with theory and research on the topic. Clinicians can use these sections in various ways: (a) read to increase own knowledge, (b) offer as recommended readings to interested colleagues, (c) share highlights with clients during interventions, and/or (d) encourage clients to read on their own to discuss during future interventions. References are included at the end of chapter for the clinician who is interested in reading the original citations.	Each content chapter includes an overview of a topic of body image based on information from experts. Clients/readers can read the information as well as share with important others (family, friends, and partners) to increase understanding and sensitivity to body image issues. Clients in therapy can share relevant topics with their clinician.	
	Talking Points	Talking points can be used to **start a conversation** on specific body image topics during interventions with clients.	Clients can circle talking points to address during treatment interventions.	Readers can journal about relevant talking points.
	Goals and Objectives	Sample goals and objectives that we have used in the care of our own clients are offered for treatment plans. The goals and objectives reflect various theoretical orientations. Clinicians can work collaboratively with clients to select relevant goals and objectives based on individual needs and preferences.	Sample goals and objectives are offered related to change. Goals are desired outcomes that are broadly defined, while objectives are smaller achievable steps	The listed goals and objectives provide guidelines for the body image journey. Goals are desired outcomes that are broadly defined, while objectives are smaller achievable steps towards

Table 1.1 (cont.)

Section	Portion	Clinicians	Clients	Readers
			towards goals. Clients can check relevant goals and objectives to include in treatment.	goals. Readers can check relevant goals and objectives to work toward.
	Additional Resources	Books, workbooks, websites, and more are offered as additional resources to deepen understanding of the body image topics in areas that extend beyond the scope of this workbook.		
	Assessments	Most chapters include at least one assessment that corresponds with the theme of the body image topic that has been authorized for use by the original cited author(s). Some of the assessments were slightly modified to be inclusive of gender fluidity, improve clarity, and increase relevance for a range of client concerns. Interpretive scores are presented. Clinicians can use assessments in various clinical pursuits: (a) to determine client progress (beginning, middle, end of treatment), (b) to tailor treatment goals and objectives unique to the client, (c) to educate about different aspects and/or nuances of a topic, (d) to open dialogue about related topics, (e) to increase client self-awareness that can translate into change, (f) to sharpen treatment focus, (g) to inform homework assignments, and (h) to demonstrate objective response to treatment interventions. Integration of these assessments can be beneficial for those clinicians who are required to demonstrate a client's response to treatment to an **external entity** (e.g., accrediting body, third party payor). Clinicians can complete assessments for their own personal growth. If clinicians wish to use the assessments for research purposes, they will need to contact the original authors.	Most chapters include an assessment focused on a topic of positive body image. Clients and readers can complete the assessments at various points throughout the positive body image journey. Guides for how to interpret high, medium, and low scores are presented. Comparing the scores between timepoints is a useful way to determine progress.	
	Assessment Applications	All assessments include corresponding applications to facilitate self-awareness via thought-provoking comments and questions. Clinicians can use the applications: (a) to stimulate dialogue during interventions, (b) to identify future treatment interventions, and/or (c) to encourage clients to complete as take-home assignments. Clinicians can complete assessment applications for their own benefit.	All assessments include applications to guide and deepen reflection by way of thought-provoking comments and questions.	

Table 1.1 (cont.)

Section	Portion	Clinicians		Clients	Readers
	Assignments	The purpose of the assignments is to apply and extend information on the body image topics. Different formats are offered to be of interest to a wide range of individuals: open ended-questions, journal entries, thought experiments, behavioral experiments, and more. Clinicians can integrate assignments in the following ways: (a) serve as talking points during clinical interventions for education purposes, (b) complete during clinical interventions, and/or (c) assign as homework between interventions. Additionally, the same assignments can be completed at the beginning and end of treatment to assess change and progress. Clinicians can complete assignments for their own benefit.		The purpose of the assignments is to apply and deepen information on body image. Different formats are offered: open ended-questions, journal entries, thought experiments, behavioral experiments, and more. Clients/readers can **choose which ones to complete based on interest**, paying attention to themes that may emerge. The assignments **can be completed multiple times** to review change and progress. Also, clients/readers can share either the completed assignments or the themes from the assignments with important others (family, friends, partners). Additionally, clients/readers can invite important and trusted others to also complete the assignments with the goal to share ideas after.	
III. Continuing Our Journeys (Chapter 23)		This chapter serves as a wrap-up to the workbook. Intentional activities are offered along with encouragement to develop a plan to maintain them in daily life. Clinicians can reinforce the use of the activities with clients along with completion of the final assignment that highlights journey reflections. Clinicians can review this chapter for their own benefit.		This chapter serves as a wrap-up to the workbook. Intentional activities are offered along with encouragement to develop a plan to maintain positive body image gains and prevent setbacks. Clients/readers can review this chapter when needing a resource to get back on track toward positive body image.	

- *Application*. An array of assignments is offered with the purpose of applying and extending information on body image topics. Readers can choose based on interest.
- *Sustainability*. A final chapter is devoted to "intentional activities" to ensure that the progress achieved is thereby maintained.

How to Use This Workbook

Because the chapters are independent of each other, you can choose how to use this workbook: read it sequentially from beginning to end, pick chapters to read that are of particular interest, and/or any combination. We encourage clinicians to own a copy of the workbook to: (a) share general information about the different components of positive body image with clients during sessions, (b) make copies of chapters and assignments for clients to complete during the session or as homework, and (c) use for their own self-guided work on positive body image. We recommend that clients have their own copy of this workbook to serve as a useful companion to therapy.

In Table 1.1, we provide an overview of the various sections and components written from the perspective of the clinician, client in therapy, and general reader.

Applicability and Limitations

We are honored for the opportunity to create this workbook and intend for it to be applicable to a range of people by:

- Including scholarly works from reputable resources around the world.
- Ensuring that samples of people with various identities are recognized and highlighted.
- Using the term "they" throughout the workbook to acknowledge that anyone can experience body image concerns regardless of gender identity.
- Integrating currently acceptable language to describe groups of people, acknowledging that this language is rooted within a Westernized lens and may not appeal to all.

We also understand that the field of positive body image is relatively young, there is still much to be learned, and what is understood as relevant today will likely morph over time. As a result, we acknowledge the following limitations along with our efforts to address them.

- Some of the information in this workbook may be interpreted as complicated and dense. We have tried to present the information so that it is accessible for the general reader.

- We promote "body acceptance" throughout the workbook while acknowledging that this experience may not be fully relatable for all. For example, those who identify as transgender may choose various forms of transition in order to promote congruence with their gender expression(s) and ultimately body acceptance. We encourage future research endeavors to focus specifically on positive body image in transgender and gender nonconforming individuals in order to fully appreciate and honor these experiences.

- We mindfully refrained from integrating trauma-focused content in the workbook. This decision was based on the collective philosophy that trauma-focused issues are most appropriately addressed within a therapeutic context, in which the client's unique needs and experiences are honored. Trauma-focused therapy necessitates assessment by a trained clinician to determine the appropriate stage of trauma work and to offer a recommended treatment modality based on the client's unique trauma history and treatment goals. It is important to note that those with histories of trauma may experience additional concerns related to their bodies such as self-protection, intimacy, body awareness, body trust, and body control. We encourage clinicians and clients to tailor the treatment tools, assessments, applications, and assignments within this workbook as clinically indicated to best fit the experiences of the client. Additionally, we recommend discretion when selecting workbook interventions in order to promote the client's sense of personal choice, validation, and empowerment throughout this process.

Be the Change!

As mentioned in our guiding beliefs, we believe that change is necessary at numerous levels to lower the incidence of body image issues and to simultaneously promote positive body image. This workbook specifically targets change at the individual level by teaching skills to recognize and resist harmful body-related messages while also promoting self-acceptance. Individuals can then create a rippling effect of change by inspiring loved ones, friends, community members, and others to move toward positive body image. Ultimately this change can permeate at a societal level. For example, individuals who apply the skills from this workbook can get others involved by discussing the harms of weight stigma and the benefits of body acceptance, mentor others to have a positive body image, boycott companies that perpetuate weight stigma, and engage in social action in many other ways.

We envision a collective effort of challenging appearance ideals and combating weight stigma; a movement toward what really matters. We, the authors, commit to promoting body acceptance within society, and we hope to inspire you (clinicians, clients, and readers) to join us in this mission. We are excited that you are taking this step with us!

References

1. C. J. Gelso, E. N. Williams, and B. R. Fretz. *Counseling Psychology* (3rd ed.). Washington: American Psychological Association, 2014.

2. S. J. Lopez, J. T. Pedrotti, and C. R. Snyder. *Positive Psychology: The Scientific and Practical Exploration of Human Strengths* (4th ed.). Thousand Oaks: Sage, 2019.

3. M. E. P. Seligman, T. Rashid, and A. C. Parks. Positive psychotherapy. *Am Psychol* 2006; **61**: 774–88.

4. Y. Brooks, D. R. Black, D. C. Coster, et al. Body mass index and percentage of body fat as health indicators for young adults. *Am J Health Behav* 2007; **31**: 687–700.

5. K. M. Flegal, B. K. Kit, H. Orpana, et al. Association of all-cause mortality with overweight and obesity using standard body mass index categories: A systematic review and meta-analysis. *JAMA* 2013; **309**: 71–82.

6. J. S. Beck. *Cognitive Behavior Therapy: Basics and Beyond* (2nd ed.). New York: Guilford Press, 2011.

7. M. M. Linehan. *DBT Skills Training Manual* (2nd ed.). New York: Guilford Press, 2015.

8. S. C. Hayes, K. D. Strosahl, and K. G. Wilson. *Acceptance and Commitment Therapy: The Process and Practice of Mindful Change* (2nd ed.). New York: Guilford Press, 2012.

9. L. S. Greenberg. *Emotion-Focused Therapy: Coaching Clients to Work Through Their Feelings*. Washington: American Psychological Association, 2015.

10. P. Gilbert. *Compassion Focused Therapy: Distinctive Features*. London: Routledge, 2010.

11. M. M. Weissman, J. C. Markowitz, and G. L. Klerman. *The Guide to Interpersonal Psychotherapy: Updated and Expanded Edition*. New York: Oxford University Press, 2018.

12. J. S. Abramowitz, B. J. Deacon, and S. P. H. Whiteside. *Exposure Therapy for Anxiety: Principles and Practice* (2nd ed.). New York: Guilford Press, 2019.

13. E. Aldarando (Ed.). *Advancing Social Justice Through Clinical Practice*. New York: Routledge, 2007.

14. W. R. Miller and S. Rollnick. *Motivational Interviewing: Helping People Change* (3rd ed.). New York: Guilford Press, 2013.

Chapter 2

Client and Reader Preparation

Welcome!

So you've decided that you want to address your body image issues with the goal of moving toward positive body image – good for you! It's likely that you have had some concerns for a while and are now trying to figure out how to make positive changes. Maybe you've tried different strategies to improve body acceptance; some worked, some didn't. Whatever your journey has been to date, we welcome you to our approach on how to embrace positive body image.

Some quick information about how this workbook is structured.[1] Each content chapter (Chapters 4–22) includes the following sections:

- *"Theory and Research" – information from experts about a body image topic;*
- *"Treatment Planning" ("Talking Points", "Goals", "Objectives") – suggestions on topics to discuss with others; sample goals and objectives for your journey;*
- *"Additional Resources" – recommendations for additional information;*
- *"Assessments" with "Applications" – assessments related to body image that you can complete along with questions for reflection;*
- *"Assignments" – different types of activities to apply and deepen information on body image. You can choose which ones to complete and which ones to share with important others (e.g., family, friends, partners).*

In this chapter, we offer frequently asked questions and answers about positive body image. We encourage you to read this chapter and complete the corresponding assignments before moving on to the following chapters. These assignments will serve as a foundation for your work toward positive body image and remind you of your reasons for this work.

So let's get started! Remember to be persistent, patient, and compassionate with yourself during this process.

Warmly,
Nichole, Tracy, and Casey

What is the problem with my body image? It is helpful to identify the specific problem(s) related to your body image. Take a moment to clearly define the current problem(s) in one sentence:

_____

_____

What can I do to prepare myself for body image work? Body image work requires time and effort along with consistent practice. Additionally, it involves approaching uncomfortable emotions and thoughts along with behavioral changes. Remember that you have a choice; you can choose to do nothing, keep doing things in the same way, or do things differently. Simply wishing or thinking about things will not result in change. There are pros and cons associated with working on these issues versus not working on them at different points in your life. Complete Assignment 2.1 "Pros/Cons of Working on Body Image Issues" to identify costs and benefits of changing versus keeping things the same.

Even after you have decided that you want to make changes, it can be challenging because motivation naturally waxes and wanes. Some days you might feel inspired and other days you might wonder whether the work is worth it. It's normal to feel stuck and overwhelmed. During those times, it can be helpful to refer back to your original reason(s) for wanting to make change. Complete Assignment 2.2 "Preparing for Positive Body Image Work" which focuses on the reason(s) why you want to make change, desired outcomes, what coping skills you can use during this process, and sources of support.

Upon responding to these questions, if you notice that your ultimate focus is *to change your body* (e.g., lose weight, cosmetic surgery), then this workbook might not best fit your goals. If you notice that your ultimate focus is *to change your mindset about your body*, then this workbook will help you on your journey.

What has impacted my current body image? Before any change toward positive body image can take place, it's important to determine what your body image is currently like and the life experiences that have shaped it. Many factors influence body image over time, such as comments from family members, exposure to messages in media, body-related changes with age, and more. These experiences can be interpreted as negative, neutral, or positive and correspond with different emotions, thoughts, stories, and behaviors. Assignment 2.3 "Body Image across Lifespan" offers suggestions on how to create a visual representation of your unique body image experiences over time and how they impact your current functioning. As you review these experiences, you'll notice:

- the emotions that can range from sadness, shame, anger, and embarrassment to pride, satisfaction, and joy;
- the thoughts and stories you believe(d) about yourself then and now related to these experiences;

---

[1] A detailed description of the workbook can be found in Table 1.1: "Workbook Overview" in Chapter 1.

s from trying to change your body, avoiding table experiences, altering your appearance, trying tivities, and promoting positive change in others;

w body investment (how much time or focus you spend on your body) and body evaluation (how you judge your body) change at different points;

- how specific feedback and comments from others such as family members, friends, partners, medical professionals, coaches, teachers, mentors, community leaders, acquaintances, and even strangers impact your experience with your body.

What is important to me? As part of this journey, it is important to consider your core values which serve as guideposts in life. Values offer a point of focus and direction for moving out of a stuck place [1]. Examples of core values include justice, equality, freedom, love, compassion, service, intellect, success, respect, appreciation of beauty, humor, artistic expression, achievement, and financial security. Core values can change throughout life depending on circumstances and experiences. Complete Assignment 2.4 "Core Values" to identify your top five core values and examine the degree to which behaviors in your life are currently aligned with your core values.

As unique individuals, we all have different combinations of character strengths [2]. Examples of these character strengths include bravery, teamwork, forgiveness, curiosity, zest, and perseverance. Check out the VIA Institute on Character to learn more about character strengths and to complete a free online scientific survey to determine your top strengths. Consider how your "Character Strengths" (Assignment 2.5) relate to your body image.

Values and character strengths correspond with our sense of purpose. Purpose is our reason for moving forward when times are difficult. It is what energizes and inspires us to create change for ourselves and sometimes others. Reflect on your unique "Purpose in Life" in Assignment 2.6 with special consideration of how it relates to moving toward positive body image.

What are my body image goals? It is important to identify goals related to positive body image as they lead us in a desired direction towards our values. Goals can range from short-term to long-term. Try to be specific about what you want versus what you don't want. Imagine having achieved your goal(s), including associated emotions, thoughts, and behaviors. Complete Assignment 2.7 "Body Image Goals".

What if my goal is to change my body including lose weight? Research shows that weight loss is not effective long-term; most people gain back the weight they lost and more [3]. Examine your various intentions or reasons for wanting to lose weight. Examples might include not liking your current shape/size/weight, wanting to fit into certain types/size of clothing, being instructed by your medical provider to do so for health reasons, receiving negative appearance-based feedback from a partner, or believing that weight loss will increase your positive body image or overall quality of life. Upon identifying the reasons, it is helpful to consider whether internalized weight bias (judging ourselves or others negatively based on weight) is part of these reasons. Research shows that weight stigma actually reinforces negative body image [4]. It is helpful to shift the focus from weight loss to challenging internalized weight bias. Chapter 5 explains weight stigma and internalized weight bias in depth.

Moving toward positive body image is about internal acceptance versus changing external appearance. Our approach focuses on treating the mind and body with respect, such as getting consistent nourishment, engaging in life-enhancing movement, and fostering self-acceptance. The body will respond in whatever ways it needs to.

What will it take to change my body image from negative to positive? Simply wishing or hoping for things to change will likely not result in that outcome. Committed action, or the process of making small steps toward change [5], is necessary. Keeping your values, character strengths, and purpose in mind is part of committed action. Each small step should be in the direction of your values. When engaging in committed action remember to choose behaviors that aren't too easy and not too challenging; choose those that are just right. Take small steps that are challenging but not impossible, in order to build a sense of accomplishment and to motivate for additional action. Complete Assignment 2.8 "Committed Action toward Positive Body Image".

It is helpful to recognize how engaging in certain behaviors prevents you from moving toward positive body image. Examples of such behaviors include excessive body checking or weighing, dieting, purging (e.g., self-induced vomiting, use of laxatives or diet pills to control weight), excessive exercise, self-injurious behaviors, consistent substance use, and more. Complete Assignment 2.9 "Behaviors that Move Me Toward or Away from Positive Body Image". This assignment can help you identify what behaviors move you further from or closer to positive body image (e.g., eating when hungry, stopping when full, being around others who accept your body, engaging in life-enhancing movement), and make specific goals to increase these behaviors.

Additionally, respecting and protecting your body from potential threats and harm corresponds with moving toward positive body image [6]. Examples of these protective behaviors can be asserting your needs, using sunblock, taking medications as needed, and getting vaccines. Review "Protection of the Body" (Assignment 2.10) to identify ways that you are currently caring for your body and to learn additional ideas of how to do so.

Your **mental perspective** also impacts the transition from negative to positive body image. If you notice that your thoughts are negative or pessimistic, try to be open to new ways of viewing yourself and your body without judgment. Practice replacing negative thoughts with positive thoughts. Complete Assignments 2.11 "Practicing Body Acceptance" and 2.12 "Self-Affirmations".

What challenges might get in the way of moving toward positive body image? It is helpful to identify and anticipate barriers associated with change so that you can problem solve in advance. Complete Assignment 2.13 "Barriers and

Solutions" to know how you would like to respond if and when various challenges come your way.

How can I track my realizations as I progress through this work? It is helpful to identify one or more key points you would like to take from each chapter (Chapters 4–22) using Assignment 2.14 "My 'Take-Home' Realizations". You can also record your overall realizations as you move toward positive body image.

How will I know once I've achieved positive body image? Realize that you're always moving toward positive body image but it might not ever be "finalized" because the body and mind are constantly changing. Your specific definition of positive body image might change or evolve over time based on different factors in your life, and that's okay.

Having identified your core values, character strengths, sense of purpose, goals, and willingness to participate in committed action, you're ready to begin your journey!

Assignment 2.1: Pros/Cons of Working on Body Image Issues

Brainstorm pros and cons for both working on body image issues and not working on body image issues at this point in your life.

	Pros	Cons
Working on body image issues		
Not working on body image issues		

Realizations about working on body image issues:

_____

_____

_____

Realizations about *not* working on body image issues:

_____

_____

_____

N. L. Wood-Barcalow, T. L. Tylka, and C. L. Judge. *Positive Body Image Workbook: A Clinical and Self-Improvement Guide.* Cambridge: Cambridge University Press, 2021.

Assignment 2.2: Preparing for Positive Body Image Work

Reflect on the questions below as you begin the process of moving toward positive body image. Your answers to these questions can serve as motivation when you experience challenging times in the future.

- What's the *purpose* for moving toward positive body image at this time in my life?

  _____

  _____

- How much of this is driven by *my* wants/needs? By the wants/needs of *others* (e.g., partner, family, friends)?

  _____

  _____

- Is moving toward positive body image *necessary* at this time? Is it *possible*?

  _____

  _____

- What change(s) do I want to make?

  _____

  _____

- What outcome(s) do I want?

  _____

  _____

- How can I tolerate the uncomfortable thoughts and emotions that might come up while moving toward positive body image?

  _____

  _____

- Do I have the *resources* I need in order to make change(s)?

  _____

  _____

- What *coping skills* can I use during challenging times?

  _____

  _____

- Who can I rely on for support and encouragement?

  _____

  _____

- I will remind myself of the following when I need inspiration:

  _____

  _____

N. L. Wood-Barcalow, T. L. Tylka, and C. L. Judge. *Positive Body Image Workbook: A Clinical and Self-Improvement Guide.* Cambridge: Cambridge University Press, 2021.

Assignment 2.3: Body Image across Lifespan

Create a body image timeline across your life that includes important body image experiences that you view as positive, negative, and neutral. This timeline is a representation of both the things that contribute to and maintain your unique body image. It's important that while completing this assignment you recognize the events without becoming consumed by them.

Be creative with the timeline, using whatever materials you prefer. For example, you can use a pen to make a timeline on paper, create a collage with different images, review important photographs at different times in your life, create artistic pieces, and more.

Explore this timeline and journal about the following:

- What patterns do I notice?
  _____
  _____
  _____

- What factors contribute(d) to my **body investment** (how much time or focus is spent on the body)? Examples might include puberty, body changes, influence of others, life experiences, the aging process, loss of functioning, and more.
  _____
  _____
  _____

- What factors contribute(d) to my **body evaluation** (how the body is judged)? Examples might include puberty, body changes, influence of others, life experiences, the aging process, loss of functioning, and more.
  _____
  _____
  _____

Negative Experiences

- What **emotions** correspond with these experiences?
  _____
  _____
  _____

- What **thoughts** correspond with these experiences?
  _____
  _____
  _____

- What **stories** do I tell myself now about these experiences?
  _____
  _____
  _____

- How do negative experiences impact my current functioning?
  _____
  _____
  _____

N. L. Wood-Barcalow, T. L. Tylka, and C. L. Judge. *Positive Body Image Workbook: A Clinical and Self-Improvement Guide.* Cambridge: Cambridge University Press, 2021.

Positive Experiences

- What **emotions** correspond with these experiences?

_____
_____
_____

- What **thoughts** correspond with these experiences?

_____
_____
_____

- What **stories** do I tell myself now about these experiences?

_____
_____
_____

- How do positive experiences impact my current functioning?

_____
_____
_____

Neutral Experiences

- What **emotions** correspond with these experiences?

_____
_____
_____

- What **thoughts** correspond with these experiences?

_____
_____
_____

- What **stories** do I tell myself now about these experiences?

_____
_____
_____

- How do neutral experiences impact my current functioning?

_____
_____
_____

Overall Reflections

- Does thinking about *past events* impact my ability to move toward positive body image?

_____
_____
_____

- Does thinking about *future events* impact my ability to move toward positive body image?

_____
_____
_____

N. L. Wood-Barcalow, T. L. Tylka, and C. L. Judge. *Positive Body Image Workbook: A Clinical and Self-Improvement Guide.* Cambridge: Cambridge University Press, 2021.

- Do I feel comfortable sharing this timeline with a trusted individual(s)?
  - If not, what are the reasons:

  _____
  _____

  - If so, who and for what reasons:

  _____
  _____

- My overall reflections:

  _____
  _____
  _____

N. L. Wood-Barcalow, T. L. Tylka, and C. L. Judge. *Positive Body Image Workbook: A Clinical and Self-Improvement Guide.* Cambridge: Cambridge University Press, 2021.

Assignment 2.4: Core Values

What values are important in how I live my life? Examples of values include justice, equality, compassion, love, freedom, service, intellect, success, respect, appreciation of beauty, humor, artistic expression, achievement, financial security, and more. You can do a search for core values on the Internet and select the top five that are most important to you at this time. Also, *The Good Project*[2] has an online value-sort activity to assist you in determining top values.

The top five core values that are important to me are:

1. _____
2. _____
3. _____
4. _____
5. _____

Do my values correspond with *how I think and feel* about my body?

_____
_____
_____

Do I *treat my body* in ways that correspond with my values?

_____
_____
_____

I want to make these changes in order to practice my values:

_____
_____
_____

I commit to making this change in the *next week*:

_____
_____
_____

I commit to making this change in the *next month*:

_____
_____
_____

I commit to making this change in the *next year*:

_____
_____
_____

N. L. Wood-Barcalow, T. L. Tylka, and C. L. Judge. *Positive Body Image Workbook: A Clinical and Self-Improvement Guide.* Cambridge: Cambridge University Press, 2021.

[2] www.thegoodproject.org/value-sort

Assignment 2.5: Character Strengths

Examples of character strengths include bravery, teamwork, forgiveness, curiosity, zest, and perseverance. Check out the VIA Institute on Character[3] website to complete a free online scientific survey (i.e., the VIA Survey of Character[4]) to determine your top strengths.

My top character strengths are:

1. _____
2. _____
3. _____
4. _____
5. _____

What *similarities* are there between my character strengths and my body image?

_____
_____
_____

What *differences* are there between my character strengths and my body image?

_____
_____
_____

How can I rely on my character strengths when I'm feeling overwhelmed with body image work?

_____
_____
_____

How can I *enhance my current strengths* as I work toward improving my positive body image?

_____
_____
_____

How can I *enhance other personality traits* that are not my strengths as I work toward positive body image?

_____
_____
_____

How can I turn my focus to my character strengths when I am thinking about perceived limitations or weaknesses about my body?

_____
_____
_____

Overall reflections on character strengths and body image:

_____
_____
_____

N. L. Wood-Barcalow, T. L. Tylka, and C. L. Judge. *Positive Body Image Workbook: A Clinical and Self-Improvement Guide.* Cambridge: Cambridge University Press, 2021.

---

[3] www.viacharacter.org/

[4] www.viacharacter.org/survey/account/register. For a list of the twenty-four character strengths, see www.viacharacter.org/character-strengths.

Assignment 2.6: Purpose in Life

Often our lives become busy with everyday tasks and activities, resulting in a lack of awareness of our sense of purpose in life. Having a sense of purpose can help guide decision-making, create a sense of fulfillment and enhance the quality of life. For this journal activity, consider the following: How would I describe my purpose in life? How am I moving toward my purpose? What barriers get in the way? Has my purpose changed over time? What values correspond with my purpose? What character strengths correspond with my purpose? Am I engaging in activities/pursuits that fulfill my purpose? Do body image issues interfere with my ability to pursue my purpose? How will moving toward positive body image impact my sense of purpose?

N. L. Wood-Barcalow, T. L. Tylka, and C. L. Judge. *Positive Body Image Workbook: A Clinical and Self-Improvement Guide.* Cambridge: Cambridge University Press, 2021.

Assignment 2.7: Body Image Goals

It is important to identify goals in order to move toward having a positive body image. Goals help point us in a desired direction that is consistent with our values. Respond to the following questions and identify one to three goals associated with moving toward positive body image.

- How I describe my *current body image*:

  _____
  _____
  _____

- My *problem(s)* related to body image is/are:

  _____
  _____
  _____

- What do I *want*?

  _____
  _____
  _____

- What do I want to *change*?

  _____
  _____
  _____

- What do I want to *keep the same*?

  _____
  _____
  _____

- What do I imagine positive body image to be like? How would I *think differently*? How would I *experience emotions differently*?

  _____
  _____
  _____

- How close am I to the current outcome I desire?

  _____
  _____
  _____

- My goals for positive body image:
  1. _____
  2. _____
  3. _____

N. L. Wood-Barcalow, T. L. Tylka, and C. L. Judge. *Positive Body Image Workbook: A Clinical and Self-Improvement Guide.* Cambridge: Cambridge University Press, 2021.

Assignment 2.8: Committed Action toward Positive Body Image

For further information see [7].

What have I done *to make improvements to my body image so far?*

_____

_____

What has *worked?*

_____

_____

What hasn't worked?

_____

_____

Thoughts about my *willingness to put in the effort* needed to make change(s):

_____

_____

These are my *core values* that motivate me toward committed action:

_____

_____

My current sense of purpose:

_____

_____

I commit to the following:

_____

_____

_____

_____

_____

_____

N. L. Wood-Barcalow, T. L. Tylka, and C. L. Judge. *Positive Body Image Workbook: A Clinical and Self-Improvement Guide.* Cambridge: Cambridge University Press, 2021.

Assignment 2.9: Behaviors that Move Me Toward or Away from Positive Body Image

You will learn how some behaviors move you closer toward a positive body image and how other behaviors move you further from it. Listed below are examples of different types of behaviors that can correspond with body image. First, indicate whether the behavior applies to you by circling either yes or no. Second, make a mark on the continuum where each behavior exists from moving toward positive body image (e.g., acceptance, appreciation, gratitude) versus moving away from it (e.g., distress, sense of obligation, worries). Record reflections including how these behaviors impact your progress toward positive body image. An example is provided. Additionally, it may be helpful to return to this assignment upon completing Chapters 4–22 to determine whether any of your responses have changed.

Example:

Dieting: (Yes) or No

|—————————————————————————————X——————————————————————————————————|
Away   Positive Body Image   Toward

Reflections: *I diet in order to feel better about myself. I want to lose weight so that I can look better and feel better. I notice that when I'm dieting, I say mean things to myself and am grouchy with others.*

Dieting: Yes or No

|——|
Away   Positive Body Image   Toward

Reflections:

_____

_____

Eating when hungry, stopping when full: Yes or No

|——|
Away   Positive Body Image   Toward

Reflections:

_____

_____

Being around others who accept my body: Yes or No

|——|
Away   Positive Body Image   Toward

Reflections:

_____

_____

Excessive body checking (including weighing): Yes or No

|——|
Away   Positive Body Image   Toward

Reflections:

_____

_____

Over exercise: Yes or No

|——|
Away   Positive Body Image   Toward

Reflections:

_____

_____

N. L. Wood-Barcalow, T. L. Tylka, and C. L. Judge. *Positive Body Image Workbook: A Clinical and Self-Improvement Guide.* Cambridge: Cambridge University Press, 2021.

Engaging in movement that I enjoy: Yes or No

|--|

Away　　　　　　　　　　　　　*Positive Body Image*　　　　　　　　　　　Toward

Reflections:

_____

_____

Focusing on weight loss: Yes or No

|--|

Away　　　　　　　　　　　　　*Positive Body Image*　　　　　　　　　　　Toward

Reflections:

_____

_____

Negative self-talk and body talk: Yes or No

|--|

Away　　　　　　　　　　　　　*Positive Body Image*　　　　　　　　　　　Toward

Reflections:

_____

_____

Compassionate self-talk and body talk: Yes or No

|--|

Away　　　　　　　　　　　　　*Positive Body Image*　　　　　　　　　　　Toward

Reflections:

_____

_____

Avoidance of pleasurable activities: Yes or No

|--|

Away　　　　　　　　　　　　　*Positive Body Image*　　　　　　　　　　　Toward

Reflections:

_____

_____

Purging (self-induced vomiting, use of laxatives or diet pills): Yes or No

|--|

Away　　　　　　　　　　　　　*Positive Body Image*　　　　　　　　　　　Toward

Reflections:

_____

_____

Hydrating regularly: Yes or No

|--|

Away　　　　　　　　　　　　　*Positive Body Image*　　　　　　　　　　　Toward

Reflections:

_____

_____

Self-injurious behaviors: Yes or No

|---|

Away   *Positive Body Image*   Toward

Reflections:

_____

_____

Expressing gratitude toward my body: Yes or No

|---|

Away   *Positive Body Image*   Toward

Reflections:

_____

_____

Consistent substance use: Yes or No

|---|

Away   *Positive Body Image*   Toward

Reflections:

_____

_____

I commit to **reducing or eliminating** these behaviors:

- _____
- _____
- _____
- _____
- _____
- _____

I commit to **increasing or enhancing** these behaviors:

- _____
- _____
- _____
- _____
- _____
- _____

N. L. Wood-Barcalow, T. L. Tylka, and C. L. Judge. *Positive Body Image Workbook: A Clinical and Self-Improvement Guide.* Cambridge: Cambridge University Press, 2021.

Assignment 2.10: Protection of the Body

Below is a list of ways to protect the body. Review the items and consider which ones are relevant by rating each item on a scale from 0 (not at all) to 10 (very). Write reflections about how the issue corresponds with protecting your body, and create an action plan with any changes to make. An example is provided.

Issue	Level of relevance: 0 = *not at all* to 10 = *very*	Reflections	Action plan for change(s)
Example: *Preventative health behaviors (e.g., breast/prostate exams)*	5	*I know it's important to do these things, but I don't have the time. I probably should do it considering my family history of cancer.*	*I'll set a reminder in my calendar to do this.*
Asserting my needs			
Setting comfortable boundaries and limits			
Preventative health behaviors (e.g., breast/ prostate exams)			
Saying "no" when I don't have time or don't want to do something			
Testing for sexually transmitted infection/ disease			
Getting vaccines			
Engagement in consensual experiences			
Communicating desires			
Sense of safety (physical, psychological)			
Use of contraception			
Engagement in physical movement			
Eating enough to support my activity			
Taking medications/ supplements			
Behaviors to prevent unintended pregnancy			
Refraining from excessive substance use			
Use of sunblock			
Other:			
Other:			
Other:			

N. L. Wood-Barcalow, T. L. Tylka, and C. L. Judge. *Positive Body Image Workbook: A Clinical and Self-Improvement Guide.* Cambridge: Cambridge University Press, 2021.

Assignment 2.11: Practicing Body Acceptance

These are *unique characteristics* of my body:

_____
_____
_____
_____

These are the *unique physical contributions from my family members and ancestors*:

_____
_____
_____
_____

My body has been *resilient and faced these challenges*:

_____
_____
_____
_____

I commit to saying the following body acceptance comments on a daily basis (examples: "I accept my body as it is," "I appreciate that my body can function in these ways"):

_____
_____
_____
_____

N. L. Wood-Barcalow, T. L. Tylka, and C. L. Judge. *Positive Body Image Workbook: A Clinical and Self-Improvement Guide.* Cambridge: Cambridge University Press, 2021.

Assignment 2.12: Self-Affirmations

Self-affirmations are positive statements that we say to ourselves to promote self-esteem and confidence. They are effective when they are specific, individualized, genuine, and practiced on a consistent basis. In the space below, write as many self-affirmations as possible. Make sure that they are actual statements that you are willing to say to yourself as a way to counter negative body image thoughts. Examples could include, "I am capable," "I can do hard things," and "I can handle what comes my way."

_____
_____
_____
_____
_____
_____
_____
_____

N. L. Wood-Barcalow, T. L. Tylka, and C. L. Judge. *Positive Body Image Workbook: A Clinical and Self-Improvement Guide.* Cambridge: Cambridge University Press, 2021.

Assignment 2.13: Barriers and Solutions

Check the boxes for possible barriers that might impact your journey toward positive body image. For those that apply, identify potential solutions to these barriers. Review this assignment at different points in your work to determine what challenges exist and how you can overcome them.

❏ Fatigue, getting tired of trying:

_____

_____

❏ Uncomfortable emotions – fear, anxiety, shame, disgust, embarrassment, despair, being overwhelmed:

_____

_____

❏ Negative beliefs – "I can't do this," "things will never change," "things have never worked in the past, why would they now?":

_____

_____

❏ Focusing on past failures:

_____

_____

❏ Focusing on future worries:

_____

_____

❏ Desire to avoid uncomfortable experiences:

_____

_____

❏ Lack of support from others:

_____

_____

❏ High expectations from self and others:

_____

_____

❏ Life events/circumstances that come up:

_____

_____

❏ Time to devote to this work:

_____

_____

❏ Pressure from others to lose weight or change my body:

_____

_____

N. L. Wood-Barcalow, T. L. Tylka, and C. L. Judge. *Positive Body Image Workbook: A Clinical and Self-Improvement Guide.* Cambridge: Cambridge University Press, 2021.

❑ Other:

_____

_____

❑ Other:

_____

_____

❑ Other:

_____

_____

N. L. Wood-Barcalow, T. L. Tylka, and C. L. Judge. *Positive Body Image Workbook: A Clinical and Self-Improvement Guide.* Cambridge: Cambridge University Press, 2021.

Assignment 2.14: My "Take-Home" Realizations

Identify one or more key themes you would like to "take" or remember from Chapters 4–22 and your overall realizations as you move toward positive body image.

Chapter 4: "Appearance Ideals and Media Literacy"

_____
_____
_____
_____

Chapter 5: "Weight Stigma versus Weight Inclusivity"

_____
_____
_____
_____

Chapter 6: "Body Acceptance by Others"

_____
_____
_____
_____

Chapter 7: "Defining Beauty and Cultural Pride"

_____
_____
_____
_____

Chapter 8: "Self-Compassion and Body Image Flexibility"

_____
_____
_____
_____

Chapter 9: "Approaching Our Bodies"

_____
_____
_____
_____

Chapter 10: "Body Appreciation"

_____
_____
_____
_____

N. L. Wood-Barcalow, T. L. Tylka, and C. L. Judge. _Positive Body Image Workbook: A Clinical and Self-Improvement Guide._ Cambridge: Cambridge University Press, 2021.

Chapter 11: "Functionality Appreciation"

_____
_____
_____
_____

Chapter 12: "Embodiment"

_____
_____
_____
_____

Chapter 13: "Objectification and Self-Objectification"

_____
_____
_____
_____

Chapter 14: "Sexual Intimacy"

_____
_____
_____
_____

Chapter 15: "Social Comparison"

_____
_____
_____
_____

Chapter 16: "Body Talk"

_____
_____
_____
_____

Chapter 17: "Protective Filtering"

_____
_____
_____
_____

Chapter 18: "Rippling Effect: Mentorship"

_____
_____
_____
_____

N. L. Wood-Barcalow, T. L. Tylka, and C. L. Judge. _Positive Body Image Workbook: A Clinical and Self-Improvement Guide._ **29** Cambridge: Cambridge University Press, 2021.

Chapter 19: "Self-Care"

_____
_____
_____
_____

Chapter 20: "Fueling Our Bodies"

_____
_____
_____
_____

Chapter 21: "Life-Enhancing Movement"

_____
_____
_____
_____

Chapter 22: "Adaptive Appearance Investment and Quality of Life"

_____
_____
_____
_____

Overall realizations:

_____
_____
_____
_____
_____
_____

N. L. Wood-Barcalow, T. L. Tylka, and C. L. Judge. _Positive Body Image Workbook: A Clinical and Self-Improvement Guide._ Cambridge: Cambridge University Press, 2021.

References

1. S. C. Hayes, K. D. Strosahl, and K. G. Wilson. *Acceptance and Commitment Therapy: The Process and Practice of Mindful Change* (2nd ed.). New York: Guilford Press, 2012.

2. VIA Institute on Character. *The VIA Character Strengths Survey: Your Greatest Strengths Lie Within*. Retrieved from www.viacharacter.org/account/register

3. A. G. Dulloo and J.-P. Montani. Pathways from dieting to weight regain, to obesity and to the metabolic syndrome: An overview. *Obes Rev* 2015; **16**: 1–6.

4. L. R. Vartanian and J. G. Shaprow. Effects of weight stigma on exercise motivation and behavior: A preliminary investigation among college-aged females. *J Health Psychol* 2008; **13**: 131–8.

5. S. C. Hayes, K. D. Strosahl, and K. G. Wilson. *Acceptance and Commitment Therapy: The Process and Practice of Mindful Change* (2nd ed.). New York: Guilford Press, 2012.

6. N. L. Wood-Barcalow, T. L. Tylka, and C. L. Augustus-Horvath. "But I like my body": Positive body image characteristics and a holistic model for young-adult women. *Body Image* 2010; 7: 106–16.

7. S. C. Hayes, K. D. Strosahl, and K. G. Wilson. *Acceptance and Commitment Therapy: The Process and Practice of Mindful Change* (2nd ed.). New York: Guilford Press, 2012.

Chapter 3

Clinician Preparation

We have been asked by clinicians over the years how to best help individuals with body image issues. Just as it is important for clients and readers to educate themselves about positive body image, it is also important that clinicians: (a) know how to help clients in meaningful and effective ways, and (b) have an awareness and understanding of their own body image experiences. We offer frequently asked questions and answers about clinical interventions for positive body image. Additionally, we offer assignments specifically designed for clinicians to promote increased self-awareness.[1]

Do I need to know this information if I don't provide direct clinical care? The information contained in this workbook is applicable to clinicians in a variety of clinical settings (e.g., medical services, mental health counseling, dietary services). Additionally, this information is applicable to teachers, educators, coaches, physical/personal trainers, and more. You are likely already interacting with individuals with body image issues in personal relationships or community settings as no person or group is immune to body image pressures.

Where can I find information about positive body image to increase my knowledge and skills? This workbook synthesizes up-to-date information about positive body image from researchers and clinical experts around the world (Chapters 4–22, in particular). Read the following scholarly books: *Body Image: A Handbook of Science, Practice, and Prevention* [1]; *Body Positive: Understanding and Improving Body Image in Science and Practice* [2]; and the *Handbook of Positive Body Image and Embodiment: Constructs, Protective Factors, and Interventions* [3]. Review the latest research via peer-reviewed articles in *Body Image: An International Journal of Research*. Join organizations that promote positive body image such as *The Body Positive* and the *Health at Every Size* (HAES). Learn clinical techniques by watching webinars from skilled practitioners. Connect with clinicians from various disciplines in your community to learn how they address body image issues. Create a network of trusted colleagues with whom you can consult. Keep up with sociocultural trends regarding body image topics, as these trends will likely emerge in clinical encounters. Finally, remember that clients are a source of knowledge and expertise as well. What you learn when interacting with one client may be helpful with another.

Do I have to be an expert on positive body image in order to provide services/care? You don't have to master all of this information to be a competent provider.

Why specialize in this area? As mentioned previously, it is common for individuals to have experienced body image concerns during the course of their lives. Negative body image can result in medical complications from unhealthy behaviors, impaired social relations, poor quality of life, and more. Additionally, there are too few clinicians who have received training and education on how to promote positive body image in a way that is informed by theory and research.

How can this workbook be relevant for clients of various backgrounds and experiences? We include research articles that include diverse samples in terms of **social identities** (e.g., gender, race, age, gender identity, sexual orientation, geographic location, and more). Also, we considered clients' social identities and experiences as we designed treatment planning tools, assessments, and assignments. The resources we provide also take into consideration various social identities and experiences.

How can I confidently and competently address medical and nutrition issues related to body image disturbance if I'm not a physician or dietitian? It can be challenging to know fact from fiction related to medical and nutrition information due to how it can be distorted or portrayed. As a result, you might have difficulty challenging a client's distorted beliefs without solid factual information. It is essential to have frequent consultation with medical and dietary colleagues to address the actual science behind the social trends in order to provide effective and appropriate clinical interventions. Consider how you can establish a consultation network of reputable clinicians. In particular, we recommend medical and dietary colleagues who practice from a weight-inclusive approach (see Chapter 5) to reduce the likelihood of weight stigma influencing the medical and nutrition information provided.

Why do some people with body image issues engage in behaviors that are destructive or harmful? Individuals with body image disturbance will often try to change their bodies using different behaviors that range from relatively benign to extreme (e.g., exercise, dietary restriction, self-induced vomiting, cosmetic surgery) in order to feel better about their bodies. They typically view the behaviors as helpful and constructive and experience fear in the thought of relinquishing them. As a clinician, it is important to recognize that these behaviors are rooted in ingrained beliefs and strong emotions, and they serve various purposes or functions. Having this awareness will help you to decrease judgment and cultivate compassion, both of

---

[1] A detailed description of the workbook can be found in Table 1.1: "How to Use This Workbook" in Chapter 1.

which are integral components of providing care to those with body image issues.

Is it helpful for me as a clinician to ignore, minimize, or dismiss body image disturbance to reduce the impact of it? It is common for individuals with body image disturbance to experience significant anguish and despair. This pain is real and legitimate. Ignoring, minimizing, or dismissing a client's experience is neither helpful nor effective. Rather, it is helpful to validate the body image distress and acknowledge the impact on the client's quality of life. A reduction in body image disturbance typically occurs when an individual addresses the issue directly with the use of effective coping skills.

The way that clients see themselves can be vastly different from the reality. Is it helpful to try to convince clients to see how beautiful they are? Trying to convince someone to recognize their own beauty can be a challenging and often futile endeavor, resulting in frustration for both individuals. Intellectual reasoning alone often does not resolve this issue due to the complexity of thoughts and emotions associated with body image. It can be helpful to validate the client's discomfort while simultaneously offering hope through learning new coping skills to work through moments of body image distress.

Is it okay to comment on a client's body to let them know that they don't look bad? It is important that you refrain from commenting on your client's appearance in general. Even offering perceived "positive" comments can be misconstrued by the client and potentially lead to undesirable outcomes such as a heightened focus on their appearance and a rupture in your clinical relationship. Rather than comment on their appearance, you can redirect focus to their emotions, cognitions, and behaviors.

In my field and training, I've been taught that inducing some guilt or shame in clients can serve as positive motivation for change. Is this effective? Shame and guilt do *not* lead to positive change, and in fact, often create additional distress, secrecy, and avoidance. You can inform clients that shaming themselves is not helpful. What is helpful is to focus on self-compassion and self-acceptance instead, which correspond with hope, inspiration, and motivation.

When a client wants to lose weight to feel better about themselves, is it okay if I endorse or recommend it? Do not recommend or praise weight loss efforts, as it does not correspond with improved body image. Instead, you can educate on how appearance and weight bias are prevalent within society, which reinforces body image disturbance. You can inform how positive body image is about internal acceptance versus changing external appearance. You can encourage clients to engage in nurturing behaviors such as consistent nourishment, life-enhancing movement, and other types of self-care practices that are promoted in this workbook. The body will respond in whatever ways it needs to.

How do I know what to focus on in treatment? In addition to asking questions of your clients, it's also helpful to use body image assessments to determine your client's unique body image concerns. Common barriers for not including assessments in clinical work include difficulty finding valid and reliable assessments, challenges in seeking permission from authors to use the assessments, and lack of awareness of how to incorporate assessments in an effective manner. We offer an array of reliable and valid body image assessments along with corresponding applications (suggestions for discussion) in the text to assist in streamlining treatment focus.

How can I communicate effectively about this complex issue? What if I say the wrong thing? As with any sensitive topic, we encourage you to be open, honest, humble, respectful, and curious. Recognize that you will make mistakes, say the wrong thing, and might unintentionally offend a client, just as we have over the years. Don't allow this fear to prevent you from providing care or having important conversations that could be beneficial to your clients. If any of these challenges occur, take accountability, make a repair, and move on. We offer sample language to use during your interactions with clients in Assignment 3.1 "Ways to Dialogue with Clients about Sensitive Topics".

How can my own worldview and beliefs impact caring for clients? Your training, education, social identities, and life experiences shape how you view the world and your clients. It can be helpful to recognize potential biases related to shape, weight, and size. Explore how your own worldview interfaces with those of your clients in Assignment 3.2 "Personal Viewpoints that Shape Clinical Responses".

What if a client judges me based on my appearance? It's important to accept the reality that all people judge and are judged based on appearance. As clinicians, we too are judged based on our appearance such as our age, gender identification, height, weight, hairstyle, skin color, clothing, grooming, jewelry, and more. These appearance-based judgments by our clients can impact how they perceive our knowledge, expertise, and even our ability to understand their experiences. When it is clinically relevant and beneficial, there can be honest and direct dialogue between clinicians and clients about client assumptions, impressions, and comparisons.

What if a client comments on my appearance? The reality is that a client will make appearance-based comments about you that you will perceive on a range from positive to negative. When a comment is made, it is helpful to maintain a neutral stance and respond in a way that is focused on the client, not you. It can be beneficial to have stock phrases available in advance. Review Assignment 3.3 "How to Respond upon Receiving an Appearance-Based Comment from a Client" to consider what responses you might utilize in your client interactions.

What if I'm struggling with or have struggled with my own body image issues? Good for you for being aware of and honest about your experiences. You don't have to fully or completely embrace your own positive body image to offer assistance with those moving toward it, and it is important to be aware of how your relationship with your own body can impact your clinical interventions. Explore how your "Own Body Image Experiences" (Assignment 3.4) can impact your clinical work with clients. You may also find it beneficial to read and complete information in the content chapters (assessments, applications and assignments) to continue your own journey towards a positive body image.

If you are unsure of whether to address your own body image issues at this time, you can complete Assignment 3.5 "Pros/Cons of Working on My Own Body Image Issues" to help guide your decision. It is helpful to know your own strengths and challenges associated with body image issues to assist in your own work.

How can I advocate for clients? In the clinical setting, you can teach clients about complex sociocultural factors that promote negative body image and empower them to make positive changes along with committed action. In a broader context, you can advocate by speaking up about these topics with colleagues, educating community members about weight stigma, and challenging policies that interfere with positive body image development. Additional advocacy examples are offered in Assignment 3.6 "Advocating for Positive Body Image". Check which advocacy actions you are already engaged in and consider what ones you would like to pursue.

Having reviewed common questions about how to best help clients and understand your own body image experiences, you're ready to complete the following assignments to prepare you for this valuable work!

Assignment 3.1: Ways to Dialogue with Clients about Sensitive Topics

It can be challenging to know how to respond in the moment to clients when discussing sensitive topics related to body image. In addition to demonstrating a genuine curiosity, choice of language is important. Below are some direct quotes that can be considered when discussing sensitive topics to encourage openness, introspection, and dialogue.

Weight/Weight Loss

- How is this weight for you?
- What do you believe your ideal weight would provide you?
- Do you think it's possible to separate your sense of self-worth from your weight?
- What do you believe will change in your life as a result of weight loss?
- What do you hope weight loss will change about your life? About what you will do and/or won't do? About the emotions you will or won't experience? About how you will think about and treat yourself? About how you think others will treat you?
- (When client wants to pursue weight-loss surgery) How do you imagine this surgery will impact your relationship with your body?

Weight Stigma

- What are your personal experiences with weight stigma?
- Do you believe that others should be treated differently based on their weight? How do you treat yourself based on your weight?
- How do you respond to weight-related compliments from others?
- Do mental health and medical health providers take your health concerns seriously without focusing solely on your weight?
- Does weight stigma impact your physical health and psychological well-being?
- How do you feel about yourself after experiencing or witnessing weight stigma?

Eating Behaviors

- How would you describe your relationship with eating or food?
- What labels or categories do you use for different foods: healthy/unhealthy, good/bad?
- Do you eliminate certain food groups or types of food? If so, what are the reasons?
- Do you label eating behaviors as "cheating?" Or as "permission" to do certain activities?
- Are you aware of your internal cues that signal when you are hungry and full? Do you listen and respond to these signals?
- Do you cope with emotions by using food or eating?
- Do you practice unconditional permission to eat?

Life Enhancing Movement

- What is your relationship with movement and exercise?
- Have there been times that you've engaged in compulsive or obligatory exercise? (If so) What is that like for you? (If currently exercising compulsively) Are you willing to make changes?
- What types of exercise do you avoid?
- Are you aware of attuned exercise and how to practice it?

When Wanting to Pursue Cosmetic Surgery

- What are your thoughts on cosmetic surgery procedures?
- Do you consider this procedure necessary?
- How do you imagine this surgery will impact your relationship with your body?
- Have you considered the possibility that surgery will not necessarily result in positive body image?

Are Any of the Topics above Uncomfortable to Discuss with Clients?

- If yes, which ones and why?

_____
_____
_____
_____

- How might you increase your comfort with discussing these topics?

_____
_____
_____
_____

N. L. Wood-Barcalow, T. L. Tylka, and C. L. Judge. *Positive Body Image Workbook: A Clinical and Self-Improvement Guide.* Cambridge: Cambridge University Press, 2021.

Assignment 3.2: Personal Viewpoints that Shape Clinical Responses

For this journal activity, reflect and write about your viewpoints on these various topics that are complex, nuanced, and can impact relationships between clinicians and clients. Questions and points of reflection are offered to stimulate responses. You can complete this application in advance of and after reading this workbook to determine how your responses might change.

"Healthy Weight"
- What measures are used to determine a "healthy weight?" Are these measures flawed?
- What personal factors can impact a client's weight status (e.g., gender, age, pregnancy)?
- How do I endorse the "weight-normative approach" (i.e., focusing on weight loss)?
- How do I endorse the "weight-inclusive approach" (i.e., focusing on well-being, not weight, and challenging weight stigma)?
- How does my own weight potentially impact the dialogue that I have with clients?

Weight Loss
- What are my thoughts about the ability or ease of losing weight?
- Am I inclined to endorse specific weight-loss methods?
- How would I respond to weight-loss goals based on a client's current weight (high weight, medium weight, low weight)?
- How would I respond to weight-loss goals based on a client's former weight (high weight, medium weight, low weight)?
- Would I respond differently about weight loss goals based on a client's age?
- What are my philosophical viewpoints on different types of weight loss surgeries?
- How might I respond to a client whose weight is in the higher range and believes that weight loss is the only path to body acceptance?
- How might I respond to a client whose weight is in the lower range and believes that weight loss is the only path to body acceptance? Do my responses for these questions differ?

Weight Stigma
- In what ways have I unintentionally participated in forms of weight stigma?
- In what ways have I purposefully participated in forms of weight stigma?
- Is it possible that I have participated in weight-related microaggressions with clients?
- What are my personal experiences with weight stigma?
- Do I believe that others should be treated differently based on their weight?
- Do I make remarks akin to complimenting weight loss or engaging in body-related talk with friends, loved ones, community members, colleagues, or clients?
- Do I take the emotional concerns related to weight of clients seriously?
- Do I tend to view issues solely from a weight-loss perspective?
- Do I have appropriately sized medical equipment and/or furniture to accommodate individuals with larger body sizes?
- Do I believe that weight stigma can impact physical health and psychological well-being?
- In what ways have I experienced internalized weight bias?

Eating Behaviors
- How would I describe my current relationship with eating or food?
- How would I describe my past relationship with eating or food?
- What labels do I use for foods: healthy/unhealthy, good/bad?
- Do I support elimination of certain food groups or types of food?
- Do I encourage the use of herbal remedies or supplements to assist with nutritional health?
- What do I deem as "too much" food to be eaten in one setting to be considered an objective binge episode? What amount do I deem to be a subjective binge episode?
- Do I equate certain eating practices with "permission?"
- Do I listen to my own internal cues for hunger and fullness?
- Do I practice forms of dietary restraint/restriction?
- Do I cope with my emotions by using food or eating?
- Do I offer myself unconditional permission to eat?

Life Enhancing Movement
- What is my relationship with movement and exercise?
- Have there been times that I've engaged in compulsive or obligatory exercise?

N. L. Wood-Barcalow, T. L. Tylka, and C. L. Judge. *Positive Body Image Workbook: A Clinical and Self-Improvement Guide.* Cambridge: Cambridge University Press, 2021.

- Have I experienced a dysfunctional relationship with exercise, such as exercising despite an injury or ignoring my body cues while doing it?
- What types of exercise do I avoid?
- Do I practice attuned exercise?

Cosmetic Surgery

- What are my overall thoughts on cosmetic surgery procedures as they relate to enhancing positive body image?
- How do my beliefs and values impact my views on cosmetic surgery?
- What do I view as pros and cons of cosmetic surgery for aesthetic reasons?
- What do I believe are valid reasons for surgery? Invalid reasons for surgery?
- What procedures do I deem appropriate? Inappropriate?
- What procedures do I deem necessary? Unnecessary?
- How would I respond if a client wanted to proceed with a procedure that I deem invalid, unnecessary, and/or inappropriate?
- Should my personal viewpoints impact decision-making as it relates to client care?

Appearance Investment

- How much importance do I place on my appearance?
- What appearance-related practices do I engage in that I consider adaptive? Maladaptive?
- How many of my appearance-related practices are based on health, self-care, and expressing my personal style versus experiencing pressures (internal, external) to do so?
- Who do I compare myself with in my personal life? In the media?
- What beautification appearance-related practices do I engage in? (Motivation is based on how it looks to others.)
- What signification appearance-related practices do I engage in? (Motivation is based on personal meaning.)
- How do I practice my own body sovereignty? (Your right to determine what's best for your body.)
- How would I describe how my own body image impacts my quality of life?

N. L. Wood-Barcalow, T. L. Tylka, and C. L. Judge. *Positive Body Image Workbook: A Clinical and Self-Improvement Guide.* Cambridge: Cambridge University Press, 2021.

Assignment 3.3: How to Respond upon Receiving an Appearance-Based Comment from a Client

It's important to accept the reality that all people judge and are judged based on appearance. As clinicians, we too are judged based on our appearance such as our age, gender identification, height, weight, hairstyle, skin color, clothing, grooming, jewelry, and more. These appearance-based judgments by our clients can impact how they perceive our knowledge, expertise and even our ability to relate to their experiences. We clinicians cannot control these judgments; however, we can control how we respond when a client makes an appearance-based comment directed toward us. For this assignment, reflect on the following:

Past Experiences

- How have clients commented on my appearance in the past?
  - How did I interpret the comment (e.g., positive, neutral, negative)?
  - What emotions came up?
  - What thoughts came up?
  - How did I respond in the moment?
  - Did I view my response as effective in the moment?
  - Is there anything I would have done differently?
  - What impact did this comment have on me then? And now?
  - Have I altered my clinical interventions?
  - Additional realizations:

Future Experiences

- How would I like to respond to appearance-based comments?
- If a client makes an appearance-based comment about me, how would I respond if it was offered:
  - as a compliment?
  - as a judgment?
  - in a derogatory manner?

- Imagine some potential scenarios in advance to have stock phrases readily available.

  Check those below that might work for you:
  - ❏ "It's common to comment on others' appearance in our society. How is it for you when others make comments about your appearance?"
  - ❏ "Is this a comment that you've received before? What impact did it have on you?"
  - ❏ "What are you wanting to express in this moment?"
  - ❏ "What assumptions are you making about me based on how I look? What is it like for others to make assumptions about you based on your appearance?"
  - ❏ "I appreciate your effort to offer me a compliment. Let's talk about how appearance-based comments are prevalent in society and how it impacts you."
  - ❏ "I'm not sure what to say to that. Do you ever feel at a loss for words when someone comments on your body or appearance?"
  - ❏ Other:
  - ❏ Other:
  - ❏ Other:

General Issues to Consider

- How can I create a safe environment to discuss openly comments that my clients make about me?
- How can I address the comment with the focus being on the client versus myself?
- How can I use what is stated by the client to serve as helpful information to be processed?
- What appearance-based comments do I consider inappropriate or unacceptable?
  - How would I like to respond to those comments?
  - What limits or boundaries might I need to set?

- These are trusted individuals whom I can consult about these issues:
- Additional realizations:

N. L. Wood-Barcalow, T. L. Tylka, and C. L. Judge. *Positive Body Image Workbook: A Clinical and Self-Improvement Guide.* Cambridge: Cambridge University Press, 2021.

Assignment 3.4: Own Body Image Experiences

As noted throughout this workbook, body image issues are common for many people, including clinicians. It's important to recognize and address these issues. Reflect on the following:

• Am I willing to address my own body image issues at this time?

  o If not, for what reasons?

  o If so, in what ways?

• Can I work on my body image while actively working with clients with their own body image issues?

• How might my own experiences with negative body image enhance interactions with clients? Examples might include the ability to offer compassion and empathy, serve as inspiration, help with motivation, normalize experiences without judgment, and offer an honest perspective of the challenges associated with change toward positive body image.

• How might my own experiences with negative body image serve as challenges in the clinician/client relationship? Examples might include being focused on myself versus the client, offering personal advice versus recommendations based on research/theory, experiencing discomfort with challenging the client when necessary and possibly not viewing issues through an objective lens.

• How can I tell if my own issues impact that of my clients?

• What aspects of positive body image do I currently embrace? What aspects am I moving toward?

N. L. Wood-Barcalow, T. L. Tylka, and C. L. Judge. *Positive Body Image Workbook: A Clinical and Self-Improvement Guide.* Cambridge: Cambridge University Press, 2021.

Assignment 3.5: Pros/Cons of Working on My Own Body Image Issues

Brainstorm lists of pros and cons for both working on my body image issues and not working on my body image issues.

	Pros	Cons
Working on my body image issues		
Not working on my body image issues		

Realizations about working on body image issues:

_____

_____

_____

Realizations about *not* working on body image issues:

_____

_____

_____

Assignment 3.6: Advocating for Positive Body Image

It is important to support clients and teach them how to be advocates. This workbook is designed to assist clients in implementing their own change. Additionally, it can be helpful for us clinicians to serve as advocates on systems levels. Examples of advocacy initiatives are provided below. Consider what forms of advocacy you're currently engaged in and what you're willing to commit to in the future (check all that apply):

- ❑ Educate colleagues, community members, and others about topics related to body image (e.g., impact of weight bias and weight stigma, objectification, body talk)
- ❑ Present at conferences about these issues
- ❑ Teach courses or workshops on these topics
- ❑ Provide training on these topics
- ❑ Write to Congress members about policy issues that impact body image
- ❑ Challenge policies that interfere with positive body image development or maintenance
- ❑ Speak about these issues on social media forums
- ❑ Follow social media influencers who promote positive body image
- ❑ Encourage dialogue with colleagues about practices that promote positive body image
- ❑ Purchase products from businesses that support positive body image
- ❑ Support campaigns that promote positive body image
- ❑ Other:
- ❑ Other:
- ❑ Other:

N. L. Wood-Barcalow, T. L. Tylka, and C. L. Judge. *Positive Body Image Workbook: A Clinical and Self-Improvement Guide.* Cambridge: Cambridge University Press, 2021.

References

1. T. F. Cash and L. Smolak. *Body Image: A Handbook of Science, Practice, and Prevention*. New York: Guilford, 2011.

2. E. A. Daniels, M. M. Gillen, and C. H. Markey. *Body Positive: Understanding and Improving Body Image in Science and Practice*. Cambridge: Cambridge University Press, 2018.

3. T. L. Tylka and N. Piran. *Handbook of Positive Body Image and Embodiment: Constructs, Protective Factors, and Interventions*. New York: Oxford University Press, 2019.

Appearance Ideals and Media Literacy

Theory and Research Overview

During my pre-teen and teenage years, I (Tracy) desperately wanted to look different: my skin was "too pale," my hair was "too thin," my weight was "too high," my arms were "too large," my height was "too short," my eyes were "too brown," and my cheeks were "too chubby." I was constantly comparing myself against models who were thin and tan and had long blonde hair, blue eyes, and visible cheekbones (for women, these models represented the **appearance ideal**, or the "look" that society labels as attractive, successful, healthy, and wealthy to sell more products). I assumed that the models' appearance was more beautiful than mine, making them more worthwhile than me. So, I dieted, sunbathed, went to tanning beds, highlighted my hair, and even tried to convince my parents to buy me blue contact lenses (they said, "absolutely not!"), all in the hopes of becoming "more worthwhile." Thankfully, I went on a body image journey in my late twenties and emerged with a positive body image that includes an appreciation for my physical features, many of which are different from societal appearance ideals. Now in my forties, I notice my body moving even farther away from these ideals. I am grateful that my positive body image helps me remain appreciative of my body as it continues to change.

Internalization of appearance ideals is when we adopt societal appearance ideals as an expectation (and aspiration) for our own body, and evaluate our attractiveness, and often self-worth, based on how much we look like these ideals [1]. Internalization of appearance ideals often occurs because we are surrounded by these images. When I was young, I studied make-up models in teen magazines to try to look like them, so I was constantly exposed to these images. **Cultivation theory** [2] suggests that the more we view mainstream[1] media images and messages, the more we believe that they represent real life. I accepted the messages that the magazines were selling me: I could achieve this look with the "right make-up" and the "right lifestyle" (e.g., dieting, excessive exercise, tanning) if I try hard enough and to be worthwhile as a person, I *had* to achieve this look. Cultivation theory can explain why body satisfaction decreases after looking at pictures of models [3], and even appearance-focused posts on social media (e.g., retouched selfies of others) [4–5].

Internalization of appearance ideals is not limited to evaluating our own bodies. When people internalize appearance ideals, they also tend to evaluate others' bodies based on how consistent they are with these ideals, which may promote their "**policing**" or monitoring of others' bodies (e.g., "You really should straighten your hair," "You really should try to lose fat and gain some muscle," or even "You lost so much weight – keep going, you look great!") to the extent that it is considered "breaking the (appearance) law" to look different. Policing is detrimental to the body image and well-being of those whose appearance is being policed [6–7]. We may also feel policed by our partners, who may want us to look like appearance ideals. This policing may also impact how we feel during intimate situations when our body is exposed to our partner (see Chapter 14).

It is important that we are aware that we are being constantly pressured from mainstream media, as well as others who have internalized these appearance ideals, to modify our body to look like these ideals [3, 6–7]. It is also important to take a closer look at which societal appearance ideals are promoted, the reasons they are promoted, and that they change over time. To illustrate how Western societal appearance ideals change over time, consider how today's styles are different from the late 1980s and early 1990s. During that time, permed and "big" hair, pegged jeans, mullet hairstyles, and leg warmers were popular in the US. While changes in fashion are often harmless, striving towards appearance ideals, and modifying bodies to achieve these ideals, can be dangerous. Yet, the ill health of consumers does not stop mainstream media from changing appearance ideals time and time again [for reviews, see 8–9].

In the 1930s–1950s, for White women in the US, a larger body size was promoted by mainstream media as ideal.[2] Soon after, in the 1960s–1970s, the very thin body type gained recognition with the model Twiggy. This "very thin ideal" emerged as a negative societal reaction against women's rights (e.g., access to birth control pills). Indeed, pursuing the very thin ideal keeps women submissive: it is hard to assert for rights when hungry and frail. This body type also promoted higher rates of **weight stigma** (see Chapter 5), or bullying, teasing, stereotyping, prejudice, and discriminatory treatment towards higher-weight individuals.

---

[1] It is important to recognize that Black-oriented media may be different from mainstream media. One study [38] found that, for White women, viewing mainstream media predicted higher body dissatisfaction, while viewing Black-oriented media was unrelated to body dissatisfaction. For Black women, viewing Black-oriented media predicted lower body dissatisfaction, while viewing mainstream media was unrelated to body dissatisfaction. Black women's ethnic identity predicted lower body dissatisfaction and appears to buffer media effects on body image.

[2] Advertisements for certain products were geared toward helping women gain weight; see https://prettysweet.com/vintage-weight-gain-ads/ or Google "vintage weight gain ads".

Around 2010, the "curvaceously thin ideal" (thin hourglass figure, or curvy in what society says are the "right places") and the "thin fit ideal" or "athletic ideal" (thin and muscle tone) gained popularity [10–11]. These ideals can also be harmful, as they may involve women seeking cosmetic procedures to become curvier (e.g., breast enhancement) while following rigid eating and exercise plans to increase muscle tone while pursuing a lower weight [11–13]. For men, societal appearance ideals have become more muscular and larger, and lower in body fat [14]. Trying to achieve this athletic "muscular and lean ideal" may also be harmful for men due to following rigid eating and excessive exercise plans [15]. To understand the extent to which you internalize appearance ideals related to muscularity and leanness, complete the *Sociocultural Attitudes Towards Appearance Questionnaire-4-Revised* [1] within this chapter.

It is helpful to examine why societal appearance ideals exist. These ideals direct people to continuously buy products (e.g., pre-packaged foods, nutrition bars, supplements, exercise plans, gym memberships, make-up) and regularly receive cosmetic procedures (e.g., injections every few months). Therefore, companies believe that appearance ideals are profitable and recognize that it is not in their best financial interests to have us like our bodies – if we like our bodies, we won't need their products and procedures any longer![3]

Companies selling products depend on this: the more a person does not look like the societal appearance ideal, the more they will purchase products to try and look like this ideal. Therefore, mainstream media create a narrow ideal that few people can realistically and healthfully achieve. In addition to body size and shape, media define what is ideal in terms of:

1. *Age.* Media attempt to sell products and procedures to "hide our age" and be "youthful."
2. *Race.* Media mostly employ models who are White or of lighter skin tone. Of note, the "thick body ideal" for women, often endorsed by Black and Latina women, is a form of resistance to the thinner, White-centric societal appearance ideals.
3. *Class.* Media sell a "rich" lifestyle, whereby glamour and success are tied into the ability to purchase products and procedures.
4. *Ability.* Most models do not have any visible physical limitations. Media want to pair their products with an illusion of health and functionality.

As indicated above, mainstream media promote and glamorize these narrow appearance ideals, and then many people internalize these ideals. Once internalized, appearance ideals are spread interpersonally, from others to us, and from us to others. Appearance ideals can influence how we communicate with each other (e.g., "policing," "body talk," see Chapter 16) and how we judge ourselves and each other (e.g., appearance comparison, see Chapter 15).

Social media is one popular platform which may promote appearance ideals. We may engage in social media for various reasons, such as to stay current with trends, to check in on others' lives, to create relationships, to maintain ongoing relationships, and as a source of entertainment (e.g., to use when we are bored or need a distraction). According to the Pew Research Center [16], in 2019, almost half of all US adults indicate that they use at least one photo-sharing social network site "several times a day," and about 20 percent more indicate that they use these sites "about once a day." For many age groups, browsing social networking sites is more popular than viewing traditional media (e.g., magazines, TV) [17].

In social media, appearance ideals can be spread by searching for and/or following profiles of models, celebrities, and other social influencers, which contain photos and posts, as well as viewing the profiles of the people we follow, such as friends, acquaintances, and family. For example, we may view others' sexualized selfies, posts about appearance and weight loss, etc., as well as view others' appearance-related reactions to our pictures. Time spent on social networking sites is linked to higher body dissatisfaction for adolescents, women, and men, and appearance-related activities (e.g., photo sharing, posting and viewing selfies) are especially detrimental to viewers' body image [18–21]. This outcome is likely due to the comparative process, as we tend to compare our appearance to how models look in their photo posts and how our peers look in their (often filtered) photo posts [21–23] (see also Chapter 15). The comparative process in social media increases body dissatisfaction even more so than in-person appearance comparisons [23]. In order to present our "best" appearance, we may modify photos (e.g., use filters, trim body areas, alter the angle of the photo, make other areas bigger, remove shadows from under eyes, etc.). This photo modification is associated with higher body dissatisfaction, and self-compassion may not protect against this effect [24]. The act of modifying, selecting, and attending to followers' responses may increase body dissatisfaction. Also, those dissatisfied with their appearance may be more likely to modify their selfies, as they may feel that their photos may need more "help."

Rather than internalizing and trying to meet appearance ideals, we can (a) acknowledge why media want us to try to meet appearance ideals (i.e., companies will make more money), (b) identify media's strategies to get us to internalize appearance ideals, and (c) commit (and recommit) to resisting appearance ideals.[4] **Media literacy** is being aware of appearance ideals and why they are used (e.g., to sell products), as well as resisting these ideals [25]. Media literacy interventions teach participants about how media generate images, support participants in questioning appearance ideals and resisting the internalization of these ideals, and engage participants in discussing

---

[3] In contrast, research shows that it is likely profitable to include plus-size models in advertising [29–30].

[4] We may need to occasionally recommit to resisting these ideals to protect our health and well-being. Because of the prevalence of appearance ideals, and seeing these ideals endorsed by peers and media, it is easy to "slip back" into thinking that we need to pursue appearance ideals. Indeed, a research study investigating weight-loss advertising found that more than half of all advertising made use of false, unsubstantiated claims [37].

important non-appearance parts of their life (e.g., personal qualities and abilities) [26]. Media literacy increases **protective filtering** (see Chapter 17), whereby people "filter" information in a body protective manner – that is, they accept information that is consistent with a positive view of their body and reject messages that could harm their body image. Media literacy also broadens participants' definitions of beauty (see Chapter 7).

Media literacy is often a central goal in eating disorder prevention. For example, *Media Smart* [26] includes many activities that emphasize the artificial nature of appearance ideals and encourages participants to question these ideals. Program participants also consider their personal goals and values. Overall, a review of media literacy interventions found that these programs were effective in improving participants' body image, lowering participants' internalization of appearance ideals, and increasing participants' knowledge of media strategies and motives for profit [25]. In addition, media literacy protects adolescent girls, even those with high levels of internalization and appearance comparison, from higher body dissatisfaction after viewing appearance-focused media [27]. Being able to critique advertising images protects against increased body dissatisfaction after viewing appearance-focused media for women, but appears to be less effective for men [19].

While media literacy interventions are beneficial, there are also ways to increase our media literacy, such as:

1. **View "body positive" social media posts**. These posts depict a broad range of body types and appearances. A research study found that body positive posts on social media were consistent with how the body image field defines positive body image, and how we define positive body image in this workbook [28].

2. **View size-inclusive images**. Brands, designers, and models who have fought for body diversity and inclusivity in fashion and media can have a positive impact on women. Examples are the Dove Campaign for Real Beauty® and Aerie Real®. One study showed that women who viewed plus-size models had the highest body satisfaction, women who viewed thin-size models had the lowest body satisfaction, and the body satisfaction of women who viewed medium-size models fell in between these two groups [29]. Therefore, when women look at thin models, they feel less confident in their own size, make more comparisons between themselves and the thin models, and pay less attention to media. In contrast, when women look at images of plus-size models, they are happier with their bodies, make fewer appearance comparisons, and remember more about the models and clothing they see. One study found that this effect may be particularly strong for women and men who have high appearance-ideal internalization [30]. Another study explored women's reactions to the Aerie Real™ campaign, which includes models that have not been digitally modified and models diverse in race; some models also have physical traits that have traditionally been marginalized (e.g., scars, amputations, colostomy bag) [31]. Most participants reacted to the images positively and perceived them as representing body diversity in many ways and believed that they would likely promote positive body image and body confidence.

These participants expressed being more likely to purchase products from Aerie. Collectively, these findings suggest that incorporating models diverse in appearance is not only good for viewers, but also good for the advertising company. Investing our time, energy, and money in body positivity advertising sends signals to companies, as they are likely to promote body positivity if their consumer base calls for it. It is important to mention that some people argue against body positivity, indicating that it "promotes obesity" and "unhealthy behaviors." This argument is associated with weight stigma, as health cannot be determined by body size (also see Chapter 5).

3. **Use media literacy strategies to think critically about media messages and content we create on social media.** Before we post on social media, we can ask ourselves why we are sending our message, who we want to reach, and determine whether it is body positive [32]. Also, whenever we see media messages and content, we can ask ourselves these questions [32]:

   - Are the bodies depicted in media realistic or digitally modified?
   - What is the message being sent and what does it mean?
   - What is the purpose of the message?
   - Who is creating and profiting from the message?
   - How may the message or content impact a viewer's body image? Our body image?

4. **Recognize that people tend to present themselves (their appearance, their life) in a more favorable light on social media**; they only select the most attractive photos and videos of themselves to post. According to Steven Fustick, "The reason why we struggle with insecurity is because we compare our behind the scenes with everyone else's highlight reel." Indeed, those who use social media frequently tend to base their evaluation of others' quality of life on what they see in the photos (i.e., referred to as the **availability heuristic**) and to rate others as happier than themselves [33].

5. **View models/celebrities/influencers without make-up or unretouched photos**. A study examined the impact of viewing (a) various pictures of models who all wore make-up or (b) various pictures of models in which some wore make-up and others did not [34]. Women who viewed the "all make-up" pictures reported less satisfaction with the appearance of their face, hair, and skin, whereas women who viewed the "some make-up, some no-make-up" pictures did not experience decreased satisfaction with the appearance of their face, hair, and skin.

6. **View self-compassion quotes on social media**. A study found that brief five-minute exposure to self-compassion quotes increased women's body satisfaction, body appreciation, and self-compassion, and reduced their negative mood [35]. Additionally, the inclusion of self-compassion quotes alongside media images of lean and toned bodies resulted in participants feeling more positively towards their body when compared to the images of lean and toned bodies alone, suggesting that self-compassion may weaken the negative impact of appearance

ideals in social media on women's body image and mood (see Chapter 8).

7. **Make fun of media images**. For example, in 2015, Celeste Barber (an Australian comedian) began to poke fun at popular celebrity Instagram images using the hashtag #CelesteChallengeAccepted. Celeste's posts highlight the absurdity of popular celebrity posts and the unattainable nature of such images. In these posts, Celeste is photographed in a similar, yet comedic, pose as the original celebrity image, which is also shown in "split screen," along with a humorous caption. For example, on the left side in one of Celeste's posts, supermodel Miranda Kerr is shown eating a sandwich and fries with her fingers pressing food against her pursed lips with a sexy expression on her face as she looks at the camera; she apparently is not wearing any clothes (a napkin covers parts of her body). On the right side of this post is Celeste with chicken nuggets, fries, and a loaf of white bread, pressing a fry against her lips as she looks at the camera; apparently, she also is not wearing any clothes (a blanket and fast food wrapper cover parts of her body). The caption reads "I love pretending to eat what I want so my fans can feel even worse about themselves. #celestechallengeaccepted #nailedit #funny #funnywomen #thefatjewish." One study documented that young adult women who viewed several of Celeste's images reported greater body satisfaction and happiness compared to those who only viewed the celebrity images [36].[5] Therefore, reminders that appearance ideals are absurd can help offset our internalization of these ideals and protect our body image.

8. **Understand how social media strategies, such as algorithms, work in order to create the content in your feed**. Social networks prioritize which content appears in our feed, and this prioritization is based on the likelihood that we will actually want to see it. The algorithms are based on our behavior: what shows up first in our feed is determined by what posts and accounts we engage with the most.

9. **Engage with body positive content**. Search for body positive posts and hashtags, and once you find ones that you like, tag the accounts in your posts, which serves as an invitation for other users to check out and share your content. Determine whether there are ways to "hide" appearance-related posts (e.g., diet products, cosmetic surgery), which tells the social networking site that you want to see fewer posts with this type of content.

10. **Talk back to media!** Voice your displeasure with advertisers who promote narrow appearance ideals and applaud advertisers who promote body positivity and body diversity. We may think that we are powerless to change media. Yet, with social media, we have a voice, and collectively it can be strong. As an example, certain social media sites enforced an updated set of community guidelines that place tighter restrictions on

advertisements related to diet products and cosmetic surgery. This change was led by actress and body positivity advocate Jameela Jamil, who acknowledged her many supporters for making "noise" about the need for these restrictions.

By increasing our awareness of industry motives for getting us to adopt appearance ideals, we can make informed decisions that support our self-care and well-being, such as the suggestions for media literacy listed above. Also, the more we turn our attention to people we interact with on an everyday basis and the more we are exposed, and receptive, to see and hear alternative messages that challenge narrow appearance ideals, the more we notice that it is extremely uncommon to look like appearance ideals.

Treatment Planning Tools
Talking Points for Sessions

- Identify important appearance ideals and standards for the client currently, as well as in the past
- Discuss how appearance ideals shift across time
- Discuss how appearance ideals differ across cultures
- Identify different types of appearance-related behaviors and routines, and then consider how each practice is motivated by "choice" as compared to "obligation" to fit societal appearance ideals
- Discuss how media promote certain appearance ideals
- Notice how media portray individuals with physical traits that have traditionally been marginalized (e.g., higher-weight individuals).

Treatment Plan
Goals

❏ Identify current appearance ideals that contribute to negative body image and lower positive body image
❏ Increase awareness of how media images impact body acceptance
❏ Consider how and why appearance ideals are unrealistic
❏ Shift from the perspective of trying to look like appearance ideals toward a perspective of accepting aspects of appearance that cannot be changed
❏ Identify personal motives associated with appearance-related activities
❏ Look at media images in a critical manner
❏ Consider the influence of media on positive body image

Objectives

❏ Learn how editing software can impact media messages
❏ Learn about appearance ideals in different cultures
❏ Learn about appearance ideals from the past

---

[5] See also: https://mymodernmet.com/celeste-barber-instagram-parody/ .

❏ Identify specific grooming/beauty practices used to achieve appearance ideals
❏ Learn how certain industries or businesses benefit from creating or maintaining negative body image as a way to promote their products or services
❏ Learn how to critique media messages
❏ Consider how access to money and resources relates to attainment of appearance ideals
❏ Consider how majority culture influences beauty standards
❏ Ask trusted others whether they try to meet appearance ideals and, if so, which ones
❏ Contact industries or businesses to provide feedback about how their practices impact the body image of others
❏ Identify portrayals of positive body image in media
❏ Listen to music that promotes positive body image
❏ Identify specific counter-messages in response to unrealistic appearance ideals
❏ Reflect on any transformative experiences from negative to positive body image including key people who have helped
❏ Identify those people around whom I feel good or safe
❏ Identify specific environments that promote positive body image
❏ Identify examples of when my appearance-related behaviors conflict with my attitudes or values
❏ Engage in one activity this week that goes against an unhelpful established attitude/belief based on appearance ideals about what "I should do"
❏ Write a journal entry to argue against unrealistic appearance ideals
❏ Identify what makes me a worthwhile person
❏ Consider costs and benefits of moving away from or rejecting appearance ideals

❏ Consider costs and benefits of not meeting appearance ideals
❏ Imagine how embracing aspects of positive body image can buffer against pressures associated with appearance ideals
❏ Identify emotions and thoughts before and after viewing social media information to determine if any changes occur
❏ Identify level of body acceptance on a scale (0 = none to 10 = high) before, during, and after viewing social media information to determine if any changes occur.

Additional Resources

A. Brashich and S. Banner. *All Made Up: A Girl's Guide to Seeing through the Celebrity Hype and Celebrating Real Beauty.* London: Walker Childrens, 2006.
C. Barber. *Challenge Accepted!* Newark: Audible Studios, 2018.
S. R. Taylor. *The Body is Not an Apology: The Power of Radical Self-Love.* Oakland: Berrett-Koehler, 2018.
M. Bennett and V. Dickerson. *Recovering the Black Female Body: Self-representations by African American Women.* Piscataway: Rutgers University Press, 2001.
N. Wolf. *The Beauty Myth: How Images of Beauty Are Used Against Women.* New York: HarperCollins, 1990.
S. Blood. *Body Work: The Social Construction of Women's Body Image.* New York: Routledge, 2005.
R. Engeln. *Beauty Sick: How the Cultural Obsession with Appearance Hurts Girls and Women.* New York: HarperCollins, 2017.
Get Real: Digital Media Literacy Toolkit, California State University Northridge and National Eating Disorders Association. Available online at: www.nationaleatingdisorders.org/sites/default/files/Toolkits/getrealmedialliteracytoolkit/index.html

Assessment 4.1: Sociocultural Attitudes Towards Appearance Questionnaire-4 (SATAQ-4 R)

Internalization Subscales

Using the following scale, indicate your level of agreement with each item. Write the number to the right of the item.

1	2	3	4	5
Definitely Disagree	Mostly Disagree	Neither Agree Nor Disagree	Mostly Agree	Definitely Agree

	Number
1. It is important to me to look muscular.	
2. I think a lot about looking muscular.	
3. I want my body to look muscular.	
4. I would like to have a body that looks muscular.	
Total Internalization: Muscular score: Add items 1–4 then divide by 4	
5. I want my body to look thin.	
6. I think a lot about looking thin.	
7. I want my body to look lean.	
8. I think a lot about having low body fat.	
Total Internalization: Thin/Low Body Fat score: Add items 5–8 then divide by 4	

Total subscale score between:

- **4–5** = high levels of internalization
- **3–3.9** = moderate levels of internalization
- **below 3** = low levels of internalization

Note. Reprinted with permission. Authors of the SATAQ-4 R are Schaefer et al.[*] The SATAQ-4 R can be used with people of diverse ages and geographic locations, as its measurement properties (i.e., reliability and validity) and structure are well supported with many samples. Three items were slightly modified with permission from the authors to be consistent with current appearance ideals (i.e., "very" was removed in front of "thin" in one item and in front of "lean" in another item, "little fat" was replaced with "low body fat" in another item). Please contact the authors of the SATAQ-4 R for permission to use it within research; there is no need to contact them to use it with clients or to complete on your own.

[*] L. M. Schaefer, J. A. Harriger, L. J. Heinberg, et al. Development and Validation of the Sociocultural Attitudes Towards Appearance Questionnaire-4-Revised (SATAQ-4 R). *Int J Eat Disord* 2017; **50**: 104–17.

Sociocultural Attitudes Towards Appearance Questionnaire-4 (SATAQ-4)

Internalization Subscales Applications

- If you think "a lot" about looking muscular and/or lean (in other words, you reported "agree" or "strongly agree" for many items), what triggers this type of thinking for you? For example, are these thoughts prompted by exposure to media, social media content, and/or conversations with others who endorse societal appearance ideals?

  o What might you be doing or thinking about if you weren't focused on looking muscular/athletic or thin/lean?

  o What situations and/or factors are associated with decreased thoughts about looking muscular/athletic or thin/lean? Perhaps you don't think a lot about your appearance on days when you are more engaged in hobbies you enjoy and have less exposure to social media.

  o Based on your answers to the above questions, what is one change you would like to make to move you closer to positive body image in the next week?

- Consider the amount of time you spend in pursuit of appearance ideals (i.e., to look more athletic, muscular, thin, or lean) as you consider these questions:

  o What are your reasons and personal motives for dedicating your time in this manner?

  o What are the values associated with deciding to spend your time this way?

  o Does the amount of time and energy you spend pursuing appearance ideals ever feel like it is "enough?"

  o Would you like to make a change to spend a portion of this time differently, in order to pursue more positive body image? If so, what action will you take towards this change within the next week?

Assignment 4.1: Challenging Media Messages

I notice that these messages or "ideals" about the body are promoted in the media:

_____
_____
_____
_____

These messages can be destructive in the following ways:

_____
_____
_____
_____

These messages can be helpful in the following ways:

_____
_____
_____
_____

I don't agree with these messages:

_____
_____
_____
_____

I commit to doing the following when I experience media messages that I don't agree with:

_____
_____
_____
_____

N. L. Wood-Barcalow, T. L. Tylka, and C. L. Judge. *Positive Body Image Workbook: A Clinical and Self-Improvement Guide.* Cambridge: Cambridge University Press, 2021.

Assignment 4.2: Investment in Ideals

A lot of resources can go into the pursuit of appearance ideals such as grooming, working out, applying make-up, eating in specific manners, shopping for items, researching health information, changing outer appearance such as hair color, and more. Take a moment to consider your habits and which are related to the pursuit of a certain appearance ideal. In this activity, you will consider and estimate your total investment in pursuing appearance ideals. Also, feel free to reflect on your answers in the spaces provided.

I engage in these behaviors/actions to try to appear a certain way:

_____
_____
_____

I spend this *amount of time each day* engaging in these behaviors:

_____
_____
_____

I spend this *amount of time each week/month* engaging in these behaviors:

_____
_____
_____

I spend this *amount of money each day* engaging in these behaviors:

_____
_____
_____

I spend this *amount of money each week/month* engaging in these behaviors:

_____
_____
_____

I spend this *amount of mental energy* thinking about my appearance each day:

_____
_____
_____

I spend this *amount of mental energy* thinking about my appearance each week/month:

_____
_____
_____

I notice these overall patterns with my investment in ideals:

_____
_____
_____

This is how my investment in ideals moves me away from positive body image:

_____
_____
_____

This is how my investment in ideals moves me toward positive body image:

_____
_____
_____

N. L. Wood-Barcalow, T. L. Tylka, and C. L. Judge. *Positive Body Image Workbook: A Clinical and Self-Improvement Guide.* Cambridge: Cambridge University Press, 2021.

Assignment 4.3: Challenge an Appearance Ideal

A specific appearance ideal that is currently important to me such as a certain body shape/type/weight, amount of muscularity, height, amount of hair, color of skin, eye shape, etc.:

_____
_____
_____

How much I invest in pursuing this ideal in terms of time, money, effort, mental energy, and more:

_____
_____
_____

Now It's Time to Challenge It . . .

Who created this appearance standard?

_____
_____
_____

Who says that this appearance standard is ideal?

_____
_____
_____

How long has this appearance standard been ideal?

_____
_____
_____

Was this appearance standard ever considered undesirable?

_____
_____
_____

Now It's Time to Consider . . .

What's the purpose of appearance ideals? Who benefits financially from societal appearance ideals?

_____
_____
_____

My life would be different in these ways if I didn't pursue this appearance ideal:

_____
_____
_____
_____

I would focus on these things instead of the appearance ideal:

_____
_____
_____
_____

 N. L. Wood-Barcalow, T. L. Tylka, and C. L. Judge. *Positive Body Image Workbook: A Clinical and Self-Improvement Guide.* Cambridge: Cambridge University Press, 2021.

Assignment 4.4: Weight In Our Solar System

Weight can be a component of various appearance ideals that can vary across cultures. Often there are low and high ranges associated with weight ideals for various genders. This particular metric has been socialized over time to be associated with attractiveness. Trying to alter or change weight often occurs at the expense of happiness and contentment.

Now consider what weight is from a purely scientific viewpoint: a metric to measure the force of gravity pulling downward on an object. Let's poke some fun at this appearance ideal in the following thought experiment. Imagine yourself living on these different planets in our solar system[6] and notice what emotions and thoughts emerge:

To *maintain my weight,* I could live on Saturn which is approximately the same as Earth.

To *gain weight,* I could live on Jupiter where my weight would be more than twice that of Earth.

To *weigh a little less,* I could live on Venus or Uranus.

To *weigh considerably less,* I could live on Mercury or Mars which would be one-quarter of my weight on Earth.

What I notice about my relationship with weight:

_____
_____
_____

My thoughts and emotions about what I'm willing to do in order to change my weight:

_____
_____
_____

A more helpful and balanced perspective on weight includes reminding myself:

_____
_____
_____

N. L. Wood-Barcalow, T. L. Tylka, and C. L. Judge. *Positive Body Image Workbook: A Clinical and Self-Improvement Guide.* Cambridge: Cambridge University Press, 2021.

[6] Numbers based on calculations from solarviews.com.

Assignment 4.5: Alternate Identity Thought Experiment

For this thought experiment, imagine that one day you wake up and are living in an alternate reality that includes vastly different appearance ideals from the ones that are relevant to you now. Examples include existing during a previous era, living in a different country, or identifying with a different gender. The purpose of this thought experiment is to consider how your current perspective on appearance ideals might be altered based on different circumstances. Reflect on the following: What are your reactions to these appearance ideals? What kind of behaviors or practices might you engage in? What would you imagine as being challenging in trying to attain these standards? What would you imagine as being easy in trying to attain these standards?

_____
_____
_____
_____
_____
_____
_____
_____
_____
_____
_____
_____
_____
_____
_____
_____

Now consider whether this thought experiment resulted in any different realizations about your relationship with current appearance ideals:

_____
_____
_____
_____
_____
_____
_____

N. L. Wood-Barcalow, T. L. Tylka, and C. L. Judge. _Positive Body Image Workbook: A Clinical and Self-Improvement Guide._ Cambridge: Cambridge University Press, 2021.

Assignment 4.6: Appearance Trends through the Years

Appearance ideals shift over time due to different trends for hairstyles, clothing, make-up applications, adornments, and even preferred body types. Take time to look back through the years to determine what trends you participated in and your reactions to them now at this point in your life. It can be helpful to look at old photographs as visual reminders of these trends.

This Was A Favorite Trend

_____
_____
_____

I remember doing the following activities/behaviors to achieve this trend:

_____
_____
_____

I made these sacrifices to achieve this trend (e.g., money invested):

_____
_____
_____

I Wish This Trend Would Come Back

_____
_____
_____

This Is A "What Was I Thinking?!" Trend

_____
_____
_____

I Wish This Trend Would Never Come Back

_____
_____
_____

Now reflect on . . .

These are themes I notice associated with these trends:

_____
_____
_____

I now have these changed perspectives of former trends:

_____
_____
_____

N. L. Wood-Barcalow, T. L. Tylka, and C. L. Judge. _Positive Body Image Workbook: A Clinical and Self-Improvement Guide._ Cambridge: Cambridge University Press, 2021.

Assignment 4.7: Body Dissatisfaction

Part A. Review common examples of thoughts associated with body dissatisfaction. For those that you relate to, identify typical situations when you have this thought, what appearance ideal(s) it relates to, and the emotions and physical/bodily sensations you typically experience with this thought. You can add your own examples as well.

Body Dissatisfaction Thoughts	Prompting Situation	Appearance Ideal(s)	Emotions	Physical/Bodily Sensations
Example: *I hate the size of my chest.*	*Comparing my chest size to that of someone I admire*	*Bigger is better*	*Anger, frustration, exasperation, agitation, embarrassment*	*Tingling, redness, hot, tension*
I hate the size of my _____.				
I dislike _____.				
Others don't find my _____ attractive.				
It's not fair that I have to look this way.				
I want to look like him/her/them.				
I will never be happy until _____ changes.				
I'm too _____.				
I'm not enough _____.				
Other:				
Other:				
Other:				

Part B. Now it's time to challenge the appearance ideal(s) and body dissatisfaction thoughts from above.

What is the origin of this appearance ideal?

_____
_____
_____

Who has the authority to define this as an ideal?

_____
_____
_____

What would it be like to reject this ideal? How would it feel?

_____
_____
_____

I imagine these things would be different if I wasn't focused on this appearance ideal:

_____
_____
_____

N. L. Wood-Barcalow, T. L. Tylka, and C. L. Judge. *Positive Body Image Workbook: A Clinical and Self-Improvement Guide.* Cambridge: Cambridge University Press, 2021.

Part C. Now it is time to shift focus from body dissatisfaction to body acceptance.

What barriers stand in the way of current acceptance?

_____
_____
_____

What would be the worst thing(s) that would happen if I accepted my body?

_____
_____
_____

What would be the best thing(s) that would happen if I accepted my body?

_____
_____
_____

N. L. Wood-Barcalow, T. L. Tylka, and C. L. Judge. _Positive Body Image Workbook: A Clinical and Self-Improvement Guide._ Cambridge: Cambridge University Press, 2021.

Assignment 4.8: Appearance Ideals

These are the appearance ideals that are promoted in my culture(s):

_____

_____

_____

These are conflicting messages about the appearance ideals:

_____

_____

_____

These are the standards or expectations that I have for my body based on the appearance ideals in my culture(s):

_____

_____

_____

General ways to challenge these specific appearance ideals:

_____

_____

_____

Here's how I want to reject these appearance ideals:

_____

_____

_____

N. L. Wood-Barcalow, T. L. Tylka, and C. L. Judge. *Positive Body Image Workbook: A Clinical and Self-Improvement Guide.* Cambridge: Cambridge University Press, 2021.

Assignment 4.9: Counter-Messages

Brainstorm on the left side of the table the various appearance ideal messages that are promoted as part of your identified culture(s), whether you accept them or not. Then, identify at least two counter-messages for each appearance ideal on the right side. Be creative with the counter-messages using different types of responses from humor, defiance, anger, compassion, and more. Consider asking a trusted friend/family member to offer suggestions for counter messages and/or sharing your responses after to recognize similarities and differences.

Appearance Ideals	Counter-Messages
Example: *Eyes should be big and round with double eyelids.*	*The "ideal" of double eyelids is based on Westernized beauty standards.*
Example: *Light skin is more attractive.*	*Who says that this is true? I'm proud of my heritage. My skin color is just what it needs to be.*

N. L. Wood-Barcalow, T. L. Tylka, and C. L. Judge. *Positive Body Image Workbook: A Clinical and Self-Improvement Guide.* Cambridge: Cambridge University Press, 2021.

Assignment 4.10: Identify and Challenge "Shoulds" and "Shouldn'ts"

It is helpful to recognize the internal "should" and "shouldn't" statements that exist regarding appearance ideals. Examples of should and shouldn't statements include: "I should weigh this amount," "I should look like this," "I should work out like this," "I shouldn't eat these foods," "I shouldn't take a day off from exercise," and more. In the space below, identify all of the "should" and "shouldn't" beliefs that you have regarding appearance ideals. After identifying them, then challenge those same beliefs in the following section. End the assignment by reflecting on how challenging these beliefs corresponds with positive body image.

✔ Identify Appearance Ideal Beliefs

Examples:

Belief: *I should work out every day.*
Belief: *I shouldn't have grey hair.*

Belief 1: I should _____

Belief 2: I should_____

Belief 3: I should_____

Belief 4: I shouldn't_____

Belief 5: I shouldn't_____

Belief 6: I shouldn't_____

✔ Challenge These Beliefs

Examples:

Challenged Belief: *Working out every day is not necessary for the health of my body, especially when sick or injured. My body needs rest days.*
Challenged Belief: *Grey hair is a natural part of aging and can be very beautiful. Big businesses are making money through messages to cover up grey hair!*

Challenged Belief 1: _____

_____

Challenged Belief 2: _____

_____

Challenged Belief 3: _____

_____

Challenged Belief 4: _____

_____

Challenged Belief 5: _____

_____

Challenged Belief 6: _____

_____

✔ Reflect On These Beliefs

How challenging appearance ideal beliefs moves me toward positive body image:

_____
_____
_____
_____
_____
_____

N. L. Wood-Barcalow, T. L. Tylka, and C. L. Judge. *Positive Body Image Workbook: A Clinical and Self-Improvement Guide.* Cambridge: Cambridge University Press, 2021.

Assignment 4.11: Impact of "Policing"

Policing is a term used to describe the process whereby an individual outwardly comments and/or critiques another individual about how or what to do with their bodies based on appearance ideals. In essence, one individual is trying to exert power or control over another person's body or appearance. For this activity, consider your own experiences of "policing" another person as well as the impact that "policing" had on you as the recipient.

An Example when I Engaged in "Policing"

- Identify facts about the situation/experience/event
- How did the situation/experience/event come about?
- What was my intention by policing this other person?
- What was I experiencing at that time in my life?
- Was I struggling with my own body acceptance or self-acceptance?
- Did my response(s) at the time align with my values then? With my values now?
- What impact, if any, did the policing have on the recipient?
- What impact did the experience have on me at that time? What impact does it have on me now?
- What is my current perspective looking back on this?
- Are there any repairs that I would like to make at this time? If so, what might that look like?
- How might I refrain from repeating this behavior in the future?
- Additional reflections

_____
_____
_____
_____

An Example when Another Person was "Policing" Me

- Identify facts about the situation/experience/event
- How did the situation/experience/event come about?
- What did I do at that moment?
- What impact did the experience have on me at that time? What impact does it have on me now?
- Have I internalized information from this experience? If so, how?
- What is my current perspective looking back on this?
- How I would like to respond to situations like this in the future
- Additional reflections

_____
_____
_____
_____

N. L. Wood-Barcalow, T. L. Tylka, and C. L. Judge. *Positive Body Image Workbook: A Clinical and Self-Improvement Guide.* Cambridge: Cambridge University Press, 2021.

Assignment 4.12: Journal about Appearance Ideals

In the space below, write about the various appearance ideals that are relevant to you currently. Consider the following: how much importance each ideal holds for me personally, what appearance ideals I accept and endorse, what appearance ideals I refuse or reject, what factors influence which ideals I accept versus those that I reject, who in my life endorses similar appearance ideals, what efforts I have invested in trying to attain these ideals, whether I will ever feel a sense of satisfaction while pursuing these ideals, how I have pursued ideals that I once considered healthy and now view as harmful, and more.

N. L. Wood-Barcalow, T. L. Tylka, and C. L. Judge. *Positive Body Image Workbook: A Clinical and Self-Improvement Guide.* Cambridge: Cambridge University Press, 2021.

Assignment 4.13: The National Eating Disorder Association Questions for Social Media

The National Eating Disorder Association (NEDA) offers educational information about Media and Eating Disorders[7] including questions to ask when determining whether social media messages promote **body positivity**. We offer additional topics for consideration on how it relates to moving toward positive body image.

The next time you are on a photo-based social media site, ask yourself these questions:

- **Are the body depictions realistic or digitally altered?** How do altered images impact my own body satisfaction? Am I able to analyze the message without believing it?

- **What does the message really mean? Why are they sending it?** What is this product/person promoting? What's the intention behind it? Do I agree with what they are "selling"?

- **How might it affect someone's body acceptance?** What are my emotions and thoughts while viewing this information? How do I feel after viewing it?

- Who created and profits from the message?

- Before you text, tweet, post comments, and share photos and videos, **ask yourself why you are sending the message, who you want to reach, and analyze its body positivity.** Am I promoting images consistent with positive body image?

My overall reflections:

_____
_____
_____
_____

N. L. Wood-Barcalow, T. L. Tylka, and C. L. Judge. *Positive Body Image Workbook: A Clinical and Self-Improvement Guide.* Cambridge: Cambridge University Press, 2021.

---

[7] https://www.nationaleatingdisorders.org/media-eating-disorders

Assignment 4.14: Balance Beam Metaphor

A balance beam is an apparatus used in gymnastics that stands above the ground (heights can vary) and is typically four inches wide. While walking on a balance beam, a gymnast must engage in concentrated effort and focus on what is immediately below and in front while performing challenging feats. Gymnasts block out what surrounds them in order to be fully occupied with the balance beam. Precision and rigidity are required with the awareness that one slight misstep can result in imbalance and falling off. As a result, there is little room for error and the stakes are high.

Trying to achieve and maintain narrow definitions of appearance ideals is similar to walking on a balance beam. One must continually be concentrating and focusing on current appearance standards to determine what is and is not attractive by reviewing media (including social media postings), identifying trends, and comparing with others. Focusing on appearance ideals can be consuming and leave little opportunity to be aware of and enjoy other areas of life. Following specific trends and appearance investment activities in a rigid manner can result in feeling pressure with the fear that undesirable missteps can result in negative outcomes.

Imagine how this metaphor relates to your investment in appearance ideals and consumption of media and ask yourself the following questions:

- Do I focus on achieving appearance ideals at the expense of focusing on other areas of my life? If so, what are the other areas of my life that are not getting my full focus and/or attention?
- Do I feel as though one misstep could result in negative outcomes?
- How long have I been consumed with appearance ideals?
- What forms of media do I use to shape my expectations of attractiveness?
- What external and internal pressures do I experience about how I should look?
- How does my focus on appearance ideals impact my movement toward positive body image?

Overall reflections:

_____
_____
_____
_____

N. L. Wood-Barcalow, T. L. Tylka, and C. L. Judge. *Positive Body Image Workbook: A Clinical and Self-Improvement Guide.* Cambridge: Cambridge University Press, 2021.

Assignment 4.15: How to Respond to Body Shaming in Social Media

An experience in social media networking can be to purposefully "body shame" others for numerous reasons. Even though shaming or bullying has existed in various forms throughout time, social media body shaming can have a particularly negative effect due to the ability to communicate information to many people in instantaneous time as well as the permanent impact it can have.

Know that it can be common to experience a range of emotions (e.g., anger, shock, disappointment, fear) and reactions (e.g., not knowing what to say, wanting to strike back, removing self from the situation) if you've experienced body shaming from another. It is important to consider the context of shaming (e.g., who made the comment, how public was the comment, who might have seen the negative information) and what you feel comfortable doing in that specific moment as well as how to respond to that event or ones similar to that in the future. Consider the following interventions below to enhance or protect your self-worth and sense of control:

- Talk to a trusted friend or loved one about how the shaming affected you.
- Connect with a supportive group of others who have had similar experiences.
- Identify the various emotions that you felt such as anger, annoyance, agitation, irritation, indignation, fury, offense, fear, anxiety, sadness, hurt, despair, hopelessness, helplessness, embarrassment, shame, guilt, remorse.
- Allow yourself to experience a range of emotions without judging them.
- Notice any urges to respond in an aggressive manner without acting on them.
- Identify the different ways that you can respond before doing so to find an option that fits with your values.
- Consider what action(s) you'd like to take and what action(s) you will take.
- Spend time breathing and reflecting before responding online.
- Express disagreement with the body shaming.
- Ask for clarification of what was communicated.
- Challenge appearance ideals associated with the body shaming.
- Inform the perpetrator that their behavior/comments were offensive.
- Educate the perpetrator on the impact of their actions.
- Interrupt the communication and redirect it.
- Consider the motive(s) or intention(s) of the person(s) doing the body shaming.
- Focus on creating and maintaining your protective shield (see Chapter 17) that keeps the negative information from penetrating.
- Engage in behaviors that allow you to feel good about your body.
- Practice body affirmations that counteract the negative comments.
- Remind yourself that one person's inappropriate comment(s) does not mean that the information is true.
- Access your wise mind in trying to determine how to respond both inwardly and outwardly.
- Remind yourself of your positive qualities.
- Engage in a loving kindness meditation.
- Instead of hiding and avoiding which is a natural response to shame, consider doing things that focus on your strengths.
- Use humor to offset the pain.
- Rely on the comfort and inspiring words from others.
- Consider using intense or strenuous physical activity as a way to respond to anger.
- Engage in self-care acts if any urges for self-directed violence arise.
- Demonstrate power by reminding yourself that those comments cannot break you.
- Participate in a relaxing or soothing activity.
- Be direct and assertive of what is not appropriate in terms of your rights, limits, and boundaries.
- Confront the situation in a way(s) that is congruent with your core values.
- Ask for others' input on how to respond.
- Consider disconnecting from certain forms of social media outlets and/or allowing certain people to access your information.
- Determine whether there is a forum for reporting body shaming.
- Commit to yourself not to do the same behaviors to others.
- Determine whether legal action is available or appropriate.
- Investigate whether there is a process of removing the information from the social media page.
- Share with others the pain that you experience and the toll that body shaming can take on a person to increase awareness and compassion.
- Seek therapy or counseling.
- Use spiritual and/or religious practices.

N. L. Wood-Barcalow, T. L. Tylka, and C. L. Judge. *Positive Body Image Workbook: A Clinical and Self-Improvement Guide.* Cambridge: Cambridge University Press, 2021.

References

1. L. M. Schaefer, J. A. Harriger, L. J. Heinberg, et al. Development and validation of the Sociocultural Attitudes Towards Appearance Questionnaire-4-Revised (SATAQ-4 R). *Int J Eat Disord* 2017; **50**: 104–17.

2. G. Gerbner, L. Gross, M. Morgan, et al. Growing up with television: The cultivation perspective. In: Bryant, J., Zillmann, D., eds. *Media Effects: Advances in Theory and Research.* Hillsdale: Erlbaum, 1994: 17–41.

3. S. Grabe, L. M. Ward, and J. S. Hyde. The role of the media in body image concerns among women: A meta-analysis of experimental and correlational studies. *Psychol Bull* 2008; **134**: 460–76.

4. R. Cohen, T. Newton-John, and A. Slater. The relationship between Facebook and Instagram appearance-focused activities and body image concerns in young women. *Body Image* 2017; **23**: 183–7.

5. G. Holland and M. Tiggemann. A systematic review of the impact of the use of social networking sites on body image and disordered eating outcomes. *Body Image* 2016; **17**: 100–10.

6. D. J. Schwartz, V. Phares, S. Tantleff-Dunn, et al. Body image, psychological functioning, and parental feedback regarding physical appearance. *Int J Eat Disord* 1999; **25**: 339–43.

7. S. Herbozo and J. K. Thompson. Development and validation of the Verbal Commentary on Physical Appearance Scale: Considering both positive and negative commentary. *Body Image* 2006; **3**: 335–44.

8. N. Wolf. *The Beauty Myth: How Images of Beauty are Used Against Women.* London: Chatto & Windus, 1990.

9. S. C. Gilbert, H. Keery, and J. K. Thompson. The media's role in body image and eating disorders. In: Cole, E., Daniel, J. H., eds. *Psychology of Women Book Series. Featuring Females: Feminist Analyses of Media.* Washington: American Psychological Association, 2005: 41–56.

10. C. Benton and B. T. Karazsia. The effect of thin and muscular images on women's body satisfaction. *Body Image* 2015; **13**: 22–7.

11. N. M. Overstreet, D. M. Quinn, and V. B. Agocha. Beyond thinness: The influence of a curvaceous body ideal on body dissatisfaction in Black and White women. *Sex Roles* 2010; **63**: 91–103.

12. L. R. Uhlmann, C. L. Donovan, M. J. Zimmer-Gembeck, et al. The fit beauty ideal: A healthy alternative to thinness or a wolf in sheep's clothing. *Body Image* 2018; **25**: 23–30.

13. H. S. Bell, C. L. Donovan, and R. Ramme. Is athletic really ideal? An examination of the mediating role of body dissatisfaction in predicting disordered eating and compulsive exercise. *Eat Behav* 2016; **21**: 24–9.

14. R. A. Leit, H. G. Pope Jr., and J. J. Gray. Cultural expectations of muscularity in men: The evolution of playgirl centerfolds. *Int J Eat Disord* 2000; **29**: 90–3.

15. G. Cafri, J. K. Thompson, L. Ricciardelli, et al. Pursuit of the muscular ideal: Physical and psychological consequences and putative risk factors. *Clin Psychol Rev* 2005; **25**: 215–39.

16. Pew Research Center. Share of US adults using social media, including Facebook, is mostly unchanged since 2018. Available at: www.pewresearch.org/fact-tank/2019/04/10/share-of-u-s-adults-using-social-media-including-facebook-is-mostly-unchanged-since-2018/ .

17. C. E. Bair, N. R. Kelly, K. L. Serdar, et al. Does the Internet function like magazines? An exploration of image-focused media, eating pathology, and body dissatisfaction. *Eat Behav* 2012; **13**: 398–401.

18. S. A. McLean, S. J. Paxton, E. H. Wertheim, et al. Photoshopping the selfie: Self photo editing and photo investment are associated with body dissatisfaction in adolescent girls. *Int J Eat Disord* 2015; **48**: 1132–40.

19. N. C. Tamplin, S. A. McLean, and S. J. Paxton. Social media literacy protects against the negative impact of exposure to appearance ideal social media images in young adult women but not men. *Body Image* 2018; **26**: 29–37.

20. M. Tiggemann and A. Slater. NetGirls: The Internet, Facebook, and body image concern in adolescent girls. *Int J Eat Disord* 2013; **46**: 630–3.

21. G. Holland and M. Tiggemann. A systematic review of the impact of the use of social networking sites on body image and disordered eating outcomes. *Body Image* 2016; **17**: 100–10.

22. A. R. Lonergan, K. Bussey, J. Mond, et al. Me, my selfie, and I: The relationship between editing and posting selfies and body dissatisfaction in men and women. *Body Image* 2019; **28**: 39–43.

23. J. Fardouly, R. T. Pinkus, and L. R. Vartanian. The impact of appearance comparisons made through social media, traditional media, and in person in women's everyday lives. *Body Image* 2017; **20**: 31–9.

24. J. V. Hogue and J. S. Mills. The effects of active social media engagement with peers on body image in young women. *Body Image* 2018; **28**: 1–5.

25. S. A. McLean, S. J. Paxton, and E. H. Wertheim. The role of media literacy in body dissatisfaction and disordered eating: A systematic review. *Body Image* 2016; **19**: 9–23.

26. S. Wilksch. Media literacy interventions to facilitate positive body image and embodiment. In: Tylka, T. L., Piran, N. eds. *Handbook of Positive Body Image and Embodiment: Constructs, Protective Factors, and Interventions.* New York: Oxford University Press, 2019: 374–84.

27. S. A. McLean, S J. Paxton, and E. H. Wertheim. Does media literacy mitigate risk for reduced body satisfaction following exposure to thin-ideal media? *J Youth Adolesc* 2016; **45**: 1678–95.

28. R. Cohen, L. Irwin, T. Newton-John, et al. #bodypositivity: A content analysis of body positive accounts on Instagram. *Body Image* 2019; **29**: 47–57.

29. R. B. Clayton, J. L. Ridgway, and J. Hendrickse. Is plus size equal? The positive impacts of average and plus sized media fashion models on women's cognitive resource allocation, social comparisons, and body satisfaction. *Commun Monogr* 2017; **84**: 406–22.

30. P. C. Diedrichs and C. Lee. Waif goodbye! Average-size female models promote positive body image and appeal to consumers. *Psychol Health* 2011; **26**: 1273–91.

31. R. F. Rodgers, L. Kruger, A. S. Lowy, et al. Getting Real about body image: A qualitative investigation of the usefulness of the Aerie Real campaign. *Body Image* 2019; **30**: 127–34.

32. National Eating Disorders Association. Get real! Digital media literacy toolkit. Available at: www.google.com/url?sa=t&rct=j&q=&esrc=s&source=web&cd=1&ved=2ahUKEwiF-YiAqOfkAhXGrZ4KHeorBVEQFjAAegQIAxAC&url=https%3A%2F%2Fwww.nationaleatingdisorders.org%2Fsites%2Fdefault%2Ffiles%2FToolkits%2FGetRealToolkit.pdf&usg=AOvVaw0wR45MqtB1hmY_7_lgX1Zg .

33. H-T. G. Chou and N. Edge. "They are happier and having better lives than I am": The impact of using Facebook on perceptions of others' lives. *Cyberpsychol Behav Social Networking* 2012; **15**: 2.

34. J. Fardouly and R. M. Rapee. The impact of no-makeup selfies on young women's body image. *Body Image* 2019; **28**: 128–34.

35. A. Slater, N. Varsani, and P. C. Diedrichs. #fitspo or #loveyourself? The impact of fitspiration and self-compassion Instagram images on women's body image, self-compassion, and mood. *Body Image* 2017; **22**: 87–96.

36. A. Slater, N. Cole, and J. Fardouly. The effect of exposure to parodies of thin-ideal images on young women's body image and mood. *Body Image* 2019; **29**: 82–9.

37. Federal Trade Commission. *Weight Loss Advertising: An Analysis of Current Trends Staff Report.* Available at: www.ftc.gov/reports/weight-loss-advertisingan-analysis-current-trends .

38. D. Schooler, L. M. Ward, A. Merriwether, et al. Who's that girl: Television's role in the body image development of young White and Black women. *Psychol Women Q* 2004; **28**: 38–47.

Weight Stigma versus Weight Inclusivity

Theory and Research Overview

We are often evaluated and judged based on our body size and amount of body fat. We are pressured constantly by media to try to "shed that fat" and "firm up" to achieve a "healthy and attractive" body. Such media messages are fear-based and try to connect our body fat with poor health and appearance. Media want us to think, "the lower body fat we have, the better we look and feel." After all, this mindset sells fat-loss products and exercise programs and equipment. However, research does not support the assertion that body fat causes poor health [1–4]. There are additional variables that impact the association between weight and health, such as weight stigma [5].

Weight stigma (also known as weight bias, weight discrimination, fat shaming, fat prejudice, and anti-fat attitudes) consists of negative attitudes, stereotypes, or beliefs held toward higher-weight individuals [6–8].[1] There are many forms of weight stigma, including weight-related teasing, bullying, harassment, violence, hostility, rejection, neglect, inadequate care, and microaggressions. **Microaggressions** communicate hostility or negativity toward higher-weight individuals and/or promote the "thin is good, fat is bad" bias [3]. Pressures to lose weight and negative appearance comments are weight-related microaggressions, even if such pressure is done out of a concern for health (e.g., "Have you thought about dieting? I'm just concerned about your health"). Telling a loved one that they "look great" when they lost weight or body fat also can be a weight-related microaggression. Although it is intended as a compliment, and the loved one may interpret it positively, the comment still communicates the "thin is good, fat is bad" bias. Comments such as these are called **complimentary weightism** [9].

Media portrayals of higher-weight individuals are often stigmatizing and inaccurate, thereby perpetuating false beliefs about weight [10]. For example, a *Daily Mail* article headline read, "Why I refuse to let my daughter be taught by a fat teacher," and a *Herald Sun* article headline read, "Obese? You're probably too lazy to exercise." Weight stigma also appears in schools, healthcare facilities, public health programs, workplace settings, and even conversations with friends, family, partners, and strangers. Higher-weight children are often stigmatized by peers, classmates, teachers, and school administrators [11–12]. Higher-weight patients are often stigmatized by healthcare professionals and insurance companies [8, 13–15]. In a large sample of higher-weight women, 69 percent experienced weight stigma by a physician (with over half reporting stigma over multiple times), 46 percent from nurses, 37 percent from dietitians, and 21 percent from additional health professionals [16]. Examples may include doctors and other medical staff making negative or inappropriate weight-related comments to patients, not having or using medical equipment (e.g., blood pressure cuffs) and hospital gowns for higher-weight individuals, engaging in mandatory weighing, having only chairs with fixed armrests, etc.

Weight stigma can be especially harmful in healthcare settings, such as suggesting weight loss to a patient who comes in for a concern unrelated to weight. As an example, Ellen Maud Bennett, a sixty-four-year-old higher-weight woman, experienced weight stigma from the medical profession – she felt unwell for years, and when she sought help, no medical professional offered any diagnostics, treatment, support, or suggestions beyond "lose weight." Days before her death, she was finally diagnosed – with inoperable cancer. She died on May 11, 2018. Her obituary includes her dying wish that higher-weight people advocate strongly for their health and not accept that being fat is the only relevant health issue [17]. Indeed, experiencing weight stigma in healthcare settings may discourage higher-weight patients from seeking routine and preventative care and treatment [18–19].

Medical professionals may also overlook symptoms of anorexia nervosa and bulimia nervosa in medium-weight and higher-weight individuals, as they may believe the myth that those with eating disorders should be lower weight. Weight stigma practices can even occur among eating disorder professionals [20]. For example, they may attribute high weight to lifestyle causes, recommend behavioral weight loss and low-calorie diets (even though such restriction can be a symptom of eating disorders), and require weight loss as a mandate to remain in treatment. Even low- and medium-weight individuals can experience negative effects from weight-related stigma [3]. For example, medical professionals may ignore the symptoms of sleep apnea and type 2 diabetes in these

---

[1] Throughout, we use the descriptive terms low weight, medium weight, high weight, and very high weight rather than evaluative terms such as thin, normal or "healthy," overweight, and obese. The latter terms tend to be stigmatizing (e.g., "over who's weight?," equating BMI with health), while the terms low weight, medium weight, high weight, and very high weight are descriptors. At times in this review, we combine high weight and very high weight into "higher weight" and low and medium weight into "lower weight."

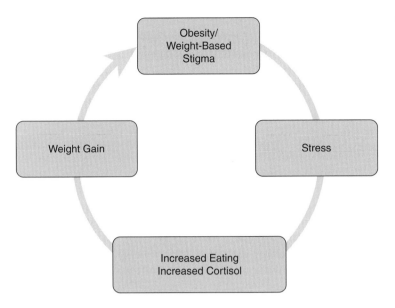

Figure 5.1 The harmful cycle of weight stigma. By Janet Tomiyama [32]; reproduced with permission.

individuals because these conditions have been stereotyped as diagnoses that affect higher-weight individuals.

When medical and other health professionals prioritize weight as a main indicator of health and prescribe weight loss to treat many health problems of higher-weight individuals, they are following the **weight normative approach**. This approach assumes that the likelihood of disease increases as weight increases [3, 21]. It emphasizes personal responsibility for "healthy lifestyle choices" and the maintenance of "healthy weight."

However, the weight normative approach is problematic for many reasons. First, as in the case of Ms. Bennett, it may overlook various health problems, attributing these problems to fat instead of another issue, and then treating the concern by telling patients to lose weight [3, 21]. Second, it assumes that high weight causes poor health, when poor health may be best attributed to other factors such as weight stigma, lower socio-economic status, insulin resistance (at all weights), and the lack of physical movement (at all weights) [5, 22–23]. Large national data sets have revealed that having low weight does not automatically equal better health and longevity [1–2]. Third, it suggests that weight can be controlled through "life-style changes" and "will-power" related to eating. Yet, voluntarily restricting what we eat may trigger a biological urge to eat and a preoccupation with food, emotional eating, binge eating, eating in the absence of hunger, and weight cycling (repeatedly losing and gaining weight) [24–27]. Findings from twenty-nine studies on weight loss programs found that participants regained, on average, 77 percent of their initial weight loss within five years [28] – given that some participants dropped out before the end of the study, the percentage of weight gain could be even higher. When shown pictures of high calorie foods, dieters had increased activation in brain regions associated with craving those foods and noticing and paying attention to them [29]. In short – the more we deprive ourselves of certain foods in the name of weight loss, the more appetizing and tougher to resist these restricted foods become.

Importantly, lower-income households may not be able to afford fresh fruits and vegetables, and lower-income communities may not have parks, green spaces, bike paths, and recreational facilities to support "lifestyle changes" [22, 30–31], making messages emphasizing individual responsibility to "maintain a healthy weight" both uninformed and unfair [3]. If attempts to reach and maintain a "healthy weight" fail and are seen as impossible, engaging in healthy behaviors may be viewed as pointless [3].

For many years, high weight has been thought to cause ill health. An alternative viewpoint is that weight stigma, rather than simply weight itself, impacts physical health and psychological well-being [3]. Daly, Sutin, and Robinson [5] found that weight stigma explained the association between weight and declining cardiovascular, metabolic, and immune health. That is, weight stigma, rather than simply weight alone, contributed to these adverse health issues. Weight stigma is a "vicious cycle" – it is a stressor that prompts negative emotions and biochemical responses such as cortisol release (which prompts fat storage and eating behavior) that, in turn, results in weight gain, which may then expose individuals to additional weight stigma [32] and exercise avoidance [33]. See Figure 5.1.

Weight stigma is connected to internalized weight bias and healthism. **Internalized weight bias** occurs when an individual believes negative weight-based stereotypes and judges themselves and others negatively based on these stereotypes [34–36]. This judgment contributes to body blame and shame, which harms body image (e.g., "If only I wasn't so fat. I hate my body!") and is also linked to binge eating, emotional eating, purging, distress, and lower quality of life [37]. To understand your level of internalized weight bias, complete the measure of internalized weight bias within this chapter. While the original *Weight Bias Internalization Scale* (WBIS [35]) was written to be used with higher-weight individuals, items were reworded in a modified version (WBIS-M [36]) to be able to be used with all individuals, as a person of any weight can experience internalized weight bias. This scale has good reliability and validity with adult community samples of all body weights [35–36]. **Healthism** moralizes lower weight bodies as "healthy and good," while judging higher-weight bodies as "unhealthy and bad." Under healthism, higher-weight individuals are thought to be failing to live up to the lifestyle choices that promise health [4, 38–39].

Fortunately, we can challenge weight stigma, internalized weight bias, and healthism by adopting a weight-inclusive approach. The **weight-inclusive approach** aims to support the well-being and health of people of all body sizes [3, 21]. It seeks to end the stigma of health problems and weight in all areas of life. It acknowledges that weight is not a personal choice that can be voluntarily controlled, and appreciates that bodies come in a variety of shapes and sizes. It finds alternatives to the ineffective and harmful practice of pursuing weight loss. The weight-inclusive approach is *not* "giving up" on our bodies' health. Quite the contrary, it helps protect health by giving up methods that have been shown to be ineffective and harmful. Also, the weight-inclusive approach does *not* mean that all individuals, regardless of their body size, are healthy. Instead, it suggests that weight alone cannot be used to determine health. Further, it suggests that all people should receive non-stigmatizing care and treatment to enhance their health and well-being to the degree that they choose.

The weight-inclusive approach can be applied in healthcare, informing the work of professionals, thereby bettering the lives of their clients, as it is based on the principle of "do no harm" [3, 21]. Specifically, it assists clients in developing long-term health practices (e.g., intuitive eating, life enhancing movement, self-care) rather than pursuing weight loss. It integrates scientifically supported practices into prevention and treatment efforts. It works with the community to provide safe means of physical activity for all bodies and access to nutritious food. The weight-inclusive approach can also be adopted in other settings that have been found to perpetuate weight stigma (e.g., media, schools, work, conversations with loved ones).

One example of the weight-inclusive approach is Health at Every Size® (HAES) [3, 40]. This approach does not suggest that people at every size are healthy. Rather, it promotes access to healthy behaviors and practices for people of all sizes. HAES is a registered trademark of the Association for Size Diversity and Health [41], and its principles are:

- **Weight Inclusivity:** Accept and respect the wide range of body shapes and sizes, and reject idealizing and pathologizing certain bodies.
- **Health Enhancement:** Support health policies that improve access to information and services. Support personal practices that improve well-being, including physical, economic, social, spiritual, emotional, and other needs.
- **Respectful Care:** Acknowledge and work toward ending weight stigma. Provide information and services from an understanding that socioeconomic status, race, gender, sexual orientation, age, and other identities impact weight stigma. Support environments that address these inequities.

- **Eating for Well-Being:** Promote flexible, intuitive eating based on hunger, satiety, nutritional needs, and pleasure, rather than any externally regulated eating plan focused on weight control.
- **Life-Enhancing Movement:** Support physical activities that allow people of all sizes, abilities, and interests to engage in enjoyable movement to the degree that they choose.

Data support the weight-inclusive approach [3, 21]. Interventions designed to be weight-inclusive resulted in improved physiological measures (e.g., blood pressure), health practices (e.g., increased physical activity), and psychological measures (e.g., self-esteem and disordered eating) [42]. Weight-inclusive interventions achieved these health improvements more successfully than interventions that emphasized dieting. Participants who received weight-inclusive interventions also demonstrated reduced dropout rates and no negative outcomes [42]. In one example, a weight-inclusive intervention was evaluated against a dieting-based intervention [43–44]. Participants, who were women with higher weights, received weekly group interventions (weight inclusive or dieting) for six months followed by monthly aftercare group support for another six months. Findings yielded more positive results for the weight-inclusive intervention over the one-year and two-year follow-ups [43–44]. Specifically, the weight-inclusive intervention group decreased total cholesterol, low-density lipoprotein (LDL cholesterol), triglycerides, and systolic blood pressure at the two-year follow-up. The weight-inclusive group decreased eating restraint, physical hunger rating, disinhibited (out of control) eating, drive for thinness, bulimic symptoms, body dissatisfaction, depression, and body image avoidance and increased self-esteem at both one-year and two-year follow-up. Whereas the dieting intervention group lost weight and showed initial improvements on many variables at the one-year follow-up, they had regained weight and did not sustain these improvements at the two-year follow-up. Participants in the dieting intervention reduced disinhibited (out of control) eating but reported decreased self-esteem. Furthermore, drop-out rates were higher in the dieting intervention group (41 percent) compared to the weight-inclusive intervention group (8 percent).

These findings suggest that weight-inclusive interventions demonstrate better adherence to practices that promote physical health and psychological well-being than dieting interventions, and these effects can be sustained over time [3, 21]. Clinicians can offer weight-inclusive principles through the clinician-client relationship and by connecting individuals to support groups (in person or online) that follow the weight-inclusive approach.[2] To conclude, it is important to understand that moving away from focusing on weight and dieting and toward weight inclusivity is not a simple and easy process. Compassion is essential to this journey. According to Dr. Rachel Millner, a licensed psychologist and certified eating disorder

---

[2] A website that may be useful is www.haescommunity.org/ .

specialist who works with clients who present with food and body issues:

> "Even if we say 'no' to participating in diet culture doesn't mean diet culture no longer impacts us. Divesting is a process. We say 'no.' Diet culture tries to pull us back in. We say 'no' again.
>
> Diet culture is the air we breathe. It doesn't just lure us with promises of thinness, but with promises of belonging, acceptance, happiness, love, health, freedom from stigma, and a longer life. We identify the lies. We say 'no' again.
>
> Not saying 'no' is understandable especially when dealing with many forms of oppression. Judging those who continue to participate is contributing to the very system that diet culture is contained in. We can choose to not blame the individual and still choose not to be around people whose participation in diet culture harms us.
>
> Recognizing the personal and systemic harm of diet culture doesn't automatically mean we are able to stop participating, but it is the start of the process.
>
> Remember that many in the HAES community and fat positive community not only do this work as their career, but are surrounded by HAES and fat positive community all the time. Community is a powerful antidote to diet culture.
>
> If you find yourself having to say 'no' to participating every day, you're not doing it wrong. If you have to remind yourself multiple times a day that you have divested, you're not doing it wrong. If one day you don't participate and the next day you do, you're not doing it wrong. Divestment isn't a destination, it's a process. Wherever you are in the process, trust yourself. You're doing it exactly the right way for you."

Treatment Planning Tools

Talking Points for Sessions

- Discuss immediate thoughts and emotions associated with a wide range of weights, including specific numbers identified in session(s) as ideal, feared, acceptable, and unacceptable weights
  - Consider the meaning attached to these various weights, highlighting inconsistencies
- Discuss various forms of weight stigma in both society and self (internalized beliefs)
  - Identify examples of weight stigma directed toward others and self
  - Identify impact of weight stigma directed towards others and self
- Discuss how developing a weight-inclusive approach would "look" as applied to the client's life (e.g., identify various ways diet culture is embedded in daily life and its negative impacts, advocate for individuals who are mistreated because of their weight, consult HAES or weight-inclusive resources, commit to resisting diet culture)
- Discuss how developing a weight-inclusive approach would "look" in therapy in terms of the client's goals and objectives

Treatment Plan

Goals

- ❏ Identify the various types of microaggressions I have personally experienced or witnessed related to weight stigma
- ❏ Consider how internalized weight bias influences positive body image
- ❏ Identify challenges associated with moving toward positive body image
- ❏ Increase experience(s) of feeling comfortable in my own skin
- ❏ Consider the role of mindreading about weight/shape/size when interacting with others
- ❏ Identify unhelpful avoidance associated with weight concerns and practice "approach" activities
- ❏ Consider how to respond to compliments (e.g., accept, deflect, challenge)
- ❏ Investigate explicit and implicit messages that equate weight with health
- ❏ Explore whether weight status and concerns about what medical providers might say impacts my decision to seek medical care, including both preventative measures (e.g., regular check-ups) and treatment for an illness or injury
- ❏ Explore how fear can be related to eating patterns and physical movement
- ❏ Identify examples of healthcare appointments when my weight was/is discussed and explore associated emotions and thoughts
- ❏ Explore how the "weight normative approach" has influenced my thoughts, emotions and behaviors
- ❏ Recognize how the cycle of food restriction leads to craving and preoccupation with food which leads to overeating
- ❏ Explore how much self-blame and shame relates to weight issues *and* how to alter the process
- ❏ Recognize when a focus on "healthism" influenced participation in enjoyable activities, relationships, and more

Objectives

- ❏ Identify emotions and thoughts associated with experiencing comments on weight, both solicited and unsolicited
- ❏ Learn how certain industries or businesses benefit from creating or maintaining negative body image as a way to promote products or services
- ❏ Learn how to critique media messages
- ❏ Contact industries or businesses to provide feedback about how their practices impact the body image of others
- ❏ Identify people around whom I feel good/safe
- ❏ Engage in one activity this week that goes against an unhelpful established attitude/belief based on appearance ideals about what "I should do"
- ❏ Identify what makes me a worthwhile person
- ❏ Imagine how embracing aspects of positive body image can buffer against pressures associated with appearance ideals
- ❏ Identify examples of the message "low fat = healthy body" in media

❏ Recognize examples of weight stigma in different environments such as school, work, and healthcare settings

❏ Label and challenge mindreading about weight in the moment

❏ Identify examples of negative weight-based stereotypes and judgments about others and myself

Additional Resources

R. S. Scritchfield. *Body Kindness: Transform Your Health from the Inside Out and Never Say Diet Again*. New York: Workman Publishing Company, 2016. Podcast available at: www.bodykindnessbook.com/podcast/

L. Bacon and L. Aphramor. *Body Respect*. Dallas: BenBella Books, 2014.

A. Pershing and C. Turner. *Binge Eating Disorder: The Journey to Recovery and Beyond*. New York: Routledge, 2018.

L. Bacon. *Health at Every Size: The Surprising Truth about Your Weight*. Dallas: BenBella Books, 2010. See also: www.thebodypositive.org/

C. Sobczak. *Embody: Learning to Love Your Unique Body (and Quiet that Critical Voice!)*. Carlsbad: Gurze Books, 2014.

P. Campos. *The Obesity Myth: Why America's Obsession with Weight is Hazardous to Your Health*. New York: Gotham, 2004.

K. Koenig and P. O'Mahoney. *Helping Patients Outsmart Overeating: Psychological Strategies for Doctors and Health Care Providers*. Lanham: Rowman and Littlefield, 2017. See also: https://benourished.org/

Clinicians (being a recovered clinician): www.jessihaggerty.com/blog/blp20

Clinicians (being a Body Trust® provider): https://benourished.org/training-institute/

Clients (finding a Body Trust® provider): https://benourished.org/certified-body-trust-providers/

Assessment 5.1: Modified Weight Bias Internalization Scale (WBIS-M)

Please indicate the extent to which you agree with each statement by **circling the number** to the right of each item.

	Strongly Disagree	Moderately Disagree	Slightly Disagree	Neutral	Slightly Agree	Moderately Agree	Strongly Agree
1. Because of my weight, I feel that I am just as competent as anyone.	7	6	5	4	3	2	1
2. I am less attractive than most other people because of my weight.	1	2	3	4	5	6	7
3. I feel anxious about my weight because of what people might think of me.	1	2	3	4	5	6	7
4. I wish I could drastically change my weight.	1	2	3	4	5	6	7
5. Whenever I think a lot about my weight, I feel depressed.	1	2	3	4	5	6	7
6. I hate myself for my weight.	1	2	3	4	5	6	7
7. My weight is a major way that I judge my value as a person.	1	2	3	4	5	6	7
8. I don't feel that I deserve to have a really fulfilling social life, because of my weight.	1	2	3	4	5	6	7
9. I am OK being the weight that I am.	7	6	5	4	3	2	1
10. Because of my weight, I don't feel like my true self.	1	2	3	4	5	6	7
11. Because of my weight, I don't understand how anyone attractive would want to date me.	1	2	3	4	5	6	7
Total Weight Bias Internalization score: add items 1–11 and then divide by 11 =							

Total Weight Bias Internalization score between:

- **4.5–7** = high levels of internalized weight bias

- **2.5–4.4** = moderate levels of internalized weight bias

- **below 2.5** = low internalized weight bias

Note. Reprinted with permission. The authors of the WBIS-M are Pearl and Puhl, [*] who modified the original WBIS to be inclusive of respondents of all weights. The authors of the original WBIS are Durso and Latner. [**] Please contact the authors of the WBIS-M for permission to use it within research; there is no need to contact them to use it with clients or to complete on your own.

[*] R. L. Pearl and R. M. Puhl. Measuring internalized weight attitudes across body weight categories: Validation of the Modified Weight Bias Internalization Scale. *Body Image* 2014; **11**: 89–92.

[**] L. E. Durso and J. D. Latner. Understanding self-directed stigma: Development of the Weight Bias Internalization Scale. *Obes* 2008; **16**: S80–6.

Modified Weight Bias Internalization Scale (WBIS-M) Applications

- If you agree with item 4 (*I wish I could drastically change my weight*), what do you hope weight loss will change about your life? About what you will do and/or won't do? About the emotions you will or won't experience? About how you will think about and treat yourself? About how you think others will treat you?

- Regarding item 7 (*My weight is a major way that I judge my value as a person*), what are other ways that you judge your value as a person? Imagine a time in the future when you endorse more positive body image. Make a list of the non-weight-related ways you will use when thinking about your value as a person, such as based on being a friend, parent, volunteer, member of a spiritual/religious community, and more. In the week to come, take a planned action in one of the listed areas and notice the impact on your sense of self.

- Can you imagine a situation in which you achieved health and happiness regardless of your weight? What do you imagine your life would be like? What would be similar? What would be different? How would your happiness be measured?

- How might your quality of life change if internalized weight bias was no longer an issue? What activities would you engage in? What behaviors would you let go of? How might it impact judgments of yourself and others? Would there be any changes in your relationships? How would letting go of this bias get you closer to positive body image?

Assignment 5.1: Attachment to Weights

These are the emotions, thoughts, and behaviors I have attached to the following weights, as well as my ideas for more helpful thoughts and behaviors I can use to manage related emotions:

	Emotions	Thoughts	Behaviors	More Helpful Thoughts and Behaviors
Example: Feared weight	Angry Uncomfortable Panicked Afraid	I can't handle this. No one will love me at this weight.	Go on a diet Exercise Avoid swimming	I can do tough things. I can find ways to cope with my emotions that aren't about food, size, and shape. I'm still going to swim, because I enjoy it.
Current weight:				
Ideal weight:				
Feared weight:				
Highest weight:				
Lowest weight:				
Other weight:				

Meanings and attachments to different weights over time, including my thoughts, behaviors, emotions, and their impact on my body acceptance:

_____

_____

_____

_____

_____

How has attachment to weight caused me to postpone valued and enjoyable experiences? For example, "I will only go on that vacation once I weigh X," or "I cannot (interview/volunteer/attend the class reunion) until I weigh X"

_____

_____

_____

_____

How has my attachment to weight impacted my journey toward positive body image?

_____

_____

_____

_____

_____

N. L. Wood-Barcalow, T. L. Tylka, and C. L. Judge. *Positive Body Image Workbook: A Clinical and Self-Improvement Guide.* Cambridge: Cambridge University Press, 2021.

What is one step I want to take in the next week in order to challenge attachment to weight as a barrier to my valued goals and/or enjoyable activities?

_____
_____
_____
_____
_____
_____
_____

N. L. Wood-Barcalow, T. L. Tylka, and C. L. Judge. *Positive Body Image Workbook: A Clinical and Self-Improvement Guide.* Cambridge: Cambridge University Press, 2021.

Assignment 5.2: Reasons for Weighing

I weigh myself for the following reasons:

Reasons for Weighing	Yes or No	Realizations
Plan how my day will be		
Figure out how much I need to eat		
Figure out how much I need to exercise		
Check that I'm doing okay		
Check whether what I ate impacted my weight		
Punish myself for what I did		
Punish myself for what I didn't do		
Keep myself from doing certain things		
Decrease my stress or anxiety		
My health provider encouraged me to do so		
Trying to lose/maintain/restore weight		
Reduce body image discomfort		
Someone is encouraging me to do so		
Increase my motivation		
Minimize obsessive thoughts		
Track my health status		
To make sure that I'm not "getting out of" or "losing" control		
I feel like I have to		
To watch the trend over time		
Because it's what I've always done		
Other:		
Other:		
Other:		
Other:		

What I notice about my reasons for weighing:

_____

_____

_____

_____

N. L. Wood-Barcalow, T. L. Tylka, and C. L. Judge. *Positive Body Image Workbook: A Clinical and Self-Improvement Guide.* Cambridge: Cambridge University Press, 2021.

What I imagine would be different if I changed my reasons for weighing:

_____
_____
_____
_____

I realize these reasons for weighing move me away from positive body image:

_____
_____
_____
_____

I realize these reasons for weighing move me toward positive body image:

_____
_____
_____
_____

I commit:

_____
_____
_____
_____

N. L. Wood-Barcalow, T. L. Tylka, and C. L. Judge. _Positive Body Image Workbook: A Clinical and Self-Improvement Guide._ Cambridge: Cambridge University Press, 2021.

Assignment 5.3: Weighing Experiment

Weighing practices often follow a routine that has a significant impact on body image. Consider the many reasons why you weigh and the routine(s) associated with it (e.g., frequency, specific time of day, what clothing is worn/not worn). To move toward positive body image, it can be helpful to refrain from extremes associated with weighing such as excessive behaviors (e.g., weighing numerous times a day) to avoidant behaviors (e.g., refusing to weigh yourself). Imagine where you fall on this continuum from excessive to avoidant and consider trying out an experiment with the opposite behavior. For example, if you tend to do excessive amounts of weighing try to refrain from doing so for a certain amount of time (e.g., one day). Or if you tend to avoid weighing yourself try an experiment whereby you weigh yourself more frequently (e.g., one time a month). The purpose of this experiment is to understand the various thoughts, emotions, and behaviors associated with weighing and how it impacts your body image.

Complete these items *before* the experiment

The reason(s) I typically refrain from weighing myself OR excessively weigh myself include(s):

_____

_____

_____

I commit to refraining from weighing OR exposing myself to weighing for this *amount of time*:

_____

_____

_____

I anticipate that I will *feel like this* while trying this experiment:

_____

_____

_____

I anticipate that I will *think like this* while trying this experiment:

_____

_____

_____

I will use these *coping strategies* to combat the urge to either weigh OR avoid weighing myself:

_____

_____

_____

Additional thoughts:

_____

_____

_____

Complete these items *after* the experiment

I experienced these thoughts:

_____

_____

_____

I experienced these emotions:

_____

_____

_____

N. L. Wood-Barcalow, T. L. Tylka, and C. L. Judge. *Positive Body Image Workbook: A Clinical and Self-Improvement Guide.* Cambridge: Cambridge University Press, 2021.

I noticed these changes in my behaviors:

_____
_____
_____

I'm surprised by:

_____
_____
_____

I learned this about myself from trying this experiment:

_____
_____
_____

I commit to this for the future as I move toward positive body image:

_____
_____
_____

Additional reflections:

_____
_____
_____

N. L. Wood-Barcalow, T. L. Tylka, and C. L. Judge. _Positive Body Image Workbook: A Clinical and Self-Improvement Guide._ Cambridge: Cambridge University Press, 2021.

Assignment 5.4: Shifting Focus from Weight

Focusing on my weight affects me in these ways:

_____
_____
_____

Focusing on my weight affects my relationships in these ways:

_____
_____
_____

I commit to doing these things when I have the urge to judge myself based on weight:

_____
_____
_____

Shifting my focus away from weight includes:

_____
_____
_____

These are the ways that I want to define myself that do not include weight:

_____
_____
_____

Moving toward positive body image, I'd like to have the following relationship with my weight:

_____
_____
_____

N. L. Wood-Barcalow, T. L. Tylka, and C. L. Judge. *Positive Body Image Workbook: A Clinical and Self-Improvement Guide.* Cambridge: Cambridge University Press, 2021.

Assignment 5.5: Weight Does Not Equal Health

Society equates weight with health status, suggesting that lower weights are "healthy" and higher weights are "unhealthy." Using weight alone to define health can result in a narrow definition of health, ignore other important variables, promote shame and blame, and contribute to weight stigma.

For this journal activity, reflect on your own experiences of equating weight with health status for yourself and others (preferably those who are close to you). Also consider what standards you use to determine what is "healthy" and "unhealthy," such as numbers that you believe are outside of a certain range, BMI, recommendations from medical providers, and more. Ask, "What do these numbers mean to me?"

_____
_____
_____
_____
_____

Now, reflect on the various beliefs that you have about these numbers. What narratives (or stories) do you have about various weights? Examples of narratives associated with lower weights might include "success," "great restraint," "being better than others," "personal control," or "perfection." Examples of narratives associated with higher weights might include "failure," "need to eat less," "need to change," "less than others," and/or "don't have control."

_____
_____
_____
_____
_____

Next, consider the emotions that are tied to various numbers. What emotions do you experience when reflecting on your (or someone close to you) lowest weights? What emotions do you experience when reflecting on your (or someone close to you) highest weights?

_____
_____
_____
_____
_____

Reflect on how the belief that "weight equals health" impacts your actions. What do you do with these beliefs? What do you _not_ do? How do you treat yourself? How do you treat others?

_____
_____
_____
_____
_____

Finally, consider how things might be different without the belief that "weight equals health" as you move toward positive body image.

_____
_____
_____
_____
_____

N. L. Wood-Barcalow, T. L. Tylka, and C. L. Judge. _Positive Body Image Workbook: A Clinical and Self-Improvement Guide._ Cambridge: Cambridge University Press, 2021.

Assignment 5.6: Experiences of Weight Stigma

Identify which of the following you have experienced:

Weight Stigma Experience	Yes/No	How I Would Like Myself or Others to Respond if I Encounter This Experience in the Future
Example: *Avoided routine medical care due to concerns of how weight would be addressed*	*Yes*	*I will attend medical appointments with providers who use a weight-inclusive approach and with whom I'm comfortable.*
Teased about my weight		
Bullied about my weight		
Received unsolicited comments from others about my weight		
Offered smaller portions of food than others		
Dismissed by someone else due to my weight		
Unable to identify furniture that could support my weight		
Treated as invisible due to my weight (e.g., not acknowledged, no eye contact)		
Told to change my eating habits		
Told to change my movement habits		
Received scare tactics about the impact of my weight		
Believed that I would not experience love due to my weight		
Believed that I don't deserve love due to my weight		
Ignored when shopping for clothing		
Actual health issues were minimized by a healthcare provider who focused on my weight		
Informed that certain medical procedures could/would not happen without weight loss first		
Avoided preventative medical care due to concerns of how weight would be addressed		
Avoided routine medical care due to concerns of how weight would be addressed		
Avoided recommended medical procedures		
Avoided physical intimacy		
Other:		
Other:		
Other:		

N. L. Wood-Barcalow, T. L. Tylka, and C. L. Judge. *Positive Body Image Workbook: A Clinical and Self-Improvement Guide.* Cambridge: Cambridge University Press, 2021.

What I notice about my experiences with weight stigma:

_____
_____
_____

What I imagine would or could be different if I had not experienced weight stigma:

_____
_____
_____

How I would like to respond (inwardly, outwardly) to future experiences of weight stigma:

_____
_____
_____

I commit:

_____
_____
_____

N. L. Wood-Barcalow, T. L. Tylka, and C. L. Judge. *Positive Body Image Workbook: A Clinical and Self-Improvement Guide.* Cambridge: Cambridge University Press, 2021.

Assignment 5.7: Pressures from Others about My Weight/Shape

For this journal experience, identify the various people who have pressured you about weight: parents, siblings, extended family members (grandparents, aunts/uncles, cousins), romantic partners, peers/friends, children, health providers, personal trainers, and more. Now consider the collective toll or impact of these pressures on your psychological health (body image, self-esteem, self-talk), willingness to seek medical treatment, engagement in physical intimacy, comfort with wearing certain clothing, participating in physical activity, willingness to date, taking risks, comfort in having candid conversations about weight, and more. What themes do you notice about how this pressure impacts your quality of life? What things might change if this pressure no longer existed? As you move toward positive body image, how do you imagine responding to these pressures?

_____
_____
_____
_____
_____
_____
_____
_____
_____
_____
_____
_____
_____

N. L. Wood-Barcalow, T. L. Tylka, and C. L. Judge. _Positive Body Image Workbook: A Clinical and Self-Improvement Guide._ Cambridge: Cambridge University Press, 2021.

Assignment 5.8: Types of Internalized Weight Bias

Internalized Weight Bias Experiences	Yes/No	More Helpful Response
Example: *Believed that I am less attractive than others*	Yes	*I have positive qualities. Appearance is not the most important thing in life. How I am feeling now is probably influencing my thoughts, and the intensity of this feeling won't last forever.*
Anticipated what others may think negatively about me		
Anticipated what others may say negatively about me		
Fantasized about ways to lose weight to increase acceptance		
Experienced self-hatred due to my weight		
Consistently put myself down as a way to punish myself		
Believed that I am less attractive than others		
Believed that attractive people will reject me		
Consistently put myself down as a way to "motivate" myself to change		
Judged myself as less worthy than others due to my weight		
Believed that I'm not worthy of love		
Believed that others would reject me because of my weight		
Other:		
Other:		

What I notice about my experiences with internalized weight bias:

_____
_____
_____
_____

What I imagine could or would be different without internalized weight bias:

_____
_____
_____
_____

How internalized weight bias impacts my movement toward positive body image:

_____
_____
_____
_____

 N. L. Wood-Barcalow, T. L. Tylka, and C. L. Judge. *Positive Body Image Workbook: A Clinical and Self-Improvement Guide.* Cambridge: Cambridge University Press, 2021.

How I would like to respond differently to internalized weight bias:

_____
_____
_____
_____

I commit:

_____
_____
_____
_____

N. L. Wood-Barcalow, T. L. Tylka, and C. L. Judge. *Positive Body Image Workbook: A Clinical and Self-Improvement Guide.* Cambridge: Cambridge University Press, 2021.

Assignment 5.9: Avoidance Behaviors Due to Weight Concerns

I recognize that I avoid the following due to weight concerns:

Experience	Yes/No	Reflections
Example: *Engaging in physical intimacy with others*	*Yes*	*I notice that I don't initiate physical contact due to embarrassment with how I look.*
Shopping for clothing		
Shopping for groceries		
Going to stores that sell clothing		
Attending preventative medical appointments due to concerns of how my weight will be addressed		
Attending routine medical appointments due to concerns of how my weight will be addressed		
Following recommended medical procedures		
Engaging in physical intimacy with others		
Engaging in self-care practices		
Engaging in beauty routines that I enjoy		
Dating		
Eating certain foods		
Wearing certain types of clothing		
Going out with others in public settings		
Eating in public		
Doing activities that might focus on my weight		
Doing activities that require me to wear uncomfortable clothing or shoes		
Engaging in certain physical activities		
Other:		
Other:		
Other:		

Insights about what I avoid due to weight concerns:

_____

_____

_____

_____

 N. L. Wood-Barcalow, T. L. Tylka, and C. L. Judge. *Positive Body Image Workbook: A Clinical and Self-Improvement Guide.* Cambridge: Cambridge University Press, 2021.

I imagine my life could or would be different if I didn't avoid:

_____
_____
_____
_____

How avoidance impacts my movement toward positive body image:

_____
_____
_____
_____

How I would like to respond differently to the urge to avoid:

_____
_____
_____
_____

I commit:

_____
_____
_____
_____

N. L. Wood-Barcalow, T. L. Tylka, and C. L. Judge. *Positive Body Image Workbook: A Clinical and Self-Improvement Guide.* Cambridge: Cambridge University Press, 2021.

Assignment 5.10: Receiving Weight-Specific Comments

It is common for weight to be discussed in social situations, including the desire to lose weight, types of weight loss methods, lowest weights as an adult, and weights associated with specific life events (e.g., high school graduation, wedding day, reunion, etc.). It is also common practice for people to make comments about others' weight.

Listed below are some typical weight-specific comments that are commonly said by loved ones, friends/family members, medical health providers, and more. Read each one and journal your reactions to having received a similar comment. Consider the degree to which you: questioned the motive of the other individual, engaged in body monitoring/checking after receiving this comment, experienced comfortable or positive emotions, experienced uncomfortable or negative emotions, felt obligated to respond in a certain way to the comment, experienced a sense of obligation to do (not do) certain things, and/or felt a sense of pressure to maintain expectations.

- "Have you lost weight?"
- "Have you gained weight?"
- "(You look like) you've lost weight."
- "(You look like) you've gained weight."
- "You need to lose weight."
- "You need to gain weight."
- "You look so much better now."
- "You were so big/fat."
- Other:
- Other:
- Other:

I notice these patterns associated with weight-based comments:

I imagine these differences if I didn't receive weight-based comments:

How weight-based comments impact my movement toward positive body image:

I commit:

N. L. Wood-Barcalow, T. L. Tylka, and C. L. Judge. *Positive Body Image Workbook: A Clinical and Self-Improvement Guide.* Cambridge: Cambridge University Press, 2021.

Assignment 5:11: "So What?!"

There comes a time when being upset about your body (e.g., weight, shape, size) requires a lot of unwanted and unnecessary energy with the realization that it could be directed elsewhere. You become fed up with blaming yourself, saying negative things about yourself, and feeling awful. You tire of doing things in a certain way in order to keep yourself "safe," only to find that it doesn't get you any closer to body acceptance. When this time arrives, this assignment is for you.

The following assignment is in honor of a wise client who spent the majority of his life with negative body image and pursuing weight loss as the solution. During therapy that focused on body image, this client made a remarkable change: He shifted his goal from weight loss toward positive body image. He shifted judgmental, negative self-talk (e.g., "I'm fat, I hate my weight") to descriptive evaluations instead (e.g., "I am this tall, I weigh this amount"). By doing so, he transformed his judgmental thoughts to neutral thoughts, something that had never been done before. He then added a simple quip to the end of his descriptive evaluations, "*So what?!*" which became a powerful symbol of this transformation.

You, too, can work towards this transition by practicing the following steps below. A common example is included to assist in the process.

My negative body judgments or thoughts
Example: *I hate my weight*

_____
_____
_____

How these negative body judgments affect my emotions
Example: *I hate my weight→ disgust, disappointment, fear, anger, desperation, shame, embarrassment, pity*

_____
_____
_____

How these negative body judgments affect my behaviors
Example: *isolate from others, avoid dating, not doing activities that I used to enjoy*

_____
_____
_____

The solutions I have tried
Example: *try new diets, overexercise, make fun of myself in an attempt to increase motivation to lose weight, consider surgery*

_____
_____
_____

How these negative body judgments affect my quality of life
Example: *lonely, constantly on edge, miserable, refrain from doing fun things*

_____
_____
_____

Now, switch each judgment from negative to neutral
Example: *I hate my weight → I weigh this much* (identify the number)

_____
_____
_____

Practice saying, "So what?!" after each time you notice a judgmental, negative thought. Do it over and over again with the goal of making this a permanent response.

N. L. Wood-Barcalow, T. L. Tylka, and C. L. Judge. *Positive Body Image Workbook: A Clinical and Self-Improvement Guide.* Cambridge: Cambridge University Press, 2021.

Assignment 5.12: I Commit to Weight-Inclusive Approaches

I commit to working towards the following weight-inclusive principles

- I will accept my own body shape, weight, and size
- I will accept and respect others for who they are regardless of body shape, weight, and size
- I will inform others about resources associated with the weight-inclusive approach
- I will engage in self-care
- I will respond to my body's needs
- I will reject appearance ideals that promote the thin ideal as the only form of beauty
- I will recognize and challenge my own experiences of weight stigma directed toward others
- I will recognize and challenge my own experiences of weight stigma directed toward myself
- I will stop blaming myself for who/what I am
- I will stop blaming others for who/what they are
- I will advocate for healthcare policies that are fair for individuals of all sizes
- I will educate others about weight stigma
- I will dialogue with healthcare providers about the weight-inclusive approach
- I will support the efforts of those who work toward ending weight stigma
- I will advocate for healthcare resources that accommodate people of different weights and sizes
- I will encourage weight-inclusive language and behaviors with others
- I will not objectify myself based on my appearance (e.g., weight, size, shape)
- I will not objectify others based on their appearance (e.g., weight, size, shape)
- I will not comment on the appearance of others, including their weight
- I will not comment on my own appearance, including weight
- I will practice eating habits that are based on my needs
- I will engage in life-enhancing movement
- I will support others in their pursuit of life-enhancing movement
- I will support public policy that promotes the weight-inclusive approach
- I will not comment on the weight gain or loss of others
- I will not engage in diets
- I will not promote dieting behavior in others
- I will challenge the diet mentality
- I will not create or promote rules regarding my eating habits or patterns
- I will not create or promote rules regarding the eating habits or patterns of loved ones, friends, and family
- I will not judge foods: good or bad, healthy or unhealthy
- I will not judge someone based on their eating habits
- I will not use "shame" to encourage change in myself
- I will not use "shame" to encourage change in others
- I will encourage myself and others to move toward positive body image
- I will express gratitude for the functioning of my body
- I will focus on quality of life
- Other: _____
- Other: _____
- Other: _____
- Other: _____

 N. L. Wood-Barcalow, T. L. Tylka, and C. L. Judge. *Positive Body Image Workbook: A Clinical and Self-Improvement Guide.* Cambridge: Cambridge University Press, 2021.

References

1. K. M. Flegal, M. D. Caroll, B. K. Kit, et al. Prevalence of obesity and trends in the distribution of body mass index among US adults, 1999–2010. *JAMA* 2012; **307**: 491–7.

2. K. M. Flegal, B. K. Kit, H. Orpana, et al. Association of all-cause mortality with overweight and obesity using standard body mass index categories: A systematic review and meta-analysis. *JAMA* 2013; **309**: 71–82.

3. T. L. Tylka, R. A. Annunziato, D. Burgard, et al. The weight-inclusive versus weight-normative approach to health: Evaluating the evidence for prioritizing well-being over weight loss. *J Obes* 2014; **2014**: 983495.

4. A. LaMarre and S. Danielsdottir. Health at Every Size: A social justice-informed approach to positive embodiment. In: Tylka, T. L. and Piran, N. eds. *Handbook of Positive Body Image and Embodiment: Constructs, Protective Factors, and Interventions.* New York: Oxford University Press, 2019: 300–11.

5. M. Daly, A. R. Sutin, and E. Robinson. Perceived weight discrimination mediates the prospective association between obesity and physiological dysregulation: Evidence from a population-based cohort. *Psychol Sci* 2019; **30**: 1030–9.

6. R. M. Puhl and C. A. Heuer. The stigma of obesity: A review and update. *Obesity* 2009; **17**: 941–64.

7. R. M. Puhl and K. D. Brownell. Bias, discrimination, and obesity. *Obes Res* 2001; **9**: 788–905.

8. K. D. Brownell, R. M. Puhl, M. B. Schwartz, et al. eds. *Weight Bias: Nature, Consequences, and Remedies.* New York: Guilford Press, 2005.

9. R. M. Calogero, S. Herbozo, and J. K. Thompson. Complimentary weightism: The potential costs of appearance-related commentary for women's self-objectification. *Psychol Women Q* 2009; **33**: 120–32.

10. S. W. Flint, J. Nobles, P. Gately, et al. Weight stigma and discrimination: A call to the media. *The Lancet: Diabetes & Endocrinology* 2018; **6**: 169–70.

11. J. C. Lumeng, P. Forrest, D. P. Appugliese, et al. Weight status as a predictor of being bullied in third through sixth grades. *Pediatrics* 2010; **125**: e1301–7.

12. R. M. Puhl and J. D. Latner. Stigma, obesity, and the health of the nation's children. *Psychol Bull* 2007; **133**: 557–80.

13. S. M. Phelan, D. J. Burgess, M. W. Yeazel, et al. Impact of weight bias and stigma on quality of care and outcomes for patients with obesity. *Obes Rev* 2015; **16**: 319–26.

14. M. B. Schwartz, H. O'Neal Chambliss, K. D. Brownell, et al. Weight bias among health professionals specializing in obesity. *Obes Res* 2003; **11**: 1033–9.

15. K. Mulherin, Y. D. Miller, F. K. Barlow, et al. Weight stigma in maternity care: Women's experiences and care providers' attitudes. *BMC Pregnancy* 2013; **13**: 19.

16. R. M. Puhl and K. D. Brownell. Confronting and coping with weight stigma: An investigation of overweight and obese adults. *Obes* 2006; **14**: 1802–15.

17. E. Cassidy. Canadian woman's obituary calls out fat-shaming in medicine. The Mighty 2018. https://themighty.com/2018/08/ellen-maud-bennett-obituary-fat-shaming-doctors/ [last accessed July 10, 2020].

18. C. A. A. Drury and M. Louis. Exploring the association between body weight, stigma of obesity, and health care avoidance. *J Am Acad Nurse Pract* 2002; **14**: 554–61.

19. J. L. Mensinger, T. L. Tylka, and M. E. Calamari. Mechanisms underlying weight status and healthcare avoidance in women: A study of weight stigma, body-related shame and guilt, and healthcare stress. *Body Image* 2018; **25**: 139–47.

20. R. M. Puhl, J. D. Latner, K. M. King, et al. Weight bias among professionals treating eating disorders: Attitudes about treatment and perceived patient outcomes. *Int J Eat Disord* 2014; **47**: 65–75.

21. R. M. Calogero, T. L. Tylka, J. L. Mensinger, et al. Recognizing the fundamental right to be fat: A weight-inclusive approach to size acceptance and healing from sizeism. *Women Ther* 2019; **42**: 22–44.

22. P. A. Estabrooks, R. E. Lee, and N. C. Gyurcsik. Resources for physical activity participation: Does availability and accessibility differ by neighborhood socioeconomic status? *Ann Behav Med* 2003; **25**: 100–4.

23. V. W. Barry, M. Baruth, M. W. Beets, et al. Fitness vs. fatness on all-cause mortality: A meta-analysis. *Prog Cardiovasc Dis* 2014; **56**: 382–90.

24. P. S. MacLean, A. Bergouignan, M. Cornier, et al. Biology's response to dieting: The impetus for weight regain. *Am J of Physiol Regul Integr Comp Physiol* 2011; **301**: R581–600.

25. P. Sumithran and J. Proietto. The defence of body weight: A physiological basis for weight regain after weight loss. *Clin Sci* 2013; **124**: 231–41.

26. T. L. Tylka, R. M. Calogero, and S. Daníelsdóttir. Is intuitive eating the same as flexible dietary control? Their links to each other and well-being could provide an answer. *Appetite* 2015; **95**: 166–75.

27. T. L. Tylka, R. M. Calogero, and S. Daníelsdóttir. Intuitive eating is connected to self-reported weight stability in community women and men. *Eat Disord* 2019; **28**: 256–64.

28. J. W. Anderson, E. C. Konz, R. C. Frederich, et al. Long-term weight-loss maintenance: A meta-analysis of US studies. *Am J Clin Nutr* 2001; **74**: 579–84.

29. E. Stice, K. Burger, and S. Yokum. Caloric deprivation increases responsivity of attention and reward brain regions to intake, anticipated intake, and images of palatable foods. *NeuroImage* 2013; **67**: 322–90.

30. N. I. Larson, M. T. Story, and M. C. Nelson. Neighborhood environments: Disparities in access to healthy foods in the U.S. *Am J Prev Med* 2009; **36**: 74–81.

31. D. Crawford, A. Timperio, B. Giles-Corti, et al. Do features of public open spaces vary according to neighbourhood socioeconomic status? *Health Place* 2008; **14**: 889–93.

32. A. J. Tomiyama. Weight stigma is stressful. A review of evidence for the Cyclic Obesity/Weight-Based Stigma model. *Appetite* 2014; **82**: 8–15.

33. L. R. Vartanian and S. A. Novak. Internalized societal attitudes moderate the impact of weight stigma on avoidance of exercise. *Obes* 2011; **19**: 757–62.

34. R. M. Puhl, C. A. Moss-Racusin, and M. B. Schwartz. Internalization of weight bias: Implications for binge eating and emotional well-being. *Obes* 2007; **15**: 19–23.

35. L. E. Durso and J. D. Latner. Understanding self-directed stigma: Development of the Weight Bias

Internalization Scale. *Obes* 2008; **16**: S80–6.

36. R. L. Pearl and R. M. Puhl. Measuring internalized weight attitudes across body weight categories: Validation of the Modified Weight Bias Internalization Scale. *Body Image* 2014; **11**: 89–92.

37. R. L. Pearl and R. M. Puhl. Weight bias internalization and health: A systematic review. *Obes Rev* 2018; **19**: 1141–63.

38. R. Crawford. Healthism and the medicalization of everyday life. *Int J Hum Serv* 1980; **10**: 365–88.

39. R. Crawford. Health as a meaningful social practice. *Health* 2006; **10**: 401–20.

40. J. Robison and K. Kratina. Health at Every Size, Health for *Every* Body. In: Kratina, K., King, N., and Hayes, D. eds. *Moving Away from Diets*, 2nd ed. Lake Dallas, Texas: Helm Publishing, 2003: 27–47.

41. Association for Size Diversity and Health. *The Health at Every Size® approach*. Available at: www .sizediversityandhealth.org/images/u ploaded/ASDAH%20HAES%20Princ iples.pdf [last accessed July 10, 2020].

42. L. Bacon and L. Aphramor. Weight science: Evaluating the evidence for a paradigm shift. *Nutr J* 2011; **10**: 9.

43. L. Bacon, J. S. Stern, M. D. Van Loan, et al. Size acceptance and intuitive eating improve health for obese, female chronic dieters. *J Am Diet Assoc* 2005; **105**: 929–36.

44. L. Bacon, N. L. Keim, M. D. van Loan, et al. Evaluating a "non-diet" wellness intervention for improvement of metabolic fitness, psychological well-being and eating and activity behaviors. *Int J Obes* 2002; **26**: 854–65.

6 Body Acceptance by Others

Theory and Research Overview

It may seem like we are surrounded by messages to focus on our appearance: to lose fat, gain muscle, have thicker hair, have a different hair texture, have a different size and/or shape of nose, have lighter skin, have darker skin, be taller, have bigger breasts, have smaller breasts, have a more defined chest, have a smaller stomach, have a shapely bottom, have almond-shaped eyes, have double eyelids, have fewer wrinkles, have whiter teeth, and the list goes on. Some of these messages come from media, but they may also come from our family members, friends, partners, acquaintances, those in health or service professions, and even strangers.

What does the lack of body acceptance by others look like? It could take many forms. Some instances may be relatively harmless, others somewhat hurtful, and others extremely hurtful. Examples include a brother teasing his sister about her weight or appearance, a parent who puts a child on a diet, a person who comments on the changed appearance of their partner, a parent who tells a child not to eat something because it will make the child "fat," a person who gains sexual gratification from pornography because they are "no longer attracted" to their partner, a stranger who comments on the food in a person's grocery cart, a stranger who makes negative or threatening comments to another person about their gender expression, and more. What about when loved ones "encourage" us to lose weight out of their concern for our "health?" This also can reflect a lack of body acceptance. In fact, this "encouragement" has been found ineffective for weight loss and can damage body image [1–2, see also Chapter 5]. Perhaps loved ones have never said anything directly to us about our appearance, but have let us know in other ways that they highly value appearance (e.g., they may have criticized or made fun of another person's appearance in front of us). Actions like this may make us feel vulnerable: loved ones may criticize or make fun of our appearance at any point or do so behind our backs. Even having our appearance frequently complimented by others shows us that they value appearance, which is associated with harmful consequences for our body image and directs us to spend time and energy habitually monitoring our appearance [2–3].

Alternatively, we may have some people (e.g., family members, friends, a support group) that serve as a safe place in which we can be (and look like) ourselves, where we are accepted and appreciated for who we are regardless of what we look like. It is within these encounters that we feel **body acceptance by others** [4–5]. Perhaps these people tell us that we are beautiful or attractive just as we are, perhaps we feel that they do not focus on appearance but instead appreciate us for who we are inside, perhaps they perceive beauty in all individuals, and/or perhaps they challenge unrealistic societal notions of beauty and attractiveness by offering statements such as, "Who makes up these ridiculous rules for what is considered attractive?!? Corporations who want to sell products, that's who!"

What is the role of body acceptance by others (or the lack of body acceptance by others) in body image? People with positive body image have provided an answer. When interviewed, adolescent girls and boys from Sweden [6] and college women from the US [7] reported that they perceive that loved ones (e.g., family, dating partners, friends) unconditionally accept their bodies and are not critical of them. They felt loved and valued for their inner qualities rather than their appearance. Overall, they perceived that this acceptance helped build and maintain their positive body image.

Findings from these interviews were used to guide theory and research on the development of positive body image. Body acceptance by others has become an important variable in theoretical frameworks of the development of positive body image and adaptive eating. The **acceptance model** [4, 8] proposes that when we perceive that our bodies are accepted by others, we are able to value our bodies for more than our appearance and feel more appreciative about our bodies. A framework that speaks to the lack of body acceptance by others is the **tripartite influence model**. This model proposes that when we feel pressured by others to change our appearance, we come to value having an "ideal appearance," which promotes negative body image [9, see also Chapter 4].

The findings from examining these models are clear. Body acceptance by others is strongly associated with higher body appreciation and valuing our bodies for more than our appearance [4, 8, 10–11], supporting the acceptance model. Pressures to be thin are strongly associated with internalizing thin beauty standards, body comparison, and body dissatisfaction among women [10–11], and pressures to be muscular and lean are strongly associated with internalizing a muscular and lean body ideal, muscularity dissatisfaction, and body fat dissatisfaction among straight and gay men [12–13], thereby supporting the tripartite influence model.

Body acceptance by others is also linked to intuitive eating [4, 8, 10, 14], which is an adaptive and flexible pattern of eating whereby people listen to and trust in their internal hunger and satiety cues to determine when, what, and how much to eat [4, 14, see also Chapter 20]. Conversely, appearance-related pressures, especially among partners, are associated with greater disordered eating in women and men [12, 15]. Among gay men, appearance-related pressures from partners and the gay community are associated with more maladaptive muscularity enhancement behaviors, and appearance pressures from friends are associated with greater disordered eating [13].

It is important to realize the messages we receive about a variety of appearance-related characteristics and whether they have been accepting or not accepting. After all, these messages are closely tied to how much we value our appearance over other aspects of our bodies and ourselves (e.g., how our bodies feel and function, our personalities), how much we compare our bodies with others' bodies, and how we feel about our own bodies. The *Body Acceptance by Others Scale* (BAOS), which is included in this chapter, can be used to measure the extent we feel body acceptance from five sources (i.e., friends, family, partners, society, and media) [4].

Treatment Planning Tools

Talking Points in Sessions

- Discuss which individuals/role models have played a key role in promoting *negative* body image
- Discuss which individuals/role models have played a key role in promoting *positive* body image
- Discuss the role of rejection when others do not accept the body
- Identify environments that promote comfort and positive body image
- Explore how eating and comparison are impacted by being around "safe people," as compared to those who are critical of appearance

Treatment Plan

Goals

❏ Identify when I feel rejected by someone based on my appearance and use positive coping skills
❏ Surround myself with others who accept me as I am
❏ Learn how others respond effectively to negative body image information

❏ Create a healthy home environment that promotes positive body image
❏ Reduce appearance-based language
❏ Recognize others in my life who accept me as I am

Objectives

❏ Recognize examples of perceived and real rejection from others
❏ Ask those I care about to offer feedback on valued qualities they see in me, unrelated to my body
❏ Explore how interactions with family members have shaped my beliefs and attitudes about body acceptance over time
❏ Interview someone with positive body image to learn about their experiences
❏ Identify "safe people" in my life who accept me as I am
❏ Role play how I can respond when others make uncomfortable body-focused comments
❏ Plan specific coping skills for when I feel pressured to change the way I look or conform to others' standards
❏ Practice assertive statements about how I want to be treated
❏ Identify a list of supportive others I can contact when experiencing negative body image

Additional Resources

We encourage you to share useful resources in other chapters, such as the ones below, with loved ones who you would like to be more accepting of your body and foster dialogue with them about what they can do to support it:

R. Scritchfield. *Body Kindness: Transform Your Health from the Inside Out and Never Say Diet Again*. New York: Workman Publishing, 2016. Podcast available here: www.bodykindnessbook.com/podcast/

L. Bacon and L. Aphramor. *Body Respect*. Dallas: BenBella Books, 2014.

C. Sobczak. *Embody: Learning to Love Your Unique Body (and Quiet that Critical Voice!)* Carlsbad: Gurze Books, 2014.

P. Campos. *The Obesity Myth: Why America's Obsession with Weight is Hazardous to Your Health*. New York: Gotham, 2004.

Assessment 6.1: Body Acceptance by Others Scale (BAOS)[1]

Using the following scale, please indicate the response that best captures your own experience with others. Write the number to the right of the item.

1	2	3	4	5
Never	Rarely	Sometimes	Often	Always

	Number
1. I've felt acceptance from my friends regarding my body.	
2. My friends have sent me the message that my body is fine.	
3. I've felt acceptance from my family regarding my body.	
4. My family has sent me the message that my body is fine.	
5. I've felt acceptance from people I've dated regarding my body.	
6. People I've dated have sent me the message that my body is fine.	
7. I've felt acceptance from the media (e.g., social media, TV, magazines) regarding my body.	
8. I feel that the media have sent me the message that my body is fine.	
9. I've felt acceptance from society (e.g., school, spiritual gatherings, gym, strangers, acquaintances) regarding my body.	
10. I feel that society has sent me the message that my body is fine.	
Total Body Acceptance by Others score: **Add items 1–10 then divide by 10**	

Total Body Acceptance by Others score between:
- **4–5** = high levels of body acceptance by others
- **3–3.9** = moderate levels of body acceptance by others
- **below 3** = low levels of body acceptance by others

You may find that you feel acceptance from certain individuals (e.g., friends), but not others (e.g., family, dating partners). Or you may feel acceptance by others in your life, but not media or society. You can calculate subscales by averaging:

Items 1 and 2 = acceptance from friends

Items 3 and 4 = acceptance from family

Items 5 and 6 = acceptance from dating partners

Items 7 and 8 = acceptance from media

Items 9 and 10 = acceptance from society

*Total average subscale scores between:
- **4–5** = high levels of body acceptance by the source
- **3–3.9** = moderate levels of body acceptance by the source
- **below 3** = low levels of body acceptance by the source

*The original items indicated "body shape and/or weight." In the BAOS version presented in this chapter, we exchanged "body shape and weight" with "body" to be more inclusive of a variety of potential body concerns.

[1] The original items indicated "body shape and/or weight." In the BAOS version presented in this chapter, we exchanged "body shape and weight" with "body" to be more inclusive of a variety of potential body concerns.

Note. The authors of the original BAOS are Avalos and Tylka.[**] The BAOS has been supported (in terms of reliability and validity) with samples of adolescents and adults of various ages and cultures. Please contact the authors of the BAOS for permission to use it within research; there is no need to contact them to use it with clients or to complete on your own.

[**]L. C. Avalos and T. L. Tylka. Exploring a model of intuitive eating with college women. *J Couns Psychol* 2006; **53**: 486–97.

Body Acceptance by Others Scale Applications

- How does your overall Body Acceptance by Others Scale score relate to your body image?

- What specific messages about your body being acceptable as it is have you received from: Family? Friends? Acquaintances? Dating partners? Society (groups, certain individuals)? Social media?

- How important is it for you to receive acceptance from others about your body?

- Were there times when you felt as though your body was **not** accepted by others? How did that affect your relationship with your body? How much was your reaction influenced by the role of the person (e.g., dating partner)?

- Do you notice people represented in media who look like you in terms of your body shape, size, and weight? In terms of other attributes?

- Go through each item and rather than respond to "body," respond to body features that are important (or concerning) to you. Examples may be, *I've felt acceptance from my family regarding my weight* and *My partner has sent me the message that my breasts are fine.* Here are some body features to consider:

  o Body shape

  o Body size

  o Weight

  o Hair

  o Skin tone/color

  o Nose

  o Lips

  o Breasts or chest

  o Complexion

  o Eyes

  o Arms

  o Thighs

  o Stomach/abdominals

  o Buttocks

  o Shoulders

  o Calves

  o Feet/toes

  o Hands/fingers

  o Teeth

- Is it possible for you to accept your body even if others do not accept your body? What might that be like?

Assignment 6.1: Here are Things that I Want You to Know

Complete this assignment and share with a loved one or friend to start a conversation about body acceptance.

I appreciate having you in my life because:

_____
_____

I've struggled with the following body image issues/concerns:

_____
_____

It makes me uncomfortable when others/you say the following about my body:

_____
_____

It makes me uncomfortable when others/you do the following:

_____
_____

I want you to know that these comments impact me by:

_____
_____

I'm working towards positive body image by:

_____
_____

I request your support in these ways:

_____
_____

I offer to do the following:

_____
_____

N. L. Wood-Barcalow, T. L. Tylka, and C. L. Judge. *Positive Body Image Workbook: A Clinical and Self-Improvement Guide.* Cambridge: Cambridge University Press, 2021.

Assignment 6.2: My Community of Acceptance

Many types of people can offer unconditional acceptance such as family, friends, mentors, spiritual members, coaches, colleagues/ co-workers, and more. They create a safe place (physical, psychological, social, relational) to allow self-expression, freedom to be authentic, and an opportunity to take risks.

These are the people in my life who accept me and my body as is:

_____
_____
_____
_____

They demonstrate body acceptance by:

_____
_____
_____
_____

They demonstrate body acceptance by not:

_____
_____
_____
_____

Because of their acceptance, I feel comfortable:

_____
_____
_____
_____

Because of their acceptance, I know that:

_____
_____
_____
_____

N. L. Wood-Barcalow, T. L. Tylka, and C. L. Judge. *Positive Body Image Workbook: A Clinical and Self-Improvement Guide.* Cambridge: Cambridge University Press, 2021.

Assignment 6.3: Reaching Out to Others

It is normal to feel a sense of rejection when receiving direct or indirect information that our bodies or appearance are not okay. Rejection can hurt emotionally, physically, and relationally. Reaching out for acceptance or reassurance from others is common. We can receive different types of support from various people in our lives.

I can reach out to these people, support networks, or groups when experiencing the following emotions . . .

Rejection:

_____
_____

Doubt:

_____
_____

Shame or guilt:

_____
_____

Embarrassment:

_____
_____

Fear:

_____
_____

Anger:

_____
_____

Envy/jealousy:

_____
_____

Sadness:

_____
_____

Other:

_____
_____

N. L. Wood-Barcalow, T. L. Tylka, and C. L. Judge. *Positive Body Image Workbook: A Clinical and Self-Improvement Guide.* Cambridge: Cambridge University Press, 2021.

Assignment 6.4: Reassurance from Others

Reassurance from others can lower discomfort with negative body image by providing comfort and validation. (Too much reassurance-seeking can indicate other issues/concerns that might need to be addressed).

I seek reassurance in the following situations:

_____

_____

I seek reassurance from these people:

_____

_____

I ask for reassurance about:

_____

_____

I often experience these emotions after seeking reassurance:

_____

_____

I often experience these thoughts after seeking reassurance:

_____

_____

The sense of reassurance tends to last this long:

_____

_____

It is possible that I can reassure myself by:

_____

_____

N. L. Wood-Barcalow, T. L. Tylka, and C. L. Judge. *Positive Body Image Workbook: A Clinical and Self-Improvement Guide.* Cambridge: Cambridge University Press, 2021.

Assignment 6.5: This One Person in My Life

When I think about people who have offered body acceptance to me throughout my life, this one person was/is highly influential:

_____
_____

This one person has demonstrated unconditional love by:

_____
_____

This one person has taught me:

_____
_____

This one person has guided me:

_____
_____

This one person has encouraged me to:

_____
_____

This one person understands:

_____
_____

I am grateful to this one person for:

_____
_____

N. L. Wood-Barcalow, T. L. Tylka, and C. L. Judge. *Positive Body Image Workbook: A Clinical and Self-Improvement Guide.* Cambridge: Cambridge University Press, 2021.

Assignment 6.6: Gender Identity within Social Experiences Journal

For this journal assignment,* consider your gender identity in relation to social experiences and ultimately body acceptance by others. Reflect on the following:

What are my experiences of gender code switching (switching how I present or express my gender) in different social environments? In what environments do I feel restricted by gender norms? In what environments do I adopt gender roles to avoid bullying and/or physical violence? What physical traits do I worry about that might not be perceived as "passing" with others? What are my thoughts and emotions when being misgendered, socially isolated, or ridiculed by others? How does it impact my body acceptance?

In what environments do I experience liberation and freedom? In what environments do I experience gender-affirming acceptance? What thoughts and emotions occur when strangers address and/or treat me as my preferred gender? When friends and family members treat me as my preferred gender?

How will I know when others accept my body? How would I like others to support me? What is helpful in how they treat me? What would I like to express to them?

_____
_____
_____
_____
_____
_____
_____
_____
_____
_____
_____
_____

* This assignment was inspired by the work from J. K. McGuire, J. L. Doty, J. M. Catalpa, et al. Body image in transgender young people: Findings from a qualitative community-based study. *Body Image* 2016; **18**: 96–107.

N. L. Wood-Barcalow, T. L. Tylka, and C. L. Judge. *Positive Body Image Workbook: A Clinical and Self-Improvement Guide.* Cambridge: Cambridge University Press, 2021.

References

1. S. Helfert and P. Warschburger. A prospective study on the impact of peer and parental pressure on body dissatisfaction in adolescent girls and boys. *Body Image* 2011; **8**: 101–9.

2. S. Herbozo, S. D. Stevens, C. P. Moldovan, et al. Positive comments, negative outcomes? The potential downsides of appearance-related commentary in ethnically diverse women. *Body Image* 2017; **21**: 6–14.

3. R. M. Calogero, S. Herbozo, and J. K. Thompson. Complimentary weightism: The potential costs of appearance-related commentary for women's self-objectification. *Psychol Women Q* 2009; **33**: 120–32.

4. L. C. Avalos and T. L. Tylka. Exploring a model of intuitive eating with college women. *J Couns Psychol* 2006; **53**: 486–97.

5. M. Tiggemann. Body acceptance by others. In Tylka, T. L., Piran, N. eds. *Handbook of Positive Body Image and Embodiment: Constructs, Protective Factors, and Interventions.* New York: Oxford University Press, 2019: 214–22.

6. A. Frisén and K. Holmqvist. What characterizes early adolescents with a positive body image? A qualitative investigation of Swedish girls and boys. *Body Image* 2010; **7**: 205–12.

7. N. L. Wood-Barcalow, T. L. Tylka, and C. L. Augustus-Horvath. "But I like my body": Positive body image characteristics and a holistic model for young-adult women. *Body Image* 2010; **7**: 106–16.

8. C. L. Augustus-Horvath and T. L. Tylka. The acceptance model of intuitive eating: A comparison of women in emerging adulthood, early adulthood, and middle adulthood. *J Couns Psych* 2011; **58**: 110–25.

9. H. Keery, P. van den Berg, and J. K. Thompson. An evaluation of the Tripartite Influence Model of body dissatisfaction and eating disturbance with adolescent girls. *Body Image* 2004; **1**: 237–51.

10. R. Andrew, M. Tiggemann, and L. Clark. Predictors and health-related outcomes of positive body image in adolescent girls: A prospective study. *Dev Psych* 2016; **52**: 463–74.

11. T. L. Tylka and K. J. Homan. Exercise motives and positive body image in physically active college women and men: Exploring an expanded acceptance model of intuitive eating. *Body Image* 2015; **15**: 90–7.

12. T. L. Tylka. Refinement of the tripartite influence model for men: Dual body image pathways to body change behaviors. *Body Image* 2011; **8**: 199–207.

13. T. L. Tylka and M. J. Andorka. Support for an expanded tripartite influence model with gay men. *Body Image* 2012; **9**: 57–67.

14. T. L. Tylka and A. M. Kroon Van Diest. The Intuitive Eating Scale-2: Item refinement and psychometric evaluation with college women and men. *J Couns Psychol* 2013; **60**: 137–53.

15. T. L. Tylka and R. M. Calogero. Perceptions of male partner pressure to be thin and pornography use: Associations with eating disorder symptomatology in a community sample of adult women. *Int J Eat Disord* 2019; **52**: 189–94.

Defining Beauty and Cultural Pride

Theory and Research Overview

Media often portray an extremely narrow depiction of beauty. For example, in Western media, women are often lean, toned, young, and busty; men are often lean, fit, muscular, and tall – and they both are often clothed in the latest fashions with body hair removed or at least groomed, white or light skin tone that is blemish free, and hair styled perfectly [1–2, see also Chapter 4]. Media equate beauty with what is considered attractive in a particular culture, which is influenced by the "dominant appearance ideals" of those who hold power and influence [3–5]. Having appearance-related features that are inconsistent with these ideals may become a source of body anxiety and shame, unless these narrow beauty ideals are challenged.

Beauty is much more than attractiveness. **Attractiveness** is a person's consistency with desirable physical attributes (thus it focuses on the external appearance) that are connected to societal power and influence, whereas **beauty** is more of a personal evaluation of someone based on their internal (personality) and external (appearance) characteristics that may or may not be consistent with societal power and influence [6]. Looking at someone through an "attractiveness lens" reduces a person to their physical appearance (i.e., we compare a person to cultural appearance ideals to see where they "rank"). On the other hand, looking at someone through a "beauty lens" allows us to see beauty based on the interaction of their internal and external features; for instance, internal features, such as self-acceptance, intelligence, kindness, and confidence, can "shine through" to influence our perception of their external features.

Typically, beauty is a term reserved for feminine traits [2, 6], and terms such as "handsome" and "good looking" are often used to describe people who are perceived to be less feminine. Yet, because "attractiveness," "handsome," and "good looking" simply reflect external appearance, these terms do not consider internal features in the same way that "beauty" does. For this reason, it is important to consider beauty as applicable to all individuals, regardless of their gender.

It is also important to define beauty broadly, not based on one particular body type and appearance ideal. Trying to meet rigid and narrow appearance ideals is harmful and oppressive [5, 7–8, see also Chapters 4 and 22]. For example, women who believe that their appearance represents "currency" that they can use to get ahead in society report higher self-objectification (i.e., they must work at their appearance) [7, see also Chapter 13]. In contrast, **defining beauty broadly** is perceiving many

looks, appearances, and body sizes/shapes as beautiful, as well as drawing from inner characteristics (e.g., confidence) when determining a person's beauty [2, 6]. Defining beauty broadly reduces the importance of "achieving beauty," as we are beautiful already, and acknowledges that beauty is not limited to physical appearance. In fact, defining beauty broadly is related to lower, rather than higher, self-objectification [6].

Defining beauty broadly has been identified as a theme in interviews with adolescents and adult women who hold a positive body image. Adolescents from Sweden mentioned that many different body sizes are beautiful, and that inner characteristics, such as happiness and self-acceptance, shape their perceptions of a person's beauty [9]. African American adolescent girls emphasized the importance of defining beauty in a flexible and individualized manner [10]. They believed that creating a style that makes a personal statement and conveys a unique presence (e.g., making "what you've got work for you") reflects beauty, not trying to look like media appearance ideals. Adolescent Aboriginal girls from Canada viewed beauty as originating from inside the self, which then is reflected outward via cultural practices (e.g., powwow dance) and self-care [11]. College women from the US emphasized that beauty can be defined and expressed in many ways and believed that individuals should not be compared in terms of "who is more beautiful" [12]. Canadian adults with spinal cord injuries emphasized that all body shapes and sizes are beautiful, and that beauty includes external and internal characteristics that are largely ignored by media [13].

During interviews, many participants indicated that they found beauty in their own features that may not be consistent with media appearance ideals. For example, Canadian Aboriginal girls considered their Aboriginal identity to be key for their positive body image, and they emphasized the importance of being proud of their cultural identity. They provided a number of examples of how young Aboriginal women show their body pride through powwow dance, fiddle dance, colors and symbols in their regalia, and various Native symbols such as beads, feathers, and moccasins. In addition, they admired their physical features that reflect their cultural heritage. They acknowledged being impacted by negative appearance stereotypes of Aboriginal women in media, and they criticized media for not including positive representations of their Aboriginal identity [11].

Overall, participants with a positive body image perceived a wide range of physical appearances as beautiful, whether these appearances were largely unchangeable (e.g., body shape, weight) or more easily modifiable (e.g., personal style of dress, hairstyle, style accessories). They viewed positive internal characteristics, such as confidence and self-acceptance, as shaping their perception of others, as well as themselves, as beautiful.

It is not enough to perceive that a wide range of body shapes, appearances, and characteristics can be beautiful in others, we must also do it for ourselves. For many people, recognizing beauty within themselves is the most challenging part: we see the beauty in others, but hold ourselves to unrealistic standards. It may be similar to being able to offer others compassion when they make a mistake, but not extending this compassion toward ourselves when we make a mistake. Research shows that when we define beauty broadly for ourselves *and* others, it is linked to even higher body appreciation, self-compassion, and body image quality of life compared to when we define beauty broadly for others alone [6].

Defining beauty broadly (for ourselves and others) may prevent or counteract some of the harm caused by **internalizing appearance ideals**, or adopting the belief that a certain appearance (e.g., thinness, leanness, muscularity) is the most desirable body type and holding oneself to that standard [6, see also Chapter 4]. Internalizing appearance ideals is a strong predictor of body image disturbance and eating disorder symptoms [14–15], and is a main target for eating disorder prevention programs [16]. If a child is raised to define beauty broadly, or at least is exposed to this perspective, they may be less likely to internalize cultural appearance ideals and hold themselves to this standard. Appreciating cultural and/or age-related characteristics that are inconsistent with media appearance ideals may be one path toward developing a broad definition of beauty. At any age, we can learn to define beauty broadly, which likely will help us appreciate ourselves as we grow older, and move further away from cultural appearance ideals that emphasize and value youth.

To understand the degree to which you define beauty broadly, complete the *Broad Conceptualization of Beauty Scale* (BCBS) [6] in this chapter. Participants who broadly defined beauty reported higher body appreciation, functionality appreciation, self-compassion, and body image quality of life, and lower weight stigma, body surveillance, appearance-ideal internalization, and social comparison of appearance, eating habits, and exercise behaviors[1] [6, 17]. Importantly, findings support that defining beauty broadly is adaptive, meaningful, and important in relation to positive body image.

Treatment Planning Tools

Talking Points for Sessions

- Discuss how beauty is understood within the client's culture(s) and other cultures
- Identify the degree to which the beauty ideals of the client's culture(s) are represented within media images

Treatment Plan

Goals

- ❏ Identify reasons for engaging in beauty rituals (e.g., a response to feeling pressured or wanting change, a reflection of personal style, self-expression, cultural expression)
- ❏ Embrace beauty according to my own standards
- ❏ Embrace helpful beauty ideals of my identified culture(s)
- ❏ Challenge practices that go against embracing cultural beauty

Objectives

- ❏ Look through photographs of my ancestors to determine familial similarities in appearance
- ❏ Consider ways that I've defined beauty narrowly and broadly
- ❏ Consider how a narrow definition of beauty has resulted in discomfort
- ❏ Acknowledge examples of beauty in older individuals
- ❏ Acknowledge examples of beauty in individuals from other cultures
- ❏ Acknowledge examples of beauty in individuals with physical traits that have been traditionally marginalized (e.g., scars, burns, paralysis)
- ❏ Identify examples of personality traits in others associated with beauty
- ❏ Identify examples of personality traits in myself associated with beauty
- ❏ Journal about what characteristics make my family lineage unique (hair texture, skin color, prominent features)
- ❏ Identify examples of doing "whatever it takes" to achieve attractiveness including the costs and benefits (e.g., erasing my unique beauty and features of my culture)
- ❏ Examine how my "personal style" reflects my sense of self
- ❏ Identify direct and indirect messages about attractiveness and gender in my identified culture(s)
- ❏ Identify specific rituals/practices within my culture(s) that are consistent with attractiveness

Additional Resources

S. R. Taylor. *The Body is Not an Apology: The Power of Radical Self-Love.* Oakland: Berrett-Koehler, 2018.

J. Stanley. *Every Body Yoga.* New York: Workman Publishing, 2017.

M. Klein. *Yoga Rising: 30 Empowering Stories from Yoga Renegades for Every Body.* Woodbury: Llewellyn Publications, 2018.

---

[1] See Chapters 4, 5, 8, 10, 11, 13, 15, and 22 for more discussion of these body image variables.

Assessment 7.1: Broad Conceptualization of Beauty Scale (BCBS): Gender-Neutral Version

How do YOU define beauty? Please indicate the extent to which you agree with each statement by **circling the number** below each item. Focus on YOUR beliefs, which may or may not be reflected by others or society.

	Strongly Disagree	Moderately Disagree	Slightly Disagree	Neutral	Slightly Agree	Moderately Agree	Strongly Agree
1. Even if a physical feature is not considered attractive by others or by society, I think that it can be beautiful.	1	2	3	4	5	6	7
2. A person's confidence level can change my perception of their physical beauty.	1	2	3	4	5	6	7
3. I think that a wide variety of body shapes are beautiful.	1	2	3	4	5	6	7
4. I think that people who are lean are more beautiful than those who have other body types.	7	6	5	4	3	2	1
5. A person's soul or inner spirit can change my perception of their physical beauty.	1	2	3	4	5	6	7
6. I define a person's beauty differently than how it is portrayed in the media.	1	2	3	4	5	6	7
7. A person's self-acceptance can change my perception of their physical beauty.	1	2	3	4	5	6	7
8. I appreciate a wide range of different looks as beautiful.	1	2	3	4	5	6	7
9. I think that people of all body sizes can be beautiful.	1	2	3	4	5	6	7
Total Broad Conceptualization of Beauty score: Add item 1–9 scores and then divide by 9 =							

Total Broad Conceptualization of Beauty score between:

- **6.1–7** = high levels of broadly defining beauty
- **3.6–6** = moderate levels of broadly defining beauty
- **3.5 and below** = low levels of broadly defining beauty

Note. This is a gender neutral version of the BCBS, which was adapted from Tylka and Iannantuono's BCBS.* Reprinted with permission. Research on the BCBS has supported its use, as its measurement properties (i.e., reliability and validity) have been upheld. Please contact the authors of the BCBS for permission to use it within research; there is no need to contact them to use it with clients or to complete it on your own.

* T. L. Tylka and A. C. Iannantuono. Perceiving beauty in all women: Psychometric evaluation of the Broad Conceptualization of Beauty Scale. *Body Image* 2016; **17**: 67–81.

Broad Conceptualization of Beauty Scale Applications

- For item 5 (*A person's soul or inner spirit can change my perception of their physical beauty*), in what ways does a person's soul or inner spirit change your perception of their physical beauty? It may help to identify an example.

- What inner qualities and/or personality characteristics influence your perception of a person's beauty?

- What inner qualities and/or personality characteristics of yours do you consider beautiful?

- If you agreed with item 6 (*I define a person's beauty differently than how it is portrayed in the media*), how does your definition of a person's beauty differ from that portrayed in the media?

  - What physical characteristics do you consider beautiful for those you know?

  - How do natural beauty traits differ from those emphasized in media?

  - How do natural beauty traits impact your tendency to engage in social comparison and feelings later?

- For item 7 (*A person's self-acceptance can change my perception of their physical beauty*), in what ways does a person's self-acceptance change your perception of their physical beauty? It may help to identify an example.

Assignment 7.1: Beauty in Others, Beauty in Self

It is common to focus on the attractiveness of others for many reasons such as a fascination with beauty, inspiration to improve ourselves, and curiosity about how beauty is achieved. We tell ourselves stories about attractive people, including that they are successful, fulfilled, content, and happy. The tendency is to minimize their flaws while magnifying their desired traits and attributes. Seeing beauty in ourselves can be more challenging due to a focus on the negative. We magnify our own flaws and minimize our positive traits and strengths.

Let's shift the focus. Rather than focusing on the attractiveness of others, let's turn the attention to ourselves, our families, our friends, our communities, and our heritage. Let's broaden the definition of beauty by looking within and immediately around us for inspiration and fascination. Notice how beauty is demonstrated in a variety of ways.

1. These are *5–10 physical traits* that I find attractive in others that I have myself. Examples might include skin color, shape of eyes, type of hair, smile, posture, and more:

_____
_____
_____

2. These are *5–10 personality traits* that I find attractive in others that I have myself. Examples might include warmth, easy-going manner, determination, sense of humor and more:

_____
_____
_____

3. These are *5–10 expressions of body pride*. Examples might include personal style, dress/clothing, engagement in cultural practices/activities and more:

_____
_____
_____

4. My definition of beauty:

_____
_____
_____

N. L. Wood-Barcalow, T. L. Tylka, and C. L. Judge. *Positive Body Image Workbook: A Clinical and Self-Improvement Guide.* Cambridge: Cambridge University Press, 2021.

Assignment 7.2: Family Ancestry

For this assignment, explore your family ancestry through the use of photographs. Notice the similarities/differences in facial and body characteristics. Identify the unique beauty features such as hair texture/color, skin color, and prominent features exhibited in different family members. Reflect on how many generations and genetic pairings resulted in your unique expression of traits. Write your realizations below.

_____
_____
_____
_____
_____
_____
_____
_____
_____
_____
_____

N. L. Wood-Barcalow, T. L. Tylka, and C. L. Judge. *Positive Body Image Workbook: A Clinical and Self-Improvement Guide.* Cambridge: Cambridge University Press, 2021.

Assignment 7.3: A Different Culture

For this assignment, think about your current appearance routines (e.g., putting on make-up, shaving). Next, imagine existing in a different culture and/or time, being surrounded by appearance ideals important to that culture. What did/does the majority consider attractive in terms of specific clothing, body type, skin color, adornments (e.g., jewelry), size of body parts, and more? Now, imagine living in this culture and answer the following about appearance ideals:

These are important appearance ideals to this culture:

_____
_____
_____

I would engage in these behaviors to try to meet these ideals:

_____
_____
_____

I would feel like this:

_____
_____
_____

This is how I would feel if I didn't meet the standards of this culture:

_____
_____
_____

Reflections and realizations:

_____
_____
_____

N. L. Wood-Barcalow, T. L. Tylka, and C. L. Judge. *Positive Body Image Workbook: A Clinical and Self-Improvement Guide.* Cambridge: Cambridge University Press, 2021.

Assignment 7.4: Body Pride

Being connected to your identified culture(s) is associated with body pride. This form of pride begins internally and is then demonstrated outwardly through various practices and rituals. As an example, Aboriginal women in Canada emphasized the following expressions of body pride: accepting all aspects of the body, reflecting who you are, being connected to your culture, engaging in healthy behaviors, and expressing gratitude in being Native.* They demonstrated this pride through dance regalia, participating in powwows, and displaying Native symbols and tattoos.

For this activity, reflect on the following:

This/These is/are the culture(s) that I identify with: _____
_____
_____

These are the ways I accept my body: _____
_____
_____

These are ways I demonstrate body pride: _____
_____
_____

This is how I like to present myself: _____
_____
_____

These are the activities, rituals and/or practices important within my culture(s): _____
_____
_____

I am proud of the following aspects of my culture(s): _____
_____
_____

I am thankful for the following components of my culture(s): _____
_____
_____

* T. F. McHugh, A. M. Coppola, and C. M. Sabiston. "I'm thankful for being Native and my body is part of that": The body pride experiences of young Aboriginal women in Canada. *Body Image* 2014; **11**: 318–27.

N. L. Wood-Barcalow, T. L. Tylka, and C. L. Judge. *Positive Body Image Workbook: A Clinical and Self-Improvement Guide.* Cambridge: Cambridge University Press, 2021.

Assignment 7.5: Differences between Attractiveness and Beauty

As defined in this chapter, attractiveness is related to how closely a person resembles cultural ideals. Alternatively, beauty is more of a personal evaluation of someone based on a combination of appearance and personality traits. Such personality traits can include agreeableness, patience, intelligence, kindness, confidence and more. For this assignment, consider the differences between attractiveness and beauty by exploring the topics below:

Examples of *attractive* people:
- in media: _____
- in my life: _____

Common characteristics of those I consider attractive:
_____

Aspects of attractiveness that are:
- important to me: _____
- aspects that I already have: _____

Examples of *beautiful* people: _____
- in media: _____
- in my life: _____

Common characteristics of those I consider beautiful: _____
_____

Aspects of beauty that are:
- important to me: _____
- aspects that I already have: _____

My overall reflections on the differences between attractiveness and beauty:
_____
_____
_____

N. L. Wood-Barcalow, T. L. Tylka, and C. L. Judge. *Positive Body Image Workbook: A Clinical and Self-Improvement Guide.* Cambridge: Cambridge University Press, 2021.

Assignment 7.6: Beauty as We Age

Most appearance ideals emphasize youthfulness, known as the "youthful ideal." In fact, many beauty practices emphasize maintaining youth or trying to appear younger. It can be challenging to find examples of older individuals who are acknowledged and celebrated for their beauty. For this activity, reflect on depictions of elderly individuals within media, characteristics of elderly individuals you know personally, and qualities you would like to embrace as you age.

Media

I notice the following direct or indirect messages about how elderly individuals are portrayed in media, including messages that encourage pursuit of the "youthful ideal" (e.g., "get younger looking skin," "get rid of crepey skin," "feel ten years younger"):

_____

_____

_____

Examples of elderly individuals in media programming that do NOT focus on the "youthful ideal" and/or show elderly persons in an undesirable manner (e.g., portrayed as unattractive due to normal aging issues, dependent, fragile, incapable) include:

_____

_____

_____

Personal Life

These are the beauty characteristics of the elderly people in my life including their physical and personality traits:

_____

_____

_____

I admire these qualities of the elderly people in my life:

_____

_____

_____

My Focus as I Age

These are the specific physical and personality traits I would like to embrace:

_____

_____

_____

This is how I would like to respond to the "youthful ideal":

_____

_____

_____

N. L. Wood-Barcalow, T. L. Tylka, and C. L. Judge. *Positive Body Image Workbook: A Clinical and Self-Improvement Guide.* Cambridge: Cambridge University Press, 2021.

References

1. V. M. Buote, A. E. Wilson, E. J. Strahan, et al. Setting the bar: Divergent sociocultural norms for women's and men's ideal appearance in real-world contexts. *Body Image* 2011; **8**: 322–34.

2. T. L. Tylka. Broad conceptualization of beauty. In: Tylka, T. L. and Piran, N. eds. *Handbook of Positive Body Image: Constructs, Protective Factors, and Interventions.* New York: Oxford University Press, 2019: 52–7.

3. R. Kuo. Four ways our socially accepted beauty ideals are racist. *Everyday Feminism* 2017. Retrieved from: https://everydayfeminism.com/2017/05/beauty-ideals-racist/ [last accessed July 11, 2020]"> [last accessed July 11, 2020].

4. D. N. Greenwood and S. Dal Cin. Ethnicity and body consciousness: Black and White American women's negotiations of media ideals and others' approval. *Psychol Pop Media Cult* 2012; **1**: 220–35.

5. N. Wolf. *The Beauty Myth: How Images of Beauty are Used Against Women.* London: Chatto & Windus, 1990.

6. T. L. Tylka and A. C. Iannantuono. Perceiving beauty in all women: Psychometric evaluation of the Broad Conceptualization of Beauty Scale. *Body Image* 2016; **17**: 67–81.

7. R. M. Calogero, T. L. Tylka, L. C. Donnelly, et al. Trappings of femininity: A test of the "beauty as currency" hypothesis in shaping college women's gender activism. *Body Image* 2017; **21**: 66–70.

8. R. M. Calogero, M. Borroughs, and J. K. Thompson. The impact of Western beauty ideals on the lives of women and men: A sociocultural perspective. In Swami, V. and Furnham, A. eds. *Body Beautiful: Evolutionary and Sociocultural Perspectives.* New York: Palgrave Macmillan, 2007: 259–98.

9. K. Holmqvist and A. Frisén. "I bet they aren't that perfect in reality": Appearance ideals viewed from the perspective of adolescents with a positive body image. *Body Image* 2012; **9**: 388–95.

10. S. Parker, M. Nichter, M. Nichter, et al. Body image and weight concerns among African American and White adolescent females: Differences that make a difference. *Hum Organ* 1995; **54**: 103–14.

11. T. F. McHugh, A. M. Coppola, and C. M. Sabiston. "I'm thankful for being Native and my body is part of that": The body pride experiences of young Aboriginal women in Canada. *Body Image* 2014; **11**: 318–27.

12. N. L. Wood-Barcalow, T. L. Tylka, and C. L. Augustus-Horvath. "But I like My Body": Positive body image characteristics and a holistic model for young-adult women. *Body Image* 2010; **7**: 106–16.

13. K. A. Bailey, K. L. Gammage, C. van Ingen, et al. "It's all about acceptance": A qualitative study exploring a model of positive body image for people with spinal cord injury. *Body Image* 2015; **15**: 24–34.

14. K. Homan. Athletic-ideal and thin-ideal internalization as prospective predictors of body dissatisfaction, dieting, and compulsive exercise. *Body Image* 2010; **7**: 240–5.

15. J. K. Thompson and E. Stice. Thin-ideal internalization: Mounting evidence for a new risk factor for body-image disturbance and eating pathology. *Curr Dir Psychol Sci* 2001; **10**: 181–3.

16. C. B. Becker and E. Stice. From efficacy to effectiveness to broad implementation: Evolution of the Body Project. *J Consult Clin Psychol* 2017; **85**: 767–82.

17. J. M. Alleva, T. L. Tylka, and A. M. Kroon Van Diest. The Functionality Appreciation Scale (FAS): Development and psychometric evaluation in US community women and men. *Body Image* 2017; **23**: 28–44.

Chapter 8

Self-Compassion and Body Image Flexibility

Theory and Research Overview

When we are faced with difficult situations in which we suffer, fail, or feel inadequate, how do we respond? Do we criticize ourselves, obsess about what we did wrong, and distract ourselves from our feelings (such as shame, guilt, or pain)? We may even believe that we "deserve" treating ourselves this way, that it is "tough love" so we will "be better" in the future. However, treating ourselves this way can be damaging and ineffective. In fact, beating ourselves up during and after difficult situations moves us further away from our goals [1].

An alternative, adaptive way to respond that moves us towards our goals is self-compassion. **Self-compassion** is acting in a caring way towards ourselves when we are faced with difficult situations or when we feel inadequate [2]. Self-compassion has three components. Rather than judging ourselves for feeling or being deficient, we react in kind, warm-hearted ways towards ourselves, known as **self-kindness**. Rather than thinking that we are "alone" in our failure, we understand that everyone is imperfect, makes mistakes, and experiences difficult situations, known as **common humanity**. Rather than obsessing about what we did wrong or trying to avoid our emotional reactions, we are aware of our feelings in a more balanced way, known as **mindfulness**.

Self-compassion has many benefits for our well-being because it helps us feel cared for, connected, and emotionally calm in difficult situations [3]. Self-compassion is not the same as self-esteem, self-pity, or self-complacency, which are related to lower psychological well-being. Instead, self-compassion is associated with higher psychological well-being, such as greater productivity, optimism, life satisfaction, and happiness, as well as less anxiety and sadness [4]. Self-compassion can improve body image as well. Among a multi-generational group of women, those who received three weeks of a guided self-compassion meditation reduced their body dissatisfaction, body shame, and the extent to which they based their self-worth on their appearance, as well as increased body appreciation relative to a control group [5]. All improvements were maintained three months after the intervention ended. Thus, self-compassion meditation may be a useful and cost-effective means of improving women's body image.

We can activate self-compassion when we are faced with many difficult situations, including **body image threats** [6–7]. Body image threats direct our attention to certain aspects of our bodies and provoke distress or shame. Examples include: a loved one suggests (or hints) that we should go on a diet, we don't fit into a piece of clothing that used to fit comfortably,

a friend who is thinner than us mentions that they are fat and hates their body, we are rejected from a love interest, we see age-related changes in our bodies, and so on. Activating self-compassion in these situations may include treating our bodies with kindness by engaging in self-care (e.g., yoga, rest, see Chapter 19), understanding that others experience body image threats as well from time to time, and being aware of the negative feelings that may emerge without obsessing about or avoiding them. Offering ourselves self-compassion during these difficult situations goes beyond simply reminding ourselves of our good qualities. To understand your level of self-compassion, complete the *Self-Compassion Scale* [8] within this chapter.

Self-compassion may build **body image flexibility** [9], which helps us respond positively to body image threats [10–11]. Body image flexibility includes:

1. Our ability to "sit with" or remain aware of our uncomfortable thoughts and feelings about our bodies without judgment.
2. Our willingness to create and work toward adaptive goals in intentional and committed ways, even in the presence of uncomfortable thoughts and feelings about our bodies.

Like self-compassion, body image flexibility is related to higher body appreciation and functionality appreciation (see Chapters 10 and 11) as well as lower body dissatisfaction, body shame, and disordered eating [10–11]. Body image flexibility is also protective of psychological health. For example, body image flexibility may help prevent women from engaging in eating disorder behaviors when they experience body dissatisfaction [12]. Weak levels of body image flexibility may leave us susceptible to disordered eating and distress when we experience body image threats. In contrast, strong levels of body image flexibility may promote body appreciation when we feel negatively about our bodies [13]. To understand your level of body image flexibility, complete the *Body Image-Acceptance and Action Questionnaire* (BI-AAQ) [10] presented within this chapter.

Thus, body image flexibility is a key target in order to enhance positive body image and psychological well-being. One approach to improve body image flexibility with research support is **Acceptance and Commitment Therapy (ACT)** [14–15]. ACT aligns well with body image flexibility and self-compassion. Specifically, in times of distress, it teaches skills that help us be open to (and mindful of) our difficult feelings and thoughts while also moving toward behaviors that we value. This process happens without self-judgment or distressing thoughts and feelings dominating our attention. Some of the assignments in this workbook are focused on building these skills.

To summarize, self-compassion and body image flexibility are valuable characteristics for positive body image that can be fostered through approaches such as ACT. It is important that we have self-compassion for ourselves, our bodies, and all body image issues we may have. It is important that we cultivate body image flexibility to pursue our meaningful goals even when situations call negative attention to our bodies. This self-compassion and body image flexibility can allow room for the growth of our positive body image and for us to approach our bodies with kindness, humanity, and mindfulness.

Treatment Planning Tools

Talking Points for Sessions

- Discuss examples of self-compassion
- Encourage your client to identify specific examples of their own body image threats (e.g., comparison with others and/or through use of social media, comparison to a "former, remembered" self, weight fluctuations during different times of the month/year)
- Discuss barriers to demonstrating body image flexibility

Treatment Plan

Goals

- ❏ Engage in self-compassionate practices when I experience negative or judgmental thoughts
- ❏ Practice self and body kindness when I experience bad body image days/experiences
- ❏ Increase patience with myself
- ❏ Reach out to compassionate others when I feel negatively about myself
- ❏ Focus on my values in life, instead of my appearance
- ❏ Practice self-acceptance not determined by my body weight/shape/size
- ❏ Decrease the focus on trying to control my body
- ❏ Recognize unrealistic standards/goals that I have about myself and my body

Objectives

- ❏ Identify self-judgmental thoughts about my body and identify alternate statements that reflect self-compassion

- ❏ Identify specific phrases or words that I can repeat when bad body image occurs (e.g., *it's going to be okay, I can get through this, I'm more than just my body*)
- ❏ Recognize when body image threats result in destructive behaviors and create a plan to respond more effectively to future threats
- ❏ Identify examples of listening to my body following traumatic or uncomfortable experiences
- ❏ Identify specific ways to reconnect with my body following traumatic or uncomfortable experiences
- ❏ Identify potential barriers to accepting my "new body" following traumatic or uncomfortable experiences
- ❏ Identify ways that I have demonstrated strength and resilience following traumatic or uncomfortable experiences

Additional Resources

C. Germer and K. Neff. *Teaching the Mindful Self-Compassion Program: A Guide for Professionals.* New York: Guilford Press, 2019.

K. Neff and C. Germer. *The Mindful Self-Compassion Workbook.* New York: Guilford Press, 2018.

E. Sandoz and T. DuFrene. *Living with Your Body and Other Things You Hate: How to Let Go of Your Struggle with Body Image Using Acceptance and Commitment Therapy.* Oakland: New Harbinger Publications, Inc., 2013.

C. K. Germer. *The Mindful Path to Self-Compassion: Freeing Yourself from Destructive Thoughts and Emotions.* New York: Guilford Press, 2009.

K. Bluth. *The Self-Compassion Workbook for Teens: Mindfulness and Compassion Skills to Overcome Self-Criticism and Embrace Who You Are.* Oakland: Raincoast Books, 2017.

T. Desmond. *Self-Compassion in Psychotherapy: Mindfulness-Based Practices for Healing and Transformation.* New York: W. W. Norton & Company, Inc., 2015.

L. Silberstein-Tirch. *How to Be Nice to Yourself: The Everyday Guide to Self-Compassion.* Emeryville: Althea Press, 2019.
The Center for Mindful Self-Compassion: www.CenterforMSC.org

Making Friends with Yourself: Mindful Self-Compassion for Teens: www.centerformsc.org/msc-teens

Guided Self-Compassion Meditations and other resources available at: www.self-compassion.org

Assessment 8.1: Self-Compassion Scale-Short Form (SCS-SF)

Please read each statement carefully before answering. Indicate how often you behave in the stated manner by **circling the number** to the right of the item.

	Almost Never	Seldom	Sometimes	Often	Almost Always
1. When I fail at something important to me, I become consumed by feelings of inadequacy.	5	4	3	2	1
2. I try to be understanding and patient towards those aspects of my personality I don't like.	1	2	3	4	5
3. When something painful happens, I try to take a balanced view of the situation.	1	2	3	4	5
4. When I'm feeling down, I tend to feel like most other people are probably happier than I am.	5	4	3	2	1
5. I try to see my failings as part of the human condition.	1	2	3	4	5
6. When I'm going through a very hard time, I give myself the caring and tenderness I need.	1	2	3	4	5
7. When something upsets me, I try to keep my emotions in balance.	1	2	3	4	5
8. When I fail at something that's important to me, I tend to feel alone in my failure.	5	4	3	2	1
9. When I'm feeling down, I tend to obsess and fixate on everything that's wrong.	5	4	3	2	1
10. When I feel inadequate in some way, I try to remind myself that feelings of inadequacy are shared by most people.	1	2	3	4	5
11. I'm disapproving and judgmental about my own flaws and inadequacies.	5	4	3	2	1
12. I'm intolerant and impatient towards those aspects of my personality I don't like.	5	4	3	2	1
Total Self-Compassion score: add items 1–12 then divide by 12 =					

Total Self-Compassion score between:

- **4–5** = high self-compassion
- **3–3.9** = moderate self-compassion
- **below 3** = low self-compassion

Note. Reprinted with permission. Authors of the SCS-SF are Raes, Pommier, Neff, and Van Gucht.* The measurement properties of this scale (reliability and validity) have been supported with various samples of individuals from many countries. Please contact the authors for permission to use the SCS-SF within research; there is no need to contact them to use it with clients or to complete on your own. For questions about the scale, contact Kristin Neff at https://self-compassion.org/ and www.CenterforMSC.org .

  * F. Raes, E. Pommier, K. D. Neff, et al. Construction and factorial validation of a short form of the Self-Compassion Scale. *Clin Psychol Psychother* 2011; **18**: 250–5.

Self-Compassion Scale-Short Form Applications

- Review your response to item 1 (*When I fail at something important to me, I become consumed by feelings of inadequacy*). List the expectations you have for your body.

    o Ask yourself how realistic are these expectations, and why they are important to you.

    o Think about how you may be using those standards to judge yourself as either good or bad, a success or failure. Now consider how your response might be different if you were able to challenge or even eliminate these expectations.

- Notice how item 4 (*When I'm feeling down, I tend to feel like most other people are probably happier than I am*) is about comparison with others. Consider how often you compare your internal experiences with the exteriors of others. What information do you use as your basis of comparison (e.g., photos of others on social media, stories about the successes of others)?

- Consider item 9 (*When I'm feeling down, I tend to obsess and fixate on everything that's wrong*). Reflect on your tendency to focus negatively on your body when you feel down.

    o What areas of your body do you focus on? What kinds of thoughts do you have? What actions do you take?

    o Now imagine responding to the experience of feeling down without focusing on your body. What might you do instead?

- If you responded "agree" or "strongly agree" to item 11 (*I'm disapproving and judgmental about my own flaws and inadequacies*):

    o Are these perceived flaws and inadequacies communicated to a partner, friend, child, or loved one either directly or indirectly?

    o Does a focus on flaws and inadequacies impact your ability to move toward positive body image?

    o How might practicing self-affirmations impact a focus on flaws or inadequacies?

Assessment 8.2: The Body Image-Acceptance and Action Questionnaire (BI-AAQ) (Body Image Flexibility)

Below you will find a list of statements. Please rate the truth of each statement as it applies to you. Use the following rating scale to make your choices. For instance, if you believe that a statement is "Always True," you would write a "1" next to that statement.

1	2	3	4	5	6	7
Always True	Almost Always True	Frequently True	Sometimes True	Seldom True	Very Seldom True	Never True

	Number
1. Worrying about my weight makes it difficult for me to live a life that I value.	
2. I care too much about my weight and body shape.	
3. I shut down when I feel bad about my body shape or weight.	
4. My thoughts and feelings about my body weight and shape must change before I can take important steps in my life.	
5. Worrying about my body takes up too much of my time.	
6. If I start to feel fat, I try to think about something else.	
7. Before I can make any serious plans, I have to feel better about my body.	
8. I will have better control over my life if I can control my negative thoughts about my body.	
9. To control my life, I need to control my weight.	
10. Feeling fat causes problems in my life.	
11. When I start thinking about the size and shape of my body, it's hard to do anything else.	
12. My relationships would be better if my body weight and/or shape did not bother me.	
Total Body Image Flexibility score: add items 1–12 then divide by 12 =	

Total Body Image Flexibility score between:

- **5.5–7** = high levels of body image flexibility
- **4–5.4** = moderate levels of body image flexibility
- **below 4** = low levels of body image flexibility

Note. Reprinted with permission. Authors of the BI-AAQ are Sandoz, Wilson, Merwin, and Kellum.* The measurement properties of this scale (reliability and validity) have been supported with various samples of individuals from many countries. Please contact the authors of the BI-AAQ for permission to use it within research; there is no need to contact them to use it with clients or to complete on your own.

* E. K. Sandoz, K. G. Wilson, R. M. Merwin, et al. Assessment of body image flexibility: The Body Image-Acceptance and Action Questionnaire. *J Contextual Behav Sci* 2013; **2**: 39–48.

The Body Image-Acceptance and Action Questionnaire (Body Image Flexibility) Applications

- If you responded sometimes true, frequently true, almost always true, or always true to item 1 (*Worrying about my weight makes it difficult for me to live a life that I value*), consider: (a) what are your top five values,[1] (b) why are these values important to you, and (c) how does weight relate to these core values?

- If you responded sometimes true, frequently true, almost always true, or always true to Item 2 (*I care too much about my weight and body shape*), consider what it means to "care too much" about your appearance. What do you do (or not do) because of caring "too much?"

- If you responded sometimes true, frequently true, almost always true, or always true to item 4 (*My thoughts and feelings about my body weight and shape must change before I can take important steps in my life*), and/or item 7 (*Before I can make any serious plans, I have to feel better about my body*), identify what specific things you are waiting to do in life.

  o Consider how life might be different if you just did these things even if you don't change how you think and feel about your body beforehand.

- If you responded sometimes true, frequently true, almost always true, or always true to item 5 (*Worrying about my body takes up too much of my time),* consider how your energy could be used if you weren't worrying about your body. What would you do? What would you think about?

- If you responded sometimes true, frequently true, almost always true, or always true to item 12 (*My relationships would be better if my body weight and/or shape did not bother me*), imagine how your relationships would be different if you weren't concerned with your body weight or shape.

  o How might you interact differently with your friends? Your family members? Romantic partners?

  o Imagine experiencing positive body image and how that would impact your thoughts, emotions, and behaviors. Challenge yourself to embrace those thoughts, emotions, and behaviors now even if you have yet to attain a positive body image.

---

[1] Check out the Good Project online to identify your values, available at: www.thegoodproject.org/value-sort.

Assignment 8.1: Body Image Threats

Body image threats direct our attention to aspects of our bodies and provoke distress or shame. Examples include: a loved one suggests (or hints) that we should go on a diet, we don't fit into a piece of clothing we used to fit into comfortably, a friend who is thinner than us mentions that they are fat and hate their body, we perceive rejection from a love interest, we notice age-related changes in our bodies. Reflect on the following items below:

Examples of my body image threats include:

_____
_____
_____
_____
_____

What I do (and/or don't do) when experiencing these body image threats:

_____
_____
_____
_____
_____

When I experience body image threats, I can rely on these people to help me:

_____
_____
_____
_____
_____

When I experience body image threats, I plan to respond in these ways:

_____
_____
_____
_____
_____

N. L. Wood-Barcalow, T. L. Tylka, and C. L. Judge. *Positive Body Image Workbook: A Clinical and Self-Improvement Guide.* Cambridge: Cambridge University Press, 2021.

Assignment 8.2: Living Life Now

How often have I said that I will do certain things only once I feel better about myself or after I make changes to my body (e.g., weight, shape, size, fitness)? Write examples and reflections here:

_____
_____
_____
_____
_____
_____
_____

Here's how I will practice accepting those aspects that I have not liked about myself:

_____
_____
_____
_____
_____
_____
_____

Here's what I will start doing, regardless of my thoughts and feelings about my body:

_____
_____
_____
_____
_____
_____
_____

How I plan to start living my life now:

_____
_____
_____
_____
_____
_____
_____

N. L. Wood-Barcalow, T. L. Tylka, and C. L. Judge. _Positive Body Image Workbook: A Clinical and Self-Improvement Guide._ Cambridge: Cambridge University Press, 2021.

Assignment 8.3: Seeking Body Perfection

Seeking perfection in life, especially related to the body, can affect the ability to experience self-compassion. Trying to obtain body perfection involves setting unrealistic expectations or goals that result in self-judgment and self-criticism.

I have these expectations of how my body should *look*:

_____
_____
_____
_____

I have these expectations of how my body should *perform*:

_____
_____
_____
_____

These expectations are based on messages from (me, family members, friends, peers, media figures):

_____
_____
_____
_____

When these expectations are not met,

I feel: _____

I think:_____

I do: _____

I don't do: _____

These expectations are unrealistic in the following ways:

_____
_____
_____
_____

I'm willing to challenge or change these expectations:

_____
_____
_____
_____

I will practice the following to increase self-compassion:

_____
_____
_____
_____

N. L. Wood-Barcalow, T. L. Tylka, and C. L. Judge. *Positive Body Image Workbook: A Clinical and Self-Improvement Guide.* Cambridge: Cambridge University Press, 2021.

Assignment 8.4: Using Self-Compassion to Cope with Body Dissatisfaction

On a day when my body dissatisfaction is strong . . .

I will remember past times I've been resilient and tell myself:

_____
_____
_____
_____

I will think about these people who struggle with similar issues or other difficulties to remember that I'm not alone in facing challenges:

_____
_____
_____
_____

I will say these kind things to myself:

_____
_____
_____
_____

N. L. Wood-Barcalow, T. L. Tylka, and C. L. Judge. _Positive Body Image Workbook: A Clinical and Self-Improvement Guide._ Cambridge: Cambridge University Press, 2021.

Assignment 8.5: Love and Kindness Experiment

I will try a thought experiment in which I imagine that I'm a being who can only experience love and kindness without any judgment or dislike.

These are the loving things that I'd say about my *body*:

_____
_____
_____
_____

These are the loving things that I'd say about my *personality*:

_____
_____
_____
_____

These are the loving things that I would do in my life:

_____
_____
_____
_____

This is how I would share love and kindness with others:

_____
_____
_____
_____

❏ I will practice this experiment on a consistent basis and notice any changes over time.

N. L. Wood-Barcalow, T. L. Tylka, and C. L. Judge. *Positive Body Image Workbook: A Clinical and Self-Improvement Guide.* Cambridge: Cambridge University Press, 2021.

Assignment 8.6: Self-Compassion Meditations

Practicing self-compassion meditation via podcast (twenty minutes a day for three weeks) results in decreased body shame and body dissatisfaction, and increased self-compassion and body appreciation.* These podcasts are free and can be found at www.self-compassion.org.

Week 1: Compassionate Body Scan meditation
Week 2: Affectionate Breathing meditation
Week 3: Self-Compassion/Loving-Kindness meditation

Week 1: I will practice a **Compassionate Body Scan meditation** daily and journal my observations and realizations from the meditation practice.
- ❏ Sunday
- ❏ Monday
- ❏ Tuesday
- ❏ Wednesday
- ❏ Thursday
- ❏ Friday
- ❏ Saturday

This is what I noticed during my practice:

Week 2: I will practice an **Affectionate Breathing meditation** daily and record my observations and realizations from the meditation practice.
- ❏ Sunday
- ❏ Monday
- ❏ Tuesday
- ❏ Wednesday
- ❏ Thursday
- ❏ Friday
- ❏ Saturday

This is what I noticed during my practice:

Week 3: I will practice a **Self-Compassion/Loving-Kindness meditation** daily and record my observations and realizations from the meditation practice:
- ❏ Sunday
- ❏ Monday
- ❏ Tuesday
- ❏ Wednesday
- ❏ Thursday
- ❏ Friday
- ❏ Saturday

This is what I noticed during my practice:

* E. R. Albertson, K. D. Neff, K. E. Dill-Shackleford. Self-compassion and body dissatisfaction in women: A randomized controlled trial of a brief meditation intervention. *Mindfulness* 2015; **6**: 444–54.

N. L. Wood-Barcalow, T. L. Tylka, and C. L. Judge. *Positive Body Image Workbook: A Clinical and Self-Improvement Guide.* Cambridge: Cambridge University Press, 2021.

Assignment 8.7: Letting Go of Negative Body Thoughts

The average human brain has between 50,000–70,000 thoughts every day, including negative and positive judgments. It is common to "hold on to" negative body thoughts, which results in additional negative thoughts and uncomfortable emotions. Rather than focus on and believe these negative body thoughts, it is helpful to notice them without judgment and let them go. It can be helpful to gently repeat a statement such as "this thought is just a thought and nothing more" or "let it go." For this assignment, identify your most common negative body image thoughts and try the following recommendations:

These are the negative body image thoughts that I experience the most:

_____
_____
_____

These thoughts and emotions follow the original negative body image thoughts:

_____
_____
_____

I will gently repeat the following upon experiencing negative body image thoughts:

_____
_____
_____

I will imagine letting go of these thoughts (over and over again):

_____
_____
_____

This is what I notice when I try to let go of these thoughts and redirect my attention to the present moment:

_____
_____
_____

N. L. Wood-Barcalow, T. L. Tylka, and C. L. Judge. *Positive Body Image Workbook: A Clinical and Self-Improvement Guide.* Cambridge: Cambridge University Press, 2021.

References

1. K. D. Neff, Y.-P. Hsieh, and K. Dejitterat. Self-compassion, achievement goals, and coping with academic failure. *Self Identity* 2005; **4**: 263–87.

2. K. D. Neff, K. L. Kirkpatrick, and S. S. Rude. Self-compassion and adaptive psychological functioning. *J Res Pers* 2007; **41**: 139–54.

3. P. Gilbert. Compassion and cruelty: A biopsychological approach. In: Gilbert P, ed. *Compassion: Conceptualisations, Research and Use in Psychotherapy*. London: Routledge, 2005: 9–74.

4. L. K. Barnard and J. F. Curry. Self-compassion: Conceptualizations, correlates, and interventions. *Rev Gen Psych* 2011; **15**: 289–303.

5. E. R. Albertson, K. D. Neff, K. E. Dill-Shackleford. Self-compassion and body dissatisfaction in women: A randomized controlled trial of a brief meditation intervention. *Mindfulness* 2015; **6**: 444–54.

6. T. F. Cash, M. T. Santos, and E. F. Williams. Coping with body-image threats and challenges: Validation of the Body Image Coping Strategies Inventory. *J Psychosom Res* 2005; **58**: 191–9.

7. K. J. Homan and T. L. Tylka. Self-compassion moderates body comparison and appearance self-worth's inverse relationships with body appreciation. *Body Image* 2015; **15**: 1–7.

8. F. Raes, E. Pommier, K. D. Neff, et al. Construction and factorial validation of a short form of the Self-Compassion Scale. *Clin Psychol Psychother* 2011; **18**: 250–5.

9. S. J. Schoenefeld and J. B. Webb. Self-compassion and intuitive eating in college women: Examining the contributions of distress tolerance and body image acceptance and action. *Eat Behav* 2013; **14**: 493–6.

10. E. K. Sandoz, K. G. Wilson, R. M. Merwin, et al. Assessment of body image flexibility: The Body Image-Acceptance and Action Questionnaire. *J Contextual Behav Sci* 2013; **2**: 39–48.

11. C. B. Rogers, J. B. Webb, and N. Jafari. A systematic review of the roles of body image flexibility as a moderator, mediator, and in intervention science (2011–2018). *Body Image* 2018; **27**: 43–60.

12. C. Ferreira, J. Pinto-Gouveia, and C. Duarte. The validation of the Body Image Acceptance and Action Questionnaire: Exploring the moderator effect of acceptance on disordered eating. *Rev Int Psicol Ter Psicol* 2011; **11**: 327–45.

13. J. B. Webb. Body image flexibility contributes to explaining the link between body dissatisfaction and body appreciation in White college-bound females. *J Contextual Behav Sci* 2015; **4**: 176–83.

14. S. C. Hayes, K. D. Strosahl, and K. G. Wilson. *Acceptance and Commitment Therapy: An Experiential Approach to Behavior Change.* New York: Guilford Press, 1999.

15. J. Linardon, J. Gleeson, K. Yap, et al. Meta-analysis of the effects of third-wave behavioural interventions on disordered eating and body image concerns: Implications for eating disorder prevention. *Cogn Behav Ther* 2018, **48**: 15–38.

Chapter 9

Approaching Our Bodies

Theory and Research Overview

When we dislike how we look, we may either "check" aspects of our appearance obsessively in the mirror, avoid looking at ourselves in the mirror, or both. When I (Tracy) was seven years old and on the swim team, I would stand in front of the mirror and check how much my upper thighs would "puff" out from under my bathing suit. Then, in my early twenties, I would avoid looking at all reflective surfaces, such as store windows and display cases. When I successfully avoided seeing my reflection, I was relieved momentarily, but then I felt even more distress when I realized how much I feared seeing my body – avoiding my reflection actually increased my initial distress. In fact, research shows that frequently checking or avoiding our appearance are both maladaptive in that they increase appearance dissatisfaction, shame, and guilt [1–2].

Body avoidance includes behaviors that help to avoid situations in which the body may be exposed or perceived in a negative manner and may also involve neglecting the body by ignoring its needs for nutrition, hygiene, movement, medical and preventative care, rest, and pleasure [1–3]. Body avoidance can correspond with different aspects of appearance such as body fat, body shape, hair thinning or loss, moles, scars, acne, excessive hair, wrinkles, asymmetrical features, and masculine or feminine physical traits. Behaviors that reflect body avoidance include:

- Avoiding mirrors and reflective surfaces
- Camouflaging the body with clothing
- Avoiding certain types of clothes that expose the body
- Avoiding sexual intimacy or intimate situations that expose the body (e.g., activity during the daytime or with the lights on)
- Avoiding weighing or measuring the body because of feeling uncomfortable with the numbers
- Avoiding engaging in certain activities in which the body (or how the body moves) is the focus (e.g., waving, bowling, swimming, dancing, jogging)
- Not touching the body (e.g., using a washcloth in order to not touch the skin)
- Avoiding looking at the face or naked body
- Avoiding taking pictures of oneself, looking at pictures of oneself, and/or having pictures taken of oneself
- Avoiding posting pictures of the body for others to see
- Avoiding medical appointments and procedures that expose the body to others (e.g., skin cancer screening)
- Covering the body with objects to prevent others from seeing one's body

Body checking includes repeatedly scrutinizing aspects of appearance (e.g., body fat, body shape, hair thinning or loss, moles, scars, acne, excessive hair, wrinkles, asymmetrical features), which can include obsessively checking one's appearance in the mirror (also known as **mirror gazing** [2]). Checking may include rigid behaviors to alter or "measure" aspects of appearance [3] such as:

- Gazing in mirrors and other reflective surfaces to examine appearance
- Weighing multiple times a day
- Measuring the size of body parts (e.g., with tape measures, fingers, rings, belts, etc.)
- Pinching areas of the body to determine the amount of fat
- Checking for a "thigh gap"
- Checking for protruding bones or defined muscles
- Checking body composition (e.g., body fat and muscle percentages)
- Engaging in compulsive exercise followed by measuring whether the body changes as a result
- Engaging in various forms of food restriction (e.g., calorie counting, eating only "clean foods") followed by measuring whether the body changes as a result.

Body avoidance and body checking often bring momentary relief from discomfort, fear and anxiety [4]. Yet, both involve judgment – either inspecting the body closely to determine how "flawed" it is (body checking) or dismissing it and its needs because of what it looks like (body avoidance). This judgment perpetuates appearance anxiety and negative body image [5–6]. In particular, repeated body checking, such as mirror gazing, focuses our attention on our perceived appearance defect(s) [7]. These defects are then over-represented and over-processed in the brain's sensory cortex [2], thereby reinforcing their presence in our minds. Frequent and extreme engagement in both avoidance and checking can correspond with postponing important life activities (e.g., vacations, class reunions, one's own wedding, clothes shopping), thereby reducing overall quality of life.

Rather than judgment, positive body image involves striving toward a more flexible view of our bodies, whereby we approach our bodies with compassion, acceptance, and appreciation rather than judgment [8]. We call this process **approaching the body**. Many therapy interventions suggest that approaching uncomfortable experiences (e.g., situations, thoughts, behaviors, and emotions) with awareness, mindfulness, and compassion can help restore well-being, while ignoring, brooding over, and judging our discomfort enhances our distress [9–11]. It may be difficult approaching the body at first, as being in contact with a source of discomfort is not comfortable. Yet, with repeated practice, approaching the body reduces judgment, appearance anxiety, and negative body image [5–6].

Mirror exposure is one way we can approach our bodies that is different from mirror gazing [2]. **Mirror exposure therapy** involves viewing our bodies in a mirror repeatedly, while following guidance from a therapist. In **guided mirror exposure**, clients are instructed to describe their reflection without judging it, typically starting with their head and progressing down to their toes, followed by describing their "whole body" [12]. In **pure mirror exposure**, clients are instructed to express their thoughts and feelings as they describe their reflection – it is common to have clients look at, touch, and describe emotions related to dissatisfied body parts [13]. Both types are effective in treating body checking and body avoidance, although pure mirror exposure has been found to be superior over guided mirror exposure for reducing distress during and after the mirror exposure sessions [13]. Mirror exposure should be carried out under the supervision of an experienced clinician.

How does mirror exposure work? First, it helps clients to interpret their bodies in an objective, neutral, holistic, and perhaps even positive manner [14] and to direct attention away from disliked areas [15]. Using mirror exposure therapy to focus on areas that clients like about their bodies is especially beneficial for reducing negative body image [14, 16]. Second, mirror exposure therapy may create **cognitive dissonance**, or discomfort that occurs when our attitudes conflict with our behavior [17]. This discomfort motivates us to change our attitudes to be consistent with our behavior. Therefore, in mirror exposure, clients' negative body attitudes could be reduced as they use neutral or positive language to describe their bodies.

One study examined three mirror exposure approaches: (a) *neutral, non-judgmental approach* whereby clients describe their bodies as "precisely and neutrally as possible" during the mirror exposure, (b) *mindfulness-based* whereby clients make non-judgmental observations about each body part aloud during mirror exposure, and (c) *cognitive dissonance-based* whereby clients describe positive aspects of their physical, emotional, intellectual, and social qualities during mirror exposure [14]. All three approaches reduce body checking, body avoidance, depression, shape and weight concern, and eating pathology, but only cognitive dissonance-based mirror exposure improved body satisfaction [14]. Thus, creating dissonance by discussing positive self-qualities during mirror exposure may be especially beneficial for clients high in body dissatisfaction. Clinicians may wish to focus on the client's most positively perceived body parts and encourage the use of positive descriptors [2, 14, 18]. Additionally, clinicians do not have to choose one approach for a client; they may wish to incorporate all three types of mirror exposure within therapy. For example, clinicians could incorporate one approach each session for three sessions.

While approaching the body may be difficult at first, it is important for us to connect with our bodies in a non-judgmental, accepting, and positive manner. Approaching the body can help facilitate the development of many of the positive body image skills presented in this workbook, such as body appreciation (Chapter 10), functionality appreciation (Chapter 11), embodiment (Chapter 12), sexual intimacy (Chapter 14), protective filtering (Chapter 17), mindful self-care (Chapter 19), fueling the body (Chapter 20), life-enhancing movement (Chapter 21), and adaptive appearance investment (Chapter 22), as well as reduce the urge to engage in social comparison (Chapter 15) and body talk (Chapter 16). Because approaching the body is needed to "open" positive body image growth, we think of it metaphorically as a "heart opener." In yoga practice, a **heart opener** is when we position our body in an "open" way that allows us to grow in compassion, appreciation, and connection to ourselves, our bodies, and others [19]. Heart openers unlock the cage around our heart that has formed from years of emotionally challenging or damaging experiences, which can include negative body image, through releasing negative emotions and sparking joyful emotions. Approaching our bodies, then, is a gift to ourselves, as it allows us to be able to do the work in our positive body image journey and enhance our well-being.

Treatment Planning Tools

Talking Points for Sessions

- Discuss what it would be like to reduce or eliminate body checking and/or avoidant behaviors
- Describe what approaching the body would be like

Treatment Plan

Goals

❑ Identify my current and past experiences with body checking and/or body avoidance
❑ Consider how effectively my distress is managed (e.g., short-term, long-term) through body checking and/or body avoidance
❑ Identify examples of how I've neglected my body by engaging in body avoidance
❑ Identify examples of how I've hurt myself or my body by engaging in body checking
❑ Identify coping strategies I can use when tempted to engage in body checking and/or body avoidance
❑ Identify specific coping strategies that I can use when practicing approaching my body
❑ Explore how frequent and extreme body avoidance/checking behaviors affect my quality of life
❑ Explore how my quality of life will likely improve with body approaching activities

Objectives

❑ Practice mirror exposure in therapy weekly for a month
❑ Practice using positive self-talk while I look in the mirror

- Create a list of body avoidant activities and schedule a time to practice each activity
- Practice compassionate self-talk during exposure to a disliked body part
- Focus on the function of the body part when my dissatisfaction arises
- Record my negative self-talk that occurs during body checking and reframe into neutral or positive statements
- Refrain from engaging in one form of body checking behavior for a specific amount of time (e.g., one day, one week, one month)
- Practice exposure to one form of body avoidant behavior for an identified timeframe (e.g., one day, one week, one month) whereby I approach my body using mindfulness and acceptance skills
- Identify emotions and thoughts before, during, and after an incident of body checking or avoidance
- Identify authentic and compassionate responses to repeat to myself when experiencing body judgment
- Identify at least five neutral aspects of my body and focus on them at least once a day for an extended period of time
- Identify at least five positive aspects of my body and focus on them at least once a day for an extended period of time
- Identify specific fear(s) associated with approaching the body and create an action plan to address the fear(s)
- Incorporate positive, kind thoughts about the body while engaging in body checking behavior
- Incorporate positive, kind thoughts about the body while engaging in body avoidant activities
- Create a pros/cons list of approaching the body

Additional Resources

A. N. Pearson, M. Heffner, and V. M. Follette. *Acceptance and Commitment Therapy for Body Image Dissatisfaction.* Oakland: New Harbinger Publications, Inc., 2010.

E. K. Sandoz, K. G. Wilson, and T. DuFrene. *Mindfulness and Acceptance Workbook for Body Image: Letting Go of the Struggle with What You See in the Mirror Using Acceptance and Commitment Therapy.* Oakland: New Harbinger Publications, Inc., 2013.

E. Sandoz and T. DuFrene. *Living with Your Body and Other Things You Hate.* Oakland: New Harbinger Publications, Inc., 2014.

Assignment 9.1: Pros/Cons of Avoiding and Approaching the Body

There are advantages and disadvantages of avoiding, checking, and approaching uncomfortable aspects of my body in the short-term and long-term.

	Pros	Cons
Avoiding the body		
Checking the body		
Approaching the body		

Realizations about *avoiding* the body:

_____

_____

_____

Realizations about *checking* the body:

_____

_____

_____

Realizations about *approaching* the body:

_____

_____

_____

N. L. Wood-Barcalow, T. L. Tylka, and C. L. Judge. *Positive Body Image Workbook: A Clinical and Self-Improvement Guide.* Cambridge: Cambridge University Press, 2021.

Assignment 9.2: "Mirror Checking" Experiment

I engage in **mirror checking** (repeatedly scrutinizing aspects of appearance in the mirror):

Never	Monthly	Weekly	Daily	Several times/day

Before **mirror checking**
I *feel* this way before engaging in mirror checking:

_____

_____

I *think these things* before engaging in mirror checking:

_____

_____

I hope that mirror checking will:

_____

_____

During **mirror checking**
I *feel* this way during mirror checking:

_____

_____

I *think these things* during mirror checking:

_____

_____

I hope that mirror checking will:

_____

_____

After **mirror checking**
I *feel* this way after engaging in mirror checking:

_____

_____

I *think these things* after engaging in mirror checking:

_____

_____

Mirror checking:

_____

_____

_____

Now, let's focus on approaching the body (approaching our bodies with compassion, acceptance, and appreciation not judgment) **rather than "mirror checking".**

Before **approaching my body**
I *feel* this way before approaching my body:

_____

_____

I *think these things* before approaching my body:

_____

_____

N. L. Wood-Barcalow, T. L. Tylka, and C. L. Judge. *Positive Body Image Workbook: A Clinical and Self-Improvement Guide.* Cambridge: Cambridge University Press, 2021.

I hope that approaching my body will:

_____

_____

During approaching my body

I *feel* this way as I am approaching my body:

_____

_____

I *think these things* as I am approaching my body:

_____

_____

I hope that approaching my body will:

_____

_____

After approaching my body

I *feel* this way after approaching my body:

_____

_____

I *think these things* after approaching my body:

_____

_____

Approaching my body:

_____

_____

_____

Overall reflections

I engage in mirror checking when:

_____

_____

I typically feel this way after mirror checking:

_____

_____

I typically feel this way after approaching my body:

_____

_____

Mirror checking impacts my progress toward positive body image:

_____

_____

Approaching my body impacts my progress toward positive body image:

_____

_____

I commit to:

_____

_____

 N. L. Wood-Barcalow, T. L. Tylka, and C. L. Judge. *Positive Body Image Workbook: A Clinical and Self-Improvement Guide.* Cambridge: Cambridge University Press, 2021.

Assignment 9.3: Body Checking Behavior

These are the types of body checking behaviors that I engage in:

_____

_____

This is one body checking behavior that I'd like to change:

_____

_____

I engage in this checking behavior:

Never   Monthly   Weekly   Daily   Several times/day

Before checking
I *feel* this way before engaging in body checking:

_____

_____

I *think these things* before engaging in body checking:

_____

_____

I hope that body checking will:

_____

_____

During body checking
I *feel* this way during body checking:

_____

_____

I *think these things* during body checking:

_____

_____

I hope that body checking will:

_____

_____

After body checking
I *feel* this way after engaging in body checking:

_____

_____

I *think these things* after engaging in body checking:

_____

_____

Body checking:

_____

_____

Overall reflections
I engage in body checking when:

_____

_____

N. L. Wood-Barcalow, T. L. Tylka, and C. L. Judge. *Positive Body Image Workbook: A Clinical and Self-Improvement Guide.* Cambridge: Cambridge University Press, 2021.

I typically feel this way after body checking:

_____

_____

Body checking impacts my progress toward positive body image:

_____

_____

I commit to:

_____

_____

N. L. Wood-Barcalow, T. L. Tylka, and C. L. Judge. *Positive Body Image Workbook: A Clinical and Self-Improvement Guide.* Cambridge: Cambridge University Press, 2021.

Assignment 9.4: Overexposure to Avoidance

Listed below are examples of different types of behaviors that can correspond with negative body image. First, indicate whether the behavior applies to you by choosing either yes or no. Second, make a mark on the continuum where you fall for each behavior from one end of the continuum (overexposure) to the other (avoidance). Record reflections including how these behaviors impact your progress toward positive body image.

Looking in reflective surfaces (e.g., mirror, windows): Yes or No

I---I
Overexposure   Moderate levels   Avoidance

Reflections:
_____
_____

Weighing: Yes or No

I---I
Overexposure   Moderate levels   Avoidance

Reflections:
_____
_____

Measuring body or body parts: Yes or No

I---I
Overexposure   Moderate levels   Avoidance

Reflections:
_____
_____

Pinching body or body parts: Yes or No

I---I
Overexposure   Moderate levels   Avoidance

Reflections:
_____
_____

Checking for bones: Yes or No

I---I
Overexposure   Moderate levels   Avoidance

Reflections:
_____
_____

Checking for muscularity (e.g., overall body, body parts, percentage): Yes or No

I---I
Overexposure   Moderate levels   Avoidance

Reflections:
_____
_____

N. L. Wood-Barcalow, T. L. Tylka, and C. L. Judge. *Positive Body Image Workbook: A Clinical and Self-Improvement Guide.* Cambridge: Cambridge University Press, 2021.

Checking for fat distribution (e.g., overall body, body parts, percentage): Yes or No

I--I
Overexposure   Moderate levels   Avoidance

Reflections:

_____

_____

Clothing (e.g., how it fits, trying on desired items, trying on former items that hold significance): Yes or No

I--I
Overexposure   Moderate levels   Avoidance

Reflections:

_____

_____

Other:

I--I
Overexposure   Moderate levels   Avoidance

_____

_____

Other:

I--I
Overexposure   Moderate levels   Avoidance

Reflections:

_____

_____

Other:

I--I
Overexposure   Moderate levels   Avoidance

Reflections:

_____

_____

N. L. Wood-Barcalow, T. L. Tylka, and C. L. Judge. *Positive Body Image Workbook: A Clinical and Self-Improvement Guide.* Cambridge: Cambridge University Press, 2021.

Assignment 9.5: Body Checking

Body checking is the practice of assessing how the body meets or does not meet some expectation or standard. Checking includes a range of behaviors from looking in reflective objects, measuring parts of the body, weighing, pinching/poking, and more. The intended purpose of checking (e.g., to reassure, serve as motivation, reduce uncomfortable emotions) can differ from the actual outcomes (e.g., increased insecurity, embarrassment, fear) which can lead to more checking behaviors. Ultimately these body checking behaviors can turn into **maladaptive appearance investment practices** (see Chapter 22) which results in moving away from body acceptance.

Body Checking Practice	Purpose/Intention	Actual Outcome	Realizations
Example: *Weighing*	*To see if there has been any change in my weight*	*Upset and frustrated that my weight has increased*	*I'm preoccupied with my weight. My day is ruined when the number goes up. I feel worse about myself rather than better.*
Looking in the mirror or another reflective surface (e.g., store window)			
Pinching			
Weighing			
Checking muscles			
Checking fat			
Measuring body parts			
Sitting/standing in certain positions			
Other:			
Other:			
Other:			

I engage in body checking when:

_____

_____

I typically feel this way after:

_____

_____

Body checking impacts my progress toward positive body image:

_____

_____

I commit to:

_____

_____

N. L. Wood-Barcalow, T. L. Tylka, and C. L. Judge. *Positive Body Image Workbook: A Clinical and Self-Improvement Guide.* Cambridge: Cambridge University Press, 2021.

Assignment 9.6: Journal about Approaching the Body

A primary reason for engaging in body avoidance and checking behaviors is to reduce negative body image. The inaccurate belief is that these behaviors will produce positive outcomes, when in reality it *only results in short-term relief* with *increased negative body image in the long-term*. In contrast, approaching the body results in *short-term discomfort* with *increased positive body image in the long-term*. Approaching the body is what actually moves us toward body acceptance.

For this journal activity, reflect on the following: what barriers exist in approaching my body (e.g., fear of the unknown, belief that things will worsen indefinitely, not knowing how to do so effectively), what judgments do I have about my ability to approach my body, how can I tolerate discomfort while approaching my body, what faulty or inaccurate beliefs do I need to let go of, what does it mean for me to be self-compassionate, which of my values correspond with approaching the body, which of my character strengths correspond with approaching the body? (See Chapter 2 for a discussion of character strengths and values.)

_____
_____
_____
_____
_____
_____
_____
_____
_____
_____
_____
_____
_____
_____
_____
_____
_____
_____
_____
_____
_____
_____
_____
_____
_____
_____

N. L. Wood-Barcalow, T. L. Tylka, and C. L. Judge. *Positive Body Image Workbook: A Clinical and Self-Improvement Guide.* Cambridge: Cambridge University Press, 2021.

Assignment 9.7: Body Judgments

These are the judgments that I make about *my body*:

_____

_____

These are the judgments that I make about *myself*:

_____

_____

These judgments impact me in the following ways:

_____

_____

These are the *things that I do* related to these judgments:

_____

_____

These are the *things that I don't do* related to these judgments:

_____

_____

These judgments impact my negative body image:

_____

_____

These judgments impact my positive body image:

_____

_____

I commit to the following regarding my judgments:

_____

_____

N. L. Wood-Barcalow, T. L. Tylka, and C. L. Judge. *Positive Body Image Workbook: A Clinical and Self-Improvement Guide.* Cambridge: Cambridge University Press, 2021.

References

1. T. Legenbauer, F. Martin, A. Blaschke, et al. Two sides of the same coin? A new instrument to assess body checking and avoidance behaviors in eating disorders. *Body Image* 2017; **21**: 39–46.

2. T. C. Griffen, E. Naumann, and T. Hildebrandt. Mirror exposure therapy for body image disturbances and eating disorders: A review. *Clin Psychol Rev* 2018; **65**: 163–74.

3. C. P. Cook-Cottone, E. Tribole, and T. L. Tylka. *Healthy Eating in Schools: Evidence-based Interventions to Help Children Thrive.* Washington: American Psychological Association, 2013.

4. V. Mountford, A. M. Haase, and G. Waller. Is body checking in the eating disorders more closely related to diagnosis or to symptom presentation? *Behav Res Ther* 2007; **45**: 2704–11.

5. R. Shafran, M. Lee, E. Payne, et al. An experimental analysis of body checking. *Behav Res Ther* 2007; **45**: 113–21.

6. D. Veale, S. Miles, N. Valiallah, et al. The effect of self-focused attention and mood on appearance dissatisfaction after mirror-gazing: An experimental study. *J Behav Ther Exp Psychiatry* 2016; **52**: 38–44.

7. D. Veale and S. Riley. Mirror, mirror on the wall, who is the ugliest of them all? The psychopathology of mirror gazing in body dysmorphic disorder. *Behav Res Ther* 2001; **39**: 1381–93.

8. T. L. Tylka and N. L. Wood-Barcalow. What is and what is not positive body image? Conceptual foundations and construct definition. *Body Image* 2015; **14**: 118–29.

9. S. C. Hayes, K. D. Strosahl, and K. G. Wilson. *Acceptance and Commitment Therapy: The Process and Practice of Mindful Change*, 2nd ed. New York: Guilford, 2012.

10. M. M. Linehan. *DBT Skills Training Manual*, 2nd ed. New York: Guilford, 2015.

11. P. Gilbert. *Compassion-Focused Therapy: Distinctive Features.* London: Routledge, 2010.

12. S. S. Delinsky and G. T. Wilson. Mirror exposure for the treatment of body image disturbance. *Int J Eat Disord* 2006; **39**: 108–16.

13. S. Moreno-Domínguez, S. Rodríguez-Ruiz, M. C. Fernández-Santaella, et al. Pure versus guided mirror exposure to reduce body dissatisfaction: A preliminary study with university women. *Body Image* 2012; **9**: 285–8.

14. C. A. Luethcke, L. McDaniel, and C. B. Becker. A comparison of mindfulness, nonjudgmental, and cognitive dissonance-based approaches to mirror exposure. *Body Image* 2011; **8**: 251–8.

15. K. A. Glashouwer, N. C. Jonker, K. Thomassen, et al. Take a look at the bright side: Effects of positive body exposure on selective visional attention with women with high body dissatisfaction. *Behav Res Ther* 2016; **83**: 19–25.

16. E. Smeets, A. Jansen, and A. Roefs. Bias for the (un)attractive self: On the role of attention in causing body (dis)satisfaction. *Health Psychol* 2011; **30**: 360–7.

17. L. Festinger. *A Theory of Cognitive Dissonance.* Stanford: Stanford University Press, 1957.

18. A. Jansen, V. Voorwinde, Y. Hoebink, et al. Mirror exposure to increase body satisfaction: Should we guide the focus of attention towards positively or negatively evaluated body parts? *J Behav Ther Exp Psychiatry* 2016; **50**: 90–6.

19. Reed, A. Opening your heart through yoga: How it works, and why they're some of our (and my) favourite experiences to include in yoga practice. *Yoga in Bowness: Yoga for Everyone, and for a Better Community* (blog). Retrieved from: www.yogainbowness.com/yoga-off-the-mat/2017/1/31/opening-your-heart-through-yoga-how-it-works-and-why-theyre-some-of-our-and-my-favourite-experiences-to-include-in-yoga-practice [last accessed July 11, 2020].

Chapter 10

Body Appreciation

Theory and Research Overview

What does it mean to appreciate our bodies? Appreciation is another word for gratitude. Gratitude is a general tendency to notice and be thankful for the positive aspects of life, and it is strongly connected to our physical health and emotional well-being [1]. That is, the more grateful we are, the healthier we are and the better we feel. **Body appreciation** is repeatedly noticing and being thankful for our bodies [2]. The more grateful we are toward our bodies, the better we feel.

To appreciate our bodies, we don't need to fit cultural beauty standards. We don't even have to be satisfied with every aspect of our appearance or how our bodies function. We just need to be able to notice and be thankful for the good in our bodies and what our bodies do for us. For example, we can notice and appreciate the strength and resilience of our bodies and our unique physical characteristics. This is important because when we appreciate our bodies, we are more likely to accept our bodies, respect our bodies, and protect our bodies by treating them well and taking care of their needs, thereby promoting our physical health and psychological well-being [3–4].

Body appreciation is a core feature of positive body image [2]. In a research study, college women from the US who self-identified as having a positive body image provided their thoughts on: "What exactly is positive body image?" [5]. Various researchers and clinicians who specialize in body image were also interviewed on this topic. Body appreciation emerged as a primary theme. Participants described appreciating, respecting, honoring, loving, and displaying gratitude toward the features, functionality, and health of their bodies. They even reported appreciating aspects of their bodies that they once disliked. Body appreciation was also a primary theme of those from other cultures and groups. Adolescent males and females from Sweden appreciated the function and appearance of their bodies, even though they considered their appearance to be "average" [6]. Aboriginal Canadian girls appreciated their Native appearance features and their ability to engage in powwow dance, which connects them to their culture and allows them to feel cultural pride [7]. Canadian adults with spinal cord injuries noticed, appreciated, and focused on improvements in the health, function, independence, and strength of their bodies [8].

Body appreciation has four core features [9–10]:

1. *Holding positive attitudes towards our bodies*, regardless of appearance

2. *Accepting our bodies and appreciating what makes them unique*
3. *Respecting our bodies by attending to their needs and engaging in healthy behaviors* to care for them
4. *Protecting our bodies by rejecting unrealistic appearance ideals found in media* (e.g., social media, TV, movies).

Body appreciation has been studied in many cultures, ages, genders, and geographic locations [11–12]. As expected, body appreciation is related to psychological well-being, such as higher optimism, self-esteem, proactive coping (i.e., imagining hurdles that could impact your progress toward your goals and figuring out ways to get past them), positive emotions (e.g., joy), life satisfaction, and happiness as well as lower negative emotions (e.g., depression) [13]. Body appreciation is also linked to healthy levels of physical activity and higher intuitive eating (see Chapter 20), as well as decreased dieting, disordered eating behaviors, and use of alcohol and cigarettes [13–14]. Further more, body appreciation is connected to greater sexual satisfaction, such as higher sexual excitement and orgasm during sexual activity [15] (see also Chapter 14). Body appreciation is also associated with higher self-compassion: we appreciate our bodies more on the days that we treat ourselves with greater self-compassion [16]. Perhaps treating ourselves compassionately minimizes the importance of appearance, which helps us appreciate our bodies even when they do not fit societal appearance ideals. In addition, body appreciation protects how we feel about our appearance when we are exposed to these ideals (e.g., leafing through fashion magazines, checking out social media profiles of celebrities and other social influencers) [17–18].

How does body appreciation emerge, especially in cultures that promote body dissatisfaction through messages to be thinner, fitter, younger, and more attractive? Currently, two theories are supported by research. First, believing that important others (family, romantic partners, and friends) accept our bodies as they are, without hints to lose weight or tone certain areas, promotes body appreciation [14, 19] (see also Chapters 5 and 6). Adolescent girls who felt that their bodies were accepted by their friends and family had higher body appreciation one year later [14]. Second, being grateful in general helps us see our own self-worth, making us less likely to need validation for our appearance and others' approval, and more likely to appreciate our bodies for what they are. Fortunately, gratitude can be increased through engaging in certain activities

[21–23], some of which will be offered in the practice assignments.

Overall, body appreciation is important to our psychological well-being, physical health, and self-care. To understand your level of body appreciation further, complete the *Body Appreciation Scale-2* [10] presented within this chapter.

Treatment Planning Tools

Talking Points for Sessions

- Discuss the topic of respect in general and how it relates to the body specifically
- Identify various needs of the body and how to attend to those needs (e.g., rest when feeling tired, eating when hungry)
- Discuss what it means to feel love and gratitude for the body

Treatment Plan

Goals

❑ Exhibit a more positive attitude toward my body
❑ Increase attentiveness to positive aspects of my body
❑ Recognize the unique qualities of my body
❑ Recognize the needs of my body
❑ Learn how to reject societal appearance ideals
❑ Learn how to increase self-compassion
❑ Engage in healthy behaviors
❑ Decrease unhealthy behaviors

Objectives

❑ Identify and record three examples of gratitude for my body on a daily basis for at least two weeks (e.g., I'm grateful that I can breathe easily)
❑ Create a list of at least five unique characteristics of my body
❑ Create a list of all the benefits that my various body parts provide for daily living
❑ Practice mindfulness and/or self-compassion practices directed toward my body at least three times per week
❑ Take five minutes each day for two weeks to identify what I appreciate about my body from that day
❑ Create a list of coping skills that promote body acceptance that can be used when I have "bad body image days"
❑ Identify potential barriers to accepting my "new body" following traumatic or uncomfortable experiences
❑ Identify specific ways to no longer take my body for granted
❑ Recognize various ways of fostering a new appreciation for my health following a medical/health crisis
❑ Identify those individuals in my life who accept my body as it is
❑ Journal about how positive body image is related to sexual health

Additional Resources

R. Scritchfield. *Body Kindness.* New York: Workman Publishing Co., Inc., 2016. Podcast available at: www.bodykindnessbook.com/podcast/

R. R. Radcliffe. *Body Prayers: Finding Body Peace.* Minneapolis: EASE Publications, 2004.

S. R. Taylor. *The Body Is Not an Apology: The Power of Radical Self-Love.* Oakland: Berrett-Koehler Publishers, Inc., 2018.

T. F. Cash. *The Body Image Workbook.* Oakland: New Harbinger Publications, Inc., 2008.

C. Sobczak. *Embody: Learning to Love Your Unique Body (and Quiet that Critical Voice!).* Carlsbad: Gurze Publications, 2014.

E. Sandoz and T. DuFrene. *Living with Your Body and Other Things You Hate: How to Let Go of Your Struggle with Body Image Using Acceptance and Commitment Therapy.* Oakland: New Harbinger Publications, Inc., 2013.

Assessment 10.1: Body Appreciation Scale-2 (BAS-2)

Please indicate how often each item is true about you using the following scale. Write the number to the right of the item.

1	2	3	4	5
Never	Seldom	Sometimes	Often	Always

	Number
1. I respect my body.	
2. I feel good about my body.	
3. I feel that my body has at least some good qualities.	
4. I take a positive attitude towards my body.	
5. I am attentive to my body's needs.	
6. I feel love for my body.	
7. I appreciate the different and unique characteristics of my body.	
8. My behavior reveals my positive attitude towards my body; for example, I hold my head high and smile.	
9. I am comfortable in my body.	
10. I feel like I am beautiful even if I am different from media images of attractive people (e.g., models, actresses/actors).	
Total Body Appreciation score: add items 1–10, then divide by 10 =	

Total Body Appreciation score between:
- **4–5** = high body appreciation
- **3–3.9** = moderate body appreciation
- **below 3** = low body appreciation

Note. Reprinted with permission. Authors of the BAS-2 are Tylka and Wood-Barcalow. The BAS-2 has been translated into different languages to be used in various countries, and its measurement properties (reliability, validity) have been supported in samples from these countries. Please contact the authors of the BAS-2 for permission to use it within research; there is no need to contact them to use it with clients or to complete on your own.

* T. L. Tylka and N. L. Wood-Barcalow. The Body Appreciation Scale-2: Item Refinement and Psychometric Evaluation. *Body Image* 2015; **12**: 53–67.

Body Appreciation Scale-2 Applications

- Complete the Body Appreciation Scale-2 based on your *current experiences.*

  ○ What *themes* do you notice in your responses? For example, perhaps you are able to identify positive aspects about your body (higher scores on items 3 and 7), but aren't currently comfortable in your body (lower score on item 9).

  ○ Take time to reflect on active changes you can make in order to increase comfort with your body. An example might be actually doing something *uncomfortable* like wearing a certain type of clothing that you usually avoid to prove to yourself that you can do it. If uncomfortable emotions, thoughts, and/or physical sensations associated with wearing certain clothing have kept you from engaging in activities you enjoy (e.g., swimming), you can practice wearing the clothing to prove to yourself that you can tolerate any associated discomfort. Another example might be trying an activity that you either haven't tried or are worried about doing due to concerns about your body.

- Complete the Body Appreciation Scale-2 while imagining a time in your life when your body image was more positive.

  ○ Try to remember what was helpful about your attitude and treatment towards your body. Challenge yourself to go beyond how society might have valued your body.

  ○ What themes do you notice in your responses? Consider what life experiences may have shifted your body image.

- Complete the Body Appreciation Scale-2 as though it's the *future and you are accepting of yourself.* What themes do you notice in your responses?

  ○ What attitudes, thoughts, and behaviors can you identify and perhaps work on now, in order to help you accept your body in the future?

- For item 1 (*I respect my body*), identify specific ways in which you respect your body. Acknowledge examples of disrespect toward the body and create an action plan for making positive change.

- Create a list of positive qualities of your body as identified in item 3 (*I feel that my body has at least some good qualities*). Review the list and ask yourself:

  ○ Do you take time to reflect on the positive qualities?

  ○ Do you receive feedback from others about these qualities?

- For item 7 (*I appreciate the different and unique characteristics of my body*), journal about the following:

  ○ Identify characteristics that are rather unique to your body that aren't typically reflected in social appearance ideals.

  ○ Identify characteristics that make your family lineage unique (hair texture, skin color, prominent features).

- Item 9 (*I am comfortable in my body*) focuses on body comfort. What does this phrase mean to you? In what ways are you comfortable with your body? In what ways are you uncomfortable with your body? Identify specific activities you're willing to try with the goal of increasing body comfort.

- Beauty is identified in item 10 (*I feel like I am beautiful even if I am different from media images of attractive people*). Journal on the following:

  ○ How does your definition of a person's beauty differ from that portrayed in media?

  ○ What unique characteristics correspond with your beauty?

Assignment 10.1: Attitude toward the Body

My *current* attitude towards my body:

_____
_____
_____
_____

How my current attitude is *different from other times in my life* (e.g., childhood, adolescence, young adulthood, adulthood, mid-life, older life):

_____
_____
_____
_____

How my current attitude is *similar to various times in my life* (e.g., childhood, adolescence, young adulthood, adulthood, mid-life, older life):

_____
_____
_____
_____

Important life events or experiences that have shaped my attitude toward my body:

_____
_____
_____
_____

How others have influenced my attitude towards my body (e.g., parents, friends, romantic partners):

_____
_____
_____
_____

When I think of a specific time that I experienced a *positive attitude* toward my body, I describe it (and how I felt / thought) as:

_____
_____
_____
_____

N. L. Wood-Barcalow, T. L. Tylka, and C. L. Judge. *Positive Body Image Workbook: A Clinical and Self-Improvement Guide.* Cambridge: Cambridge University Press, 2021.

Assignment 10.2: Body Gratitude

On a daily basis for one week, I will identify reasons I am grateful for my body. Examples can include what my body does for me, how my body works efficiently, my overall health, and the absence of pain in a specific area.

Day 1: _____
_____
_____

Day 2: _____
_____
_____

Day 3: _____
_____
_____

Day 4: _____
_____
_____

Day 5: _____
_____
_____

Day 6: _____
_____
_____

Day 7: _____
_____
_____

N. L. Wood-Barcalow, T. L. Tylka, and C. L. Judge. *Positive Body Image Workbook: A Clinical and Self-Improvement Guide.* Cambridge: Cambridge University Press, 2021.

Assignment 10.3: Body Respect

This is what it means to respect my body:

_____
_____
_____

What kinds of things _would I do_ if I honored and respected my body? Examples might be attending preventative medical appointments, eating when I'm hungry, engaging in life-enhancing movement to keep my body active, surrounding myself with others who are positive about their own bodies, and resting when I'm tired.

_____
_____
_____

What kinds of things _would I not do_ if I honored and respected my body? Examples might be smoking, dieting, or uncomfortable sexual practices.

_____
_____
_____

What commitments and specific activities will I practice in honor of respecting my body?

_____
_____
_____

I commit to do this daily:

_____
_____

I commit to do this weekly:

_____
_____

I commit to do this monthly:

_____

N. L. Wood-Barcalow, T. L. Tylka, and C. L. Judge. _Positive Body Image Workbook: A Clinical and Self-Improvement Guide._ Cambridge: Cambridge University Press, 2021.

Assignment 10.4: Coping on Bad Body Image Days

These experiences increase my negative body image (check all that apply):

❏ Trying on or wearing certain types of clothes

❏ Comparing myself to others who are perceived to be better, more attractive, more muscular, in better shape, etc.

❏ Doing activities that highlight things I don't like about my body

❏ People commenting on my appearance

❏ Weighing myself

❏ Uncomfortable physical and/or emotional experiences (e.g., feeling bloated, tension, stress, loneliness)

❏ Being the center of attention

❏ Going to unfamiliar environments

❏ Meeting someone new

❏ Failing to achieve a goal

❏ Attending a medical appointment (e.g., being weighed, how I'm treated)

❏ Other: _____

❏ Other: _____

These are coping skills I can use when my body image is negative (check all that apply):

❏ Remind myself of my positive qualities and strengths

❏ Remember a compliment that someone has offered me

❏ Focus on how my body functions effectively

❏ Practice acceptance that I'm going to have "bad body image days," and that it is okay

❏ Reduce or eliminate the use of social media for a specific period of time

❏ Remind myself that this feels uncomfortable, and feeling uncomfortable will pass with time

❏ Challenge my negative thoughts and emotions by thinking of positive examples

❏ Focus on helping someone else

❏ Practice relaxation skills

❏ Engage in activities that I find enjoyable

❏ Remind myself of what I find important in my life besides my body

❏ Connect with others who make me feel good about myself

❏ Other: _____

❏ Other: _____

N. L. Wood-Barcalow, T. L. Tylka, and C. L. Judge. *Positive Body Image Workbook: A Clinical and Self-Improvement Guide.* Cambridge: Cambridge University Press, 2021.

References

1. A. M. Wood, J. J. Froh, and A. W. A. Geraghty. Gratitude and well-being: A review and theoretical integration. *Clin Psych Rev* 2010; **30**: 890–905.

2. T. L. Tylka and N. L. Wood-Barcalow. What is and what is not positive body image? Conceptual foundations and construct definition. *Body Image* 2015; **14**: 118–29.

3. R. Andrew, M. Tiggemann, and L. Clark. Positive body image and young women's health: Implications for sun protection, cancer screening, weight loss and alcohol consumption behaviours. *J Health Psych* 2016; **21**: 28–39.

4. M. M. Gillen. Associations between positive body image and indicators of men's and women's mental and physical health. *Body Image* 2015; **13**: 67–74.

5. N. L. Wood-Barcalow, T. L. Tylka, and C. L. Augustus-Horvath. "But I like my body": Positive body image characteristics and a holistic model for young-adult women. *Body Image* 2010; **7**: 106–16.

6. A. Frisén and K. Holmqvist. What characterizes early adolescents with a positive body image? A qualitative investigation of Swedish girls and boys. *Body Image* 2010; **7**: 205–12.

7. T. L. McHugh, A. M. Coppola, and C. M. Sabiston. "I'm thankful for being Native and my body is part of that": The body pride experiences of young Aboriginal women in Canada. *Body Image* 2014; **11**: 318–27.

8. K. A. Bailey, K. L. Gammage, C. van Ingen, et al. "It's all about acceptance": A qualitative study exploring a model of positive body image for people with spinal cord injury. *Body Image* 2015; **15**: 24–34.

9. L. Avalos, T. L. Tylka, and N. Wood-Barcalow. The Body Appreciation Scale: Development and psychometric evaluation. *Body Image* 2005; **2**: 285–97.

10. T. L. Tylka and N. L. Wood-Barcalow. The Body Appreciation Scale-2: Item refinement and psychometric evaluation. *Body Image* 2015; **12**: 53–67.

11. V. Swami. Considering positive body image through the lens of culture and minority social identities. In: Daniels E., Gillen M. M., Markey C. H., eds. *Body Positive: Understanding Body Image in Science and Practice.* Cambridge: Cambridge University Press, 2018: 59–91.

12. M. Tiggemann. Considerations of positive body image across various social identities and special populations. *Body Image* 2015; **14**: 168–76.

13. T. L. Tylka. Overview of the field of positive body image. In: Daniels E. A., Gillen M. M., Markey C. H., eds. *Body Positive: Understanding Body Image in Science and Practice.* Cambridge: Cambridge University Press, 2018: 6–33.

14. R. Andrew, M. Tiggemann, and L. Clark. Predictors and health-related outcomes of positive body image in adolescent girls: A prospective study. *Dev Psych* 2016; **52**: 463–74.

15. S. Satinsky, M. Reece, B. Dennis, et al. An assessment of body appreciation and its relationship to sexual function in women. *Body Image* 2012; **9**: 137–44.

16. A. C. Kelly and E. Stephen. A daily diary study of self-compassion, body image, and eating behavior in female college students. *Body Image* 2016; **17**: 152–60.

17. E. Halliwell. The impact of thin idealized media images on body satisfaction: Does body appreciation protect women from negative effects? *Body Image* 2013; **10**: 509–14.

18. R. Andrew, M. Tiggemann, and L. Clark. The protective role of body appreciation against media-induced body dissatisfaction. *Body Image* 2015; **15**: 98–104.

19. C. L. Augustus-Horvath and T. L. Tylka. The acceptance model of intuitive eating: A comparison of women in emerging adulthood, early adulthood, and middle adulthood. *J Couns Psych* 2011; **58**: 110–25.

20. K. J. Homan and T. L. Tylka. Development and exploration of the gratitude model of body appreciation in women. *Body Image* 2018; **25**: 14–22.

21. J. Dunaev, C. H. Markey, and P. M. Brochu. An attitude of gratitude: The effects of body-focused gratitude on weight bias internalization and body image. *Body Image* 2018; **25**: 9–13.

22. K. Homan, B. Sedlak, and E. Boyd. Gratitude buffers the adverse effect of viewing the thin ideal on body dissatisfaction. *Body Image* 2014; **11**: 245–50.

23. W. L. Wolfe and K. Patterson. Comparison of a gratitude-based and cognitive restructuring intervention for body dissatisfaction and dysfunctional eating behavior in college women. *Eat Disord* 2017; **25**: 330–44.

Functionality Appreciation

Theory and Research Overview

Often, when we think about our bodies, we think in terms of how we *look* – our size, shape, muscularity, fat, and other physical features such as our hair, skin, teeth, and face. We tend to focus less on what our bodies *do* for us, such as carry a child, perform labor, walk our dog, digest food, observe a beautiful sunset, read and comprehend the ideas in this workbook, engage in a deep conversation, enjoy a massage, hug the ones we love, feel and express empathy, heal us from illness, breathe in oxygen, keep our hearts beating, and more. In short, the functions of our bodies keep us alive – not just physically but also emotionally. **Body functionality** is everything the body can do or is capable of doing [1], and can be different for everyone based on physical abilities and limitations due to illnesses, injuries, development, aging, and surgeries.

How can focusing on body functionality help our body image? Actually, it is not as useful to focus on the number of things our bodies can do. If this is the case, we may become angry at our bodies when they cannot (or can no longer) perform certain functions. Instead, it is more useful to *appreciate* what our bodies can do [1]. The process of appreciating, respecting, and honoring the body for what it is capable of doing is **functionality appreciation** [1].

Being *aware* of what our bodies, including our brains, can do is necessary for functionality appreciation, but it is only part of the story [2]. We also need to be *grateful* for what our bodies allow us to do. As an example, a group of adults with spinal cord injuries were interviewed about their body image [3]. Many of these adults revealed that they appreciated what their bodies could do – for instance, one participant indicated that they were grateful that their upper body could function well. Many also celebrated gains in functionality – for instance, they were grateful when they made gains in mobility after their injury. In a recent study, a group of adults who experience chronic pain conditions (e.g., fibromyalgia, bowel disease, back pain) reported a more positive body image when they were able to accept their pain (i.e., experience body pain without judgment, feel that their lives are going well despite pain), even when they perceived that they were unable to control or manage their pain [4].

Therefore, even when we view our bodies as less functional in some ways, we can still be grateful for how our bodies function in other ways. That said, it is okay to grieve the loss of body function. For example, I (Tracy) was 32 when I had to have a surgery that left me unable to have children. It was

devastating, and at times, I catch myself "blaming my body." The grief comes in waves, being more intense in specific moments and less intense in other moments. I allow myself to grieve as needed but also remind myself what my body does for me in other ways, like walk my dogs, connect with others in many ways (e.g., through interesting and meaningful conversations, compassion, laughter), "think on my feet" while I'm answering students' questions, and help write this workbook. My body allows me to nurture myself and others in many ways. Functionality appreciation allows me to lower body blame and shame.

Functionality appreciation may seem like the same thing as body appreciation (see Chapter 10). Indeed, they are connected: the higher body appreciation we have, the higher functionality appreciation we also have. Yet, body appreciation is more general and includes appreciation for our appearance [5–6], whereas functionality appreciation is specific to being grateful for how our bodies function [1]. Furthermore, compared to body appreciation, functionality appreciation is more strongly related to eating mindfully, or remaining attentive to how food tastes and how it impacts the body while eating [7].

Like body appreciation, functionality appreciation is related to *higher well-being*, such as higher self-compassion and body image flexibility (see Chapter 8), gratitude, life satisfaction, self-esteem, defining beauty broadly (see Chapter 7), and intuitive eating (see Chapter 20) [1]. Functionality appreciation is also related to *lower* anxiety, depression, and endorsing unrealistic and narrowly defined societal images of beauty (e.g., thin female models, muscular male athletes; see also Chapter 4). Additionally, during pregnancy, functionality appreciation is associated with fewer symptoms of depression and fewer unhealthy prenatal behaviors, even when women are self-conscious about how their bodies are changing [2].

Functionality appreciation allows us to move our bodies in ways that allow us to mindfully observe and experience them. Exercising for reasons related to body functionality such as enjoyment, flexibility, and health corresponds with greater body confidence and lower self-objectification (e.g., habitually monitoring how we look to others, see Chapter 13) than exercising to alter appearance (e.g., to lose weight, become toned, gain muscle) [8–9]. Among student athletes, functionality appreciation is linked to higher sports-related confidence and performance, being more fully engaged in the sport (i.e., being "in the zone" or in a state of "flow"), and experiencing this engagement as internally rewarding [10]. In one study, women who engaged in a four-session body positive yoga program (which included functionality appreciation as a theme) reported increased body connectedness, body appreciation, and body satisfaction after the program, and these outcomes remained one month later [11].

Writing about the body's functionality can also help. Several studies have shown this effect with the *Expand Your Horizon* program [12–13]. This online program includes a brief introduction to body functionality followed by three structured writing assignments, delivered on separate days over the course of one week. For each assignment, people describe the functions that their bodies perform and why these functions are personally important and meaningful. The first assignment concentrates on body senses and physical activity, the second concentrates on health and creative outlets, and the third concentrates on self-care and communication with others.

Expand Your Horizon helped women with a negative body image improve their body appreciation, appearance satisfaction, functionality satisfaction, and decrease their self-objectification when compared to a group of women who didn't participate in the program, and these outcomes remained one week later [12–13]. A sample of women with rheumatoid arthritis who participated in the *Expand Your Horizon* intervention improved their functionality appreciation, body appreciation, and body satisfaction, as well as reduced their depression after the intervention [14]. These outcomes remained one month later. While this program has yet to be delivered with men, men have shown improvements in their functionality satisfaction after writing only 100 words about their body functionality [15], so there is reason to think that *Expand Your Horizon* could be beneficial for men too. These studies show that focusing attention on how our bodies function in diverse ways, and how these functions are meaningful to us, can promote our positive body image, even when we have physical limitations.

In sum, appreciating how our bodies function in diverse ways is linked to higher psychological well-being and can help guide us towards developing a more positive body image. The *Functionality Appreciation Scale* (FAS) [1] is available in this chapter to better understand your level of gratitude for your body's ability to function to the extent that it can.

Treatment Planning Tools

Talking Points for Sessions

- Identify specific ways the body and mind function well
- Discuss thoughts, emotions, and behaviors that occur when the body is and is not functioning well
- Address ways the body allows interaction, communication, and connection with others

- Identify areas of grief related to loss of functioning of body parts or systems

Treatment Plan

Goals

❏ Shift my focus from appearance to my body's function and purpose

❏ Transition from a judgmental body focus to one that observes what my body (various parts of the body) can do

❏ Grieve losses of my body's functioning

❏ Increase present moment awareness of my body, instead of focusing on how my body functioned in the past or how it will function in the future

❏ Increase appreciation for how my body functions

❏ Increase appreciation for how my mind functions

Objectives

❏ Generate a list of favorite activities and hobbies that my body allows me to do

❏ Participate in a body scan that focuses on what feels good and/or content

❏ Identify the things that I can do because of how my body works

❏ Practice redirecting appearance-focused conversations with friends/family members to the benefits of how the body works

❏ Discuss how my body functions with my healthcare provider to provide relevant information

❏ Identify specific ways to reconnect with my body following traumatic or uncomfortable experiences

❏ Redefine the belief that my body "has given up" on me

❏ Identify specific ways to no longer take my body for granted

❏ Recognize various ways to have a new appreciation for health

❏ Express gratitude for how my mind functions

Additional Resources

S. Danielsdottir. *Your Body Is Awesome: Body Respect for Children*. London: Singing Dragon, 2014.

To access more information about the *Expand Your Horizon* program, see Jessica Alleva's work at www.psychologytoday.com/blog/mind-your-body .

Assessment 11.1: Functionality Appreciation Scale (FAS)

Please indicate the extent to which you agree with each of the following statements by placing the number to the right of the item.

1	2	3	4	5
Strongly Disagree	**Disagree**	**Neither Agree nor Disagree**	**Agree**	**Strongly Agree**

	Number
1. I appreciate my body for what it is capable of doing.	
2. I am grateful for the health of my body, even if it isn't always as healthy as I would like it to be.	
3. I appreciate that my body allows me to communicate and interact with others.	
4. I acknowledge and appreciate when my body feels good and/or relaxed.	
5. I am grateful that my body enables me to engage in activities that I enjoy or find important.	
6. I feel that my body does so much for me.	
7. I respect my body for the functions it performs.	
Total Functionality Appreciation score: add items 1–7 and divide by 7 =	

Total Functionality Appreciation score between:

- **4–5** = high functionality appreciation
- **3–3.9** = moderate functionality appreciation
- **below 3** = low functionality appreciation

Note. Reprinted with permission. Authors of the FAS are Alleva, Tylka, and Kroon Van Diest[*]. The FAS's measurement properties (reliability, validity) have been supported in samples from various countries. This scale is relevant to responders from diverse cultural backgrounds and physical abilities. Please contact the authors of the FAS for permission to use it within research; there is no need to contact them to use it with clients or to complete it on your own.

[*] J. M. Alleva, T. L. Tylka, and A. M. Kroon Van Diest. The Functionality Appreciation Scale (FAS): Development and Psychometric Evaluation in US Community Women and Men. *Body Image* 2017; **23**: 28–44.

Functionality Appreciation Scale Applications

- Complete the Functionality Appreciation Scale based on your current experiences. What themes do you notice in your responses? What can you learn from your responses?

- Complete the Functionality Appreciation Scale as though it's the *future and you are more accepting of your body*. What themes do you notice in your responses? What can you learn from your responses?

- Write down the following:

  o A list of all that your body does for you

  o A list of all that your body is capable of doing

  o The activities in which you can participate and enjoy – because of your body.

- Identify three specific ways you are grateful for your body's ability to function.

- Regarding item 3 (*I appreciate that my body allows me to communicate and interact with others*), reflect on the following:

  o Specific ways that your body communicates a range of requests, demands, limits, and/or needs to yourself

  o Specific ways that your body communicates a range of requests, demands, limits, and/or needs to others

  o Specific ways that your body helps you to connect with yourself

  o Specific ways that your body helps you to connect with others.

- Item 4 focuses on when the body is functioning well (*I acknowledge and appreciate when my body feels good and/or relaxed*). Focus on parts of your body that are not experiencing pain or discomfort. Create a list below of what you notice feels good, neutral, and/or comfortable.

Assignment 11.1: Body Tasks

All that my body does in approximately one day:

My lungs breathe 23,000 times.

My eyes blink 28,000 times.

My brain has 60,000–80,000 thoughts.

My heart beats 115,000 times.

Additional tasks that my body does for me every day without my asking:

_____
_____
_____
_____

In what ways do I appreciate how my body functions, overall? How do I appreciate the functioning of specific, individual body parts?

_____
_____
_____
_____

Focusing on the function of my body helps me move towards positive body image in these ways:

_____
_____
_____
_____

Reflections:

_____
_____
_____
_____

N. L. Wood-Barcalow, T. L. Tylka, and C. L. Judge. *Positive Body Image Workbook: A Clinical and Self-Improvement Guide.* Cambridge: Cambridge University Press, 2021.

Assignment 11.2: Body Purpose and Function

This is a specific body part and/or area of the body that is associated with uncomfortable thoughts, feelings, and/or physical sensations:

_____
_____
_____
_____
_____
_____

This is *why* this body part or area is uncomfortable for me:

_____
_____
_____
_____
_____
_____

Now, rather than focus on the appearance, I will list the *purpose, function, and resilience* of this body part/area. For example, if I dislike my abdomen (i.e., belly), then I will focus on all that this area *does for me*: digests food, keeps organs inside, helps keep my body upright, may provide a place for a baby, provides core strength to help me move through the world, and more:

_____
_____
_____
_____
_____
_____

When I find myself focusing on my appearance, I will take time to refocus on what my body does for me including these reminders:

_____
_____
_____
_____
_____
_____

N. L. Wood-Barcalow, T. L. Tylka, and C. L. Judge. *Positive Body Image Workbook: A Clinical and Self-Improvement Guide.* Cambridge: Cambridge University Press, 2021.

Assignment 11.3: Body Investment

The amount of time I spend thinking about my body on a daily or weekly basis in terms of estimated minutes/hours (e.g., 120 minutes/day, 14 hours/week) or percentage of the day/week (e.g., 70 percent):

_____
_____
_____

Of the total estimated time above, I spend this much time thinking about *my appearance*:

_____
_____
_____

Of the total estimated time above, I spend this much time thinking about *how my body works or functions properly*:

_____
_____
_____

What I imagine might happen if my overall focus were to shift from appearance to body functioning:

_____
_____
_____

Based on my realizations, I would like to make these changes:

_____
_____
_____

I intend to shift my focus from my appearance to that of my body's functioning by doing the following:

_____
_____
_____

N. L. Wood-Barcalow, T. L. Tylka, and C. L. Judge. *Positive Body Image Workbook: A Clinical and Self-Improvement Guide.* Cambridge: Cambridge University Press, 2021.

Assignment 11.4: What's Not Wrong with My Body?

The brain has a tendency to focus on the negative, including all that is wrong with the body. For this journal assignment, reflect on what's *not* wrong with the body.

Here are the pleasurable things my body allows me to do: sing a favorite song, dance around, read a good book, belly laugh at a funny joke, move from one place to another, smell different scents, see a sunset, hug someone I love, taste delicious food, and hear a soothing melody, for example.

These are specific things that *are not wrong* with my body:

_____

N. L. Wood-Barcalow, T. L. Tylka, and C. L. Judge. *Positive Body Image Workbook: A Clinical and Self-Improvement Guide.* Cambridge: Cambridge University Press, 2021.

Assignment 11.5: How I Feel on a Good Day

For this journal assignment, focus on what the body experiences when it feels good, neutral, and/or comfortable.

On a day when I am feeling good (e.g., emotionally, physically, spiritually), I will focus on parts of my body that are not experiencing pain or discomfort. I will create a list below of what I notice feels good, neutral, and/or comfortable. I will refer back to this journal entry as needed to remind myself of such experiences:

_____
_____
_____
_____
_____
_____
_____
_____
_____
_____
_____
_____
_____
_____
_____
_____
_____
_____
_____
_____
_____
_____

N. L. Wood-Barcalow, T. L. Tylka, and C. L. Judge. *Positive Body Image Workbook: A Clinical and Self-Improvement Guide.* Cambridge: Cambridge University Press, 2021.

Assignment 11.6: How I Feel On a Day with Chronic Body Pain

Among those who experience chronic pain, the ability to accept their pain (e.g., perceiving that their life is going well despite pain) is more closely linked to positive body image than their ability to control or manage their pain.* For this assignment, reflect on your experiences of chronic body pain while answering the items below.

These are the physical/bodily sensations associated with the pain I experience:

_____

_____

_____

The following can and may contribute to my experience of the pain (check all that apply):

- ❏ My eating/hydration habits or changes to them
- ❏ My sleep habits or changes to them
- ❏ How I'm moving my body (exercising, activity)
- ❏ How I'm not moving my body (sedentary activity)
- ❏ How I'm breathing
- ❏ How I'm holding my body (posture)
- ❏ Alcohol/substance intake, including caffeine
- ❏ Medication changes
- ❏ Physical illness
- ❏ Changes in pain levels
- ❏ Emotions (sadness, anger, fear)
- ❏ Stress
- ❏ Social support and connectedness
- ❏ Other: _____
- ❏ Other: _____
- ❏ Other: _____
- ❏ Other: _____

These are typical *thoughts* I have associated with the pain:

_____

_____

_____

These are the typical *emotions* I have associated with the pain:

_____

_____

_____

These are the things that I typically *do in response to* the pain:

_____

_____

_____

I notice that these particular thoughts and emotions *increase my pain/discomfort*:

_____

_____

_____

I notice that these particular thoughts and emotions *decrease my pain/discomfort*:

_____
_____
_____

What I can control when I experience the pain:

_____
_____
_____

What I cannot control when I experience the pain:

_____
_____
_____

What is going well in my life in addition to the experience of the pain:

_____
_____
_____

I commit to the following effective ways to manage the pain when it occurs:

_____
_____
_____
_____
_____
_____
_____
_____

*C. H. Markey, J. L. Dunaev, and K. J. August. Body Image Experiences in the Context of Chronic Pain: An Examination of Associations among Perceptions of Pain, Body Dissatisfaction, and Positive Body Image. *Body Image* 2020; **32**: 103–10.

N. L. Wood-Barcalow, T. L. Tylka, and C. L. Judge. *Positive Body Image Workbook: A Clinical and Self-Improvement Guide.* Cambridge: Cambridge University Press, 2021.

Assignment 11.7: Functional Body Scan

Participate in a functional body scan. The purpose of this scan is to acknowledge the functions of your various body parts and what each body part/area offers you in the moment. Start at the top of your head and let your focus move slowly downward over your various body parts. Mindfully consider the sensations present and various functions offered by each body part.

Next, scan your body overall and notice areas that currently feel good and relaxed. Again, scan various body parts from your head to toes as you notice positive and/or neutral sensations. It may be helpful to search the Internet and/or smart phone applications for "body scan script" for additional guidance with this exercise, or you may even like to create your own individualized functional body scan script. You may also find it helpful to record your script.

N. L. Wood-Barcalow, T. L. Tylka, and C. L. Judge. *Positive Body Image Workbook: A Clinical and Self-Improvement Guide.* Cambridge: Cambridge University Press, 2021.

Assignment 11.8: Body Resilience

The body naturally experiences times of health and times of illness throughout development and life. For this journal assignment, reflect on the various ailments or concerns throughout your life and how your body has demonstrated resilience by rebounding or healing over time. Record your thoughts here:

_____
_____
_____
_____
_____
_____
_____
_____
_____
_____
_____
_____
_____
_____
_____
_____
_____
_____
_____
_____
_____
_____

N. L. Wood-Barcalow, T. L. Tylka, and C. L. Judge. *Positive Body Image Workbook: A Clinical and Self-Improvement Guide.* Cambridge: Cambridge University Press, 2021.

Assignment 11.9: My Body as a Machine

For this assignment, imagine your body as a valuable machine that serves an important task and answer the following.

These are the ways that I invest in my machine (check all that apply):

❏ Ensure a consistent source of energy or fuel

❏ Keep it moving

❏ Keep its joints flexible

❏ Attend medical appointments

❏ Follow medical recommendations

❏ Allow time for rest

❏ Monitor its efficiency and make adjustments when needed

❏ Respond to its needs

❏ Accept that it will perform differently at various times

❏ Refrain from using substances that would impact its performance

❏ Balance my physical needs with my social, spiritual, and emotional needs

❏ Other:

❏ Other:

❏ Other:

When it comes to investing in the functioning of my body, here is what I'm doing well:

_____
_____
_____
_____

Here is what I need to improve:

_____
_____
_____
_____

I commit to making the following changes:

_____
_____
_____
_____

N. L. Wood-Barcalow, T. L. Tylka, and C. L. Judge. *Positive Body Image Workbook: A Clinical and Self-Improvement Guide*. Cambridge: Cambridge University Press, 2021.

Assignment 11.10: Focus on Function versus Shaming

If you notice someone body shaming themselves or others, make a point to speak up and encourage them to focus on all the amazing things that the body *can* do. Emphasize the importance of body functionality and how it works versus what the body looks like. Share that body shaming hurts the person it is focused on and others around them. Encourage them to pass on the message.

N. L. Wood-Barcalow, T. L. Tylka, and C. L. Judge. *Positive Body Image Workbook: A Clinical and Self-Improvement Guide.* Cambridge: Cambridge University Press, 2021.

Assignment 11.11: Day-to-Day Decisions Can Impact Body Functioning

My daily self-care decisions can impact how my body functions in the short-term, the present, and long-term (check all that apply):

- ❏ How I hold my body (posture)
- ❏ My breathing patterns
- ❏ My hydration efforts
- ❏ My nutrition choices
- ❏ The quality of my sleep
- ❏ The quantity of my sleep
- ❏ Taking vitamins/supplements
- ❏ Moving my body
- ❏ Avoiding activities that have a high potential for injury
- ❏ Engaging in mindfulness and/or meditation activities
- ❏ Protecting my body (e.g, wearing sunblock, wearing a helmet)
- ❏ Allowing my body to rest when tired
- ❏ Avoiding substances that have a negative impact
- ❏ Using appropriate precautions while practicing sexual activities
- ❏ Taking needed medications
- ❏ Treating myself with compassion
- ❏ Other: _____
- ❏ Other: _____
- ❏ Other: _____

Here is what I'm doing effectively to respond to my body on a daily basis:

_____
_____
_____

Here is what I'd like to improve:

_____
_____
_____

I commit to making the following changes:

_____
_____
_____

N. L. Wood-Barcalow, T. L. Tylka, and C. L. Judge. *Positive Body Image Workbook: A Clinical and Self-Improvement Guide.* Cambridge: Cambridge University Press, 2021.

Assignment 11.12: Grieving Changes in Body Functioning

The functioning of our bodies can change for the short-term and long-term due to various factors such as aging, developmental milestones, chronic pain, trauma reactions, physical training, injury, illness, development of new skills, disfigurement, environmental stressors, and more. These changes can be viewed as positive, neutral, and even negative depending on expectations and the overall impact on life. Regardless, the one constant about the body is that it is constantly changing.

A grieving process can occur when the functions of the body change or when the body does not perform in a desired or expected way. Grieving emotions can include sadness, frustration, disappointment, anger, numbness, disbelief, longing, and jealousy. Thoughts can include that "it's not fair," "why did this happen to me?" as well as "what ifs."

Reflect on possible grieving associated with changes in body functioning.

- Examples of when my body functioned differently or changed in its functioning:

_____

_____

- I experience(d) these emotions:

_____

_____

- I experience(d) these thoughts:

_____

_____

- My grieving is related to these expectations, dreams, or hopes:

_____

_____

- These are the ways that I've adapted or am adapting:

_____

_____

- These are things that I'm doing to increase acceptance:

_____

_____

N. L. Wood-Barcalow, T. L. Tylka, and C. L. Judge. *Positive Body Image Workbook: A Clinical and Self-Improvement Guide.* Cambridge: Cambridge University Press, 2021.

Assignment 11.13: Gratitude for the Mind

It is important to express gratitude for the mind, as it is a central part of the body. Consider these facts about the human brain:[1] it weighs approximately 3 lbs., contains one hundred billion neurons, is up to 60 percent fat, and creates 50,000–70,000 thoughts a day! Reflect on all that the brain does on a daily basis: regulates breathing and heart rate, coordinates movement, interprets and stores information from our senses, assists with emotions, aids in language and communication, helps with decision-making, is active during sleep, and so much more. Each brain is unique and has the ability to grow new neurons, which means that humans can learn new things and adapt to damage/disease throughout the lifespan. For this assignment, reflect on the following about your mind:

• I appreciate this about my mind: _____
_____
_____
_____
_____

• This is how my mind is unique: _____
_____
_____
_____
_____

• These are things that I currently do to care for my mind (e.g., participate in life-enhancing movement, learn new things, rest, refrain from substance use, provide myself with consistent nourishment and hydration): _____
_____
_____
_____
_____

• Focusing on gratitude for my mind helps me move towards positive body image in these ways:
_____
_____
_____
_____
_____
_____
_____

• These are actions that I commit to taking in the *next week* to care for my mind:
_____
_____

• These are actions that I commit to taking in the *next month* to care for my mind:
_____
_____

• These are actions that I commit to taking in the *next several months* to care for my mind:
_____
_____

• Reflections: _____
_____
_____
_____
_____

---

[1] See www.humanbrainfacts.org and www.brainfacts.org .

N. L. Wood-Barcalow, T. L. Tylka, and C. L. Judge. *Positive Body Image Workbook: A Clinical and Self-Improvement Guide.* Cambridge: Cambridge University Press, 2021.

References

1. J. M. Alleva, T. L. Tylka, and A. M. Kroon Van Diest. The Functionality Appreciation Scale (FAS): Development and psychometric evaluation in US community women and men. *Body Image* 2017; **23**: 28–44.

2. L. R. Rubin and J. R. Steinberg. Self-objectification and pregnancy: Are body functionality dimensions protective? *Sex Roles*; **65**; 606–18.

3. K. A. Bailey, K. L. Gammage, C. van Ingren, et al. "It's all about acceptance": A qualitative study exploring a model of positive body image for people with spinal cord injury. *Body Image* 2015; **15**: 24–34.

4. C. H. Markey, J. L. Dunaev, and K. J. August. Body image experiences in the context of chronic pain: An examination of associations among perceptions of pain, body dissatisfaction, and positive body image. *Body Image* 2020; **32**: 103–10.

5. T. L. Tylka and N. L. Wood-Barcalow. The Body Appreciation Scale-2: Item refinement and psychometric evaluation. *Body Image* 2015; **12**: 53–67.

6. N. A. L. Dignard and J. L. Jarry. The Body Appreciation Scale-2: Item interpretation and sensitivity to priming. *Body Image* 2019; **28**: 16–24.

7. J. B. Webb, C. B. Rogers, L. Etzel, et al. "Mom, quit fat talking–I'm trying to eat (mindfully) here!": Evaluating a sociocultural model of family fat talk, positive body image, and mindful eating in college women. *Appetite* 2018; **126**: 169–75.

8. I. Prichard and M. Tiggemann. Relations among exercise type, self-objectification, and body image in the fitness center environment: The role of reasons for exercise. *Psychol Sport Exerc* 2008; **9**: 855–66.

9. K. Homan and T. L. Tylka. Appearance-based exercise motivation moderates the relationship between exercise frequency and positive body image. *Body Image* 2014; **11**: 101–8.

10. Z. Soulliard, A. Kauffman, H. Fitterman-Harris, et al. Examining positive body image, sport confidence, flow state, and subjective performance among student athletes and non-athletes. *Body Image* 2019; **28**: 93–100.

11. E. Halliwell, K. Dawson, and S. Burkey. A randomized experimental evaluation of a yoga-based body image intervention. *Body Image* 2019; **28**: 119–27.

12. J. M. Alleva, C. Martijn, G. J. P. Van Breukelen, et al. *Expand Your Horizon*: A programme that improves body image and reduces self-objectification by training women to focus on body functionality. *Body Image* 2015; **15**: 81–9.

13. J. M. Alleva, P. C. Diedrichs, E. Halliwell, et al. A randomised-controlled trial investigating potential underlying mechanisms of a functionality-based approach to improving women's body image. *Body Image* 2018; **25**: 85–96.

14. J. M. Alleva, P. C. Diedrichs, E. Halliwell, et al. More than my RA: A randomized trial investigating body image improvement among women with rheumatoid arthritis using a functionality-focused intervention program. *J Consult Clin Psychol* 2018; **86**: 666–76.

15. J. M. Alleva, C. Martijn, A. Jansen, et al. Body language: Affecting body satisfaction by describing the body in functionality terms. *Psychol Women Q* 2014; **38**: 181–96.

Embodiment

Theory and Research Overview

Up to this point in the workbook, we have focused on body image, which is our feelings and thoughts about our bodies [1]. This chapter discusses a closely related, but broader, term: embodiment. Like body image, **embodiment** includes our feelings and thoughts about our bodies but also considers how we experience and engage our bodies in the world [1–5]. When we view our bodies as influential in the world, we have positive embodiment [3]. However, when we view our bodies as problematic within the world, we have **disrupted embodiment** [3].

Our lived experiences, past and present, shape our embodiment. That is, experiences that honor and respect who we are, our inner qualities, our unique appearance characteristics, and how we express ourselves, encourage positive embodiment. On the other hand, experiences that minimize and/or shame who we are, our inner qualities, our unique appearance characteristics, and how we express ourselves promote disrupted embodiment.

There are five components to embodiment, as identified and studied extensively by Niva Piran [1–5]. Each component can be positive or disrupted depending on our lived experiences. Examples of positive embodiment and disrupted embodiment for each component are detailed in Table 12.1.

You may be curious as to the extent you are positively embodied. Six items from the *Experience of Embodiment Scale* (EES) can be completed within this chapter to assist in learning about your level of embodiment.

Certain activities can also promote embodiment. For example, yoga can be an **embodying activity** [14]. Overall, those who practice yoga report higher positive embodiment and body appreciation (see Chapter 10) and lower self-objectification (see Chapter 13) compared to those who do not practice [15]. Yet, yoga instructors who focus on appearance (e.g., "These asanas are good for shaping your glutes!") and yoga studios that contain mirrors (which can direct participants to focus on their appearance and compare their bodies with other yogis) can disrupt yoga's positive impact on embodiment [14]. Activities that promote sexual agency, such as bellydancing, are linked to positive embodiment [16]. Bellydancing requires dancers to train their bodies to move in new ways, requiring concentration and communication with their bodies, and is practiced by dancers of diverse body types and ages.

Certain environments and experiences can promote disrupted embodiment. For example, sexually objectifying environments prompt us to "inhabit our bodies externally," or self-objectify (see Chapter 13), thereby decreasing body connection and comfort, agency, functionality, and the freedom to experience and express desire. Experiencing lack of body acceptance by others can disrupt our body comfort and connection, agency and functionality, attuned self-care, as well as experience and expression of desire. Traumatic events can disrupt each component of positive embodiment [2, 4]. For these reasons, we as a society need to work toward changing our environments through social action.

To summarize, embodiment is how we experience and engage our bodies in the world. Positive embodiment allows us to feel connected to and comfortable with our bodies and engage in self-care, so that we can interact with the world through agency and expression of who we are on the inside. Environmental factors such as objectification can disrupt positive embodiment by interfering with our sexual intimacy and prompting us to compare our appearance with others and talk negatively about our bodies. The next four chapters address this process: Objectification and Self-Objectification (Chapter 13), Sexual Intimacy (Chapter 14), Social Comparison (Chapter 15), and Body Talk (Chapter 16).

Treatment Planning Tools

Talking Points for Sessions

- Identify activities that promote a sense of agency (power, influence)
- Discuss specific times the client has felt connected with their body
- Identify specific times the client has felt comfortable with their body
- Dialogue about how negative comments from others can impact one's own body connection and comfort
- Discuss the amount of focus directed toward how the body feels, rather than how it looks
- Reflect on specific sexual desires and needs as well as the degree to which they are being acknowledged and met
- Identify environments or situations that promote the client's positive embodiment and those that promote disrupted embodiment
- Identify what needs to be done on a societal level to cultivate positive embodiment

Table 12.1 Components of Positive and Disrupted Embodiment

Component	Positive Embodiment	Disrupted Embodiment
Body Connection and Comfort	We feel connected to and comfortable within our bodies as we engage with the world. This feeling of being "at home" in our bodies helps us talk positively about ourselves and challenge threats to our body image, such as pressures to lose weight.	We are embarrassed, ashamed, fearful, and afraid of our bodies. We may try to control, repair, and monitor our bodies in unhealthy ways, such as rigidly watching what we eat.
Agency and Functionality	We act with assertiveness and agency (i.e., influence, power) in how we carry our bodies and express ourselves. We are confident and stand up for ourselves. We guide and lead others. We feel influential and believe that our ideas and opinions matter. We don't sacrifice our needs to fit another's agenda. We value how our bodies function in the world more so than how they appear in the world.	We tend to follow what others do, even if something doesn't feel right to us. We look to others to choose activities rather than voicing our opinion of what we would like to do. We engage in exercise primarily for weight and shape control rather than feeling a sense of empowerment from moving our bodies.
Experience and Expression of Desire	We are in touch with and respond to our desires in nurturing ways. For example, we are in tune with our sexual needs and can express them in our relationships. We eat food we enjoy when hungry and stop when full.	We do not let our partners know what pleases us sexually. We minimize our needs for our own sexual pleasure. We may engage in sexual acts that are painful, and/or fake pleasure. We punish ourselves by not eating ("I don't deserve to eat because I've gained weight"), degrade ourselves and certain foods ("I'm a bad person because I want to eat cake"), and ignore our hunger cues ("If I wait long enough, I'll lose the desire to eat," "I'll just drink water when I'm hungry to trick my stomach that it is full").
Attuned Self-Care	We are in touch with, or attuned to, our bodies' needs and respond to these needs in a nurturing way. We move our bodies in a pleasurable way for physical activity, rest when tired, drink water to stay hydrated, take breaks in work to avoid burnout, bond with comforting others for social support, reach out to friends for laughter and companionship, and are compassionate toward ourselves when we are distressed. We also engage in meaningful, passionate, or spiritual activities such as walking in nature [6], attending services [7], and creating new things (e.g., artwork, cooking) [8] that help us connect with the world at a higher level.	We push ourselves when we are physically, emotionally, behaviorally, and/or spiritually fatigued [9] and drive ourselves without fueling our bodies with food, water, and rest. We may not regularly take medication for our bodies to function properly. We may not nurture our souls with spiritual or other activities. We are likely to be critical toward ourselves and/or avoid our emotions rather than comfort ourselves when distressed. We do not "pause" to savor the good in our life.
Inhabiting the Body Internally	We believe that our internal qualities matter more than our appearance. For example, when we exercise, we may have health and well-being as our primary goal, rather than appearance or weight reduction [10–11]. We may engage in mind-body activities, such as yoga or team sports that support many different body types and comfortable clothing [12–13]. We allow our bodies to be their natural size. We have many interests and hobbies that nurture our minds, bodies, and souls that are unrelated to managing, monitoring, and altering our appearance.	We examine our bodies for "flaws," like a critical observer would. We try to change our bodies by "repairing them" through harmful cosmetic procedures in an attempt to fit societal appearance ideals. While it is normal to take care of our bodies and appearance (see Chapters 19 and 22), it is disruptive to try to alter our bodies through practices that may hurt them in order to achieve societal appearance ideals. This orientation likely negatively impacts our mood, confidence, relationships, and outlook on life. For example, a scale reading that shows weight gain may correspond with anger and irritability for the rest of the day.

Treatment Plan

Goals

- ❏ Increase a positive connection with my body
- ❏ Respond to my body's needs on a regular basis rather than ignore them
- ❏ Respond to my body's desires
- ❏ Reduce body-checking behaviors
- ❏ Be assertive about my sexual desires and needs
- ❏ Identify which environments promote positive embodiment versus disrupted embodiment

Objectives

- ❏ Engage in at least one body-nurturing activity each week
- ❏ Identify and participate in a form of physical activity each week that increases my agency, connection, and/or comfort
- ❏ Identify my needs that are routinely neglected and the reason(s) for doing so
- ❏ Identify at least one experience a week of being disconnected from my body

- ❏ Communicate with my partner(s) about preferred sexual experiences
- ❏ Identify examples of listening to my body following traumatic or uncomfortable experiences
- ❏ Identify specific ways to reconnect with my body following traumatic or uncomfortable experiences
- ❏ Identify specific ways to claim/reclaim power of my body
- ❏ Identify and limit exposure to environments that involve disrupted embodiment
- ❏ Identify and increase exposure to environments that enhance my positive embodiment
- ❏ Limit participation in specific activities that worsen disrupted embodiment
- ❏ Increase participation in specific activities that enhance my positive embodiment

Additional Resources

N. Piran. *Journeys of Embodiment at the Intersection of Body and Culture: The Developmental Theory of Embodiment.* San Diego: Elsevier, 2017.

C. P. Cook-Cottone. *Embodiment and the Treatment of Eating Disorders: The Body as a Resource for Recovery.* New York: W. W. Norton & Company, Ltd., 2020.

Assessment 12.1: Sample Items from the Experience of Embodiment Scale (EES)

Please read each statement carefully before answering. Indicate how often you agree with each item by circling the number to the right of the item.

	Strongly Disagree	Disagree	Neutral	Agree	Strongly Agree
1. I feel in tune with my body.	1	2	3	4	5
2. My body reduces my sense of self-worth in the world.	5	4	3	2	1
3. I believe in my ability to accomplish what I desire in the world.	1	2	3	4	5
4. I express what I want and need sexually.	1	2	3	4	5
5. I put a priority on listening to my body and its needs (e.g., stress, fatigue, hunger).	1	2	3	4	5
6. I care more about how my body feels than about how it looks.	1	2	3	4	5
Total Embodiment Score: add items 1–6 together and divide by 6 =					

Total Embodiment score between:

- **4–5** = high positive embodiment
- **3–3.9** = moderate positive embodiment
- **below 3** = low positive embodiment

Note. Reprinted with permission. The author of these items is Niva Piran.[*] These items represent the components of embodiment identified by Piran, but do not represent Piran's full EES, which contains thirty-four items. These six items are useful to determine embodiment within clients and readers. To access the full thirty-four-item scale and use within research, contact Niva Piran at niva.piran@utoronto.ca

[*] N. Piran. The Experience of Embodiment Construct: Reflecting the Quality of Embodied Lives. In Tylka, T. L., and Piran, N., eds. *Handbook of Positive Body Image and Embodiment: Constructs, Protective Factors, and Interventions.* New York: Oxford University Press, 2019: 11–21.

Sample Items from the Experience of Embodiment Scale Applications

- What experiences/activities help you to feel "in tune" with your body as addressed in item 1 (*I feel in tune with my body*)? Examples might include playing an instrument, practicing martial arts, sitting mindfully in the sun, playing a favorite sport, singing, engaging in a hobby, and more.

- For item 3 (*I believe in my ability to accomplish what I desire in the world*), what do you hope to accomplish in this world?

- If you responded neutral, disagree or strongly disagree to item 4 (*I express what I want and need sexually*), reflect on what barriers exist in expressing your specific sexual wants/needs. Are you able to identify what you want sexually? What things could increase the likelihood of you expressing your needs? Are you able to communicate your needs to a partner(s)?

- Consider your response to item 5 (*I put a priority on listening to my body and its needs (e.g., stress, fatigue, hunger)*). If you responded agree or strongly agree, identify the specific ways in which you're listening to your body. If you responded neutral, disagree, or strongly disagree, identify specific things that you can do on a daily or weekly basis to increase responsiveness to your body.

- What does your total score reflect in terms of embodiment? Are you surprised by this outcome? Are there any changes that you want to make?

Assignment 12.1: Comfort, Connection, and Activity

I am *uncomfortable* with how my body feels while engaging in these types of activities:

_____
_____
_____

I feel *comfortable* with my body while engaging in these types of activities:

_____
_____
_____

I am *disconnected* with/from my body while engaging in these types of activities:

_____
_____
_____

I feel *connected* with my body while engaging in these types of activities:

_____
_____
_____

I commit to the following embodying activities to promote connection and comfort with my body:

_____
_____
_____

N. L. Wood-Barcalow, T. L. Tylka, and C. L. Judge. *Positive Body Image Workbook: A Clinical and Self-Improvement Guide.* Cambridge: Cambridge University Press, 2021.

Assignment 12.2: Disrupted Embodiment Experience

Disrupted embodiment can occur when we view the body as problematic or deeply flawed, focus solely on its appearance rather than function, and disregard its needs.

A recent example of disrupted embodiment occurred when:

_____
_____
_____

I experienced the following *thoughts* and *emotions* after this experience:

_____
_____
_____

I *responded* in these ways:

_____
_____
_____

When my embodiment is disrupted in the future, I commit to the following activities (check all that apply):

- ❏ Notice my experience of disrupted embodiment *without* trying to control or change my appearance
- ❏ Investigate the reason for my experience of disrupted embodiment and focus on that issue
- ❏ Consider how my core values conflict with disrupted embodiment
- ❏ Use soothing activities to cope
- ❏ Engage in relaxation techniques
- ❏ Identify what my body actually needs and respond to those needs
- ❏ Recognize how my thoughts contribute to disrupted embodiment
- ❏ Focus on what my body does versus what it looks like
- ❏ Other: _____
- ❏ Other: _____
- ❏ Other: _____

N. L. Wood-Barcalow, T. L. Tylka, and C. L. Judge. *Positive Body Image Workbook: A Clinical and Self-Improvement Guide.* Cambridge: Cambridge University Press, 2021.

References

1. N. Piran. New possibilities in the prevention of eating disorders: The introduction of positive body image measures. *Body Image* 2015; **14**: 146–57.

2. N. Piran and T. L. Teall. The developmental theory of embodiment. In: McVey, G., Levine, M. P., Piran, N., and Ferguson, H. B., eds., *Preventing eating-related and weight-related disorders: Collaborative research, advocacy, and policy change.* Waterloo, Ontario: Wilfred Laurier Press, 2012: 171–99.

3. N. Piran. Embodied possibilities and disruptions: The emergence of the Experience of Embodiment construct from qualitative studies with girls and women. *Body Image* 2016; **18**: 43–60.

4. N. Piran. *Journeys of Embodiment at the Intersection of Body and Culture: The Developmental Theory of Embodiment.* San Diego: Elsevier, 2017.

5. N. Piran. The experience of embodiment construct: Reflecting the quality of embodied lives. In Tylka, T. L., and Piran, N., eds. *Handbook of Positive Body Image and Embodiment: Constructs, Protective Factors, and Interventions.* New York: Oxford University Press, 2019: 11–21.

6. V. Swami, D. Barron, and A. Furnham. The impact of exposure to films of natural and built environments on state body appreciation. *Body Image* 2018; **24**: 82–94.

7. M. Tiggemann and K. Hage. Religion and spirituality: Pathways to positive body image. *Body Image* 2019; **28**: 135–41.

8. H. L. Stuckey and J. Nobel. The connection between art, healing, and public health: A review of current literature. *Am J Public Health* 2010; **100**: 254–63.

9. C. P. Cook-Cottone and W. M. Guyker. The development and validation of the Mindful Self-Care Scale (MSCS): An assessment of practices that support positive embodiment. *Mindfulness* 2017; **9**: 161–75.

10. K. J. Homan and T. L. Tylka. Appearance-based exercise motivation moderates the relationship between exercise frequency and positive body image. *Body Image* 2014; **11**: 101–8.

11. T. L. Tylka and K. J. Homan. Exercise motives and positive body image in physically active college women and men: Exploring an expanded acceptance model of intuitive eating. *Body Image* 2015; **15**: 90–7.

12. D. Neumark-Sztainer, R. F. MacLehose, A. W. Watts, et al. Yoga and body image: Findings from a large population-based study of young adults. *Body Image* 2018; **24**: 69–75.

13. N. Piran. New possibilities in the prevention of eating disorders: The introduction of positive body image measures. *Body Image* 2015; **14**: 146–57.

14. D. Neumark-Sztainer, A. W. Watts, and S. Rydell. Yoga and body image: How do young adults practicing yoga describe its impact on their body image? *Body Image* 2018; **27**: 156–68.

15. L. Mahlo and M. Tiggemann. Yoga and positive body image: A test of the embodiment model. *Body Image* 2016; **18**: 135–42.

16. M. Tiggemann, E. Coutts, and L. Clark. Belly dance as an embodying activity? A test of the embodiment model of positive body image. *Sex Roles* 2014; **71**: 197–207.

Objectification and Self-Objectification

Theory and Research Overview

As I (Tracy) look around me, I see many objects: a coffee mug, my laptop, my cell phone, a pen, and my planner. I use these objects for my goals: namely to work and give me energy to work. One of my two dogs, Ryley, is sleeping at my feet. He provides me joy, eases my anxiety, warms my feet, and is my companion while I write. Yet, he is not an object; he is alive, and I consider his needs, feelings, and personality. I take breaks in my workday to take him and his sister, Lacey, on walks. I stop so they can sniff bushes, flowers, grass, and mulch as well as chase rabbits, squirrels, and birds, because that is what they love to do. I can tell he is happy and rejuvenated when we get home – that golden retriever "smile" comes out – which also brings me joy. After receiving a treat, he falls asleep again at my feet as I resume my work.

This example distinguishes objects (non-living things) from non-objects (living things with personalities and feelings that require care, love, and personal connection). While it seems easy to determine what is and what is not an object, the distinction is often blurred within society and our relationships. **Objectification** occurs when people are treated as objects or "things" for someone else's personal gain or satisfaction with little or no regard for feelings, needs, personality, or care [1]. When a person is treated as an object, it is easy to neglect, abuse, manipulate, and otherwise hurt them because there is no consideration of, or empathy for, their feelings or experience.

Sexual objectification occurs when a person's body or body parts are separated from their personal identity and used for the sexual enjoyment of others [1-2]. Although sexual objectification can impact anyone, it is more often directed toward women than men [1, 3-4]. According to the author John Berger [5], "Women are depicted in a quite different way from men – not because the feminine is different from the masculine – but because the 'ideal' spectator is always assumed to be male and the image of the woman is designed to flatter him." Think about examples of women you see in media. Often, women are shown with little (or tight) clothing in sexualized poses. The primary focus is to sexualize body parts (e.g., legs, buttocks, breasts), with their heads (which represent their personality, feelings, and thoughts) often removed. Even professional female athletes, who gain recognition for their ability and skill within their sport, are often sexualized in media (i.e., lying on the ground in sexually suggestive poses with little clothing on) [6-7].

Not only is sexual objectification seen in media, but it can be experienced when interacting with others. Women routinely encounter experiences of sexual objectification with not only strangers, but also acquaintances, partners, family, and friends. One subtle but frequent way sexual objectification is expressed is through the **objectifying gaze**, which is the scrutiny and sexual evaluation of bodies (e.g., staring, leering) [1, 8]. This gaze can be a "look up, look down," which seems minor, but sends the message that the body is "on display" for others to critique.

Society gives the impression that it is acceptable, and even entertaining, to judge and evaluate the bodies of others through this objectifying gaze [9]. For example, women are often rated by others on a 1–10 "attractiveness" scale; their bodies scrutinized to determine where they fall (e.g., "She is a perfect 10!" or "I can't date her; she is only a 4.5"). Notice how a woman is a number – all other aspects of her identity are discarded. Because sexual objectification is viewed as playful, and perhaps even flattering to women, many believe that it doesn't harm women and that it is just "locker-room talk." Another possibility is that some people aren't actually concerned about whether it harms women: after all, they believe that women are objects used for men's gratification.

There are a number of harmful consequences of being sexually objectified. **Objectification theory** is a model that details the progression of these harmful consequences [1]. First, being treated as an object may lead us to view ourselves as objects. We may come to "internalize the objectification," or see ourselves through the eyes of those objectifying us. We care about what we look like to others at the expense of how we feel. When we view our bodies as objects to be looked at, and that our appearance matters more than our inner experiences (thoughts, feelings, comfort, intellect), we engage in **self-objectification** [1, 10]. If we believe that others value us primarily for our appearance, we begin to equate our value and self-worth with how we look. We then monitor how we look, making sure we "look good" at all angles that we may be viewed. This is **body surveillance**, or spending considerable time monitoring how we look to others [11].

Checking our bodies in the mirror for potential "flaws" to hide, thinking about how we look to our partners during sexual experiences, and wearing shoes that are stylish but painful are examples of body surveillance. In an experiment that highlights body surveillance, women wore either swimsuits or sweaters while completing a math test [12]. Those wearing swimsuits had a harder time focusing, as their thoughts wandered to how they looked in the swimsuit. Moreover, they experienced greater body shame compared to those wearing sweaters. The more often we are exposed to situations that draw attention to our bodies, the more likely we are to monitor how our bodies look in *all* situations, objectifying or not [8].

Second, while the objectifying gaze is often subtle, it is associated with fear. This fear is **personal safety anxiety**, which restricts what we do [13]. When I was twelve years old, my parents had the large windows replaced throughout our home, including my bedroom. It was summer, and I was in shorts and a short-sleeve shirt, reading a book, and lying on my bed. One of the men replacing my bedroom window kept staring at me. I felt exposed and ashamed – I thought I did something wrong. Also, I felt scared. I left my room and went in the bathroom (all other rooms had windows), my heart pounding, until they left hours later. Another example is, while at the gym a man told me "we need to get you a tan" (I must have been too pale for his taste) and another told me "The honey bee cannot resist the honey; I have plans for you." Experiences with sexual objectification can be frightening (I feared I may be sexually assaulted) as well as restrictive (I stopped going to that gym to avoid continued harassment).

We don't even have to experience sexual objectification directly; just hearing that it happens to others is enough to raise this fear [13]. When one of my best friends passed away in a car accident, I wanted to visit her gravesite. I mentioned this to my mom and she exclaimed, "I read a story about how a woman was assaulted at a cemetery, and that men can easily find places to hide and sexually assault women there, so don't go alone!" I still went to the cemetery. I couldn't truly "be there" for my friend and process my grief because I was looking over my shoulder the entire time. Think of all the things we may do as a result of personal safety anxiety. The list may include: carrying our keys in a defensive manner, avoiding public restrooms when alone, walking with another person for safety, keeping distance when walking past strangers on the street or in dark areas, parking in well-lit areas, avoiding the parking garage while alone at night, planning a route with safety in mind, staying at home for fear of going out alone, checking the back seat of the car for intruders, changing our routine or activities, and pretending to talk on our cell phone when alone [13–14].

In addition to increasing our personal safety anxiety, self-objectification:

1. Increases our **appearance anxiety** (i.e., we become tense when others are looking at us due to worrying that they will see our appearance as flawed) [10, 15].

2. Increases our feelings of **body shame** because our bodies do not "measure up" to media appearance ideals, do not smell fresh, grow hair in unwanted areas, jiggle when we wave, and more [4, 10–13].

3. Makes it difficult to determine how our bodies feel (e.g., hungry), which is **poor interoceptive awareness** [13, 16].

4. Makes it difficult to experience **flow**, or becoming engaged and "fully present" in a task. When we self-objectify, we are too concerned about how we look doing the task to focus on the task itself. Flow is enjoyable, and we need flow activities

in our lives to enhance our well-being [17]. The more attention is called to our appearance, the more we detach from activities that produce flow [18].

When we experience self-objectification and these consequences, we are at increased risk for disordered eating, depression, and lower sexual well-being [1, 13, 15–16]. This makes sense – if we are focused on and anxious about our appearance, feel shameful towards our bodies, and ignore our inner experiences (e.g., hunger cues), it puts us at increased risk of disordered eating. If we are anxious about our appearance and safety, feel shameful toward our bodies, and find it hard to focus on tasks, it puts us at risk for depression. If we have anxiety about our appearance and focus on how we look during sexual activity instead of enjoying the experience in the moment and within our bodies, then that interferes with our sexual enjoyment.

Much research has supported objectification theory [3–4, 8–13, 15–16]. In fact, it is one of the largest areas of research investigating body image. While most research on objectification theory has sampled young, predominantly White, able-bodied, straight college women, there is evidence that objectification theory also explains the experiences of gay men [19], lesbian women [20], women who are deaf [21], women across the adult lifespan [10, 22], and women who are Hispanic, African American, and Asian [23–24]. Sexual objectification can also be racialized for certain ethnic groups of women, meaning that features of their race, culture, and sexuality are sexually objectified. Only certain aspects of objectification theory hold for straight men; being sexually objectified is closely linked to their body shame, which is then closely linked to their disordered eating [4, 25]. Among straight men, believing in traditional masculine gender roles (e.g., "I must be strong and powerful," "I cannot be vulnerable") is related to greater body dissatisfaction and a drive to become more muscular [25].

Therefore, we do experience sexual objectification in different ways based on our social identities, such as gender, race, sexual orientation, age, and ability. These differences are tied to the power structures within society. When we hold less power, we are exposed to more discrimination, and we then experience additional variations of sexual objectification that could negatively impact our well-being. We need to recognize the harmfulness of sexual objectification and combat it at a societal level [26–27]. Recently, **positive masculinity** has emerged as a way to lower sexual objectification and promote men's well-being at the same time [28]. Positive masculinity rejects the "toxic" aspects of masculinity, such as domination, power over others, aggression, control, excessive self-reliance, restricting emotional expression, and objectifying others, which are also linked to lower well-being for men (e.g., anger issues, problems with the law) and their partners (e.g., interpersonal violence). Instead, positive masculinity reflects the healthy parts of masculinity, and then uses these parts to improve men's well-being, their relationships, and society. For example, men can work together to fight violence against women and behaviors that promote it. To illustrate, the *Men's Program* [29] includes aspects of positive masculinity, such as courage, strength, action, and protection in its structure to prevent sexual assault. This program has been found to increase men's understanding of sexual violence and its relevance to them and their loved ones and motivation to act against it (e.g., challenging rape jokes, helping survivors seek assistance, and intervening when they witness sexual violence or objectification).

Additionally, we can resist some of the harmful effects of sexual objectification by developing a **contextualization schema** [26–27]. To do so, it is important to first recognize when sexual objectification occurs and our negative reactions to it and then place the responsibility for our negative reactions on the objectifier (rather than ourselves and engage in self-objectification). In other words, when we are exposed to sexual objectification, we place the blame on the objectifier (e.g., "that was wrong to objectify me like that!") rather than place the blame on ourselves ("I caused it to happen") and self-objectify (e.g., "I must pay attention to how I look"). To understand your level of self-objectification, complete the *Self-Objectification Beliefs and Behaviors Scale* (SOBBS) [30] in this chapter. The exercises and handouts within this chapter will help you develop a contextualization schema for sexually objectifying encounters.

Treatment Planning Tools

Talking Points for Sessions

- Discuss the definitions of objectification and self-objectification
- Discuss how sexual objectification impacts expression and pleasure in intimate relationships and sexual encounters
- Discuss how sexual objectification impacts body image, appearance anxiety, perceptions of safety, and awareness of the body's needs
- Discuss contextualization schemas and how they may offset self-objectification and promote positive body image
- Practice role plays of effective responses for situations that include objectification of self or others
- Address how sexual objectification results from an inadequate society, not personal inadequacy

Treatment Plan

Goals

- Decrease the frequency and intensity of my appearance anxiety
- Decrease the frequency and intensity of my body shame
- Recognize the frequency and intensity of my own body monitoring
- Recognize how often I monitor others' bodies
- Examine the purpose and intention behind trying to change my body

- Learn more about objectification and self-objectification and how they relate to my experience(s)
- Reduce destructive behaviors when I experience body shame and engage in self-care activities
- Practice scripts of how I want to respond when I receive appearance-focused comments
- Identify ways that I can respond effectively in situations that include an objectifying gaze
- Decrease my involvement in situations or environments that promote objectification/sexual objectification

Objectives

- Engage in self-monitoring assignments to identify the frequency of my body monitoring thoughts and behaviors
- Eliminate taking selfies for a week to explore the impact on my body image
- Identify activating events associated with my experience(s) of body shame
- Identify activating events associated with my experience(s) of body anxiety
- Identify the number of times over the course of a week that I engage in behaviors to change my body
- Journal about how my focus on physical attractiveness can interfere with my focus on body functionality
- Explore how comments from others about my body can correspond with self-objectification
- Journal about my emotions, thoughts, and behaviors associated with both real or imagined experiences of body monitoring by others
- Identify a specific self-care plan to use upon receiving unsolicited "body-focused" comments from others
- Identify personal examples of objectifying others (within a framework of self-compassion and commitment to change)
- Identify examples of my agency, mastery, and achievement that extend beyond my physical attributes, sexuality, and/or appearance
- Identify and label examples of objectification on a continuum from criticisms to compliments
- Identify red flags associated with self-objectification
- Create and rehearse a script of how to respond to objectifying comments
- Identify examples of engaging in self-objectification
- Generate personal affirmations that focus on my personality, character, and abilities
- Identify the pros and cons of engaging in objectification both in the short-term and long-term
- Practice grounding techniques to promote empowerment
- Identify what a "safe environment" is in respect to objectification
- Protest offensive media images and messages that include sexual objectification
- Identify specific examples of objectification that have occurred throughout my life and consider both the immediate and long-term impacts

❏ Identify my specific thoughts, emotions and behaviors experienced upon receiving "negative body talk" comments, including those comments from respected or loved ones

❏ Identify examples of listening to my body following traumatic or uncomfortable experiences

❏ Identify specific ways to reconnect with my body following traumatic or uncomfortable experiences

❏ Identify specific ways to claim/reclaim power of my body

❏ Identify potential barriers to accepting my "new body" following traumatic or uncomfortable experiences

❏ Identify ways that I have become stronger and/or more resilient following traumatic or uncomfortable experiences

Additional Resources

S. L. Bartky. *Femininity and Domination: Studies in the Phenomenon of Oppression*. New York: Routledge, 1990.

J. Berger. *Ways of Seeing*. New York: Penguin, 1972.

N. Wolf. *The Beauty Myth*. New York: HarperCollins Publishers, Inc., 1990.

S. Jhally. *Codes of Gender: Identity and Performance in Popular Culture* [DVD]. Northampton, MA: Media Education Foundation, 2009.

N. Clark. *Cover Girl Culture: Awakening the Media Generation* [DVD]. New York: Women Make Movies, 2009.

E. Zurbriggen et al. *Report of the APA Task Force on the Sexualization of Girls*, 2007. Available at: www.google.com/url?sa=t&rct=j&q=&esrc=s&source=web&cd=7&ved=2ahUKEwjIk4ib8trlAhUFF6wKHVY3BnIQFjAGegQIBBAC&url=https%3A%2F%2Fojp.gov%2Fnewsroom%2Fevents%2Fpdfs%2Fapa_report.pdf&usg=AOvVaw3KD2-pRsiJUzjJHnyfiy1r [last accessed July 11, 2020].

J. Swift and H. Gould. *Not an Object: On Sexualization and Exploitation of Women and Girls*, 2019). Available at: www.unicefusa.org/stories/not-object-sexualization-and-exploitation-women-and-girls/30366 [last accessed July 11, 2020].

Assessment 13.1: Self-Objectification Beliefs and Behaviors Scale (SOBBS)

Use the following scale to indicate your level of agreement with each item. Please write the number to the right of the item.

1	2	3	4	5
Strongly Disagree	Disagree	Neither Agree Nor Disagree	Agree	Strongly Agree

Body as Self Subscale	Number
1. Looking attractive to others is more important to me than being happy with who I am inside.	
2. How I look is more important to me than how I think or feel.	
3. My physical appearance is more important than my personality.	
4. My physical appearance says more about who I am than my intellect.	
5. How sexually attractive others find me says something about who I am as a person.	
6. My physical appearance is more important than my physical abilities.	
7. My body is what gives me value to other people.	
Total Body as Self Subscale Score: add items 1–7 then divide by 7 =	
Observer's Perspective Subscale	**Number**
8. I try to imagine what my body looks like to others (i.e., like I am looking at myself from the outside).	
9. I choose specific clothing or accessories based on how they make my body appear to others.	
10. When I look in the mirror, I notice areas of my appearance that I think others will view critically.	
11. I consider how my body will look to others in the clothing I am wearing.	
12. I often think about how my body must look to others.	
13. I try to anticipate others' reactions to my physical appearance.	
14. I have thoughts about how my body looks to others even when I am alone.	
Total Observer's Perspective Subscale score: add items 8–14 then divide by 7 =	
Total SOBBS score: add items 1–14 then divide by 14 =	

Total Self-Objectification Beliefs and Behaviors score between:
- **3.5–5** = high self-objectification
- **2.5–3.4** = moderate self-objectification
- **below 2.5** = low self-objectification

Note. Reprinted with permission. Authors of the SOBBS are Lindner and Tantleff-Dunn.* The SOBBS's measurement properties (i.e., reliability and validity) and structure are well supported with college and community women and men. Please contact the authors of the SOBBS for permission to use it within research; there is no need to contact them to use it with clients or to complete it on your own.

* D. Lindner and S. Tantleff-Dunn. The Development and Psychometric Evaluation of the Self-Objectification Beliefs and Behaviors Scale. *Psychol Women Q* 2017; 41: 254–72.

Self-Objectification Beliefs and Behaviors Scale Applications

- If you responded either "agree" or "strongly agree" to item 1 (*Looking attractive to others is more important to me than being happy with who I am inside*), reflect on the following:

  ○ Why is attractiveness so important?

  ○ What are your thoughts and emotions if you're not judged as "attractive" by another person?

  ○ What do you do in order to be attractive?

  ○ How do you define happiness?

- If you responded either "agree" or "strongly agree" for item 3 (*My physical appearance is more important than my personality*), consider the aspects of your personality that are unique.

- For item 8 (*I try to imagine what my body looks like to others*), consider:

  ○ The amount of time each day/week given to imagining what your body looks like to others

  ○ The types of activities/things you do to make your body look as best as it can to others.

- Item 10 (*When I look in the mirror, I notice areas of my appearance that I think others will view critically*) addresses self-objectification while looking at reflective sources (e.g., mirrors, windows). How much time do you spend checking your appearance in reflective sources? How do you feel after you check your appearance? What areas or body parts do you tend to focus on? What do you imagine others will think of you? How can you challenge these critical thoughts?

- To what degree does your concern about how others perceive you affect your decision-making and well-being?

  ○ What situations and/or activities do you *avoid* because of how your appearance might be perceived by others?

  ○ How would your life and body image be different if you could make decisions in the direction of your values, even if you still have concerns about how others perceive your appearance?

- In reference to item 13 (*I try to anticipate others' reactions to my physical appearance*), what information do you use to anticipate the reactions of others to your appearance?

  ○ How would you know whether the information is accurate? Are there times you might have misinterpreted the reactions of others?

  ○ What is the function/reason/purpose of trying to anticipate others' reactions to your appearance (for example, to try to prevent or reduce anxiety, embarrassment)?

Assignment 13.1: Make a Change with Objectification

Identify examples of media messages that focus on the objectification of the body including sexualized themes. Create a thoughtful written response (e.g, letter, social media posting) that includes the following: identification of the problem associated with objectification, how this issue impacts various individuals, and recommendations for how the problem of objectification can be addressed. Consider the pros and cons for yourself and others of sending/posting this response.

_____
_____
_____
_____
_____
_____
_____
_____
_____
_____
_____
_____
_____

N. L. Wood-Barcalow, T. L. Tylka, and C. L. Judge. _Positive Body Image Workbook: A Clinical and Self-Improvement Guide._ Cambridge: Cambridge University Press, 2021.

Assignment 13.2: Positive Role Models

Consider important, positive role models for whom their bodies are not the main source of self-worth. Identify individuals who are both famous and that you know on a personal level while completing this assignment.

- These are people whom I admire for their talents, achievements, strengths, and contributions to society:
  _____
  _____
  _____

- These are the specific qualities and traits that I admire in these role models:
  _____
  _____
  _____

- These are the contributions of my role models:
  _____
  _____
  _____

- I would like to exhibit or demonstrate these similar qualities:
  _____
  _____
  _____

- Focusing on these qualities will help me move toward positive body image by:
  _____
  _____
  _____

N. L. Wood-Barcalow, T. L. Tylka, and C. L. Judge. *Positive Body Image Workbook: A Clinical and Self-Improvement Guide.* Cambridge: Cambridge University Press, 2021.

Assignment 13.3: Interpreting Comments from Others

Receiving comments about our bodies from others, including unwanted advice, can result in various emotions ranging from anger, confusion, and ambivalence to satisfaction and pleasure. The context of the situation (e.g., who made the comment, where it occurred, and under what circumstances) can influence if the comment is interpreted as a compliment, criticism, threat, or even a combination. It can be normal to feel happy when receiving positive appearance-related comments and uncomfortable when receiving negative comments. It also can be uncomfortable to receive seemingly positive comments about the body, as these comments may promote body monitoring and unwanted attention. Additionally, objectifying comments have an impact in the moment that they occur as well as a lingering impact.

In the space below, explore your reactions to different situations in which you received comments about your body:

Situation 1: Negative Body Comment

The situation including where, who, when, and what was said:

_____
_____
_____
_____
_____
_____

My *immediate* responses:
- emotion(s): _____
- thought(s): _____
- behavior(s): _____

My responses *over time*:
- emotion(s): _____
- thought(s): _____
- behavior(s): _____

How I'd like to respond in the future if a similar experience occurs:

_____
_____
_____
_____

Additional thoughts/reflections:

_____
_____

Situation 2: Positive Body Comment

The situation including where, who, when, and what was said:

_____
_____
_____
_____
_____
_____

My *immediate* responses:
- emotion(s): _____
- thought(s): _____
- behavior(s): _____

My responses *over time*:
- emotion(s): _____
- thought(s): _____
- behavior(s): _____

N. L. Wood-Barcalow, T. L. Tylka, and C. L. Judge. *Positive Body Image Workbook: A Clinical and Self-Improvement Guide.* Cambridge: Cambridge University Press, 2021.

How I'd like to respond in the future if a similar experience occurs:

_____
_____
_____
_____

Additional thoughts/reflections:

_____
_____

Situation 3: Confusing Body Comment

The situation including where, who, when, and what was said:

_____
_____
_____
_____
_____
_____

My *immediate* responses:

- emotion(s): _____
- thought(s): _____
- behavior(s): _____

My responses *over time*:

- emotion(s): _____
- thought(s): _____
- behavior(s): _____

How I'd like to respond in the future if a similar experience occurs:

_____
_____
_____
_____

Additional thoughts/reflections:

_____
_____

Overall Reflections

I notice that my body image is affected in these ways when others comment on my body:

_____
_____
_____
_____

I commit to making these changes:

_____
_____
_____
_____

N. L. Wood-Barcalow, T. L. Tylka, and C. L. Judge. *Positive Body Image Workbook: A Clinical and Self-Improvement Guide.* Cambridge: Cambridge University Press, 2021.

Assignment 13.4: My Role in Objectification

An honest and realistic look at ourselves likely reveals our own participation in objectification not only directed at others (e.g., siblings, friends, peers, strangers) but also ourselves. Objectification experiences can range from internal judgments and comparisons to external communication such as making comments, offering perceived compliments, and/or teasing/bullying others about their respective bodies. It can be helpful to explore some of these experiences in-depth, while also remaining compassionate towards ourselves, in order to make positive changes moving forward. Choose one objectifying or self-objectifying experience at a time and reflect on the following questions. You can complete this assignment for as many experiences as desired.

Objectifying Someone Else

- Facts about the situation/experience/event.
- How did this situation come about?
- What was the purpose or intent associated with objectifying this person/people?
- What was I experiencing at that time in my life?
- Was I struggling with my own body acceptance or self-acceptance?
- Did my response(s) at the time align with my values *then*? With my values *now*?
- What impact, if any, did the objectification have on the recipient(s)?
- What impact did the experience have on me *at that time*? What impact does it have on me *now*?
- How does the objectification of others impact my body image?
- What is my current perspective looking back on this experience?
- Are there any repairs that I would like to make at this time? If so, what might those look like?
- How might I refrain from repeating this behavior in the future?
- My overall reflections.

Objectifying Myself

- Facts about the situation/experience/event.
- How did this situation come about?
- What was the purpose or intent associated with the self-objectification?
- What was I experiencing at that time in my life?
- Was I struggling with my own body acceptance or self-acceptance?
- Did my response(s) at the time align with my values *then*? With my values *now*?
- What impact did the experience have on me *at that time*? What impact does it have on me *now*?
- How does objectifying myself impact my body image?
- What is my current perspective looking back on this?
- Are there any repairs that I would like to make at this time? If so, what might those look like?
- How might I refrain from repeating this behavior in the future?
- My overall reflections.

N. L. Wood-Barcalow, T. L. Tylka, and C. L. Judge. *Positive Body Image Workbook: A Clinical and Self-Improvement Guide*. Cambridge: Cambridge University Press, 2021.

Assignment 13.5: Creating a Rehearsed Script

Reflect on a real scenario when you experienced a form of objectification. It could include a comment, physical contact, a gaze, a look-up/look-down or "once-over," verbal expressions, nonverbal gestures, and more. Consider the following: the circumstances of the situation, who was present, the nature of the objectifying act, what was communicated, what was experienced internally, response(s) *in the moment* (both inward and outward), levels of discomfort (e.g., fear, panic, embarrassment, shame, anger), response(s) *after the situation* (both inward and outward), and current thoughts/feelings about the situation. Write sentiments here:

_____
_____
_____
_____
_____
_____
_____

Now imagine that you have an opportunity to re-experience this specific situation on *your terms*. In this scenario, you have *a choice* in how you respond from accepting, rejecting, resisting, pushing back, creating an alternative outcome, and more. Consider your *goal(s)* in this re-imagined scenario: maintain self-respect, set a limit, verbalize discomfort, challenge someone else, express a point, express emotion(s) (e.g., anger, indignation, fury, sadness, disappointment), fight back, engage in an objectifying act yourself, embarrass the other person, provide education and more. Write reflections here:

_____
_____
_____
_____
_____
_____
_____
_____

Now imagine creating and practicing internal scripts to use when experiencing a *future event* that includes objectification. The purpose of the script is to *protect* your sense of self, your body, and your body image while also honoring yourself and setting comfortable boundaries and limits. Instead of internalizing the objectifying experience or information, it is helpful to identify and label the act for what it is, such as "that's harassment," "that's not appropriate," and "they are objectifying me." Write examples here:

_____
_____
_____
_____
_____
_____

Your scripts can include internal coping statements such as "I don't have to feel embarrassment," "that person should be embarrassed for what they did," "I wouldn't treat someone that way," and "I deserve better than how I was treated." Write internal coping statements here:

_____
_____
_____
_____
_____

N. L. Wood-Barcalow, T. L. Tylka, and C. L. Judge. *Positive Body Image Workbook: A Clinical and Self-Improvement Guide.* Cambridge: Cambridge University Press, 2021.

A final component can be practicing the script(s) with someone you trust. You can choose to share the actual experience that occurred, how you handled it at the time, and how you re-imagined it. You can identify examples of objectification in your personal life and imagine how you want to respond in the future. Be creative with the ultimate goal of practicing responses that correspond with empowerment. Write about your experience:

_____
_____
_____
_____
_____
_____

N. L. Wood-Barcalow, T. L. Tylka, and C. L. Judge. *Positive Body Image Workbook: A Clinical and Self-Improvement Guide*. Cambridge: Cambridge University Press, 2021.

Assignment 13.6: Patterns of Objectification

Over time, you might notice patterns associated with objectifying experiences such as a tendency for them to occur at certain places, with certain people, and/or in certain environments. For this journal activity, reflect on the following: situations typically associated with experiences of objectification, the individual(s) typically involved, the many ways the objectification has impacted me, the degree to which I internalize(d) the events (i.e., blamed myself for the objectifying encounter and/or my negative reactions), the degree to which I contextualize(d) the events (i.e., placed the responsibility for the objectifying encounter and/or my negative reactions on the objectifier), my desired responses in the future, and more.

_____

_____

_____

_____

_____

_____

_____

_____

_____

_____

_____

N. L. Wood-Barcalow, T. L. Tylka, and C. L. Judge. *Positive Body Image Workbook: A Clinical and Self-Improvement Guide.* Cambridge: Cambridge University Press, 2021.

Assignment 13.7: Intimacy and Objectification

We minimize the overall value and worth of the human experience when we view or treat others or ourselves as "things" or "objects." Objectification can then affect the development and nurturance of healthy intimate relations. Imagine how a person's own preoccupation with their body (in terms of how it looks, feels, and functions) can impact their ability to be present during sexual experiences. Or imagine how you might feel when a partner engages in objectifying behavior directed toward you (e.g., making a negative comment about your body) or with others (e.g., commenting on the body parts of others). Lastly, imagine how exposure to pornography might result in unrealistic expectations related to sexual experiences and sometimes even diminished interest in a partner.

For this journal activity, reflect on the following: in what ways does my engagement in self-objectification create intimate barriers with others? How often does body surveillance affect my ability to be present in the moment? What would it be like to be free from body judgments during sexual experiences? Does my current partner(s) engage in objectifying behaviors with me or with others? Did previous partner(s) engage in objectifying behaviors with me or with others? What are the consequences of these behaviors on me and others?

N. L. Wood-Barcalow, T. L. Tylka, and C. L. Judge. *Positive Body Image Workbook: A Clinical and Self-Improvement Guide.* Cambridge: Cambridge University Press, 2021.

Assignment 13.8: Positive Masculinity

In contrast to traditional masculinity which focuses on *power over others*, **positive masculinity** focuses on power that is *shared with others*.* Positive masculinity is about collaboration and cohesion rather than competition and comparison. This form of masculinity includes men working toward a common goal of caring for loved ones with empathy and resisting behaviors that sexually objectify women.

For this journal activity, identify at least one person who demonstrates positive masculinity in your life (for example, a friend, family member, teacher, mentor, spiritual leader, instructor, partner). Identify specific characteristics and actions of positive masculinity within this person, such as compassion, empathy, resilience, fights sexual objectification, protects against sexual violence, advocates for the rights of women, supports those women who have been sexually assaulted, intervenes with other men who are engaged in inappropriate behaviors with women, and more. Consider how this positive masculinity has impacted you. Finally, consider specific ways that positive masculinity can be carried forward to others.

_____
_____
_____
_____
_____
_____
_____
_____
_____
_____
_____

*M. Englar-Carlson and M. S. Kiselica. Affirming the Strengths in Men: A Positive Masculinity Approach to Assisting Male Clients. *J Couns Dev* 2013; 91: 399–409.

N. L. Wood-Barcalow, T. L. Tylka, and C. L. Judge. *Positive Body Image Workbook: A Clinical and Self-Improvement Guide.* Cambridge: Cambridge University Press, 2021.

Assignment 13.9: Objectifying View versus Whole View

This assignment focuses on identifying situations of participating in either the "objectifying view" versus the "whole view." While in the "objectifying view," people tend to focus on the body parts, weight, shape, or size, and/or sexuality of others. This viewing process is associated with reducing another individual into parts or objects, thereby diminishing their power. When in the "whole view," people tend to focus on the totality of the person such as their overall body, their essence as well as personal characteristics and traits. This viewing process is associated with respect and dignity of the entire individual. In addition to viewing others in these ways, we can also take on an "objectifying view" or a "whole view" of ourselves.

"Objectifying View"

- Reflect on how much time I spend in this role.
- What do I notice about the percentage of time objectifying others? Percentage of time objectifying myself?
- What are the *benefits* associated with this view?
- What are the *costs or harmful outcomes* associated with this view?
- How does this view move me closer to positive body image?
- How does this view move me further from positive body image?
- What *thoughts* are associated with this view?
- What *emotions* are associated with this view?
- What *behaviors* go along with this perspective?
- Additional thoughts/comments.

"Whole View"

- Reflect on how much time I spend in this role.
- What do I notice about the percentage of time observing others in a whole perspective? Percentage of time observing myself in a whole perspective?
- What are the *benefits* associated with this view?
- What are the *costs or harmful outcomes* associated with this view?
- How does this view move me closer to positive body image?
- How does this view move me further from positive body image?
- What *thoughts* are associated with this view?
- What *emotions* are associated with this view?
- What *behaviors* go along with this perspective?
- Additional thoughts/comments.

N. L. Wood-Barcalow, T. L. Tylka, and C. L. Judge. *Positive Body Image Workbook: A Clinical and Self-Improvement Guide.* Cambridge: Cambridge University Press, 2021.

Assignment 13.10: My Experiences in Different Environments

Consider the various physical and virtual environments that you interact with or in such as work, school, shopping stores, restaurants, nature/parks, social media platforms, gyms, sporting events, bars, community events, places of worship, and more. Now consider your *internal experiences* in these different environments in terms of feeling personal safety and comfort, experiencing objectification by others, increased body surveillance and self-objectification, and the freedom to be yourself.

Choose one environment at a time and reflect on the following questions. You can complete this assignment for as many environments as desired. Rate each environment on the following scales and record any reflections.

Environment:_____

Objectification by Others

0	1	2	3	4	5	6	7	8	9	10
Not at all										Extremely

Self-Objectification

0	1	2	3	4	5	6	7	8	9	10
Not at all										Extremely

Comfort

0	1	2	3	4	5	6	7	8	9	10
Not at all										Extremely

Safety

0	1	2	3	4	5	6	7	8	9	10
Not at all										Extremely

Appearance Anxiety

0	1	2	3	4	5	6	7	8	9	10
Not at all										Extremely

Freedom to Be Myself

0	1	2	3	4	5	6	7	8	9	10
Not at all										Extremely

Reflections_____

_____

_____

_____

_____

N. L. Wood-Barcalow, T. L. Tylka, and C. L. Judge. *Positive Body Image Workbook: A Clinical and Self-Improvement Guide.* Cambridge: Cambridge University Press, 2021.

Assignment 13.11: Feeling Invisible

In addition to acknowledging the range of experiences associated with receiving objectifying comments, it is also important to highlight the experiences of *not* receiving body-focused comments in a society that is focused on appearance. The absence of comments can correspond with *feeling invisible*. Reflect on the following:

I feel this way when in a situation in which others receive comments about their bodies and I don't (check all that apply):

- ❏ Jealousy, envy
- ❏ Anger, irritation, frustration
- ❏ Worthless
- ❏ Shame, embarrassment, guilt, mortified
- ❏ Fear, panic, dread
- ❏ Relief, freedom from pressure(s)
- ❏ Yearning, wanting to have positive comments
- ❏ Sadness, despair, disappointment
- ❏ Satisfaction, pleasure, joy
- ❏ Other: _____
- ❏ Other: _____

These are the stories I tell myself about why I don't receive comments:

_____
_____
_____

These stories impact my thoughts, feelings, and behaviors in the following ways:

_____
_____
_____

Feeling invisible impacts me in these ways:

_____
_____
_____

N. L. Wood-Barcalow, T. L. Tylka, and C. L. Judge. *Positive Body Image Workbook: A Clinical and Self-Improvement Guide.* Cambridge: Cambridge University Press, 2021.

References

1. B. L. Fredrickson and T-A. Roberts. Objectification theory: Toward understanding women's lived experiences and mental health risks. *Psychol Women Q* 1997; **21**: 173–206.

2. S. L. Bartky. *Femininity and Domination: Studies in the Phenomenon of Oppression.* New York: Routledge, 1990.

3. B. Moradi and Y-P. Huang. Objectification theory and the psychology of women: A decade of advances and future directions. *Psychol Women Q* 2008; **32**: 377–98.

4. R. Engeln-Maddox, S. A. Miller, and D. M. Doyle. Tests of objectification theory in gay, lesbian, and heterosexual community samples: Mixed evidence for proposed pathways. *Sex Roles* 2011; **65**: 518–32.

5. J. Berger. *Ways of Seeing.* London: BBC and Penguin Books, 1972.

6. E. A. Daniels. Sex objects, athletes, and sexy athletes: How media representations of women athletes can impact adolescent girls and college women. *J Adolesc Res* 2009; **24**: 399–422.

7. S. Jhally. *Codes of Gender.* Northampton, MA: Media Education Foundation, 2009.

8. S. J. Gervais, T. K. Vescio, and J. Allen. When what you see is what you get: The consequences of the objectifying gaze for women and men. *Psychol Women Q* 2011; **35**: 5–17.

9. T. L. Tylka and N. J. Sabik. Integrating social comparison theory and self-esteem within objectification theory to predict women's disordered eating. *Sex Roles* 2010; **63**: 18–31.

10. M. Tiggemann and J. E. Lynch. Body image across the life span in adult women: The role of self-objectification. *Dev Psychol* 2001; **37**: 243–53.

11. N. M. McKinley and J. S. Hyde The Objectified Body Consciousness Scale: Development and validation. *Psychol Women Q* 1996; **20**: 181–215.

12. B. L. Fredrickson, T-A. Roberts, S. M. Noll, et al. That swimsuit becomes you: Sex differences in self-objectification, restrained eating, and math performance. *J Pers Soc Psychol* 1998; **75**: 269–84.

13. R. M. Calogero, T. L. Tylka, J. A. Siegel, et al. Smile pretty and watch your back: Personal safety anxiety and vigilance in objectification theory. Manuscript under review.

14. C. J. Sheffield. Sexual terrorism: The social control of women. In: Hess B. B. and Ferree M. M., eds. *Analyzing Gender: A Handbook of Social Science Research.* Thousand Oaks: Sage, 1987: 171–89.

15. D. M. Szymanski and S. L. Henning. The role of self-objectification in women's depression: A test of objectification theory. *Sex Roles* 2007; **56**: 45–53.

16. T. L. Tylka and M. S. Hill. Objectification theory as it relates to disordered eating among college women. *Sex Roles* 2004; **51**: 719–30.

17. M. Csikszentmihalyi. *Finding Flow: The Psychology of Engagement with Everyday Life.* New York: Basic Books, 1997.

18. S. E. O'Hara, A. E. Cox, and A. J. Amorose. Emphasizing appearance versus health outcomes in exercise: The influence of the instructor and participants' reasons for exercise. *Body Image* 2014; **11**: 109–18.

19. M. C. Wiseman and B. Moradi. Body image and eating disorder symptoms in sexual minority men: A test and extension of objectification theory. *J Couns Psychol* 2010; **57**: 154–66.

20. H. B. Kozee and T. L. Tylka. A test of objectification theory with lesbian women. *Psychol Women Q* 2006; **30**: 348–57.

21. B. Moradi and A. Rottenstein. Objectification theory and deaf cultural identity attitudes. Roles in deaf women's eating disorder symptomatology. *J Couns Psychol* 2007; **54**: 178–88.

22. C. L. Augustus-Horvath and T. L. Tylka. A test and extension of objectification theory as it predicts disordered eating: Does women's age matter? *J Couns Psychol* 2009; **56**: 253–65.

23. L. M. Schaefer, N. L. Burke, R. M. Calogero, et al. Self-objectification, body shame, and disordered eating: Testing a core mediational model of objectification theory among White, Black, and Hispanic women. *Body Image* 2018; **24**: 5–12.

24. H-L. Cheng, A. G. T. T. Tran, E. R Miyake, et al. Disordered eating among Asian American college women: A racially expanded model of objectification theory. *J Couns Psychol* 2017; **64**: 179–91.

25. C. M. Davids, L. B. Watson, and M. P. Gere. Objectification, masculinity, and muscularity: A test of objectification theory with heterosexual men. *Sex Roles* 2019; **80**: 443–57.

26. T. L. Tylka and C. L. Augustus-Horvath. Fighting self-objectification in prevention and intervention contexts. In: Calogero, R. M., Tantleff-Dunn, S., and Thompson, J. K., eds. *Self-Objectification in Women: Causes, Consequences, and Counteractions.* Washington: American Psychological Association, 2011: 187–214.

27. T. L. Tylka and R. M. Calogero. Promoting a resistant stance toward objectification. In: Tylka, T. L. and Piran, N. eds. *Handbook of Positive Body Image and Embodiment: Constructs, Protective Factors, and Interventions.* New York: Oxford University Press, 2019: 149–60.

28. M. Englar-Carlson and M. S. Kiselica. Affirming the strengths in men: A positive masculinity approach to assisting male clients. *J Couns Dev* 2013; **91**: 399–409.

29. J. D. Foubert and B. C. Perry. Creating lasting attitude and behavior change in fraternity members and male student athletes. *Violence Against Women* 2007; **13**: 70–86.

30. D. Lindner and S. Tantleff-Dunn. The development and psychometric evaluation of the Self-Objectification Beliefs and Behaviors Scale. *Psychol Women Q* 2017; **41**: 254–72.

Chapter 14

Sexual Intimacy

Theory and Research Overview

We describe **sexual intimacy** as being in touch with and responding to our bodies' sexual desires in nurturing, compassionate, and safe ways that bring us joy and sexual pleasure, either alone or within a sexual relationship. Within a sexual relationship, sexual intimacy can be complex, as it corresponds not only with how physically attracted we are to our partners, but also how emotionally connected we are to them, how safe we feel with them, the extent we trust them, how attentive they are to our bodies and our desires, our religious and spiritual beliefs, and our adoption of social and cultural messages for how we should behave (e.g., feminine and masculine gender roles). Our body image is also tied to sexual intimacy in that we are more likely to experience sexual pleasure when we feel good about, appreciate, and are connected to our bodies [1–2]. That is, when we are in tune with and respect our bodies, we are more aware of, responsive to, and likely to express our sexual desires in ways that fulfill us and our relationships.

Adverse or negative experiences can impact how we feel about our bodies, which then can impact our sexual intimacy. Examples of adverse experiences can include trauma, sexual objectification, sexual assault and its various forms (e.g., rape, non-consensual experiences), stigma, intimate partner violence, appearance-related pressures, gender role socialization (e.g., pressure for girls and women to "be feminine," which minimizes assertiveness within sexual encounters), and many more. Indeed, these experiences are associated with negative body image [3–6] which is associated with lower sexual pleasure (e.g., reaching orgasm [7]), lower levels of sexual desire and arousability [8], less frequent sexual initiation and sexual avoidance [9], dissociating (or "zoning out") from the sexual encounter [10], and higher engagement in risky sexual behaviors [11–12]. Body-related experiences, such as chronic pain, illnesses and their symptoms, appearance alterations (e.g., amputation, scars), medications, aging, and gender dysphoria (i.e., distress due to gender identity not matching sex assigned at birth) can also impact our body image and sexual intimacy [13–15].

One particular way negative body image can impact our sexual intimacy is by focusing on how we look, smell, and sound, instead of how we feel in the moment [16]. Taking an "observer's perspective" of our bodies during our sexual encounters is referred to as **spectatoring** – that is, being distracted during sexual intimacy with the thoughts of how one's body is being experienced by a partner (e.g., "What is my partner thinking as they look at my body?", "Am I smelling okay?", "How do I sound during sex?") [17]. While similar to body surveillance (see Chapter 13), spectatoring is more specific in that it happens within sexual encounters. Objectification theory can explain how spectatoring and difficulties with sexual intimacy develop. Being treated as a sexual object promotes us to take an observer's perspective of our bodies (self-objectification), which promotes general body surveillance, spectatoring, body shame, and appearance anxiety, which then disrupt various forms of psychological health, including sexual functioning [16].

When we have external support, and when we are exposed to positive role models who own their sexual desire, we are more likely to be connected to and express our own sexual desire [1]. For example, one woman who was interviewed by Niva Piran in a research study on embodiment [2] stated:

> I describe myself as a very sexual person because I was always very much in touch with the sexual feelings that my body had . . . feeling sexual was a very positive thing. I have healthy attitudes about sex. I thought, well maybe I am attracted to women and I think it's more of a continuum . . . things kind of went on hold when I met [husband] and fell in love with him . . . I do feel sex was a very good thing for my body (p. 50).

Therapists often use **sensate focus** as a tool within sex and couple therapy to reduce spectatoring and enhance sexual intimacy for partners [18]. Sensate focus includes behavioral exercises that partners do together as homework outside of therapy. These exercises refocus them on their own sensory perceptions and sensuality, instead of goal-oriented behaviors that focus on the genitals and achieving orgasm. The first step of sensate focus is touching areas of the body not associated directly with sex (e.g., back, legs, neck). Each person focuses on their own sensations while being touched and while touching their partner (thus, each person takes turns being the giver and receiver of touch). The second step incorporates touching of the breasts (if applicable) and/or genitals in the same manner– again the focus is on the sensations experienced while taking turns being touched. The third step is mutual touching, meant to integrate the sensations felt while being both the giver and receiver of touch. The final step is **sensual intercourse**, whereby partners focus on pleasure and sensation with touching that includes intercourse, without focusing on achieving orgasm. Sensate focus has been shown to be successful for partners of all ages, gender identities, and sexual orientations and is also useful for people dealing with sexual difficulties as a result of medical conditions such as breast cancer [18].

Sensate focus can help us focus on how we feel and what our senses are experiencing during sexual practices (e.g., "I love it when I am touched there," "It feels amazing when I touch myself here," "My body goes wild when I smell my partner's scent"). This perspective of the body is one characteristic of attuned sexuality. Satinsky and Winter [19] define **attuned sexuality** as a state where our sexual experiences contain desired levels of sexual connection, desire, functioning, and expression. Building on positive embodiment [2] (see also Chapter 12), attuned sexuality includes sexual agency, access to our sexual desires, use of strategies to protect and nurture our bodies during sex, and the ability to mindfully tune into our bodies' pleasures in sexual situations [19]. Attuned sexuality can be impacted by the nonsexual parts of our relationships (e.g., openness, power dynamics, communication), our diverse identities (e.g., race, gender, body size), and our partners' skills and attention to our bodies and pleasures.

Researchers have examined aspects of attuned sexuality, such as sexual subjectivity. **Sexual subjectivity** represents positive sexual agency, an important component of attuned sexuality [20–22]. Agency is when we act in the world, either through asserting ourselves physically or through "the power of voice" [2], and therefore **positive sexual agency** includes proactively engaging in wanted and desired sexual experiences, but also voicing our needs, desires, and consent/non-consent during these experiences [17, 23]. Sexual subjectivity also includes **sexual body esteem** (i.e., feelings that we are sexually desirable), entitlement to sexual desire and pleasure from self and partners, **sexual self-efficacy** (i.e., confidence in achieving sexual pleasure, both alone and with our partner), and **sexual self-reflection** (i.e., reflecting on our sexual experiences) [20–21]. To understand your level of sexual subjectivity, complete the *Sexual Subjectivity Inventory* [20–21] within this chapter.

Positive body image is connected to several aspects of sexual subjectivity and sexual health practices including higher levels of sexual pleasure (arousal, orgasm, and satisfaction) [1, 24], greater comfort communicating about sex [25], discussions of contraceptive use with partners [26], higher use of contraception such as male condom use and hormonal contraceptives [22, 27], more active engagement in preventative health behaviors such as regular breast exams and pap smears [26], undergoing regular testing for sexually transmitted infections and taking precautions to prevent these infections [26], and receiving vaccines to prevent Human Papillomavirus (HPV) [26]. Positive body image is also linked to higher levels of sex positivity, including feeling sexually liberated and holding more favorable views of unconventional sexual practices (e.g., preferring sexual activity when "it is out of the ordinary") [26].

While the majority of the research connecting body image and sexuality has focused on the sexual experiences of healthy, young, white women who identify as heterosexual and cisgender (i.e., whereby a sense of personal identity and gender identity match one's biological sex) [28], some research has been conducted among sexual minority populations. Approximately 42 percent of gay men and 27 percent of lesbian women indicated that body dissatisfaction has had a negative impact on their sex lives [29], such as elevated sexual anxiety and lower sexual self-efficacy [30]. In another study, the more people perceived themselves as sexually attractive, the higher their sexual satisfaction and sexual activity, and this trend was present among heterosexual and bisexual women and men, lesbian women, and gay men [31]. These findings highlight the need to enhance self-perceptions of sexual attractiveness, which may include expanding the definition of attractiveness beyond what is considered attractive in society (see Chapter 7).

Research on both body image and sexuality variables, such as sexual subjectivity, has yet to focus on individuals who identify as nonbinary, gender nonconforming, or transgender. We do know that body dissatisfaction is linked to gender dysphoria. These variables combine to promote disordered eating, with the goal of suppressing physical features of natal sex (sex assigned at birth) and accentuating features of gender identity [32]. Gender confirmation treatments, such as hormone treatments and gender confirmation surgeries which alter the body to be compatible with a person's identity, are related to lower anxiety and depression as well as higher body satisfaction and **transgender congruence** (i.e., the extent to which a person is comfortable with and accepts their gender identity, including their external appearance) and should not be prolonged if it is a person's desire to proceed with these treatments [32–35] (see Chapter 22). Nonbinary, gender nonconforming, and transgender individuals often fear and sometimes experience sexualized violence and sexual objectification, which negatively impacts their mental health, body image, and sexual intimacy simultaneously [35].

Certain treatments for medical conditions and diseases can alter sexual intimacy, sexual functioning, body image, and **body integrity** (e.g., experience of the body being "whole"). For example, women with breast cancer experience impaired sexual functioning and body dissatisfaction more so than women without breast cancer [14]. Chemotherapy, radiation, hormonal suppression, mastectomy, and other surgeries can impact energy, sexual desire, vaginal dryness, and body-related changes such as weight gain or loss. Furthermore, each person's experiences with breast cancer are unique, influenced by a range of factors such as age, illness stage, treatment types, and relationship status. Those with breast cancer report dissatisfaction with the amount and quality of care they receive from their healthcare providers regarding sexual health. As another illustration, men with prostate cancer experience decreased body integrity that corresponds with physical and emotional challenges with their sexual expression [36]. For example, 57 percent of men with prostate cancer were concerned with being able to satisfy their partners [37]. **Note for clinicians:** We recommend that clinicians identify, assess, and treat individuals' sexual and body image concerns, considering how they are uniquely affected by the biological, psychological, and relational changes that surface with diagnosis and treatment [14]. This recommendation is adopted for the vast number of other clinical conditions in which diagnosis and treatment could impact body image and sexuality.

In conclusion, to enhance sexual intimacy, including attuned sexuality and sexual subjectivity, it is important to understand how it may have become disrupted and address these factors. Research also indicates that the many identities of a person, such as gender, sexual orientation, and gender identity may make everyone's experience with sexual intimacy unique. The assignments within this chapter can be used to understand the complexity of body image and sexuality concerns and how best to work toward sexual intimacy.

Treatment Planning Tools

Talking Points for Sessions

- Explore the relationship between body image and sexual intimacy throughout life
- Identify ways negative body image is associated with avoidance of certain sexual behaviors
- Explore how adverse experiences (e.g., sexual and other trauma) and body-related experiences (e.g., illness, aging, chronic pain) have impacted client's sexual experiences and intimacy
- Explore how positive experiences have influenced sexual experiences and intimacy
- Define and discuss attuned sexuality, sexual agency, and sexual self-efficacy as they relate to positive body image
- Discuss components of healthy sexual intimacy

Treatment Plan

Goals

❏ Increase communication with my partner(s) about desired sexual behaviors
❏ Explore my definition of healthy sexual intimacy and how it relates to my partner selection
❏ Increase comfort in discussing sexual matters that are important
❏ Identify my values associated with sex
❏ Make decisions in sexual encounters that support my health, well-being, and values
❏ Increase mindful awareness using my five senses during sexual intimacy
❏ Establish and maintain comfortable sexual boundaries and limits
❏ Reduce frequency of anxious self-scrutiny during sexual experiences
❏ Increase sexual experimentation with behaviors I'm comfortable with
❏ Increase communication about sex and/or intimacy with my partner(s)
❏ Increase self-exploration related to my sexual desires
❏ Explore how trauma and/or uncomfortable experiences impact my sexual attitudes, behaviors, and experiences
❏ Increase my sexual agency
❏ Increase my sexual body esteem
❏ Engage in self-reflection of sexual experiences, desires, and behaviors
❏ Explore the relationships between gender incongruence, body image, and sexual expression(s)

Objectives

❏ Consider how "bad body image" days affect my sexual interest, arousal, and participation
❏ Imagine what sexual behaviors might be altered or changed upon moving toward positive body image and positive embodiment
❏ Dialogue with my partner(s) about what is desired in sexual intimacy
❏ Focus on sensitivity to my bodily experiences during sexual activity
❏ Focus on sense of smell during sexual intimacy
❏ Focus on visual sensation during sexual intimacy
❏ Focus on touch during sexual intimacy
❏ Explore different ways of connecting and fostering sexual intimacy
❏ Create a list of desired ways to express my sexuality, with the goal to fulfill one day
❏ Consider how my body image corresponds with use of sexual and reproductive health practices
❏ Consider how my evaluation of my appearance relates to how I express my sexuality
❏ Identify different types of avoided (yet safe, pleasurable, and desired) sexual behaviors including my reasons for avoiding them, and commit to approaching one
❏ Ask about my partner's sexual history
❏ Ask about my partner's status regarding sexually transmitted infections
❏ Implement components of sensual intercourse
❏ Identify characteristics of a partner(s) who will respect my attuned sexuality
❏ Explore how my body image relates to my sexual arousal and satisfaction
❏ Consider how transformations with/of my body both short-term and long-term (such as age-related changes, pregnancy, loss of limb or organ) can impact sexual intimacy
❏ Imagine what I might do or not do with increased sexual body esteem and implement at least one new behavior
❏ Speak with medical health providers about my body image and sexual health
❏ Identify spectatoring when it occurs and redirect my attention to my sensations in the moment
❏ If I experience gender dysphoria, dialogue with medical providers about gender confirmation interventions
❏ If I experience gender dysphoria, assert desired requests for gender confirmation interventions from medical providers

Additional Resources

L. Mintz. *Becoming Cliterate: Why Orgasm Equality Matters – and How to Get It*. New York: HarperCollins, 2017.

S. Haines. *Healing Sex: A Mind-Body Approach to Healing Sexual Trauma*. San Francisco: Cleis Press, 2007.

W. Maltz. *The Sexual Healing Journey: A Guide for Survivors of Sexual Abuse*. New York: William Morrow/HarperCollins, 2012.

Assessment 14.1: Sexual Subjectivity Inventory (SSI)

This measure contains various subscales, each of which is a component of sexual subjectivity. These questions are about your ways of thinking about sexual behavior and relationships. They do NOT depend on having had any particular past experiences. Rather we are asking you about general feelings, opinions, and values. Please read each statement carefully before answering. Indicate your agreement by circling the number to the right of each item.

Sexual Body Esteem Subscale	Strongly Disagree	Disagree	Neutral	Agree	Strongly Agree
1. I worry that I am not sexually desirable to others.	5	4	3	2	1
2. I am confident that a romantic partner would find me sexually attractive.	1	2	3	4	5
3. I am confident that others will find me sexually desirable.	1	2	3	4	5
4. It bothers me that I'm not better looking.	5	4	3	2	1
5. Physically, I am an attractive person.	1	2	3	4	5
Total Sexual Body Esteem score: add items 1–5 and then divide by 5 =					

Entitlement to Sexual Pleasure from Self Subscale	Strongly Disagree	Disagree	Neutral	Agree	Strongly Agree
6. It is okay for me to meet my own sexual needs through self-masturbation.	1	2	3	4	5
7. I believe self-masturbating can be an exciting experience.	1	2	3	4	5
8. I believe self-masturbation is wrong.	5	4	3	2	1
9. I believe self-masturbation can be a positive experience.	1	2	3	4	5
10. It is okay to enjoy self-masturbation.	1	2	3	4	5
Total Entitlement to Sexual Pleasure from Self score: add items 6–10 and then divide by 5 =					

Entitlement to Sexual Pleasure from Partner	Strongly Disagree	Disagree	Neutral	Agree	Strongly Agree
11. If a partner were to ignore my sexual needs and desires, I'd feel hurt.	1	2	3	4	5
12. It would bother me if a sexual partner neglected my sexual needs and desires.	1	2	3	4	5
13. I would expect a sexual partner to be responsive to my sexual needs and feelings.	1	2	3	4	5
14. I think it is important for a sexual partner to consider my sexual pleasure.	1	2	3	4	5
15. I would be concerned if my partner did not care about my sexual needs and feelings.	1	2	3	4	5
Total Entitlement to Sexual Pleasure from Partner score: add items 11–15 and then divide by 5 =					

Sexual Self-Reflection	Strongly Disagree	Disagree	Neutral	Agree	Strongly Agree
16. I spend time thinking and reflecting about my sexual experiences.	1	2	3	4	5
17. I rarely think about the sexual aspects of my life.	5	4	3	2	1
18. I think about my sexuality.	1	2	3	4	5
19. I don't think about my sexual behavior very much.	5	4	3	2	1
20. My sexual behavior and experiences are NOT something I spend time thinking about.	5	4	3	2	1
To score for Sexual Self-Reflection, add items 16–20 and then divide by 5 =					

Sexual Self-Efficacy	Strongly Disagree	Disagree	Neutral	Agree	Strongly Agree
21. If it happened, I know I would be able to be clear about my sexual desires with a partner.	1	2	3	4	5
22. I would not hesitate to ask for what I want sexually from a romantic partner.	1	2	3	4	5
23. I am able to ask a partner to provide the sexual stimulation I need.	1	2	3	4	5
24. If I were to have sex with someone, I'd show my partner what I want.	1	2	3	4	5
To score for Sexual Self-Efficacy, add items 21–24 and then divide by 4 =					

Total score between:

- **4–5** indicates high levels of the subscale
- **3–3.9** indicates moderate levels of the subscale
- **under 3** indicates low levels of the subscale

Note. Reprinted with permission. Authors of the Sexual Subjectivity Inventory are Horne and Zimmer-Gembeck.[*] It has psychometric support, including evidence of reliability and validity, with women and men.[**] Please contact the authors of this measure for permission to use the SSI within research; there is no need to contact them to use it with clients or to complete it on your own.

[*]S. Horne and M. J. Zimmer-Gembeck. The Female Sexual Subjectivity Inventory: Development and Validation of a Multidimensional Inventory for Late Adolescents and Emerging Adults. *Psychol Women Q* 2006; **30**: 125–38.
[**]M. J. Zimmer-Gembeck and J. French. Associations of Sexual Subjectivity with Global and Sexual Wellbeing: A New Measure for Young Males and Comparison to Females. *Arch Sex Behav* 2016; **45**: 315–27.

Sexual Subjectivity Inventory Applications

- If you responded "agree" or "strongly agree" to item 1 (*I worry that I am not sexually desirable to others*) on the Sexual Body Esteem Subscale:

  o How does this worry impact your willingness to participate in sexual relations with others?

  o How does this worry impact your initiation of sexual activity with a partner?

  o If this worry was not present, how might things be different?

- Reflect on your responses to the Sexual Body Esteem Subscale. Challenge yourself to expand your idea of what makes you sexually attractive – go beyond the definition of what society might consider as sexually attractive. Identify qualities and characteristics you respect and admire about yourself and your body, and consider their impact on your attractiveness.

- As you consider your responses to the Entitlement to Sexual Pleasure Subscales (both Self and Partner), reflect on the degree to which self-worth, body shame, body appreciation, and self-compassion may impact the extent to which you feel entitled to sexual pleasure. If you would like your response(s) to these subscales to be different, what is one step you can take towards that goal?

- For item 24 on the Sexual Self-Efficacy Subscale (*If I were to have sex with someone, I'd show my partner what I want*):

  o Are you aware of your sexual desires and needs?

  o How can you communicate those desires and needs during times of intimacy and at other times?

  o What barriers might get in the way of communicating your desires and needs? What strategies can you use to overcome these barriers?

- Consider your overall responses to the Sexual Subjectivity Inventory. Imagine a time in the future when you have greater body connection and appreciation. Reflect on the ways you imagine responding to your sexual desires in more attuned and/or effective ways. What would be different from now, and what is one step to take towards that goal?

Assignment 14.1: Sexual Desires and Needs

My sexual desires and needs include:

_____
_____
_____

I am comfortable expressing these sexual desires and needs:

_____
_____
_____

For these reasons:

_____
_____
_____

I am uncomfortable expressing these sexual desires and needs:

_____
_____
_____

For these reasons:

_____
_____
_____

I plan to do the following in order to meet my sexual desires and needs:

_____
_____
_____

Identifying and expressing sexual desires and needs correspond with positive body image in these ways:

_____
_____
_____

N. L. Wood-Barcalow, T. L. Tylka, and C. L. Judge. *Positive Body Image Workbook: A Clinical and Self-Improvement Guide.* Cambridge: Cambridge University Press, 2021.

Assignment 14.2: Mindful Participation in Sexual Experiences

A key part of a sexual experience is being focused in the moment without worries about the past or future or even what your body looks like. To increase mindfulness, engaging all sensory components such as vision/sight, touch, scent, taste, and sounds can be helpful. For this journal entry, reflect on the following associated with sexual experiences: these are the senses I am most focused on, I'd like to increase or enhance these senses, these are the worries/thoughts/fears that I'd like to be free from, this is how I'd like to feel during sexual experiences, this is how moving toward positive body image might enhance these experiences, and more.

_____
_____
_____
_____
_____
_____
_____
_____
_____
_____
_____

N. L. Wood-Barcalow, T. L. Tylka, and C. L. Judge. *Positive Body Image Workbook: A Clinical and Self-Improvement Guide.* Cambridge: Cambridge University Press, 2021.

Assignment 14.3: Nonsexual Components of a Relationship

Nonsexual aspects of a partnership can have a significant impact on sexual intimacy. These aspects may include communication, power dynamics, sense of connection, openness, emotional intimacy, mutual respect, appreciation, shared household labor, and more. For this assignment, journal about the strengths and positive components of partnerships, both past and current. Identify areas for growth and improvement. If appropriate, share reflections and insights with your current partner.

_____
_____
_____
_____
_____
_____
_____
_____
_____
_____
_____
_____

N. L. Wood-Barcalow, T. L. Tylka, and C. L. Judge. _Positive Body Image Workbook: A Clinical and Self-Improvement Guide._ Cambridge: Cambridge University Press, 2021.

Assignment 14.4: Setting Healthy Limits in Sexual Relationships

Individuals with positive body image identify and set healthy limits and boundaries in sexual relationships. For this journal entry, reflect on the following: these are non-negotiable components of a healthy sexual relationship for me, this is how I *want* to be treated, this is how I *expect* to be treated, I will not tolerate these behaviors/aspects, I will communicate my needs in the following ways, and more. If appropriate, share reflections and insights with your current partner.

N. L. Wood-Barcalow, T. L. Tylka, and C. L. Judge. *Positive Body Image Workbook: A Clinical and Self-Improvement Guide.* Cambridge: Cambridge University Press, 2021.

Assignment 14.5: The Role of Spectatoring

Being distracted during sex with the thoughts of how one's body appears to a partner is known as spectatoring. This focus can interfere with our ability to be in the moment and to experience pleasure.

• I engage in spectatoring on these occasions:

_____

_____

_____

• These are the worries/beliefs that I have about myself in those moments:

_____

_____

_____

• These are the worries/beliefs that I have about my partner(s) in those moments:

_____

_____

_____

• Specatoring impacts my pleasure:

_____

_____

_____

• If spectatoring were not an issue, I would feel:

_____

_____

_____

• If spectatoring were not an issue, I would do:

_____

_____

_____

• Moving toward positive body image includes:

_____

_____

_____

N. L. Wood-Barcalow, T. L. Tylka, and C. L. Judge. *Positive Body Image Workbook: A Clinical and Self-Improvement Guide.* Cambridge: Cambridge University Press, 2021.

Assignment 14.6: Initiation of Physical Intimacy

Our initiation of physical intimacy is related to various issues including, but not limited to, desire, sense of comfort, sense of safety, bodily arousal, energy levels, emotional relationship with partner, and more. Several body image-related issues can also interfere with our initiation of physical intimacy such as an overall negative body image, spectatoring, body surveillance, body checking, and more. For this activity, consider how these issues impact your initiation of physical intimacy.

Issue	Level of Relevance: 0 = Not At All to 10 = Very Important	Reflections	Action Plan for Change(s)
Example: *Spectatoring*	*10*	*I'm too focused on what my body looks like.*	*I'm going to focus on how my body feels in the moment.*
Spectatoring			
Body surveillance			
Focusing on senses			
Feeling safe			
Feeling respected			
Feeling embarrassed, humiliated, or ashamed			
Feeling proud of my body			
Physical connection with my partner			
Emotional connection with my partner			
Body's ability to function in ways that I want it to			
Belief that my partner desires me			
Mutual respect			
Feeling concerned my partner will reject my initiation			
Other:			
Other:			
Other:			

N. L. Wood-Barcalow, T. L. Tylka, and C. L. Judge. *Positive Body Image Workbook: A Clinical and Self-Improvement Guide.* Cambridge: Cambridge University Press, 2021.

Assignment 14.7: Self-Affirmations Related to Sexual Expression

Self-affirmations are positive statements that we say to ourselves to increase self-esteem and confidence. They are effective when they are specific, individualized, genuine, and practiced on a consistent basis. In the space below, write as many self-affirmations as possible specifically related to sexual expression. Make sure that they are actual statements that you are willing to say to yourself as a way to counter negative body image, spectatoring, and/or body surveillance during sexual experiences. Examples could include: "I am worthy to experience sexual pleasure," "My partner desires me," and "I can enjoy this experience even without having complete acceptance of my body."

_____

_____

_____

_____

_____

_____

_____

_____

_____

_____

_____

N. L. Wood-Barcalow, T. L. Tylka, and C. L. Judge. *Positive Body Image Workbook: A Clinical and Self-Improvement Guide.* Cambridge: Cambridge University Press, 2021.

Assignment 14.8: My Definition of Radical Consent

Radical consent is a term that describes mutual engagement in sexual activities among adults without any coercion.[*] This term can also be expanded to include other types of situations. Each person consents to activities that they feel comfortable with in that situation with a particular person. It can vary based on circumstances, environments, individuals, and more.

- My definition of radical consent:

_____

_____

- These are behaviors/activities that *I am comfortable with*:

_____

_____

- These are behaviors that *I am not comfortable with*:

_____

_____

- These are the ways that I can communicate my consent:

_____

_____

- If I experience discomfort in a particular situation, I can:

_____

_____

- If I feel coerced or pressured to do any activity that feels uncomfortable, I can:

_____

_____

- I can remind myself of the following:

_____

_____

- Engaging in radical consent promotes positive body image:

_____

_____

[*]T. L. Tylka and R. M. Calogero. Promoting a Resistant Stance toward Objectification. In: Tylka, T. L. and Piran, N. eds. *Handbook of Positive Body Image and Embodiment: Constructs, Protective Factors, and Interventions*. New York: Oxford University Press, 2019: 149–60.

N. L. Wood-Barcalow, T. L. Tylka, and C. L. Judge. *Positive Body Image Workbook: A Clinical and Self-Improvement Guide.* Cambridge: Cambridge University Press, 2021.

References

1. S. Satinsky, M. Reece, B. Dennis, et al. An assessment of body appreciation and its relationship to sexual function in women. *Body Image* 2012; **9**: 137–44.

2. N. Piran. Embodied possibilities and disruptions: The emergence of the Experience of Embodiment construct from qualitative studies with girls and women. *Body Image* 2016; **18**: 43–60.

3. J. L. Mensinger, T. L. Tylka, and M. E. Calamari. Mechanisms underlying weight status and healthcare avoidance in women: A study of weight stigma, body-related shame and guilt, and healthcare stress. *Body Image* 2018; **25**: 139–47.

4. D. L. Ordaz, L. M. Schaefer, E. Choquette, et al. Thinness pressures in ethnically diverse college women in the United States. *Body Image* 2018; **24**: 1–4.

5. M. M. Davidson and S. J. Gervais. Violence against women through the lens of objectification theory. *Violence Against Women* 2015; **21**: 330–54.

6. B. L. Velez, I. D. Campos, and B. Moradi. Relations of sexual objectification and racist discrimination with Latina women's body image and mental health. *Couns Psychol* 2015; **43**: 906–35.

7. C. Quinn-Nilas, L. Benson, R. R. Milhausen, et al. The relationship between body image and domains of sexual functioning among heterosexual emerging adult women. *J Sex Med* 2016; **4**: e182–9.

8. D. Sanchez and A. Kiefer. Body concerns in and out of the bedroom: Implications for sexual pleasure and problems. *Arch Sex Behav* 2007; **36**: 808–20.

9. T. F. Cash, C. L. Maikkula, and Y. Yamamiya. "Baring the body in the bedroom": Body image, sexual self-schemas, and sexual functioning among college women and men. *Electron J Hum Sex* 2004; 7: 1–9.

10. A. Carvalheira, C. Price, and C. F. Neves. Body awareness and bodily dissociation among those with and without sexual difficulties: Differentiation using the Scale of Body Connection. *J Sex Marital Ther* 2017; **43**: 801–10.

11. M. M. Gillen, E. S. Lefkowitz, and C. L. Shearer. Does body image play a role in risky sexual behavior and attitudes? *J Youth Adolesc* 2006; **35**: 243–55.

12. A. J. Blashill and S. A. Safren. Body dissatisfaction and condom use self-efficacy: A meta-analysis. *Body Image* 2015; **12**: 73–7.

13. I. Melis, P. Litta, L. Napi, et al. Sexual function in women with deep endometriosis: Correlation of quality of life, intensity of pain, depression, anxiety, and body image. *Int J Sex Health* 2015; **27**: 175–85.

14. D. A. Male, K. D. Fergus, and K. Cullen. Sexual identity after breast cancer: Sexuality, body image, and relationship repercussions. *Curr Opin Support Palliat Care* 2016; **10**: 66–74.

15. Y. W. Kahn, F. O'Keeffe, M. Nolan, et al. "Not a whole woman": An interpretative phenomenological analysis of the lived experience of women's body image and sexuality following amputation. *Disabil Rehabil* 2019. https://doi.org/10.1080/09638288.2019.1622797

16. B. L. Fredrickson and T-A. Roberts. Objectification theory: Toward understanding women's lived experiences and mental health risks. *Psychol Women Q* 1997; **21**: 173–206.

17. M. W. Wiederman. Women's body image self-consciousness during physical intimacy with a partner. *J Sex Res* 2000; **37**: 60–8.

18. L. Weiner and C. Avery-Clark. Sensate focus: Clarifying the Masters and Johnson's model. *Sex Relation Ther* 2014; **29**: 307–19.

19. S. Satinsky and V. Ramseyer Winter. Attuned sexuality. In: Tylka, T. L. and Piran, N. eds. *Handbook of Positive Body Image and Embodiment: Constructs, Protective Factors, and Interventions.* New York: Oxford University Press, 2019: 91–101.

20. S. Horne and M. J. Zimmer-Gembeck. The Female Sexual Subjectivity Inventory: Development and validation of a multidimensional inventory for late adolescents and emerging adults. *Psychol Women Q* 2006; **30**: 125–38.

21. M. J. Zimmer-Gembeck and J. French. Associations of sexual subjectivity with global and sexual well-being: A new measure for young males and comparison to females. *Arch Sex Behav* 2016; **45**: 315–27.

22. M. J. Zimmer-Gembeck, W. H. Ducat, and M. A. Boislard-Pepin. A prospective study of young females' sexual subjectivity: Associations with age, sexual behavior, and dating. *Arch Sex Behav* 2011; **40**: 927–38.

23. S. Satinsky and K. N. Jozkowski. Female sexual subjectivity and verbal consent to receiving oral sex. *J Sex Marital Ther* 2015; **41**: 413–26.

24. A. R. Robbins and E. D. Reissing. Appearance dissatisfaction, body appreciation, and sexual health in women across adulthood. *Arch Sex Behav* 2018; **47**: 703–14.

25. V. Ramseyer Winter, M. M. Gillen, and A. K. Kennedy. Associations between body appreciation and comfort communicating about sex: A brief report. *Health Commun* 2016; **33**: 359–62.

26. V. Ramseyer Winter. Toward a relational understanding of objectification, body image, and preventative sexual health. *J Sex Res* 2017; **54**: 341–50.

27. V. Ramseyer Winter and L. R. Ruhr. Body appreciation and contraceptive use among college women: A brief report. *Int J Sex Health* 2016; **29**: 168–72.

28. L. Woertman and F. van den Brink. Body image and female sexual functioning and behavior: A review. *J Sex Res* 2012; **49**: 184–211.

29. L. A. Peplau, D. A. Frederick, C. Yee, et al. Body image satisfaction in heterosexual, gay, and lesbian adults. *Arch Sex Behav* 2009; **38**: 713–25.

30. A. J. Blashill, J. Tomassilli, K. Biello, et al. Body dissatisfaction among sexual minority men: Psychological and sexual health outcomes. *Arch Sex Behav* 2016; **45**: 1241–7.

31. B. A. Jones, E. Haycraft, S. Murjan, et al. Body dissatisfaction and disordered eating in trans people: A systematic review of the literature. *Int Rev Psychiatry* 2016; **28**: 81–94.

32. H. B. Kozee, T. L. Tylka, and L. A. Bauerband. Measuring transgender individuals' comfort with gender identity and appearance: Development and validation of the Transgender Congruence Scale. *Psychol Women Q* 2012; **36**: 179–96.

33. A. A. Owen-Smith, J. Gerth, R. C. Sineath, et al. Association between gender confirmation treatments and perceived gender congruence, body image satisfaction and mental health in a cohort of transgender individuals. *J Sex Med* 2018; **15**: 591–600.

34. K. Wylie and J. Woodcock. Understanding sexual health and HIV in the transgender population. In: Ettner, R., Monstrey, S., and Coleman, E. eds. *Principles of Transgender Medicine and Surgery* (2nd ed.). New York: Routledge, 2016: 318–30.

35. N. Amos and M. McCabe. The importance of feeling sexually attractive: Can it predict an individual's experience of their sexuality and sexual relationships across gender and sexual orientation? *Int J Psychol* 2017; **52**: 354–63.

36. S. L. Bober and V. S. Varela. Sexuality in adult cancer survivors: Challenges and intervention. *J Clin Oncol* 2012; **30**: 3712–19.

37. S. A. Crowley, S. M. Foley, D. Wittmann, et al. Sexual health concerns among cancer survivors: Testing a novel information-need measure among breast and prostate cancer patients. *J Cancer Educ* 2016; **31**: 588–94.

Chapter 15

Social Comparison

Theory and Research Overview

When I (Tracy) was seven years old, I joined the swim team and competed in meets. Toward the end of the last lap, I would always look to my right or left when I came up for a breath to determine how far behind (or ahead) I was to give it my all (or coast in) to the finish. My father, an avid swimmer who watched my performance closely, noticed me comparing myself to others. "What are you doing?" he proclaimed. "That'll slow you down." I was embarrassed he noticed, denied doing it, and then tried to be less obvious. Out of the water, I'd compare the size of my bathing suit and the way it fit my body to that of my peers. If they caught me staring, I would have to come up with something quick like, "your suit is really nice." Even at seven years old, I knew that it wasn't socially acceptable to compare my performance, or appearance, to others.

As a child, I had no idea that everyone engages in social comparison. **Social comparison theory** states that we have a natural drive to measure our progress and standing in life, particularly with regard to the things we highly value [1]. This natural drive can help us gather information: social comparison allows us to understand where we are in relation to others and change our course of action if needed, as well as learn from the struggles and successes of others [2]. After all, knowing others' race times allowed me to determine whether I needed to be competitive and prompted me to develop goals for training. However, social comparison also taxes our mental, physical, and emotional energy [2]. In the race, this loss of energy appeared as nervousness, frustration, and disorientation if I was behind, and an overall disruption in my pace and rhythm. Social comparison can also interfere with motivation; when we are behind others we may "give up," and when we are ahead we may "coast." Further, we may use comparison-based information against ourselves to confirm deeply rooted critical thoughts (e.g., "I'll never be a great swimmer") or to pad our egos (e.g., "At least I'm better than them").

Who are we most likely to compare ourselves against? Our peers often serve as the source of social comparison [3]. Peers can be anyone we view as similar to us in age, gender, race, etc. They may be our friends or family members, people we know personally but are not close to (e.g., acquaintances at school or work, social media "friends" who we have met), and those who we know of but don't know personally (e.g., social media "friends" we haven't met, famous people).

What are the types of comparison? See Table 15.1 for the types of comparison as well as the advantages and disadvantages of each type.

Bodies are often the target of comparison, and the body features we compare are often valued and idealized in society and by those around us. Many of us are taught to place a high value on obtaining and maintaining a lean body, and therefore we may idealize a lean body ideal [6]. The **body ideal** can shift somewhat depending on our other identities (e.g., race, age, sexual orientation, gender identity). For example, while the body ideal for White women is portrayed as thin, fit, and toned [7], the ideal for Black and Latina women may be "thicker" and "curvier" [7-10]. For men, the ideal body is portrayed as muscular, tall, and having very low body fat [11]. Facial features (e.g., eye and nose shape), hair, and skin (color and smoothness) may also be connected to the body ideal due to society valuing certain tones, shapes, sizes, and textures over others [12-13]. The body ideal can be unrealistic to achieve unless we have the genetics for it, yet it is advertised as realistic and achievable when we put in sufficient effort, willpower, and money (e.g., for personal training, cosmetic procedures) [14]. We may or may not endorse the body ideal, which can be determined by our level of exposure to, interaction with, and resistance against body features idealized in society.

If we personally endorse the body ideal, we may chronically monitor our bodies, which is known as **body surveillance** (see Chapter 13) and compare our bodies with others [13]. This second process is referred to as **body comparison** [14]. In an effort to achieve a lean body ideal, we may compare with our peers' eating patterns (**eating comparison**) and exercise habits (**exercise comparison**). We include an abbreviated version of the *Body, Eating, and Exercise Comparison Orientation Measure* (BEECOM [16]) in this chapter for you to understand your level of social comparison.

How does body comparison develop and what are its potential consequences? One theory in particular has identified its role in body dissatisfaction and disordered eating. The **Tripartite Influence Model** [15] suggests that certain people (family, peers, and dating partners) and media influence us to value the body ideal appearance by pressuring us to look like the ideal. When we value this body ideal, then we compare ourselves to others who fit the ideal (upward comparison) or others who don't (downward comparison). These comparisons make appearance prominent in our mind, which prompts us to feel badly about our bodies when we are unable to achieve the ideal. When dissatisfied with our bodies, we may engage in harmful behaviors, such as disordered eating and excessive exercise to try to fit this ideal. Research supports the

Table 15.1 Types of Comparison

Type of Comparison	Description	Advantages	Disadvantages
Upward Comparison	Compare ourselves to others we view as "better off" than us in some way	Motivation to "do better," inspiration, hope, optimism; humility; a sense of direction and focus for goals	Feeling badly about ourselves and our bodies; despair, frustration, hopelessness; attention, time, and energy is spent in the comparison process
Downward Comparison	Compare ourselves to others we view as "worse off" than us in some way	Reassurance that we are not "too bad," gratitude for what we have, keeping things in perspective, recognizing what is not wanted	Guilt for using others to try to feel better about ourselves and our body; egotism, arrogance; attention, time, and energy is spent in the comparison process
Lateral Comparison	Compare ourselves to others we perceive as similar to us in some way	Reassurance that there are others out there who are similar to us	Guilt for using others to reassure ourselves that others are like us; attention, time, and energy is spent in the comparison process

Tripartite Influence Model with adolescent girls [15], women [17–18], and men [19].

To measure social comparison, most researchers have either used experimental studies that show participants images (e.g., attractive models in advertisements) and measure the effects of viewing these images on body image and mood, or have asked participants to retrospectively recall how often they engage in comparison. An alternative, newer method to measure social comparison is **ecological momentary assessment (EMA)**. In EMA studies, participants complete brief surveys multiple times a day regarding specific experiences in their daily lives [20]. These surveys are completed using a Smartphone app, computer, or tablet. EMA studies are novel, useful, and highly generalizable to "real life" (i.e., not studied within an experimental lab). Results from EMA studies show that women are more likely to compare themselves to others they perceive as more attractive (upward), than they are to others they perceive as equally attractive (lateral) or to others they perceive as less attractive (downward) [3, 21]. Of the three, upward body comparisons consistently are found to have the most negative effects on body image and mood [3, 21–22].

It is also important to consider the various contexts of comparisons. Whereas we are more likely to compare our bodies to people we interact with (in-person comparisons), we also compare ourselves with those we see on social media and traditional media (e.g., TV, magazines), and most of these comparisons are upward [20]. While in-person and traditional media comparisons are both harmful to body image, social media comparisons have been shown to be even more harmful [20]. Social media literacy underscores the comparison processes that may be activated due to the use of filters that smooth out wrinkles in the skin, reverse the discoloration of blemishes, make the skin and eyes brighter, as well as viewing the "likes" and comments on pictures. For example, when we view an image of an attractive peer or celebrity on social media, the number of "likes" and positive appearance-related comments from others may reinforce their attractiveness, which could

prompt more negative perceptions of our own bodies and decreases in our moods. This process may happen regardless if we are satisfied with our appearance or not [20], demonstrating the need to increase social media literacy for all users. Indeed, the more selfies were perceived to be edited via "filters," the less viewers valued societal standards of attractiveness [23]. **Note for clinicians:** Social media literacy is an important issue to address in therapy focused on body image, given the increasing popularity and accessibility of it [24] (see also Chapter 4).

Importantly, social media posts often contain appearance-related "inspiration" in the forms of "thinspiration" and "fitspiration" [25–27]. **Thinspiration** content contains idealized images of excessively thin bodies, glorification of extreme dieting, and emotional support for individuals struggling to maintain their thinness-oriented attitudes and behaviors. **Fitspiration** content contains idealized images of overly fit and lean bodies with visible muscle tone, glorification of exercise and fat loss in the name of health, and emotional support for individuals who wish to "chisel" their bodies. Both thinspiration and fitspiration are widespread in photo-based social media [25]. They both encourage body, eating, and exercise comparisons, and are linked to body dissatisfaction and negative mood both for individuals with and without eating disorders [22, 25, 27]. It is important to recognize that, while fitspiration content appears innocent, it can be damaging due to the upward social comparison process it evokes [22].

Overall, everyday life permits numerous opportunities for body, eating, and exercise comparisons. While it is a natural process, it can be damaging to body image and mood, in particular, if we are comparing our bodies to individuals we view as more attractive. It appears that a high level of body appreciation [28–29], self-compassion [30], and media literacy [31] may disrupt the connection between appearance comparisons, decreased body image, and negative mood (see Chapters 4, 8, and 10). We predict that building a strong protective filter and broadly conceptualizing beauty may also disrupt this connection (see

Chapters 7 and 17). While research has not yet investigated our engagement in body comparison with ourselves at a younger age (e.g., we look at pictures of ourselves from years ago and wish we looked like that now), this too may impact our body image given that youth is valued in Western culture. The assignments in this chapter contain strategies that target these variables.

Treatment Planning Tools

Talking Points in Sessions

- Discuss the costs/benefits of upward, downward, and lateral comparisons
- Identify how frequently comparison occurs and with what groups and types of people
- Consider how mood is impacted when the client engages in social comparison
- Address how comparison to self or others corresponds with body checking behaviors
- Address how comparison is related to avoidant behaviors (e.g., refusing to do certain activities, not wearing certain types of clothes)
- Discuss the role of family members in supporting specific beauty ideals or standards and promoting comparison

Treatment Plan

Goals

❏ Decrease my overall focus on others' bodies

❏ Decrease comparison with my former self (what I looked like in the past) or future self (what I anticipate to look like in the future)

❏ Decrease the amount of unhelpful time I spend on social media platforms

❏ Increase my participation in activities that are not focused on comparison

❏ Identify different forms of body checking behaviors that occur when I find myself engaged in comparison

❏ Increase my awareness of how appearance ideals are related to both positive and negative body image

❏ Reduce my tendency to compare myself to attractive others

❏ Reduce my tendency to compare myself to those I perceive as less attractive

❏ Recognize how media promotes body dissatisfaction for various corporate gains

❏ Analyze media images for direct and/or indirect messages about body image

Objectives

❏ Monitor the amount of time I spend engaged in comparison (daily, weekly, monthly)

❏ Recognize when I'm engaging in comparison in the moment and investigate the purpose

❏ At least one time, refrain from acting on urges to body check that arise after comparing to someone else

❏ Identify three ways I am grateful for my body when I engage in upward comparison

❏ Identify three ways I am grateful for my body when I engage in lateral comparison

❏ Consider the various sources that have shaped my body ideal(s)

❏ Take a deep breath and count to ten when I am tempted to compare my body, eating, or exercise habits with someone else (e.g., friend, media figure)

❏ Identify the range of emotions I experience upon engaging in comparison

❏ Read inspiring information from others about their journey from negative to positive body image

❏ Identify positive portrayals of positive body image in the media

❏ Watch inspiring videos like Smart Girls at the Party (https://amysmartgirls.com/smart-girls-at-the-party-1214fec9d8b2)

Additional Resources

R. Scritchfield. *Body Kindness*. New York: Workman Publishing Co., Inc., 2016. Podcast available at: www.bodykindnessbook.com/podcast/

C. Sobczak. *Embody: Learning to Love Your Unique Body (and Quiet That Critical Voice!)*. Carlsbad: Gurze Books, 2014.

A. D. Brashich. *All Made Up: A Girl's Guide to Seeing through the Celebrity Hype and Celebrating Real Beauty*. New York: Walker Publishing Company, Inc., 2006.

Assessment 15.1: The Body, Eating, and Exercise Comparison Orientation Measure-Revised (BEECOM-R)*

Below you will find a list of statements. Please rate the truth of each statement as it applies to you using the following rating scale. For instance, if you believe that a statement is "Always" true, you would write a 7 next to that statement.

1	2	3	4	5	6	7
Never	Almost Never	Seldom	Sometimes	Often	Almost Always	Always

	Number
1. In social situations, I think about how my body "matches up" to the bodies of those around me.	
2. I notice how I compare with my peers in terms of specific parts of the body (e.g., stomach, legs, arms, breasts or chest, hair, etc.).	
3. I compare my body shape to that of my peers.	
Total Body Comparison score: add items 1–3 and divide by 3 =	
4. During meals, I compare what I am eating to what others are eating.	
5. I find myself thinking about how my food choices compare with the food choices of my peers.	
6. When I go out to eat, I pay attention to how much I am eating compared to other people.	
Total Eating Comparison score: add items 4–6 and divide by 3 =	
7. I pay close attention when I hear peers talking about exercise (in order to determine if I am exercising as much as they are).	
8. I like to know how often my friends are working out so I can figure out if the number of times I work out "matches up."	
9. When I exercise (e.g., at the gym, running outdoors), I pay attention to the intensity level of the workouts of those around me.	
Total Exercise Comparison score: add items 7–9 and divide by 3 =	

Total subscale scores between:

- **4–7** = high body, eating, or exercise comparison
- **3–3.9** = moderate body, eating, or exercise comparison
- **below 3** = low body, eating, or exercise comparison

Note. Reprinted with permission. The BEECOM-R contains nine of the original eighteen items presented in the BEECOM. Authors of the original BEECOM are Fitzsimmons-Craft, Bardone-Cone, and Harney. Items 1 and 2 were modified with permission to be gender inclusive. The measurement properties of this scale (reliability and validity) have been supported with individuals with and without eating disorders. Authors of the BEECOM-R are Saunders, Eaton, and Fitzsimmons-Craft.** Please contact the authors of the BEECOM-R for permission to use it within research; there is no need to contact them to use it with clients or to complete it on your own.

*E. E. Fitzsimmons-Craft, A. M. Bardone-Cone, and M. B. Harney. Development and Validation of the Body, Eating, and Exercise Comparison Orientation Measure (BEECOM) among College Women. *Body Image* 2012; **9**: 476–87.
J. F. Saunders, A. A. Eaton, and E. E. Fitzsimmons-Craft. Body-, Eating-, and Exercise-Related Comparisons during Eating Disorder Recovery and Validation of the BEECOM-R. *Psychol Women Q* 2019; **43: 494–508.

The Body, Eating, and Exercise Comparison Orientation Measure Applications

- Notice how much time you spend comparing your body/eating/exercise with others based on your responses to this assessment. Do the comparisons result in negative feelings and thoughts? Do the comparisons result in destructive behaviors?

- Notice who are the people that you tend to compare yourself with such as age, body type, gender, abilities, etc. What happens when you compare yourself to others who do not fit into these categories? What is the impact on your self-worth?

- For item 2 (*I notice how I compare with my peers in terms of specific parts of the body (e.g., stomach, legs, arms, breasts or chest, hair, etc.)*), identify the specific body parts that you tend to focus on when you compare your body with others. How do you feel after the comparison(s)?

- Regarding your responses to items in the Eating Comparison subscale, do you tend to compare what and/or how much you eat when around others? If so:

  ○ What is that experience like for you?

  ○ How does it impact your choices while eating?

  ○ How do the comparisons impact your eating habits when alone and when eating with others (e.g., restricting in advance of eating with others, eating smaller portions or different types of food in front of others, emotional eating when alone)?

  ○ What would it be like to redirect your attention from comparison with others to your own experience (e.g., listening to your body throughout your eating experience)?

  ○ Refer to Chapter 20.

- Regarding your responses to items in the Exercise Comparison subscale, do you tend to compare what or how much activity you engage in when around others? If so:

  ○ What is that experience like for you?

  ○ How does it impact your decisions while exercising?

  ○ How do the comparisons impact your sense of satisfaction following the activity?

  ○ What would it be like to redirect your attention from comparison with others to your own experience (e.g., listening to your body throughout your exercise/activity session)?

  ○ Refer to Chapter 21.

- Reflect on how your responses to the BEECOM-R may correspond with self-destructive behaviors: restriction of food, pushing yourself beyond comfortable limits when exercising, avoiding pleasurable foods or activities, self-blaming, punishing yourself if an expectation isn't met, and more.

- After completing this assessment, imagine it is the future and you experience positive body image. Now complete this assessment a second time using a different colored pen/pencil from that perspective. Compare your responses between now and in the imaginary future. What do you notice? How might things be different? What would you like to change?

Assignment 15.1: Comparison to Self

For this assignment, consider how often you compare your current body with your former body or future body.

Comparison with Former Body

How often do I compare my current body with my *former* body? Examples include comparing to certain ages, life experiences, or significant life events.

_____

_____

What are the *benefits* of doing this type of comparison?

_____

_____

What are the *costs* of doing this type of comparison?

_____

_____

How do I *feel* when making these types of comparisons with myself?

_____

_____

What is the *purpose* of doing this type of comparison?

_____

_____

Comparison with Future Body

How often do I compare my current body with my *future* body? Examples include anticipating what my body will look like, how it will function, and whether I will be satisfied with it.

_____

_____

What are the *benefits* of doing this type of comparison?

_____

_____

What are the *costs* of doing this type of comparison?

_____

_____

How do I *feel* when making these types of comparisons with myself?

_____

_____

What is the *purpose* of doing this type of comparison?

_____

_____

Overall Reflections

What I notice about self-comparisons:

_____

_____

How self-comparison impacts my movement toward positive body image:

_____

_____

N. L. Wood-Barcalow, T. L. Tylka, and C. L. Judge. *Positive Body Image Workbook: A Clinical and Self-Improvement Guide.* Cambridge: Cambridge University Press, 2021.

Assignment 15.2: Comparison with Others

Comparison with Friends, Family, Acquaintances, and Others

I engage in upward comparison (of body, eating, and/or exercise) with these people:

_____
_____

I notice that I feel this way after comparing myself with these people:

_____
_____

I notice that I think these things after comparing myself with these people:

_____
_____

I notice that I do these things after comparing myself with these people:

_____
_____

I engage in *downward comparison* (of body, eating, and/or exercise) with these people:

_____
_____

I notice that I feel this way after comparing myself with these people:

_____
_____

I notice that I think these things after comparing myself with these people:

_____
_____

I notice that I do these things after comparing myself with these people:

_____
_____

Comparison with Media Personalities, Influencers, TV/Movie Stars, Musicians

I engage in **upward comparison** (of body, eating, and/or exercise) with these particular individuals from media:

_____
_____

I notice that I feel this way after comparing myself with these people:

_____
_____

I notice that I think these things after comparing myself with these people:

_____
_____

I notice that I do these things after comparing myself with these people:

_____
_____

I engage in **downward comparison** (of body, eating, and/or exercise) with these particular individuals from media:

_____
_____

N. L. Wood-Barcalow, T. L. Tylka, and C. L. Judge. *Positive Body Image Workbook: A Clinical and Self-Improvement Guide.* Cambridge: Cambridge University Press, 2021. **225**

I notice that I feel this way after comparing myself with these people:

_____

_____

I notice that I think these things after comparing myself with these people:

_____

_____

I notice that I do these things after comparing myself with these people:

_____

_____

Overall Reflections

What I notice about comparisons with others:

_____

_____

How self-comparison impacts my movement toward positive body image:

_____

_____

N. L. Wood-Barcalow, T. L. Tylka, and C. L. Judge. *Positive Body Image Workbook: A Clinical and Self-Improvement Guide.* Cambridge: Cambridge University Press, 2021.

Assignment 15.3: Mind Reading

Mind reading occurs when we think we know what other people think and feel. Typically, mindreading takes the form of negative thoughts ("He sees me as ugly," "She thinks I'm stupid") and emotions (embarrassment, shame, fear). Mindreading is associated with body comparison ("She won't be interested in me because I'm not as muscular as others"). If we convince ourselves that this information is true, then it can result in uncomfortable experiences such as feeling bad about ourselves, feeling apprehensive, avoiding certain people/activities including things we enjoy, isolating ourselves, and even damaging relationships with others.

Review the types of mindreading examples below and indicate whether you have had this thought (or something similar to it). If you respond "yes," then challenge that thought. Write in your own examples of mindreading in the "other" slots and challenge those too.

Mind Reading	Yes/No	Challenge It
Example: *They think I'm ugly.*	*Yes*	*I don't know what they think is attractive.*
They think I'm ugly.		
They are disgusted by me.		
They think I'm not smart.		
They are going to laugh at me if I wear that.		
They don't want to be seen with someone like me.		
I embarrass them.		
I can't ever be good enough for them.		
Other:		
Other:		
Other:		

N. L. Wood-Barcalow, T. L. Tylka, and C. L. Judge. *Positive Body Image Workbook: A Clinical and Self-Improvement Guide.* Cambridge: Cambridge University Press, 2021.

Assignment 15.4: Investment in Comparison

For this assignment, reflect on how much time is spent comparing yourself with others in terms of appearance, eating habits, and exercise patterns.

Estimated time spent comparing myself to others on a daily and weekly basis in terms of minutes/hours (e.g., 120 minutes/day, 14 hours/week) or percentage of the day:

_____
_____

Of the time spent comparing with others, I feel *better* about myself this amount of time:

_____

Of the time spent comparing with others, I feel *worse* about myself this amount of time:

_____

What I notice about/realizations from my answers above:

_____
_____
_____
_____
_____

I would like to change or modify these things:

_____
_____
_____
_____
_____

I intend to shift my focus from comparing myself with others by doing the following:

_____
_____
_____
_____
_____

N. L. Wood-Barcalow, T. L. Tylka, and C. L. Judge. *Positive Body Image Workbook: A Clinical and Self-Improvement Guide.* Cambridge: Cambridge University Press, 2021.

Assignment 15.5: How I Feel on Days with Significant Comparison

These are typical thoughts I have associated with comparison:

_____
_____
_____

These are the typical emotions I have associated with comparison:

_____
_____
_____

These are the things that I typically do in response to comparison:

_____
_____
_____

I notice that these thoughts and emotions increase my discomfort:

_____
_____
_____

I notice that these thoughts and emotions decrease my discomfort:

_____
_____
_____

I commit to the following effective ways to manage comparison when it occurs:

_____
_____
_____
_____
_____
_____
_____
_____
_____
_____
_____

N. L. Wood-Barcalow, T. L. Tylka, and C. L. Judge. _Positive Body Image Workbook: A Clinical and Self-Improvement Guide._ Cambridge: Cambridge University Press, 2021.

References

1. L. Festinger. A theory of social comparison processes. *Hum Relat* 1957; **7**: 117–40.

2. J. Suhls and T. A. Willis, eds. *Social Comparison: Contemporary Theory and Research*. Hillsdale: Lawrence Erlbaum Associates, 1991.

3. T. M. Leahey, J. H. Crowther, and K. D. Mickelson. The frequency, nature, and effects of naturally occurring appearance-focused social comparisons. *Behav Ther* 2007; **38**: 132–43.

4. M. M. Harris, F. Anseel, and F. Lievens. Keeping up with the Joneses: A field study of the relationships among upward, lateral, and downward comparisons and pay level satisfaction. *J Appl Psychol* 2008; **93**: 665–73.

5. K. S. O'Brien, P. Caputi, R. Minto, et al. Upward and downward physical appearance comparisons: Development of scales and examination of predictive qualities. *Body Image* 2009; **6**: 201–6.

6. K. Harrison. Media and the body. In: Nabi, R. L. and Oliver, M. B., eds. *The Sage Handbook of Media Processes and Effects*. Thousand Oaks: Sage Publications, Inc., 2009: 393–408.

7. S. Parker, M. Nichter, M. Nichter, et al. Body image and weight concerns among African American and White adolescent females: Differences that make a difference. *Hum Organ* 1995; **54**: 103–14.

8. S. M. McClure. Body image among African Americans. In: Cash, T. F., ed. *Encyclopedia of Body Image and Human Appearance*. San Diego: Elsevier Academic Press, 2012: 89–94.

9. D. Schooler, L. S. Lowry, and J. N. Biesen. Body image among Hispanics/Latinos. In: Cash, T. F., ed. *Encyclopedia of Body Image and Human Appearance*. San Diego: Elsevier Academic Press, 2012: 108–13.

10. N. M. Overstreet, D. M. Quinn, and V. Bee Agocha. Beyond thinness: The influence of a curvaceous body ideal on body dissatisfaction in Black and White women. *Sex Roles* 2010; **63**: 91–103.

11. T. L. Tylka, D. Bergeron, and J. P. Schwartz. Development and psychometric evaluation of the Male Body Attitudes Scale. *Body Image* 2005; **2**: 161–75.

12. N. Craddock. Colour me beautiful: Examining the shades related to global skin tone ideals. *J Aesthetic Nursing* 2016; **5**: 6.

13. B. H. Ching and J. T. Xu. Understanding cosmetic surgery consideration in Chinese adolescent girls: Contributions of materialism and sexual objectification. *Body Image* 2019; **28**: 6–15.

14. P. Markula. Beyond the perfect body: Women's body image distortion in fitness magazine discourse. *J Sport Soc Issues* 2001; **25**: 158–79.

15. H. Keery, P. van den Berg, and J. K. Thompson. An evaluation of the Tripartite Influence Model of body dissatisfaction and eating disturbance with adolescent girls. *Body Image* 2004; **1**: 237–51.

16. E. E. Fitzsimmons-Craft, A. M. Bardone-Cone, and M. B. Harney. Development and validation of the Body, Eating, and Exercise Comparison Orientation Measure (BEECOM) among college women. *Body Image* 2012; **9**: 476–87.

17. R. Rodgers, H. Chabrol, and S. J. Paxton. An exploration of the Tripartite Influence Model of body dissatisfaction and disordered eating among Australian and French college women. *Body Image* 2011; **8**: 208–25.

18. M. E. Lovering, R. F. Rodgers, J. E. George, et al. Exploring the tripartite influence model of body dissatisfaction in postpartum women. *Body Image* 2018; **24**: 44–54.

19. T. L. Tylka. Refinement of the tripartite influence model for men: Dual body image pathways to body change behaviors. *Body Image* 2011; **8**: 199–207.

20. J. Fardouly, R. T. Pinkus, and L. R. Vartanian. The impact of appearance comparisons made through social media, traditional media, and in person in women's everyday lives. *Body Image* 2017; **20**: 31–9.

21. T. Leahey and J. Crowther. An ecological momentary assessment of comparison target as a moderator of the effects of appearance-focused social comparisons. *Body Image* 2008; **5**: 307–18.

22. M. Tiggemann and M. Zaccardo. "Exercise to be fit, not skinny": The effect of fitspiration imagery on women's body image. *Body Image* 2015; **15**: 61–7.

23. M. A. Vendemia and D. C. DeAndrea. The effect of viewing thin, sexualized selfies on Instagram: Investigating the role of image source and awareness of photo editing practices. *Body Image* 2018; **27**: 118–27.

24. N. C. Tamplin, S. A. McLean, and S. J. Paxton. Social media literacy protects against the negative impact of exposure to appearance ideal social media images in young adult women but not men. *Body Image* 2018; **26**: 29–37.

25. S. Griffiths, D. Castle, M. Cunningham, et al. How does exposure to thinspiration and fitspiration relate to symptom severity among individuals with eating disorders? Evaluation of a proposed model. *Body Image* 2018; **27**: 187–95.

26. M. Tiggemann, O. Churches, L. Mitchell, et al. Tweeting weight loss: A comparison of #thinspiration and #fitspiration communities on Twitter. *Body Image* 2018; **25**: 133–8.

27. I. Prichard, A. C. McLachlan, T. Lavis, et al. The impact of different forms of #fitspiration imagery on body image, mood, and self-objectification among young women. *Sex Roles* 2018; **78**: 789–98.

28. E. Halliwell. The impact of thin idealized media images on body satisfaction: Does body appreciation protect women from negative effects? *Body Image* 2013; **10**: 509–14.

29. R. Andrew, M. Tiggemann, and L. Clark. The protective role of body appreciation against media-induced body dissatisfaction. *Body Image* 2015; **15**: 98–104.

30. K. J. Homan and T. L. Tylka. Self-compassion moderates body comparison and appearance self-worth's inverse relationships with body appreciation. *Body Image* 2015; **15**: 1–7.

31. Y. Yamamiya, T. F. Cash, S. E. Melnyk, et al. Women's exposure to thin-and-beautiful media images: Body image effects of media-ideal internalization and impact-reduction interventions. *Body Image* 2005; **2**: 74–80.

Body Talk

Theory and Research Overview

Imagine that someone we care about, perhaps a good friend, a child, or our romantic partner exclaims, "I hate my body! My stomach is too big." We hear frustration and disgust in their voice. We may be able to relate to the depth of how they feel, as we may have similar feelings towards our own bodies at times. We want them to feel better. We want to reassure them. Maybe we want to *normalize* their concerns by letting them know that we also have body concerns. We may even think, "Wow, if they see their own body that way, what do they think of mine?" We feel pressure to respond. In the midst of experiencing these internal reactions, what do we say to them?

In these situations, we may be inclined to draw from our own body concerns. For example, we may respond by saying, "OMG! Your stomach is flat! I wish I had your stomach" or "Wow, you think your stomach is big? Look at mine!" We also may try to change their perception of their appearance by telling them, "Your stomach looks smaller to me. I really think you've lost weight and toned up!" followed by, "Tell me how you did it, as I need to do something about my body!" They may experience similar internal reactions to our response and exclaim, "No you don't! In fact, you are looking like you've lost weight!" to try to make us feel better about our bodies. Conversations like these may lower frustration and disgust with our bodies temporarily [1]. However, long term, these conversations create a cycle that reinforces the importance of appearance to self-concept, which is detrimental to the well-being and body image for everyone involved in the conversation (i.e., the discloser of the body concern and recipients of this concern) [1–4].

This appearance-focused type of conversation was originally referred to as **fat talk** by Mimi Nichter to describe the "social phenomenon" of White women speaking negatively with each other about the weight, size, and shape of their bodies [5–6]. However, it was expanded to **negative body talk** to acknowledge that such conversations also occur about many other appearance issues [7–9], for example, the desire to look "cut" (i.e., muscular) and have a "thick bottom," that may occur in various genders, cultures, and generations. Given that many cultures stigmatize being fat, body fat is associated with shame and guilt and thus becomes a frequent source of negative body talk (see Chapter 5).

How can we identify conversations that contain negative body talk? These conversations are complex and may take varied forms, and they can occur more directly, such as in person, or more indirectly, such as within social media. They

typically include people disparaging their bodies and/or speaking with each other about their bodies in a negative manner [2–4]. We may respond by talking poorly about our bodies because we believe that mutual participation in negative body talk will make the other person (the "discloser") feel better. After all, the discloser may be expressing their body concerns to open the door for empathy and reassurance from others that their body concerns are normal. Thus, we likely feel pressure to engage in negative body talk, even though we may find it uncomfortable [5]. We also may feel a burden or a responsibility to lift the spirits of the person who talks about their body in a negative manner, even when we don't want to reciprocate the body talk – perhaps we are tired of making negative comments about ourselves and do not want to end the conversation feeling negatively about our bodies. The more we are exposed to negative body talk, the more we are likely to engage in it ourselves [2], which reinforces the need to surround ourselves with others that have a positive body image and engage in self-accepting body talk (see Chapter 17). To understand the extent to which you participate in negative body talk, complete the *Negative Body Talk Scale* within this chapter. **Note**: A female version and a male version are provided as a current gender-neutral version does not exist; however, if you do not identify as female or male, we encourage you to respond to one or both measures. You can replace "women/she/her" and "men/he/his/him" with "people/they/them/their" within the items and directions [7–8].

Who is more likely to engage in body talk, and what are its consequences for well-being? Body talk is common across people of different ages, genders, body sizes, and ethnicities [9–16], although some groups may experience it less. For example, in an age-diverse sample in the US, Black women and men reported less negative body talk and more positive body talk compared to White, Hispanic, and Asian women and men [16]. However, regardless of ethnicity, gender, age, and weight, *those who participate in negative body talk report increased body dissatisfaction and emotional distress* [2, 4, 12–14, 17–19]. In fact, the consequences of negative body talk among men are comparable to those identified among women [13]. Importantly, some people may be more vulnerable to the harmful effects of body talk than others. For example, women who habitually monitor their appearance (see Chapter 13) are especially vulnerable to increased body dissatisfaction when they overhear someone engaging in negative body talk [18].

What are the effects of negative body talk on children? Here, we would like to acknowledge a particular type of negative body talk that includes a child as the recipient. For instance, a parent or older sibling may engage in negative body talk with a younger child, who may or may not respond with additional negative body talk. This type of conversation has been shown to be quite harmful to children [1]. For example, parents' tendency to make negative comments about their own weight is associated with daughters' higher disordered eating behaviors [20–21] and lower body appreciation, body functionality, and mindful eating [22]. That is, the *more that children are exposed to parental negative body talk, the more they engage in disordered eating behaviors and the less likely they are to eat mindfully and appreciate their body*, both generally and in terms of its functionality. Negative body talk in front of children may send indirect messages that they, too, should feel ashamed about the size and shape of their body. Examples here may include parental encouragement to diet to "avoid looking like me," parents stating that they hide their "bad body areas" with clothing, and telling children, "we can't trust ourselves around tasty food" [20, 22]. Importantly, children often model their parents' body talk. Research involving a sample of mothers and daughters has revealed that daughters model how mothers speak about their bodies – when mothers talk negatively about their bodies, daughters do the same, and when mothers talk positively about their bodies, so do their daughters [23].

What can we do to avoid negative body talk conversations? Importantly, we can commit to not being the discloser of negative body talk. Whenever we feel badly about our bodies and need reassurance, or just to vent, we can practice some of the many assignments within this workbook to uncover the source of our negative feelings, treat ourselves with compassion, pursue behaviors we value and/or build our positive body image, and reflect on this experience. We can also reduce our likelihood of being the recipient of negative body talk conversations. To do this, we can monitor which relationships are more (and less) likely to contain negative body talk conversations, and interact more frequently with those who do not engage in negative body talk. Indeed, when women interact with others who are not focused on their bodies (i.e., who do not engage in negative body talk), they experience greater body appreciation, intuitive eating, and less dietary restraint over the course of a week [24]. These effects remain even when women interact with people who did engage in negative-body talk during this time. This finding suggests that *interacting with others who are not focused on their bodies is protective* in that it can lessen the negative impact of overhearing negative body talk when it does occur.

For the relationships that we want or need to maintain that include consistent negative body talk, we may want to share how we feel to the discloser and discuss the detrimental impacts of negative body talk with them. A challenging response may be, "Come on, don't be silly! I know we say things like that, but I wish we wouldn't. Media want us to believe that our appearance is the most important thing about us, but it isn't. The kind of person we are is much

more important." Other options may include ignoring (or redirecting) negative body talk by changing the subject, reassuring the discloser (e.g., "You are definitely not fat, you look great just the way you are!"), and reciprocating the talk (e.g., "If you think you're fat, I must be huge. I can't believe you are saying that about your thighs, I would love to have your legs instead of my chubby ones!"). Of these four types, challenging body talk directly seems to reduce shame and enhance support for the discloser [25]. Reassuring the discloser and reciprocating the talk may backfire, as they could reinforce negative body talk in the future. How we respond to negative body talk conversations is dependent on many factors, such as our energy at the time, the context (e.g., a holiday dinner), our cultures, our personalities, our relationships with the discloser, and more. It is important that we remain compassionate toward ourselves with our choice of response and perhaps have stock phrases available or plans on how to respond in the future.

What about positive body talk? Is talking positively about our bodies, such as in a self-accepting way, linked to a more positive body image? Indeed, it is! The more frequently we speak positively about our bodies, the higher our body satisfaction and self-esteem [26]. Therefore, the next time we find ourselves wanting to participate in negative body talk, we can reframe (or change) it to be positive. For example, instead of saying or thinking, "I hate the size of my arms," we can replace this thought with "My arms are strong and allow me to carry my children." Will others be receptive to positive body talk? Research has shown that people are liked more when they speak positively about their bodies and indicate that they accept their bodies [27]. Thus, engaging in positive body talk may be another way to counteract the impact of negative body talk.

In sum, negative body talk is inconsistent with having a positive body image. Negative body talk can "spill over" to others who overhear it, prompting them to feel badly about their bodies. To feel better about our bodies, and encourage others to do the same, we can challenge negative body talk (or if this is uncomfortable, find a way to respond that honors your experience and style), explore strategies to manage our internal reactions to negative body talk, and engage in self-accepting body talk. The assignments in this workbook will help you on this journey.

Treatment Planning Tools

Talking Points for Sessions

- Discuss the frequency of negative body talk and its impact on self-esteem and positive body image
- Identify individuals in the client's life who engage in negative body talk and those who engage in positive body talk
- Consider when, where, and how the client is exposed to negative body talk
- Identify the ultimate aims of reassurance-seeking body talk
- Discuss instances of feeling pressured to engage in body talk and effective ways to respond

Treatment Plan

Goals

- ❏ Increase awareness of the frequency and impact of body talk
- ❏ Refrain from engaging in negative body talk with others
- ❏ Refrain from initiating negative body talk with others
- ❏ Consider effective ways of responding when people are making negative comments about their own or others' bodies
- ❏ Reduce exposure to social media profiles/sites/platforms that contain negative body talk
- ❏ Investigate the degree to which people claiming to promote positive body image and positive body talk are actually doing that, rather than promoting another agenda
- ❏ Decrease reassurance-seeking about the acceptability of my body
- ❏ Increase comments about self-acceptance
- ❏ Increase self-accepting body talk
- ❏ Redirect to my core values when my body focus is strong
- ❏ Notice how I typically respond after engaging in or witnessing negative body talk
- ❏ Reduce my use of appearance-based language
- ❏ Reduce negative body talk when around children
- ❏ Help children to change negative body talk

Objectives

- ❏ Learn how to challenge negative body talk of others by using media literacy and positive body image tips
- ❏ Recognize patterns associated with body talk situations including who I am usually with, whether I feel pressured to engage in this type of talk, what purpose it serves, and how I feel during and after
- ❏ Identify concrete ways to respond to or challenge negative body talk when it is directed at me and/or someone I care about
- ❏ Investigate the impact of body talk on my self-esteem and positive body image

- ❏ Reduce or eliminate talking negatively about others' bodies (types, shapes, weight, fat distribution, muscle mass)
- ❏ Investigate whether the "real issue" is about my body or if I could be feeling uncomfortable about something else (e.g., relationship concerns, feeling incompetent at work or school, or other non-body-related difficulties)
- ❏ Remind myself of my good qualities
- ❏ Remind myself that I can influence the impact of negative body talk
- ❏ Practice mindfulness when body talk occurs
- ❏ Do something kind for myself when experiencing internal negative body talk
- ❏ Recognize how I can experience negative thoughts and emotions related to negative body image without engaging in negative behaviors or actions (i.e., voicing the negative body talk)
- ❏ Remind myself that my negative feelings which occur in response to overhearing negative body talk are temporary
- ❏ Consider the sense of "burden" that corresponds with negative body talk
- ❏ Identify specific thoughts, emotions, and behaviors experienced upon receiving negative body talk comments, especially from respected or loved ones
- ❏ Journal about the importance of appearance in society and how it is a focus of many conversations in various situations/environments
- ❏ Identify my motives for engaging in body talk (e.g., feeling pressured, wanting to participate in conversation, seeking reassurance from others, wanting to connect with others)
- ❏ Teach children specific techniques on how to respond to the negative body talk of others

Additional Resources

D. Martz. *Fat Talk: A Feminist Perspective*. Jefferson: McFarland & Company, Inc., Publishers, 2019.

M. Nichter. *Fat Talk: What Girls and Their Parents Say About Dieting*. Cambridge, MA: Harvard University Press, 2000.

Assessment 16.1: Negative Body Talk Scale (NBTS): Female Version

We're interested in the types of things women say about their bodies when they're talking to other people. Remember, we're not interested in how often you have thoughts like this. Instead, we're interested in how often you *SAY things like this aloud* when you're with others. Even if you wouldn't use these exact words, we're interested in whether you say similar things (that mean the same thing) when you're with others.

Use the following scale to indicate how frequently you SAY things like the statements below. Please write the number to the right of the item.

1	2	3	4	5	6	7
Never	Rarely	Occasionally	Sometimes	Frequently	Usually	Always

When talking with your friends, how often do you SAY things like . . .	Number
1. I wish my body looked like hers.	
2. I need to go on a diet.	
3. I feel fat.	
4. She has a perfect stomach.	
5. This outfit makes me look fat.	
6. Why can't my body look like hers?	
7. She has a perfect body.	
8. I need to start watching what I eat.	
9. She's in such good shape.	
10. I wish I was thinner.	
11. I wish my abs looked like hers.	
12. I think I'm getting fat.	
13. You never have to worry about gaining weight.	
Total Negative Body Talk score: add items 1–13 and divide by 13 =	

Total Negative Body Talk score between:
- **4–7** = high levels of negative body talk
- **2–3.9** = moderate levels of negative body talk
- **below 2** = low levels of negative body talk

Note. Reprinted with permission. Authors of the NBTS are Engeln-Maddox, Salk, and Miller.* Its measurement properties (reliability and validity) have been supported with ethnically diverse samples of women.** Please contact the authors of the NBTS for permission to use it within research; there is no need to contact them to use it with clients or to complete it on your own.

*R. Engeln-Maddox, R. H. Salk, and S. A. Miller. Assessing Women's Negative Commentary on Their Own Bodies: A Psychometric Investigation of the Negative Body Talk Scale. *Psychol Women Q* 2012; **36**: 162–78.
M. R. Sladek, R. H. Salk, and R. Engeln. Negative Body Talk Measures for Asian, Latina(o), and White Women and Men: Measurement Equivalence and Associations with Ethnic-Racial Identity. *Body Image* 2018; **25: 66–77.

Negative Body Talk Scale: Female Version Applications

- Consider how you would respond to this assessment on a "bad body image day." What would your responses be like? Now consider how you would respond to this assessment on a "good body image day." What would those responses be like?

- Are there particular items/statements that tend to increase your negative body image? If so, what may be the reason(s)?

- What type(s) of women do you typically compare yourself with when making these statements? Consider what they typically look like, their age(s), their body type, their clothing, and more.

- Do you tend to initiate these comments when with others? Do you say these statements in response to hearing comments by others?

- Item 3 refers to "feeling fat." Have you had this experience? What is it like for you? Does it correspond with uncomfortable emotions? Certain types of behaviors? Certain physical bodily sensations?

- If a friend/family member/acquaintance makes a comment to you about someone else's desirable attribute like item 7 (*She has a perfect body*), what do you notice about your own response? Will this draw attention to your own body, body areas, and/or insecurities?

- What are the overall underlying emotions, negative and possibly even positive, associated with these statements? Examples might be shame, envy, jealousy, anger, fear, joy, pride, satisfaction.

- What would it be like if you stopped saying these statements aloud? What would it be like if you stopped saying these statements internally?

- The majority of these statements are upward comparisons (see Table 13.1 for information about upward and downward comparisons). Now consider what type of downward comparisons you tend to say aloud (e.g., *"At least I don't look like her"*). Identify these different statements. What do you notice about yourself after saying these types of statements aloud? What do you notice about yourself after saying these types of statements internally (not aloud but in your thoughts)?

- Do you engage in negative body talk with certain people but not others? What about these relationships increases the likelihood of engaging in negative body talk? What about these relationships decreases the likelihood of engaging in negative body talk?

Assessment 16.2: Male Body Talk Scale (MBTS)

We're interested in the types of things men say about their bodies when they're talking to other people. We're interested in what men SAY – not what men think. When you're answering the following questions, please only give responses that are consistent with the way YOU ACTUALLY TALK to other people.

Remember, we're not interested in how often you have thoughts like this. Instead, we're interested in how often you *SAY things like this out loud* when you're having a conversation with others. Even if you wouldn't use these exact words, we're interested in whether you say similar things (that mean the same thing) when you're talking to people.

Use the following scale to indicate how frequently you SAY things like the statements below. Please write the number to the right of the item.

1	2	3	4	5	6	7
Never	Rarely	Occasionally	Sometimes	Frequently	Usually	Always

When talking with your friends, how often do you SAY things like . . .	Number
1. I want a six-pack.	
2. I wish I could lose this belly fat.	
3. I need to go on a diet.	
4. I wish I had bigger biceps.	
5. I wish my chest were more muscular.	
6. I want to add bulk.	
7. I need to lose some weight.	
8. I wish my abs were more toned.	
9. I wish I could lose this gut.	
10. I need to start watching what I eat.	
11. I need to lift weights more.	
12. I should work on my abs.	
13. I need to lose a few pounds.	
14. I wish I could bulk up a little.	
15. I want to have more muscle.	
16. I wish I had more muscular arms.	
Total Male Body Talk score: add items 1–16 and divide by 16 =	

Total Male Body Talk score between:

- **4–7** = high levels of negative body talk
- **2–3.9** = moderate levels of negative body talk
- **below 2** = low levels of negative body talk

Note. Authors of the MBTS are Sladek, Engeln, and Miller.* Its measurement properties (reliability and validity) have been supported with ethnically diverse samples of men .** Please contact the authors of the MBTS for permission to use it within research; there is no need to contact them to use it with clients or to complete it on your own.

*M. R. Sladek, R. Engeln, and S. A. Miller. Development and Validation of the Male Body Talk Scale: A Psychometric Investigation. *Body Image* 2014; **11**: 233–44.
M. R. Sladek, R. H. Salk, and R. Engeln. Negative Body Talk Measures for Asian, Latina(o), and White Women and Men: Measurement Equivalence and Associations with Ethnic-Racial Identity. *Body Image* 2018; **25: 66–77.

Male Body Talk Scale Applications

- Consider how you would respond to this assessment on a "bad body image day." What would your responses be like? Now consider how you would respond to this assessment on a "good body image day." What would those responses be like?

- Are there particular items/statements that tend to increase negative body image? If so, what may be the reason(s)?

- What type(s) of men do you typically compare with when making these statements? Consider what they typically look like, their age(s), their body type, their clothing, and more.

- Do you tend to initiate these comments when with others? Do you say these statements in response to hearing comments by others?

- If a friend/family member/acquaintance makes a comment to you about their own bodies, what do you notice about your own response? Will this draw attention to your own body parts and/or insecurities?

- What are the overall underlying emotions, negative and possibly even positive, associated with these statements? Examples might be shame, envy, jealousy, anger, fear, joy, pride, satisfaction.

- What would it be like if you stopped saying these statements aloud? What would it be like if you stopped saying these statements internally (not aloud but in your thoughts)?

- Do you engage in negative body talk with certain people but not others? What about these relationships increases the likelihood of engaging in negative body talk? What about these relationships decreases the likelihood of engaging in negative body talk?

- The majority of these statements are upward comparisons (see Table 13.1 for information about upward and downward comparisons). Now consider what type of downward comparisons you tend to say aloud (e.g., *At least I don't look like him*). Identify these different statements. What do you notice about yourself after saying these types of statements aloud? What do you notice about yourself after saying these types of statements internally (not aloud but in your thoughts)?

- Teasing about the body often occurs amongst male friends. When a friend/family member/acquaintance teases you about a specific area or amount of muscle versus fat, what is your typical outward response? What is your internal response?

Assignment 16.1: Responding to Body Talk of Others

It can be uncomfortable to be part of conversations in which others engage in negative body talk about themselves or others. There are many factors that impact what we might say or do, including the environment or location that we're in (private versus public), how well we know the person who is engaging in the body talk (friend or family, acquaintance, stranger), whether we like and/or respect this person, frequency of interactions with this person (one time versus ongoing), who else might be part of the conversation, what potential power differences might exist, past experiences of body talk with this person, our comfort in challenging the other person, and what our goals are in the situation (e.g., help a friend to feel better about themselves, decrease our own discomfort, avoid engaging in our own body talk).

For this assignment, imagine that you're in a situation in which another person engages in negative body talk. Below are examples of responses that you could say. Review the type of responses and consider the likelihood of using them. Identify the possible pros and cons of using the responses and overall reflections from using that strategy. Being compassionate towards yourself and honoring your experience as you respond are important to keep in mind. Examples are provided.

Various Approaches to Body Talk

Type of Response	Examples	Pros	Cons	Reflections
Example: *Ignore*	*"Did you hear about . . . ?"*	*I don't have the time or energy to deal with this right now.*	*By ignoring it, it's likely that he's going to keep saying these things while I'm around him.*	*Ignoring is helpful in the short-term but the problem continues when I don't address it.*
Example: *Express discomfort with body talk*	*"I'm not comfortable with this conversation."*	*It's important for him to know that it's annoying to hear about his negative body talk all the time.*	*I don't know if I can say this to his face. I don't want him to get mad at me.*	*I like the idea of being direct, but am nervous to be so. I'll have to practice saying something like this.*
Ignore	"Did you hear about . . . ?"			
	"Did I tell you about . . . ?			
	Other:			
Redirect	"Let's talk about . . ."			
	"Tell me about . . . "			
	Other:			
Offer practical tips	"Have you considered doing this . . . ?"			
	"If you tried this, you might feel better about yourself."			
	Other:			
Reciprocate	"If you don't like that about you, what about my . . .?"			
	"I get how you feel. I don't like that about me either."			
	Other:			
Reassure	"You look fine just the way you are."			

N. L. Wood-Barcalow, T. L. Tylka, and C. L. Judge. *Positive Body Image Workbook: A Clinical and Self-Improvement Guide.* Cambridge: Cambridge University Press, 2021. **239**

Type of Response	Examples	Pros	Cons	Reflections
	"I think you look great!"			
	Other:			
Offer a compliment	"I like your (body part)."			
	"You are gorgeous."			
	Other:			
Express discomfort with body talk	"I'm not comfortable with this conversation."			
	"I'm uncomfortable when we talk about … "			
	Other:			
Express a different opinion	"I don't agree with what you said."			
	"That's not how I view it."			
	Other:			
Reflect on what happens during body talk	"How do you think this kind of talk impacts us?"			
	"I feel … when we talk about … Do you feel the same?"			
	Other:			
Challenge	"I notice that you talk a lot about your body in a negative way. Is that okay with you? Is that something you want to change?"			
	"Negative body talk keeps us focused on our bodies versus talking about other important things. What if we stopped focusing on our appearance and started focusing on other things that matter?"			
	Other:			
	Other:			

N. L. Wood-Barcalow, T. L. Tylka, and C. L. Judge. *Positive Body Image Workbook: A Clinical and Self-Improvement Guide.* Cambridge: Cambridge University Press, 2021.

Assignment 16.2: How to Respond to Hurtful Body Talk in the Moment

Sometimes we are the person who receives hurtful body talk from another (e.g., "You're stomach is big," "You need to lose weight,") which can be surprising, unsettling, and uncomfortable. Here are some options of how to deal with the negative body talk in the moment. Note that it might take a few interventions to deal with the hurtful talk.

- Ask for clarification of what the person said
- Ask for clarification of what the person intended
- Acknowledge the discomfort internally
- Acknowledge the discomfort aloud ("wow, that hurt")
- Leave the conversation
- End the conversation
- Leave the situation
- Identify positive aspects of myself internally
- Reflect on why those comments hurt (e.g., who said it, what was said, that it struck a chord)
- Use humor to deflect the power of it
- Redirect the conversation
- Ask if the person intended to be hurtful
- Consider the source of the hurtful comment and whether their opinion/perspective matters
- Other:
- Other:
- Other:

N. L. Wood-Barcalow, T. L. Tylka, and C. L. Judge. *Positive Body Image Workbook: A Clinical and Self-Improvement Guide.* Cambridge: Cambridge University Press, 2021.

Assignment 16.3: Moving towards Authentic Body Positivity

Positive body image is a topic discussed by many in recent years, especially within social media forums. Many of these messages align with the true spirit of positive body image which promote body acceptance for all. Alternatively, there are some messages that appear on the surface to promote positive body image but upon closer inspection actually include ulterior motives and/or conflict with the true spirit of total body acceptance. Examples can include a social media influencer using their body in a sexualized manner for self-promotion, or a weight loss company promoting a product by highlighting a person's appearance after weight loss while simultaneously talking about the former body in a critical and shaming manner.

It can be challenging to determine what is authentic body positivity within these various messages. Here are questions to consider whether the message is in line with the values of positive body image. Ask yourself if the message . . .

- Focuses on a person's worth based solely on her/his appearance?
- Flaunts the body in degrading ways?
- Promotes self-care or meeting the body's needs?
- Objectifies bodies in any way by using all-or-nothing language (e.g., good versus bad, attractive versus unattractive)?
- Encourages body acceptance for a range of individuals?
- Shames aspects of their former selves (e.g., weight, amount of fat versus muscle) by using negative language?
- Shames others for their overall appearance or physical traits?
- Encourages body positivity in others?
- Focuses primarily on the body and/or activities related to their appearance?
- Refrains from identifying specific numbers while discussing weight?
- Focuses on how to live a good quality of life?
- Emphasizes that happiness is about attaining a certain physical appearance?
- Objectifies the bodies of others?

N. L. Wood-Barcalow, T. L. Tylka, and C. L. Judge. *Positive Body Image Workbook: A Clinical and Self-Improvement Guide.* Cambridge: Cambridge University Press, 2021.

Assignment 16.4: Positive Body Talk

We know that negative body talk can have an undesirable impact on emotions, thoughts, moods, behaviors and more. What about positive body talk; what impact does it have? Consider the following questions to determine how positive body talk impacts you.

What's the purpose or intent of engaging in positive body talk?

_____
_____
_____
_____

What are the triggers to engage in this talk?

_____
_____
_____
_____

What are examples of positive body talk that I typically say aloud about others? About myself?

_____
_____
_____
_____

Do I say positive things about others as a way to have positive things said about me? If so, what are some examples?

_____
_____
_____
_____

What happens when I want someone to say something positive about my body and they don't? How will I feel?

_____
_____
_____
_____

Are there non-appearance-focused comments that I can make about others instead?

_____
_____
_____
_____

N. L. Wood-Barcalow, T. L. Tylka, and C. L. Judge. _Positive Body Image Workbook: A Clinical and Self-Improvement Guide._ Cambridge: Cambridge University Press, 2021.

Assignment 16.5: How to Respond to Body Shaming in Social Media

An experience in social media networking can be to purposefully "body shame" others for numerous reasons. Even though shaming or bullying has existed in various forms throughout time, social media body shaming can have a particularly negative effect due to the ability to communicate information to many people in instantaneous time as well as the permanent imprint it can leave.

Know that it can be common to experience a range of emotions (e.g., anger, shock, disappointment, fear) and reactions (e.g., not knowing what to say, wanting to strike back, removing self from the situation) if you've experienced body shaming from another. It is important to consider the context of shaming (e.g., how public was the comment, who might have seen the negative information, who made the comment) and what you feel comfortable doing in that specific moment as well as how to respond to that event or ones similar to that in the future. Consider the following interventions below to enhance or protect your self-worth and sense of control:

- Talk to a trusted friend or loved one about how the shaming impacted me
- Connect with a support group of others who have had similar experiences
- Identify the various emotions that I felt such as anger, annoyance, agitation, irritation, indignation, fury, offense, fear, anxiety, sadness, hurt, despair, hopelessness, helplessness, embarrassment, shame, guilt, remorse, and more
- Notice any urges to respond in an aggressive manner without acting on them
- Allow myself to experience a range of emotions without judging them
- Express disagreement with the body shaming
- Challenge appearance ideals associated with the body shaming
- Inform the perpetrator that their behavior/comments were offensive
- Educate the perpetrator on the impact of their actions
- Interrupt the communication and redirect it
- Ask for clarification of what was communicated
- Identify the different ways that I could respond before doing so to find an option that fits with my values
- Spend time breathing and reflecting before responding online
- Consider what actions I'd *like to* take and what actions I *will take*
- Consider the motive(s) or intention(s) of the person(s) doing the body shaming
- Focus on creating and maintaining my protective shield that keeps the negative information from penetrating
- Engage in behaviors that allow me to feel good about my body
- Practice body affirmations that counteract the negative comments
- Remind myself that a person's inappropriate comments are not necessarily true
- Consider my personal values in trying to determine how to respond both externally and internally
- Remind myself of my positive qualities
- Engage in a loving kindness meditation (see Chapter 8)
- Instead of hiding and avoiding which is a natural response to shame, consider acting in ways that focus on my strengths
- Use humor to offset the pain
- Rely on the comfort and inspiring words from others to bolster me
- Engage in intense or strenuous physical activity as a way to respond to anger directed at the other person
- Engage in self-care acts if any urges to self-harm arise
- Demonstrate power by reminding myself that those comments cannot break me
- Participate in a relaxing activity
- Be direct and assertive of what is not appropriate in terms of my rights, limits, and boundaries
- Confront the situation in a way(s) that is congruent with my core values
- Ask for input from others on how to respond
- Consider disconnecting from certain forms of social media outlets and/or allowing certain people to access my information
- Determine whether there is a forum for reporting body shaming
- Commit to myself not to do the same behaviors to others
- Determine whether legal action is available and/or appropriate
- Investigate whether there is a process of removing the information from the social media page
- Share with others the pain that I experienced and the toll that body shaming can take on a person to increase awareness and compassion
- Seek therapy or counseling
- Use spiritual and/or religious practices

N. L. Wood-Barcalow, T. L. Tylka, and C. L. Judge. *Positive Body Image Workbook: A Clinical and Self-Improvement Guide.* Cambridge: Cambridge University Press, 2021.

Assignment 16.6: How to Respond to Internal Negative Body Talk

Internal negative body talk happens. It can take numerous forms and have differing impacts depending on context such as the frequency, intensity, and longevity of it as well as mood. Listed below are different techniques to try when internal negative body talk occurs. Try practicing a few at a time once you recognize that it has occurred:

- Notice how the thoughts impact my body sensations and emotions. Don't try to change anything, just notice the impact
- Accept that the thoughts have occurred *without* believing them.
- Notice the thought and then imagine letting go of it. Don't spend additional time or effort focusing on it.
- Recognize how the thought(s) is inconsistent with my values. Shift my focus on what is important in my life that isn't related to my body or appearance.
- Challenge the thought(s) by asking myself, "says who?", "this isn't true!", or "this thought is ridiculous." Identify additional thoughts that challenge internal negative body talk
- Make a commitment in the moment to refrain from negative or destructive behavior(s)
- Say to myself, "I will not allow this thought to impact my mood, emotions, or behaviors"
- Engage in deep breathing or a functional body scan (see Chapter 11)
- Observe the thought and then let go of it. Imagine the thought(s) in a balloon that then flies away
- Do something kind for myself or someone else
- Identify an alternate response that is either neutral or positive
- Do an action that is the opposite of the negative body talk
- Imagine that a silly cartoon character is saying the negative body talk in a comical way to reduce the emotional distress

N. L. Wood-Barcalow, T. L. Tylka, and C. L. Judge. *Positive Body Image Workbook: A Clinical and Self-Improvement Guide.* Cambridge: Cambridge University Press, 2021.

Assignment 16.7: Different Ways to Respond to Negative Body Talk

In a 2019 journal article, researchers* identified possible reasons people engage in negative body talk (referred to as "fat talk" in this article) as well as a minimum of four different ways to respond when it occurs. The authors noted that the outcomes of these interventions varied based on different situations and experiences.

When in a situation that includes negative body talk, try to reflect on the following in that moment or later to have a better understanding of the experience.

What Was/Were the Possible Reasons for the Negative Body Talk (Check All That Apply):

❏ Promote bonding between each other

❏ Provide support

❏ Practice vulnerability in the relationship

❏ Serving as a cue that something was wrong

❏ Wanting reassurance

❏ Trying to get attention

❏ Other:

❏ Other:

❏ Other:

How I Responded (Check All That Apply):

❏ Ignored the comment/conversation

❏ Challenged the person(s) about what was being said

❏ Engaged in the same/similar type of talk

❏ Offered reassurance to the person about accepting themselves as they are

❏ Offered practical tips on how to change/improve body image

❏ Validated the person's uncomfortable experiences

❏ Offered encouragement

❏ Used humor

❏ Redirected the conversation to another topic

❏ Noted concerns that I have for that person

❏ Helped to distract the person

❏ Expressed discomfort with the body talk

❏ Offered a compliment

❏ Shared my own experiences with body dissatisfaction

❏ Expressed a different opinion

❏ Reflected on what happens during negative body talk

❏ Other:

❏ Other:

❏ Other:

How I Would Like To Respond in the Future (Check All That Apply):

❏ Ignore the comment/conversation

❏ Challenge the person(s) about what was being said

❏ Engage in the same/similar type of talk

❏ Offer reassurance to the person about accepting themselves as they are

❏ Offer practical tips on how to change/improve body image

❏ Validate the person's uncomfortable experiences

❏ Offer encouragement

N. L. Wood-Barcalow, T. L. Tylka, and C. L. Judge. *Positive Body Image Workbook: A Clinical and Self-Improvement Guide.* Cambridge: Cambridge University Press, 2021.

- ❏ Use humor
- ❏ Redirect the conversation to another topic
- ❏ Note concerns that I have for that person
- ❏ Help to distract the person
- ❏ Express discomfort with the body talk
- ❏ Offer a compliment
- ❏ Share my own experiences with body dissatisfaction
- ❏ Express a different opinion
- ❏ Reflect on what happens during negative body talk
- ❏ Other:
- ❏ Other:
- ❏ Other:

Additional Thoughts/Reflections

_____
_____
_____
_____
_____
_____
_____

*J. Mills, O. Mort, and S. Trawley. The impact of different responses to fat talk on body image and socioemotional outcomes. *Body Image* 2019; **29**: 149–55.

N. L. Wood-Barcalow, T. L. Tylka, and C. L. Judge. *Positive Body Image Workbook: A Clinical and Self-Improvement Guide*. Cambridge: Cambridge University Press, 2021.

References

1. K. Bassett Greer, N. Campione-Barr, and A. K. Lindell. Body talk: Siblings' use of positive and negative body self-disclosure and associations with sibling relationship quality and body esteem. *J Youth Adolesc* 2015; **44**: 1567–79.

2. R. H. Salk and R. Engeln-Maddox. Fat talk among college women is both contagious and harmful. *Sex Roles* 2012; **66**: 636–45.

3. N. M. Overstreet and D. M. Quinn. Contingencies of self-worth and appearance concerns: Do domains of self-worth matter? *Psychol Women Q* 2012; **36**: 314–25.

4. J. Mills and M. Fuller-Tyszkiewicz. Nature and consequences of positively intended fat talk in daily life. *Body Image* 2018; **26**: 38–49.

5. M. Nichter. *Fat talk*. Cambridge, MA: Harvard University Press, 2000.

6. M. Nichter and N. Vuckovic. Fat talk. In: Sault, N., ed. *Many Mirrors: Body Image and Social Relations*. New Brunswick: Rutgers University Press, 1994: 109–31.

7. R. Engeln-Maddox, R. H. Salk, and S. A. Miller. Assessing women's negative commentary on their own bodies: A psychometric investigation of the Negative Body Talk Scale. *Psychol Women Q* 2012; **36**: 162–78.

8. M. R. Sladek, R. Engeln, and S. A. Miller. Development and validation of the Male Body Talk Scale: A psychometric investigation. *Body Image* 2014; **11**: 233–44.

9. M. R. Sladek, R. H. Salk, and R. Engeln. Negative body talk measures for Asian, Latina(o), and White women and men: Measurement equivalence and associations with ethnic-racial identity. *Body Image* 2018; **25**: 66–77.

10. L. Britton, D. Martz, D. Bazzini, et al. Fat talk and self-presentation of body image: Is there a social norm for women to self-degrade? *Body Image* 2006; **3**: 247–54.

11. D. M. Martz, A. B. Petroff, L. Curtin, et al. Gender differences in fat talk among American adults: Results from the psychology of size survey. *Sex Roles* 2009; **61**: 31–41.

12. E. Ahlich, E. M. Choquette, and D. Rancourt. Body talk, athletic identity, and eating disorder symptoms in men. *Psychol Men Masc* 2019; **20**: 347–55.

13. R. Engeln, M. R. Sladek, and H. Waldron. Body talk among college men: Content, correlates, and effects. *Body Image* 2013; **10**: 300–8.

14. R. Engeln and R. H. Salk. The demographics of fat talk in adult women: Age, body size, and ethnicity. *J Health Psychol* 2016; **21**: 1655–64.

15. C. B. Becker, P. C. Diedrichs, G. Jankowski, et al. I'm not just fat, I'm old: Has the study of body image overlooked "old talk?" *J Eat Disord* 2013; **1**: 6.

16. M. F. Fiery, D. M. Martz, R. M. Webb, et al. A preliminary investigation of racial differences in body talk in age-diverse US adults. *Eat Behav* 2016; **21**: 232–5.

17. E. Stice, J. Maxfield, and T. Wells. Adverse effects of social pressure to be thin on young women: An experimental investigation of the effects of "fat talk." *Int J Eat Disord* 2003; **34**: 108–17.

18. K. D. Gapinski, K. D. Brownell, and M. LaFrance. Body objectification and "fat talk": Effects on emotion, motivation, and cognitive performance. *Sex Roles* 2003; **48**: 377–88.

19. R. H. Salk and R. Engeln-Maddox. "If you're fat then I'm humongous": Frequency, content, and impact of fat talk among college women. *Psychol Women Q* 2011; **35**: 18–28.

20. D. Neumark-Sztainer, K. W. Bauer, S. Friend, et al. Family weight talk and dieting: How much do they matter for body dissatisfaction and disordered eating behaviors in adolescent girls? *J Adolesc Health* 2010; **47**: 270–6.

21. C. M. Chow and C. C. Tan. The role of fat talk in eating pathology and depressive symptoms among mother-daughter dyads. *Body Image* 2018; **24**: 36–43.

22. J. B. Webb, C. B. Rogers, L. Etzel, et al. "Mom, quit fat talking—I'm trying to eat (mindfully) here!" Evaluating a sociocultural model of family fat talk, positive body image, and mindful eating in college women. *Appetite* 2018; **126**: 169–75.

23. M. Perez, A. M. Kroon Van Diest, H. Smith, et al. Body dissatisfaction and its correlates in 5- to 7-year-old girls: A social learning experiment. *J Clin Child Adolesc Psychol* 2018; **47**: 757–69.

24. K. Miller, A. Kelly, and E. Stephen. Exposure to body focused and non-body focused others over a week: A preliminary investigation of their unique contributions to college women's eating and body image. *Body Image* 2019; **28**: 44–52.

25. J. Mills, O. Mort, and S. Trawley. The impact of different responses to fat talk on body image and socioemotional outcomes. *Body Image* 2019; **29**: 149–55.

26. J. A. Rudiger and B. A. Winstead. Body talk and body-related co-rumination: Associations with body image, eating attitudes, and psychological adjustment. *Body Image* 2013; **10**: 462–71.

27. K. B. Tompkins, D. M. Martz, C. A. Rocheleau, et al. Social likeability, conformity, and body talk: Does fat talk have a normative rival in female body image conversations? *Body Image* 2009; **6**: 292–8.

Chapter 17

Protective Filtering

Theory and Research Overview

Our immune systems help protect our bodies from illnesses caused by potentially damaging viruses, bacteria, and cancer-causing agents. We don't have to ask our immune systems to keep us well, they just do their job, nearly all of the time. However, our immune systems are not foolproof. Sometimes illnesses are too strong, or our immune systems are compromised (e.g., from stress, lack of sleep, immunosuppressive medication), and we get sick. With rest, self-care, and perhaps medication, our bodies recover.

What if we had an immune system for our body image, or something to protect it from outside assaults, such as **body image threats** (e.g., remarks made by others about our appearance, also see Chapter 8)?

We can build one or strengthen the one that already exists. Women with a positive body image described having **protective filters** that block out negative information, such as body-related threats, from harming their body image [1]. For instance, when coming across fitness celebrities on social media, our protective filters can remind us that beauty comes in diverse forms, as opposed to comparing our bodies unfavorably to the models' bodies. Also, we may choose to not interact with social media sites or individuals that result in negative feelings toward our bodies. Our protective filters also allow positive body-related information (e.g., messages of body empowerment and self-care) to flow inward to protect or even strengthen our body image [1]. Importantly, these women indicated that their protective filters helped develop and maintain their positive body image. Thus, building and strengthening the protective filter is one of the most essential tasks we can do to help us develop and maintain a healthy body image. So, what helps to build and strengthen it?

Just like our immune systems, our protective filters can grow to be healthy and robust within environments free from major negative influences that completely overwhelm them but contain minor influences that can "exercise" them. Exposure to these minor influences provides the practice we need to engage in **protective filtering**, or rejecting the negative influences and absorbing the positive influences. Women with a positive body image perceived that engaging in protective filtering strengthened their protective filters, creating an upward spiral and a more positive body image [1]. One woman indicated that her protective filter allows herself to be "standing solid" on her feet so that she can "take little assaults as they come" [1].

Many women revealed that they had a negative body image prior to building their protective filters [1]. When they had a negative body image and encountered body-related threats, they would respond with negative emotions (e.g., "I hate my body,") and thoughts (e.g., "I'll never be attractive to anyone"), inaccurate perceptions (e.g., "Oh my gosh, my body looks hideous in this outfit!"), and destructive behaviors (e.g., "I'm not going to eat again until I lose weight"). Now that they have developed protective filters and engage in protective filtering, their emotions are more positive (e.g., "I love my body, even if it looks different than models in magazines"), their thoughts are more reasonable and compassionate (e.g., "I'm not going to let this negative event define my day or how I feel about my body"), their perceptions are more accurate (e.g., "Yes, my body has changed, but it is okay; everyone's body changes with time"), and they engage in self-care (e.g., "I want to eat and move my body in ways that honor my health") in reaction to body-related threats. They also have increased awareness of unrealistic media images – they remind themselves that celebrities don't really look like the generated media images of themselves "in real life" due to digital editing, professional make-up artists, etc. In the same way, adolescents with a positive body image from Sweden spoke out about societal appearance ideals, describing these ideals as "unnatural" and "unrealistic" and realizing that media have underlying intentions for doing this, namely to sell products [2] (see also Chapter 4). Indeed, being critical toward societal appearance ideals is the protective filter in action: filtering out negative influences (i.e., pressures to look a certain way) and filtering in more positive messages (e.g., understanding that beauty is subjective).

Young adult women and men from Sweden who overcame a negative body image in early adolescence and developed a positive body image by early adulthood reflected on their journey [3]. They began intentionally using strategies to improve their body image and they put in effort to maintain their positive body image by developing a protective filter. For example, they found friends and partners that provided a sense of body acceptance and belonging (see Chapter 6). They focused on qualities other than appearance and began to experience their body as a source of agency and functionality (e.g., engaging in sports, developing and honing a talent; see Chapters 11 and 12). They avoided people and situations that made them feel badly about their bodies. They filtered media images in a manner that protected their body image (see Chapter 4). They mentored others regarding body acceptance (see Chapter 18). They engaged in adaptive appearance investment (see Chapter 22). Many realized that pursuing an unrealistic appearance ideal would require sacrificing important things in life and wasn't worth it.

Yet, just like viruses sometimes slip past our immune systems and cause infections, negative information sometimes slips past our protective filters [1–2]. A body image threat may catch us off-guard. For example, we may overhear an unflattering comment about our appearance from someone we love, or we may come across a picture from ten years ago of us with noticeable appearance differences. When we are tired or stressed, our protective filters may not as effectively shield from such body-related threats in the short term, no matter how strong our positive body image. However, people with a positive body image work through these body image threats so that these threats don't have a negative long-term impact [1]. Thus, for them, the body image threat is a temporary setback and they soon "bounce back" to a positive body image. It is important to be compassionate towards ourselves during these setbacks and learn how to cope with them in a healthy manner.

Thomas Cash and his colleagues described three ways in which we can cope with these setbacks [4]. Each way of coping involves changing our thoughts, behaviors, and emotions to manage the body-related threat.

The form of coping that is most likely to strengthen our protective filter is positive rational acceptance [4]. **Positive rational acceptance** includes accepting the body image threat and its full impact on us (e.g., sadness, frustration), and responding with positive self-care and/or positive self-talk. For example, we engage in positive rational acceptance when we are patient and compassionate with ourselves during the threat, do something that makes us feel good about ourselves (e.g., go for a nature walk), remind ourselves that our negative reaction "will pass" and we will feel better after a while, try to figure out what makes us threatened by the situation, remind ourselves of our good qualities, and tell ourselves that how we look is our least important quality. Positive rational acceptance is associated with higher self-esteem and body image quality of life (see Chapter 22) and related to lower negative body image and disordered eating [4].

Appearance fixing includes attempts to change our appearance by covering, camouflaging, or correcting the perceived defect [4]. For example, if someone tells us that our stomach is "too big," an attempt at appearance fixing would be to hide our stomach, try to diet to lose stomach fat, spend time examining our stomach in front of the mirror and comparing the size of our stomach to others, and even surgical procedures (e.g., liposuction, coolsculpting) to remove body fat. Appearance fixing may weaken our protective filter because it directs our attention to our perceived body flaws, focuses our energy on our appearance, accepts rather than challenges media ideals, and may even place our health at risk. **Avoidance** includes attempts to escape or avoid body-related threats [4]. For example, we may try to ignore the body-related threat and our reactions to it, numb the impact of the threat by mindlessly eating, and avoid looking at ourselves in the mirror. Avoidance may weaken our protective filter because we avoid dealing with the body image threat. By ignoring the threats

and/or our reactions, we cannot sort through our emotions and grow and learn from the experience. We become "stuck" [4]. Appearance fixing and avoidance are linked to higher negative body image, self-objectification (see Chapter 13), disordered eating, and lower self-esteem [4–6].

Cash and his colleagues created a measure of these coping methods called the *Body Image Coping Strategies Inventory* (BICSI) [4]. Its three subscales correspond to the three types of body image coping described above. Completing the BICSI applications and assignments in this chapter will help you understand: (a) the extent to which you engage in the three ways of coping, (b) ways you can build your protective filter, and (c) how to reduce appearance fixing and/or avoiding the body-related threats that may weaken your protective filter. Furthermore, consistent effort is needed to maintain a strong protective filter. Regularly engaging in positive strategies, such as the ones found in this chapter's assignments and the positive psychology literature [7, see also Chapter 23] can substantially help with this mission.

Treatment Planning Tools

Talking Points in Sessions

- Brainstorm ways to create and strengthen the protective filter
- Identify effective coping skills the client uses to protect against harmful messages about their body
- Discuss specific actions to help the client reject negative information
- Explore how important relationships relate to the protective filter

Treatment Plan

Goals

- ❏ Identify current coping skills that are being used to keep myself safe from absorbing negative information
- ❏ Identify additional coping skills to use when threatening information arises
- ❏ Learn how others with positive body image respond effectively to negative body image threats
- ❏ Surround myself with others who accept me as I am, as often as I can
- ❏ Create limits as needed to promote my positive body image
- ❏ Investigate how certain behaviors lead me away from accepting my body
- ❏ Reduce the tendency to compare myself to others
- ❏ Decrease the amount of unhelpful time I spend on social networking sites
- ❏ Identify when I feel rejected and use positive coping skills
- ❏ Block out destructive messages
- ❏ Reflect on how I use appearance fixing to deal with body image threats

❑ Reflect on how I use avoidance to deal with body image threats

Objectives

❑ Identify concrete ways to respond to body-related threats when they are directed at me and/or someone I care about

❑ Envision my protective filter and how it redirects incoming body-related threats

❑ Reduce or eliminate talking poorly about others' bodies (types, shapes, weight, fat distribution, muscle mass), which can weaken my protective filter by prompting me to focus on a narrow definition of beauty

❑ Remind myself of my good qualities

❑ Engage in positive self-talk about my body

❑ Engage in self-care (e.g., pamper myself, say something kind to myself) when experiencing internal negative appearance-related talk

❑ Recognize how I can experience negative thoughts and emotions without engaging in harmful behaviors

❑ Monitor the amount of time that is spent on appearance comparison (daily, weekly, monthly), which can weaken my protective filter

❑ Find inspiration by reading information others have written about their journey from negative to positive body image

❑ Journal during a moment of neutral or positive body image

❑ Recognize examples of appearance fixing and identify alternate coping that includes positive rational acceptance

❑ Recognize examples of avoidance and identify alternate coping that includes positive rational acceptance

❑ Focus on patience and compassion when experiencing a body image threat

❑ Engage in an activity that makes me feel good about myself

❑ Remind myself that the discomfort associated with the body image threat will pass

❑ Remind myself that there are more important things than what I look like and identify what they are

❑ Investigate why I am challenged or threatened by a particular situation or experience

Additional Resources

S. Lyubomirsky. *The How of Happiness: A Scientific Approach to Getting the Life You Want.* New York: Penguin Press, 2008).

Stories of Hope on the National Eating Disorder Association's (NEDA) website, available at: www.nationaleatingdisorders.org/

Assessment 17.1: Body Image Coping Strategies Inventory (BICSI)

There are situations and events that occur which can negatively affect our body image, known as "body image threats or challenges." Listed below are some of the ways that people cope with these threats and challenges. For each item, put a number to the right that represents how much it is like you to use one of these coping strategies.

0	1	2	3
Definitely Not Like Me	Mostly Not Like Me	Mostly Like Me	Definitely Like Me

Positive Rational Acceptance	Number
1. I remind myself that I will feel better after a while.	
2. I tell myself that I am probably just overreacting to the situation.	
3. I tell myself that the situation will pass.	
4. I tell myself that I probably look better than I feel that I do.	
5. I remind myself of my good qualities.	
6. I try to figure out why I am challenged or threatened by the situation.	
7. I tell myself that there are more important things than what I look like.	
8. I tell myself that I'm just being irrational about things.	
9. I tell myself that the situation is not that important.	
10. I react by being especially patient with myself.	
11. I consciously do something that might make me feel good about myself as a person.	
Total Positive Rational Acceptance score: add items 1–11 and divide by 11 =	

Appearance Fixing	Number
12. I do something to try to look more attractive.	
13. I spend extra time trying to fix what I don't like about my looks.	
14. I think about what I should do to change my looks.	
15. I compare my appearance to that of physically attractive people.	
16. I make a special effort to hide or "cover up" what's troublesome about my looks.	
17. I make a special effort to look my best.	
18. I think about how I could "cover up" what's troublesome about my looks.	
19. I fantasize about looking different.	
20. I spend more time in front of the mirror.	
21. I seek reassurance about my looks from other people.	
Total Appearance Coping score: add items 12–21 and divide by 10 =	

Avoidance	Number
22. I make no attempt to cope or deal with the situation.	
23. I try to ignore the situation and my feelings.	
24. I react by overeating.	
25. I try to tune out my thoughts and feelings.	
26. I withdraw and interact less with others.	
27. I avoid looking at myself in the mirror.	
28. I eat something to help me deal with the situation.	
29. I tell myself that I am helpless to do anything about the situation.	
Total Avoidance Coping score: add items 22–29 and divide by 8 =	

Total score between:

- **2.25–3** = high levels of body image coping strategy
- **1.75–2.24** = moderate levels of body image coping strategy
- **below 1.75** = low levels of body image coping strategy

Note. Reprinted with permission. Authors of the BICSI are Cash, Santos, and Williams.* Its measurement properties (reliability and validity) have supported its use with samples of women and men. Permission was granted by Thomas Cash to include the BICSI in this workbook. The BICSI cannot be used for research without a user's license (available at www.body-images.com).

*T. F. Cash, M. T. Santos, and E. F. Williams. Coping with body-image threats and challenges: Validation of the Body Image Coping Strategies Inventory. *J Psychosom Res* 2005; **58**: 191–9.

Body Image Coping Strategies Inventory Applications

Positive Rational Acceptance

- When faced with a body-related threat, how often are you able to remind yourself that you will "feel better after a while" as indicated in item 1 (*I remind myself that I will feel better after a while*)? How well does that reminder provide you with short-term relief? How well does it provide long-term relief? How can you use this approach effectively on "bad body image days?"

- If/when you tell yourself that "the situation will pass," as indicated in item 3 (*I tell myself that the situation will pass*), how does that impact your thoughts, emotions, and behaviors?

- Take a moment to create a list of all the positive qualities about your body, your personality, how you live your life, and more.

- If you responded "mostly like me" or "definitely like me" to item 6 (*I try to figure out why I am challenged or threatened by the situation*), what is that process like? Can you identify themes regarding situations or people that challenge or threaten you? Are these real or perceived threats or both?

- What kinds of things do you do to "feel good about yourself as a person" as indicated in item 11 (*I consciously do something that might make me feel good about myself as a person*)?

- Look at items 5 (*I remind myself of my good qualities*), 7 (*I tell myself that there are more important things than what I look like*), 9 (*I tell myself that the situation is not that important*), and 10 (*I react by being especially patient with myself*). What would you like to do and do more often to improve body image coping?

Appearance Fixing

- What's the difference between trying to "change" your looks versus trying to "improve" your looks?

- What in particular do you do as a "special effort" to look your best as indicated in item 17 (*I make a special effort to look my best*)?

- If you responded "mostly like me" or "definitely like me" to "fantasizing" about looking different in item 19 (*I fantasize about looking different*), how do you specifically imagine you would look? How would that be different from how you look now? How might you act differently if you looked the way that you fantasize?

- If you tend to seek reassurance from others as indicated in item 21 (*I seek reassurance about my looks from other people*), does the feedback from others actually provide assurance? If so, for how long? What happens when that sense of assurance goes away? Do you find the need to get assurance again either from others or from yourself?

Avoidance

- How often do you ignore your uncomfortable thoughts or emotions about your body? When is ignoring effective? When is it ineffective?

- When having a "bad body image day," how often do you withdraw from others? What is the intended purpose of withdrawing? When is this behavior effective? When is it ineffective?

- Telling yourself that you're "helpless" as indicated in item 29 (*I tell myself that I am helpless to do anything about the situation*) can impact your motivation to care for yourself properly. Reflect on how thoughts of "helplessness" impact what you do and what you don't do. Consider short-term and long-term pros/cons associated with helplessness.

Assignment 17.1: Protective Shield Metaphor

Negative information about the body surrounds us from advertisements on television, pop-up ads online, an acquaintance commenting on their body via a social media platform, and more. Just as we have the choice as to what we eat and what we do, we also have the choice of what information to allow in and what information to reject out. We are the gatekeepers of information even though we can feel as though we have no control over the amount or intensity of negative information that is around us.

To demonstrate your ability to control information, imagine a protective shield that surrounds you. Be creative in thinking about its color, design, and texture. This shield is strong against outward forces. This shield protects negative and harmful body-focused information from getting in. Examples might include negative ads online that focus on trying to change the body or disrespectful comments from others about your body shape, size, or weight. When this information gets near the shield, the information bounces away, unable to penetrate or impact your body image. You remain safe and unharmed from this information.

Now imagine that this shield includes a small door with a latch that can only be opened from the inside. This latch keeps the door closed at all times unless it is determined that it is safe to allow in beneficial information from respected sources. Examples might be positive comments about your body from a loved one or tips from a friend on how to improve self-acceptance. So when that information is present, you unlatch the door and welcome it through. Allowing the absorption of this type of information can bolster your body image.

- Practice imagining this protective shield on a consistent basis, being mindful of what to allow in and what to keep out.
- Often, this shield follows you wherever you go and whatever you do. However, sometimes it may not be raised, and you may be exposed to negative information. This is not your fault, as it requires energy and attention to keep the shield up. No one can have their shield up 100 percent of the time. For example, maybe you are having a particularly stressful day, and someone says something negative about your body, your clothes don't fit quite right that day, or you saw yourself in a picture and had an uncomfortable response (i.e., you imagined yourself looking more attractive than what the picture reflects). Or perhaps someone you love compares your body to another person they think is more attractive. Your shield is down; after all, you felt comfortable enough to lower it in certain settings. You feel the sting. This is normal. In times like these, how can you engage in self-care to nurture and heal the wound? Can you envision raising your shield to allow yourself to heal?

N. L. Wood-Barcalow, T. L. Tylka, and C. L. Judge. *Positive Body Image Workbook: A Clinical and Self-Improvement Guide.* Cambridge: Cambridge University Press, 2021.

Assignment 17.2: Creating a Safe Environment

This is what I imagine a safe environment that is body positive to be like (check all that apply and write some additional ideas in the "other" rows):

- ❏ Keeping my residence free from negative information
- ❏ Decorating my residence with positive images
- ❏ Talking with others about important issues going on in the world
- ❏ Not engaging in appearance-based conversations with others
- ❏ Refraining from watching movies/TV that focus on appearance
- ❏ Redirecting conversations that focus on appearance to other topics
- ❏ Eliminating/removing an excess of mirrors from my residence
- ❏ Monitoring my overall use of social media
- ❏ Making sure that I take care of myself
- ❏ Limiting my use of social media that fosters comparison with others
- ❏ Surrounding myself with those who exhibit positive body image
- ❏ Surrounding myself with those who have similar core values
- ❏ Surrounding myself with those who make me feel good about myself
- ❏ Surrounding myself with those who accept me as I am
- ❏ Surrounding myself with those who are positive
- ❏ Surrounding myself with those who are trying to make this world a better place
- ❏ Limiting my time with those who focus on food talk (e.g., dieting, comparing meal plans)
- ❏ Limiting my time with those who focus on negative body talk
- ❏ Limiting my time with those who focus on comparison with others
- ❏ Limiting my time with those who are negative
- ❏ Other:
- ❏ Other:
- ❏ Other:

N. L. Wood-Barcalow, T. L. Tylka, and C. L. Judge. *Positive Body Image Workbook: A Clinical and Self-Improvement Guide.* Cambridge: Cambridge University Press, 2021.

Assignment 17.3: Body Talk

Identify situations or environments where you may be likely to encounter significant body (or appearance-based) talk in all forms (negative, neutral, and positive). Examples can include work, school, the gym, hanging out with certain family members or friends, and more.

These are the situations or environments where I experience body talk:

_____
_____
_____
_____
_____

Body talk impacts me in these ways:

_____
_____
_____
_____
_____

How I can use protective filtering in these situations or environments:

_____
_____
_____
_____
_____

Specific steps towards creating a safe living environment where negative body talk is not tolerated:

_____
_____
_____
_____
_____

N. L. Wood-Barcalow, T. L. Tylka, and C. L. Judge. *Positive Body Image Workbook: A Clinical and Self-Improvement Guide.* Cambridge: Cambridge University Press, 2021.

Assignment 17.4: Practicing Assertiveness with Others

These are people currently in my life who activate my negative body image, act as body image threats, and/or say hurtful things about me or my body:

_____

_____

I can set healthy limits with them by saying these things:

_____

_____

I can set healthy limits with them by doing these things:

_____

_____

I can set healthy limits by requesting:

_____

_____

I can change my responses to them by:

_____

_____

I can use the following coping techniques before interacting with them:

_____

_____

I can use the following coping techniques while interacting with them:

_____

_____

I can use the following coping techniques after interacting with them:

_____

_____

N. L. Wood-Barcalow, T. L. Tylka, and C. L. Judge. _Positive Body Image Workbook: A Clinical and Self-Improvement Guide._ Cambridge: Cambridge University Press, 2021.

Assignment 17.5: Positive Body Image Box

Create a positive body image box with objects/items to enhance body acceptance. The purpose of this box is to provide concrete coping reminders to use on bad body image days and/or when body image threats occur. Examples of items could be a letter from a friend, a photograph of a time when body acceptance occurred, an "I commit to" list, memorabilia from a favorite destination, inspirational quotes, uplifting music, and more. The positive body image box can be a physical box with actual objects or it can be virtual in which the "box" contains images stored electronically.

N. L. Wood-Barcalow, T. L. Tylka, and C. L. Judge. *Positive Body Image Workbook: A Clinical and Self-Improvement Guide.* Cambridge: Cambridge University Press, 2021.

Assignment 17.6: Surrounding Myself with Positive Others

These are people in my life currently who promote positive body image:

_____
_____
_____

By doing:

_____
_____
_____

By saying:

_____
_____
_____

I appreciate these things about them:

_____
_____
_____

This is how I feel when I'm around them:

_____
_____
_____

This is what I do when I'm around them:

_____
_____
_____

I commit to surrounding myself with others who experience positive body image by:

_____
_____
_____

N. L. Wood-Barcalow, T. L. Tylka, and C. L. Judge. _Positive Body Image Workbook: A Clinical and Self-Improvement Guide._ Cambridge: Cambridge University Press, 2021.

Assignment 17.7: Interview Someone with Positive Body Image

Ask someone with a positive body image if you can interview them about their experiences. Consider asking questions similar to these:*

- You identify as having a positive body image. Can you please explain what you mean by that? What things are related to a positive body image?
- How do you describe your attitude toward your body?
- Tell me the story of how you feel about your body.
- How has your understanding of your own body image changed or not changed over time?
- What important information have you learned from others about your body (such as family, peers, romantic partners, and society)?
- How do your relationships with others affect your body image?
- What kinds of messages do you think society promotes about the female body, the male body (social media, TV, movies, magazines, etc.)?
- How do you understand your body in relation to these messages?
- Is there one experience that stands out for you related to how you feel or what you think about your body?
- What does your body provide you?
- How do you care for your body?
- Could you use a metaphor to describe how you feel about your body?
- What advice would you give to others who are struggling with body acceptance?
- Is there anything else you would like to share?

*We used these questions as part of our interview script in the research article by N. L. Wood-Barcalow, T. L. Tylka, and C. L. Augustus-Horvath. "But I like my body": Positive body image characteristics and a holistic model for young-adult women. *Body Image* 2010; 7: 106–16.

N. L. Wood-Barcalow, T. L. Tylka, and C. L. Judge. *Positive Body Image Workbook: A Clinical and Self-Improvement Guide.* Cambridge: Cambridge University Press, 2021.

Assignment 17.8: Coping with Body Image Threats

I experienced this negative body image thought recently:

_____
_____
_____
_____
_____

List below body image threats that could have contributed to this thought. Examples could be _internal factors_ (e.g., physical bodily sensations, bad mood) and/or _external factors_ (clothing did not fit, negative comment from a friend).

_____
_____
_____
_____
_____

I coped with this negative body image thought in these ways:

_____
_____
_____
_____
_____

Reflections on how well the coping strategies worked:

_____
_____
_____
_____
_____

How I would like to respond to body image threats in the future (e.g., use of different coping strategies):

_____
_____
_____
_____
_____

N. L. Wood-Barcalow, T. L. Tylka, and C. L. Judge. _Positive Body Image Workbook: A Clinical and Self-Improvement Guide._ Cambridge: Cambridge University Press, 2021.

Assignment 17.9: Exercising Your Protective Filter from Within: Changing Negative Body Image Thoughts

I notice myself having negative body image thoughts like these:	When I notice thoughts like these, I can remind myself of more helpful thoughts such as:
Example: *I hate the texture of my hair.*	*My hair is unique to me. It is just like my grandfather's hair.*

N. L. Wood-Barcalow, T. L. Tylka, and C. L. Judge. *Positive Body Image Workbook: A Clinical and Self-Improvement Guide.* Cambridge: Cambridge University Press, 2021.

Assignment 17.10: Common Unhelpful Thinking Patterns

Below are common unhelpful thinking patterns, called cognitive distortions, that originated from the theories of Aaron Beck[a] and gained popularity from the work of David Burns.[b] After reading about the thinking patterns, put a star next to the ones that are most common for you. Next to each thinking pattern, write an example of how this thinking pattern is associated with negative body image thoughts for you. Finally, identify more helpful and/or balanced alternative thoughts to practice instead.

Unhelpful Thinking Pattern	Negative Body Image Thoughts	More Positive, Filtered Thoughts
Example: *All-or-nothing thinking:* thinking in terms of absolute, black-or-white categories*	*My body has to be perfect.*	*My body may have flaws, but so does everyone's. I'm grateful that my body is functional in many ways.*
All-or-nothing thinking: thinking in terms of absolute, black-or-white categories		
Overgeneralization: thinking one negative event represents an unending pattern of negativity and defeat		
Mental Filter: dwelling more on the negatives than the positives		
Discounting the Positive: thinking that the positives "don't count" for a variety of reasons		
Jumping to Conclusions: arriving at a conclusion that is not fully supported by the facts of the situation		
Mind-Reading: assuming that others are thinking negatively about you		
Fortune-Telling: assuming the future will turn out negatively		
Magnification: disproportionately magnifying the importance of the negative		
Minimization: disproportionately minimizing the importance of the positive		
Emotional Reasoning: when feeling negatively, making an assumption that the reality and facts of a situation must therefore indeed be negative		
"Should, Must, Ought" Statements: thinking that often leads to guilt and shame when directed at self and anger and frustration when directed at others		
Labeling: thinking that judges the self and/or others by assigning labels to people		
Personalization and Blame: assigning undue responsibility to yourself and/or others for a negative event		

[a] A.T. Beck. *Cognitive Therapy and the Emotional Disorders*. Madison: International Universities Press, 1976.
[b] D.D. Burns. *The Feeling Good Handbook*. New York: Penguin, 1989.

N. L. Wood-Barcalow, T. L. Tylka, and C. L. Judge. *Positive Body Image Workbook: A Clinical and Self-Improvement Guide*. Cambridge: Cambridge University Press, 2021.

Assignment 17.11: Managing Difficult Interactions with People Close to Me

It can be difficult to manage uncomfortable interactions with close friends or family members who engage in negative body talk that is either directed at themselves, you, or others. Because this person is close to you, it can be helpful to consider different responses that focus on preserving your sense of body acceptance as well as the relationship.

- Role play or rehearse possible responses
- Imagine that the person who is making these comments experiences their own negative body image or pain. Can accessing their pain help to lessen the negative impact of their comments?
- Inform how these negative comments are hurtful to me and to them
- Educate that shaming comments do not result in positive change
- Request that certain topics are not discussed when together
- Remind the other person that it is not a competition
- Provide specific examples of what comments have been hurtful
- Share my ideas of what a "safe environment" is like
- Imagine a protective shield that surrounds me that is not penetrated by negative comments
- Ask for clarification of what the person means
- Try to create distance in terms of how much time is spent together
- Smile and offer the other person a genuine compliment
- Talk with another trusted individual about ways to handle these situations
- Try to eliminate being in situations in which negative comments are frequent (e.g., clothes shopping, going out in social situations)
- Use humor to offset any pain associated with the comments
- Remind myself privately that what this person says:
  - is different than how I interpret it
  - is not true
  - is their opinion and not mine
- Identify coping skills in advance of seeing this person
- Identify coping skills to use after interacting with this person
- Be firm in what my boundaries are about how I want to be treated
- Other:
- Other:
- Other:

N. L. Wood-Barcalow, T. L. Tylka, and C. L. Judge. *Positive Body Image Workbook: A Clinical and Self-Improvement Guide.* Cambridge: Cambridge University Press, 2021.

References

1. N. L. Wood-Barcalow, T. L. Tylka, and C. L. Augustus-Horvath. "But I like my body": Positive body image characteristics and a holistic model for young-adult women. *Body Image* 2010; **7**: 106–16.

2. K. Holmqvist and A. Frisén. "I bet they aren't that perfect in reality": Appearance ideals viewed from the perspective of adolescents with a positive body image. *Body Image* 2012; **9**: 388–95.

3. K. Holmqvist Gattario and A. Frisén. From negative to positive body image: Men's and women's journeys from early adolescence to emerging adulthood. *Body Image* 2019; **28**: 53–65.

4. T. F. Cash, M. T. Santos, and E. F. Williams. Coping with body-image threats and challenges: Validation of the Body Image Coping Strategies Inventory. *J Psychosom Res* 2005; **58**: 191–9.

5. S. G. Mancuso. Body image inflexibility mediates the relationship between body image evaluation and maladaptive body image coping strategies. *Body Image* 2016; **16**: 28–31.

6. K. A. Bailey, L. Lamarche, K. L. Gammage, et al. Self-objectification and the use of body image coping strategies: The role of shame in highly physically active women. *Am J Psychol* 2016; **129**: 81–90.

7. S. Lyubormirsky. *The How of Happiness: The Scientific Approach to Getting the Life You Want*. New York: Penguin Press, 2008.

Chapter 18

Rippling Effect: Mentorship

Theory and Research Overview

We are surrounded by images and messages telling us what we "should" look like: what shape our bodies should be in, how much muscle we should have (and where on our bodies this muscle should be), how much fat we should have (and the only acceptable places for it), what texture of hair we should have and how it should be styled, what skin tone we should have, how our eyelids and noses should be shaped, what clothes and accessories we should wear, how we should smell, how tall we should be, and so on [1]. These images and messages appear on social media, billboards, magazines, television, movies, and radio. We can find them in fitness centers, grocery stores, subways, and most places we go on a daily basis. We are likely to **internalize** these images and messages, or accept and use them as guidelines for how we should look, and consequently experience body dissatisfaction if we do not have the skills to challenge them [2–4] (see Chapters 4 and 17).

Hopefully, we hear **counter-messages** that challenge the ridiculous and unrealistic nature of these appearance images and messages [4–5]. While media literacy programs can provide counter-messages [6] (see Chapter 4), counter-messages can also be spread from person-to-person. For example, someone we admire may say, "I am *not* going to mold my body into what society expects me to look like. I *refuse* to hate my body. Instead, I'm going to respect, love, and care for my body." In this example, this person is *aware* of the unrealistic appearance expectations society promotes, and *models* how to challenge these expectations while treating their body with kindness and unconditional acceptance. This counter-message includes body appreciation (see Chapter 10). Hearing such counter-messages from people we respect can then impact our own responses to our bodies, shifting from negative to positive body image. We might think, "if they can believe that, I can to." We may even "pay it forward" by helping others challenge appearance ideals to develop their own positive body image.

We call this process the **rippling effect**, which is a specific type of mentorship whereby we learn from others who have a positive body image, and then "pass on" our knowledge and skills to foster positive body image in those who have not been exposed to such counter-messages. When we interviewed young adult women with a positive body image [7], many (80 percent) expressed that they had a negative body image during adolescence and reflected on how they transitioned to a positive body image. They recalled instances whereby they interacted more often with friends who were not focused on body and weight issues, and they modeled themselves after influential women who were proud of their bodies.

Women in our study made a conscious choice to surround themselves with others who have a positive body image [7]. One woman shared how her sister's positive body image impacted her: "I would just watch her and see how she could be confident and interact with different people and how she felt about herself. It gave me a goal to work up to. I knew I could reach it because it had been done." After exposure to positive role models such as this example, many said proudly that they were "never going back" to a negative body image. Women in our study not only modeled the positive body image of influential others, but also mentored others about positive body image and the importance of self-care [7]. One woman from our study reflected, "When you do become comfortable with yourself, you want to help others get to where you are."

A similar rippling effect was found in the interviews of young adult men and women from Sweden [8]. Many encouraged their children and friends to love their bodies and not to base their body image on what other people think. For example, one woman mentioned that her friends asked her about what their male dates would think about their appearance and she would reply, "It doesn't matter what he thinks, what matters is what you think. If you think that you look good, you look good. You don't need anyone else to tell you that."

Our peers can be powerful mentors [9]. Several programs geared towards improving body image use a **peer mentoring approach**, whereby those who complete the program mentor the next group of participants. For example, the prevention program *Full of Ourselves*, which is based on helping girls to claim their strengths (within their relationships and the world) and engage in self-care [10], has older girls (seventh and eighth graders) who have completed the program design and guide activities for younger girls (fourth and fifth graders) who are currently taking the program. It benefits the older girls by reinforcing the concepts learned, while it benefits the younger girls as they are more likely to absorb (and less likely to dismiss) information when it comes from an older peer compared to an adult. *Full of Ourselves* has been successfully implemented in schools, after-school programs, summer camps, churches, synagogues, and Girl Scout meetings [10].

Peer mentoring is a valuable component in the *Body Project* [11], a program which has demonstrated success in reducing negative body image and disordered eating [12–13]. The *Body Project* [11] is designed to raise **cognitive dissonance**, or an uncomfortable state whereby attitudes that maintain body dissatisfaction (e.g., "I must look like models") conflict with behavior (e.g., voicing the problems associated with trying to modify the body to look like a model). To do this, trained leaders (adults or peers) guide program participants to take part in verbal, written, and behavioral activities that argue against unrealistic appearance ideals. Some activities reflect the ripple effect. For example, program participants write a letter to a teen who is struggling with body image issues and describe the costs associated with pursuing appearance ideals. By repeatedly arguing against appearance ideals, program participants resolve their dissonance by reducing their pursuit of these ideals (e.g., "I can't hate my body because I talked to others about the problems associated with having a negative body image").

Peer leaders of the *Body Project* also benefit from the rippling effect as evidenced by the outcomes of former participants who were then trained to be peer leaders themselves [14]. These leaders reported lower disordered eating, body dissatisfaction, and appearance-ideal internalization after the program as compared to their pre-training scores. These beneficial effects were maintained both seven weeks [14] and eight months [15] later. Therefore, peer leaders continued to improve their own body image by mentoring others to accept their bodies.

Participating in activities and attending places that promote acceptance in general can also have a rippling effect on our positive body image. For example, certain yoga studios are body positive – that is, they focus on inclusion and acceptance, appreciate diversity, and emphasize the importance of listening to the body rather than focusing on appearance [16]. Those who practice yoga have higher body appreciation (see Chapter 10), higher positive embodiment (see Chapter 12), and lower self-objectification (see Chapter 13) compared to those who do not practice [17]. Yoga brings about a sense of gratitude for the body, self-confidence, an appreciation for different body sizes and shapes, and improvements in posture, flexibility, and strength [18]. Certain types of dance that do not focus heavily on the dancer's body type, such as belly dance [19] and contemporary dance [20], can also create a rippling effect, as participation is linked to higher body appreciation and lower self-objectification. Indeed, approaches to dance that allow participants to challenge negative societal appearance ideals while exploring other aspects of themselves (their emotions, social connections) show the most promise for a rippling effect on positive body image [21]. Engagement with spiritual and religious practices also create a rippling effect on body appreciation, which is likely due to the gratitude and reduced self-objectification that such practices foster [22].

Our continued involvement in actions and activities that bring out the rippling effect is important. We need to be active in both receiving and delivering counter-messages to outpace the damaging appearance-based images and messages from society. This involvement will benefit our own health and well-being, as well as others' health and well-being.

Treatment Planning Tools

Talking Points for Sessions

- Discuss which individuals/role models have influenced the client's positive body image
- Address specific experiences of positive body image
- Brainstorm ideas for promoting positive body image in others

Treatment Plan

Goals

- ❑ Inform others about the components of positive body image
- ❑ Inspire others to move towards positive body image
- ❑ Recognize people in my life who have shared knowledge and/or skills about positive body image
- ❑ Identify positive mentors in my life
- ❑ Make intentional choices on who to surround myself with

Objectives

- ❑ Interview someone with positive body image to learn about their experiences
- ❑ Identify positive portrayals of positive body image in media
- ❑ Read inspiring information from others about their journey from negative to positive body image such as *Stories of Hope* on the National Eating Disorder Association's (NEDA) website at: www.nationaleatingdisorders.org/
- ❑ Educate others on the *10 Steps to Positive Body Image*, a resource from the National Eating Disorder Association's (NEDA) website at: www.nationaleatingdisorders.org/
- ❑ Listen to and share music that promotes positive body image
- ❑ Present at established children's programs (e.g., Boy Scouts, Girl Scouts) about positive body image
- ❑ Create new programs in my community that promote positive body image
- ❑ Identify specific counter-messages in response to unrealistic appearance standards
- ❑ Reflect on any transformative experiences from negative to positive body image including key people who helped me
- ❑ Identify people around whom I feel positive and/or safe
- ❑ Identify environments that promote positive body image
- ❑ Identify examples of when my behaviors conflict with my attitudes or values in terms of my body image
- ❑ Engage in one activity a week to challenge an established attitude/belief about what "I should/shouldn't do" that is based on appearance ideals

❏ Write a journal entry to argue against unrealistic appearance ideals

❏ Repeat to myself at least daily a valuable sentiment expressed to me by one of my mentors

❏ Reflect on the ways that people with positive body image represent themselves (e.g., how they talk, speak, walk, treat their bodies) and incorporate one of these behaviors in the next week

Additional Resources

A. Brashich. *All Made Up: A Girl's Guide to Seeing Through the Celebrity Hype and Celebrating Real Beauty*. New York: Walker Publishing Company, Inc., 2006.

G. Scarano-Osika and K. Denver-Johnson. *You Grow Girl!: A Self-empowering Workbook for Tweens and Teens*. Burdett: Larson Publications, 2008.

A. Douglas, J. Douglas, and C. Davila. *Body Talk: The Straight Facts on Fitness, Nutrition, and Feeling Great about Yourself! (Girl Zone)*. Toronto: Maple Tree Press, 2006.

A. Mills, B. Osborn, and E. Neitz. *Shapesville*. Carlsbad: Gurze Books, 2003.

S. Danielsdottir and B. Bjarkdottir. *Your Body is Brilliant*. London: Singing Dragon, 2014.

T. Parr. *It's Okay to Be Different*. New York: Little, Brown and Company, 2009.

C. Steiner-Adair and L. Sjostrom. *Full of Ourselves*. New York: Teachers College Press, 2006.

Assignment 18.1: Contributions

Some people honor their own body functioning through contributing to the functioning of others. Examples of contributions include: a donation associated with the body (blood, platelets, plasma, sperm/eggs, organs), offering knowledge or expertise on how to increase body functioning or performance (coaching, instruction, rehabilitation), teaching how to care for the body (prevention, treatment), and mentoring on how to optimize a positive relationship with the functioning of the body. Reflect on whether contributing to others is important to you and if so complete the following.

Contributing relates to my core values*:

_____
_____
_____
_____
_____

I have received contributions from others in these ways:

_____
_____
_____
_____
_____

I have contributed to others in these ways:

_____
_____
_____
_____
_____

I commit to contribute in these ways:

_____
_____
_____
_____
_____

*The Good Project has an online value-sort activity to assist you in determining top values, available at: www.thegoodproject.org/value-sort

N. L. Wood-Barcalow, T. L. Tylka, and C. L. Judge. *Positive Body Image Workbook: A Clinical and Self-Improvement Guide.* Cambridge: Cambridge University Press, 2021.

Assignment 18.2: Acknowledging Those Who Have Mentored Me

When I reflect on my life, I recognize that these individuals (mentors) have promoted my positive body image:

_____
_____
_____
_____

These people said the following helpful or inspiring things:

_____
_____
_____
_____

These people did the following helpful or inspiring things:

_____
_____
_____
_____

I learned the following from these mentors:

_____
_____
_____
_____

I'd want these mentors to know:

_____
_____
_____
_____

I'd like to pay it forward by:

_____
_____
_____
_____

N. L. Wood-Barcalow, T. L. Tylka, and C. L. Judge. *Positive Body Image Workbook: A Clinical and Self-Improvement Guide.* Cambridge: Cambridge University Press, 2021.

Assignment 18.3: Why I Want to Mentor Others

Select the following as your reasons for mentoring others about positive body image:

Reasons	Yes/No	Reflections
I feel good doing it		
Help others who might not have access to these resources or information		
Help others to experience a different path than that of my own		
Challenge appearance ideals		
Challenge the status quo		
Inspire others		
It's the right thing to do		
Promote positive change		
Contribute to social justice		
It's associated with my core values		
It reinforces my own positive body image		
Promote positive change within my community		
I've been encouraged to do so		
It's part of my faith/spirituality		
Honor those who have done the same for me		
Make new connections		
Build my reputation		
Reduce loneliness		
Feel valued		
Feel needed		
Feel loved		
It's fun		
It's rewarding		
Benefits me just as much as others		
This knowledge/information should be free to all		
Pay It forward		
Other:		
Other:		
Other:		

 N. L. Wood-Barcalow, T. L. Tylka, and C. L. Judge. *Positive Body Image Workbook: A Clinical and Self-Improvement Guide.* Cambridge: Cambridge University Press, 2021.

Assignment 18.4: Volunteerism

According to Adam Grant in *Give and Take: Why Helping Others Drives Our Success* (2013), volunteering approximately two hours a week results in increased happiness, satisfaction, and self-esteem, which are all important components of positive body image. There are many ways to volunteer including, but not limited to, time spent with others, teaching others how to do something, donating money, giving blood, and more. In the table below, list different ways that you can volunteer that are of interest to you and set a timeline by which you would like to accomplish it.

Volunteer Activity	Timeline	Achieved?
Talk to cub/girl scouts about positive body image	*Within the next six months*	

* A.M. Grant. *Give and Take: Why Helping Others Drives Our Success*. New York: Penguin, 2013.

Assignment 18.5: Helping Others to Achieve Positive Body Image

It can be rewarding to contribute to others even when we have areas of growth ourselves. Instead of waiting for "the day that I feel better about myself," why not take small steps in contributing to the positive body image of others now? You don't have to be an expert on positive body image to help others in their own journeys. All you need is a genuine willingness to want to contribute to the positive outcome of others. Consider the following ways that you might promote positive body image in others. You may find it helpful to review the "take-home" themes for each chapter (see Assignment 2.14).

Idea	Commitment Strategy
Example: *I want to share information with the coach about how body image can impact athletic performance.*	*I'll ask coach if she's interested in learning about how positive body image can impact performance and help identify ways to increase it in athletes.*
Example: *I want to offer feedback to my partner about how their body-focused comments impact our children.*	*I'll ask my partner to dialogue about how our body-focused comments (toward ourselves and others) can have a negative impact on our kids. I'll leave a copy of this chapter and assignment for my partner to read.*

N. L. Wood-Barcalow, T. L. Tylka, and C. L. Judge. *Positive Body Image Workbook: A Clinical and Self-Improvement Guide.* Cambridge: Cambridge University Press, 2021.

Assignment 18.6: Transform Body Image Pain into Positive Change

Various ways that I experience negative body image pain:

_____

_____

_____

_____

_____

The toll(s) that this pain takes on my overall functioning:

_____

_____

_____

_____

_____

Ideas of how I can transform this pain into positive and productive outcomes for myself:

_____

_____

_____

_____

_____

Ideas of how I can transform this pain into positive and productive outcomes for others:

_____

_____

_____

_____

_____

N. L. Wood-Barcalow, T. L. Tylka, and C. L. Judge. *Positive Body Image Workbook: A Clinical and Self-Improvement Guide.* Cambridge: Cambridge University Press, 2021.

Assignment 18.7: Perspective Taking

Imagine a time of significant body dissatisfaction. This is how I felt, what I thought, how I acted, and what it meant to me at the time:

_____
_____
_____
_____
_____
_____

Things that were helpful to me during my difficult time:

_____
_____
_____
_____
_____

Now, imagine that someone else is experiencing similar levels of pain, discomfort, and body dissatisfaction. This is what they might feel, think, or experience:

_____
_____
_____
_____
_____
_____

How I might help this other person during their time of pain:

_____
_____
_____
_____
_____
_____

How helping others helps me:

_____
_____
_____
_____
_____

N. L. Wood-Barcalow, T. L. Tylka, and C. L. Judge. *Positive Body Image Workbook: A Clinical and Self-Improvement Guide.* Cambridge: Cambridge University Press, 2021.

Assignment 18.8: Important Topics to Address When Mentoring Others

Here is a list of possible topics to address when engaging in either formal or informal mentoring practices with others in order to promote positive body image. Check the items that you think are important in the process of switching from a focus on negative body image to that of positive body image. If there are topics that you are unfamiliar with, you can review different chapters of this workbook to gain ideas.

Positive Body Image . . .	Important to Address	Notes
Example: *is achievable regardless of body appearance*	X	*Your body doesn't have to look "perfect" in order to accept yourself.*
is achievable regardless of body appearance		
is achievable regardless of body functioning		
is appreciating the body		
is not only about appearance		
is about caring for the body (self-care)		
reflects trusting the body		
takes practice		
includes rejecting unrealistic appearance ideals		
takes commitment and investment		
includes letting go of ineffective or destructive behaviors		
is a process		
can be uncomfortable		
is not about altering or changing the body		
is not about avoiding the body		
involves examining thoughts, emotions, and behaviors		
includes setting appropriate limits/boundaries		
is appreciating how the body works or functions		
is loving the body as it is		
is accepting a range of bodies as beautiful		
recognizes unique characteristics		
includes bouncing back from body image threats		
includes celebrating our unique heritage(s)		
is talking about the body in positive ways		
includes rejecting negative/harmful information		
recognizes diverse forms of beauty		
Other:		
Other:		
Other:		

N. L. Wood-Barcalow, T. L. Tylka, and C. L. Judge. *Positive Body Image Workbook: A Clinical and Self-Improvement Guide.* Cambridge: Cambridge University Press, 2021.

Assignment 18.9: Tips for Promoting Positive Body Image in Children

- Engage in self-accepting body talk
- Provide a "body accepting" environment for everyone in the residence
- Engage the family in life-enhancing movement
- Promote a peaceful relationship with food
- Honor your child's ability to determine when they are hungry and full, and how much they should eat
- Praise your child's abilities, talents and strengths
- Accept diverse forms of beauty
- Don't joke about eating disorders or unhealthy behaviors such as vomiting or binge eating
- Know that weight doesn't translate into health
- Highlight the role and functions of the body
- Prioritize the need for breaks in busy schedules and self-care
- Acknowledge the role of spirituality/faith if applicable
- Refrain from negative body talk
- Encourage your child's own unique style rather than trying to fit them into a single mold
- Express and model how you appreciate your body
- Highlight how your heritage/ethnicity is reflected in your body
- Engage in culturally relevant activities
- Visit *the Full Bloom Project* (fullbloomproject.com) for research-informed, body-positive resources.

N. L. Wood-Barcalow, T. L. Tylka, and C. L. Judge. *Positive Body Image Workbook: A Clinical and Self-Improvement Guide.* Cambridge: Cambridge University Press, 2021.

References

1. V. M. Buote, A. E. Wilson, E. J. Strahan, et al. Setting the bar: Divergent sociocultural norms for women's and men's ideal appearance in real-world contexts. *Body Image* 2011; **8**: 322–34.

2. H. Keery, P. van den Berg, and J. K. Thompson. An evaluation of the tripartite influence model of body dissatisfaction and eating disturbance with adolescent girls. *Body Image* 2004; **1**: 237–51.

3. T. L. Tylka. Refinement of the tripartite influence model for men: Dual body image pathways to body change behaviors. *Body Image* 2011; **8**: 199–207.

4. S. A. McLean, S. J. Paxton, and E. H. Wertheim. Does media literacy mitigate risk for reduced body satisfaction following exposure to thin-ideal media? *J Youth Adolesc* 2016; **45**: 1678–95.

5. T. L. Tylka and C. L. Augustus-Horvath. Fighting self-objectification in prevention and intervention contexts. In: Calogero, R. M., Tantleff-Dunn, S., and Thompson, J. K., eds. *Self-Objectification in Women: Causes, Consequences, and Counteractions*. Washington: American Psychological Association, 2011: 187–214.

6. S. M. Wilksch and T. D. Wade. Reduction of shape and weight concern in young adolescents: A 30-month controlled evaluation of a media literacy program. *J Am Acad Child Adolesc Psychiatry* 2009; **48**: 651–61.

7. N. L. Wood-Barcalow, T. L. Tylka, and C. L. Augustus-Horvath. "But I like my body": Positive body image characteristics and a holistic model for young-adult women. *Body Image* 2010; **7**: 106–16.

8. K. Holmqvist Gattario and A. Frisén. From negative to positive body image: Men's and women's journeys from early adolescence to emerging adulthood. *Body Image* 2019; **28**: 53–65.

9. D. H. Shunk. Peer models and children's behavioral change. *Rev Educ Res* 1987; **57**: 149–74.

10. C. Steiner-Adair and L. Sjostrom. *Full of Ourselves: A Wellness Program to Advance Girl Power, Health, and Leadership*. New York: Teachers College Press, 2006.

11. E. Stice and K. Presnell. *The Body Project: Promoting Body Acceptance and Preventing Eating Disorders: Facilitator's Guide*. New York: Oxford University Press, 2007.

12. E. Stice, A. Chase, S. Stormer, et al. A randomized trial of a dissonance-based eating disorder prevention program. *Int J Eat Disord* 2001; **29**: 247–62.

13. E. Stice, C. N. Marti, S. Spoor, et al. Dissonance and healthy weight eating disorder prevention programs: Long-term effects from a randomized efficacy trial. *J Consult Clin Psychol* 2008; **76**: 329–40.

14. C. B. Becker, S. Bull, L. M. Smith, et al. Effects of being a peer-leader in an eating disorder prevention program: Can we further reduce eating disorder risk factors? *Eat Disord* 2008; **16**: 444–59.

15. C. B. Becker, S. Bull, K. Schaumberg, et al. Effectiveness of a peer-led eating disorders prevention: A replication trial. *J Consult Clin Psychol* 2008; **76**: 347–54.

16. C. Cook-Cottone and L. L. Douglass. Yoga communities and eating disorders: Creating safe space for positive embodiment. *Int J Yoga Ther* 2017; **27**: 87–93.

17. L. Mahlo and M. Tiggemann. Yoga and positive body image: A test of the Embodiment Model. *Body Image* 2016; **18**: 135–42.

18. D. Neumark-Sztainer, A. W. Watts, and S. Rydell. Yoga and body image: How do young adults practicing yoga describe its impact on their body image? *Body Image* 2018; **27**: 156–68.

19. M. Tiggemann, E. Coutts, and L. Clark. Belly dance as an embodying activity? A test of the embodiment model of positive body image. *Sex Roles* 2014; **71**: 197–207.

20. V. Swami and M. J. Tovée. A comparison of actual-ideal weight discrepancy, body appreciation, and media influence between street-dancers and non-dancers. *Body Image* 2009; **6**: 304–7.

21. V. Swami and A. S. Harris. Dancing toward positive body image? Examining body-related constructs with ballet and contemporary dancers at different levels. *Am J Dance Ther* 2012; **34**: 39–52.

22. M. Tiggemann and K. Hage. Religion and spirituality: Pathways to positive body image. *Body Image* 2019; **28**: 135–41.

Chapter 9

Self-Care

Theory and Research Overview

Self-care is any action we purposefully take to improve our physical, emotional, and/or spiritual well-being [1]. It involves being aware of and attending to our body's needs, as well as integrating self-care into our daily routine, relationships, and environment [2–6]. Self-care can include resting, eating nourishing foods, taking needed medication, seeking medical treatment, engaging in behaviors that may help prevent disease (such as flossing, regular skin cancer screenings), spending time in thoughtful reflection, being kind to ourselves, and engaging in any activity that renews us [7]. It helps build a foundation of our physical health and psychological well-being [2–3, 5, 7–8], and without it, we are more susceptible to exhaustion, emotional and physical burnout, physical health problems, and depletion [5, 9–10].

Too often, we may not plan and implement self-care. We may be too busy taking care of others, performing at our work, or we may think that we don't need it for ourselves. We may not be able to engage in some self-care practices due to financial reasons, as it often requires money and time to seek medical and preventative care, sleep, eat high nutrient foods, etc. Yet, our demands at home, at work, in our community, and in our relationships can shake our lives out of balance, and this imbalance needs to be restored. Our good friend and colleague, Dr. Catherine Cook-Cottone, often says, "We cannot pour from an empty cup." How often do we try to do this, though? When I (Tracy) was in graduate school, I did not engage in self-care. In addition to taking classes, studying for my comprehensive doctoral exams, applying for clinical internships, and being newly married, I was seeing clients in the university counseling center and working the night-shift at our local domestic violence shelter. I slept only a few hours a day and gave all my energy to my clients, my studies, the women at the shelter, and my husband. Concerned about my well-being, my mother told me to "stop and smell the flowers" and even bought me a pot of petunias for my patio. The petunias soon withered and died when I repeatedly forgot to water them. I had nothing left for the petunias, and I had nothing left for me. My physical health and psychological well-being suffered greatly in many ways during this time. As I look back, this was the period of time that I was least effective in my work and relationships. I was trying to "pour from an empty cup." I couldn't maintain this pattern long-term without serious negative effects. I needed to care for myself as well.

Mindful self-care is honoring our thoughts, emotions, and body reactions as we interact with others and our world – for example, planning activities with others who encourage us [2–5, 7]. It includes both scheduled and spontaneous self-care practices, such as being mindful as we go about our daily activities. Consistently practicing mindful self-care may help protect our physical and mental health by lowering our risk for burnout in work, school, and other areas of our lives [2–5, 7, 9–10], and is linked to more positive body image and lower symptoms of eating disorders [7]. Mindful self-care is "the thing to do now, to feel better later" [5].

Mindful self-care helps us regulate our emotions [2, 5]. **Emotional regulation** is our ability to recognize and respond to our emotions in ways that honor our experience but also don't get us into trouble [11]. For example, if we feel mistreated by a friend, we talk to this friend about how we feel (honoring our experience) without aggressively lashing out at them (which may get us into trouble by hurting the friendship). It also involves our ability to **self-soothe**, or calm ourselves when we are emotionally distressed [12–13], so that we don't engage in behaviors that we regret later. Therefore, we still acknowledge our emotions, and behave in ways that are not destructive in both the short-term and long-term.

Mindful self-care includes both mindful awareness and mindful practice [5, 14]. **Mindful awareness** occurs when we are present and notice our thoughts, emotions, sensations, and perceptions, and do not react to them or judge them. **Mindful practice** is regularly engaging in ways that help build mindful awareness, such as meditating and practicing yoga. **Beauty hunting** is another example that can include stopping to press the feet into the ground, taking a deep breath, and looking around for something beautiful, which can include a puppy playing with a ball, a ladybug on a leaf, or a couple sharing an ice cream cone [5]. Engaging in mindful practices can help stabilize our body's physiology, thereby supporting emotional regulation, and mindful practices are therefore often integrated into therapy [11, 13]. Mindful awareness and practice need a solid foundation from which to work. Regular self-care practices can help provide this base. These self-care practices can be divided into six domains [14]:

1. Getting adequate nutrition and fuel

2. Becoming and remaining hydrated

3. Engaging in life-enhancing movement (physical activities that bring us joy)

4. Engaging in self-soothing activities (e.g., meditation)

5. Getting sufficient rest

6. Taking medication as prescribed to regulate our body

What are common signs that we are in need of self-care? Our thoughts may turn negative, we may feel unappreciated and taken for granted, and we may notice that we slip into guilt trips or blame (ourselves and others) [15]. Our energy and concentration may be zapped. Our blood pressure may increase. For me, one sign was that my petunias died. While we need self-care to deal effectively with stressful situations, stress often lowers our engagement in self-care because we have to spend time and energy coping and sorting out the stress. Also, some self-care activities may require money that we simply do not have. Stress and self-care may become a downward spiral: increased stress reduces time and resources needed for self-care, and reduced self-care makes our bodies and well-being more susceptible to the depleting effects of stress.

What happens when we do not have time, money, or other resources to engage in self-care? First, it is important to treat ourselves with compassion, and know that we are doing the best that we can to cope as effectively as possible with our lives at any given moment. Second, it is important to consider whether there are small ways we can integrate self-care practices that are within the bounds of what our time, energy, and finances allow. Third, if self-care is impacted due in part to not being assertive or a reluctance

to say "no," we may want to consider ways to empower ourselves within these relationships. Fourth, sometimes we can make shifts within our lives to give us extra resources (time, energy) for self-care. Focusing on what we can do can create self-care opportunities. For example, if our current job is draining our resources and there are other job opportunities in our field, we may focus on finding another job that is less draining. If we are caring for an elderly parent or child with a disability, we may be able to reach out to others for support.

Adding consistent self-care to our lives may help us deal effectively with stressful situations [5, 12–13]. As articulated by Cook-Cottone [5], mindful self-care includes four steps: (a) being *aware* that mindful self-care is essential to our well-being, (b) assessing the extent to which we *engage* in self-care, (c) setting *goals* for self-care, and (d) taking *action* to improve our self-care. The *Mindful Self-Care Scale* (MSCS) [5, 7], which is presented in this chapter, can help with setting goals and taking action in the following six self-care domains: mindful relaxation, physical care, self-compassion and purpose, supportive relationships, supportive structure, and mindful awareness.

Research supports the connections between mindful self-care and physical health and psychological well-being [5]. For instance, good nutrition, hydration, and rest support our ability to regulate our emotions, think effectively, pay attention, and engage in exercise as well as maintain skin health, neurological, gastrointestinal, and renal function [16–18]. Exercise reduces stress by releasing endorphins into our bloodstream, decreases our muscle tension, and improves body image, strength, flexibility, and blood flow to the brain [19]. Exercise also improves body image [20] and has many benefits for our memory and learning, such as generating neurons in the circuits of the hippocampus by increasing the key molecule brain-derived neurotrophic factor (BDNF) [21]. This process is responsible for improved cognitive and emotional functioning (e.g., clear thinking, feeling more positive) that accompany exercise. Planned breaks, rest, and relaxation can help us focus more energy on our goals during the time spent working [6]. Self-soothing practices and supportive relationships help us effectively regulate our emotions and handle current and future stressors [11–13]. Personalizing our workspaces and keeping them organized helps our psychological well-being and job satisfaction [22]. Mindful awareness can be achieved through activities that bring us flow. **Flow**, or "being in the zone," happens when we are engrossed in an enjoyable task (e.g., playing a musical instrument, performing a sport) in which we challenge ourselves to meet the demands of the task [23].

Spiritual self-care involves inspiration from something greater than ourselves and does not have to be connected to religion – it can include a sense of mission, purpose, and value [5]. Spirituality has been found to be a useful resource for maintaining life satisfaction during times of stress [24], and is related to higher positive body image [25]. For example, women with a warm and secure relationship with God experience less body dissatisfaction after being exposed to images of models [26] as well as experience higher positive emotions, body appreciation, body functionality, and intuitive eating [27].

In sum, self-care can nurture our physical health and psychological well-being so that we can tackle the demands of our lives. We hope that this chapter helps raise awareness of the importance of self-care for physical and emotional health and encourages achievable actions to improve it.

Treatment Planning Tools

Talking Points for Sessions

- Define types of self-care
- Discuss overall balance in different areas of life: social, emotional, familial, professional/work/school, spiritual, physical, and psychological
- Discuss the role of joy and pleasure in life related to self-care
- Address how self-care relates to being effective in life
- Discuss the phrase, "self-care is the thing to do now, to feel better later"
- Address how compassion for self and others relates to self-care

Treatment Plan

Goals

- ❏ Create a personal definition of self-care including behaviors, thoughts, and emotions
- ❏ Increase frequency of my engagement in self-care activities
- ❏ Consider how self-care relates to my positive body image
- ❏ Consider how self-care relates to my physical health and psychological well-being
- ❏ Explore how setting limits (e.g., saying "no" to unwanted requests) corresponds with my self-care
- ❏ Implement plans to restore balance
- ❏ Incorporate spontaneous activities to increase fun and pleasure
- ❏ Increase engagement in mindful activities that I can practice regularly
- ❏ Consider potential life changes to restore balance
- ❏ Explore how relying on the help or assistance of others can enhance my self-care
- ❏ Reflect on how self-care relates to my sense of mission, purpose, and value

Objectives

- ❏ Identify and practice one self-care activity each day/week
- ❏ Identify and respond to basic daily needs (e.g., sleep, rest, nourishment, hygiene)
- ❏ Identify and implement a routine for self-care (e.g., daily, weekly, monthly, yearly)
- ❏ Identify environments that promote self-care

- ❏ Recognize "red flags" associated with my exhaustion (mental, physical, and emotional)
- ❏ Identify symptoms associated with my depletion and burnout
- ❏ Identify "red flags" that interfere with self-care and problem solve how to prevent or overcome them
- ❏ Identify specific barriers to practicing self-care and problem solve how to prevent or overcome them
- ❏ Recognize thoughts and emotions that interfere with engaging in self-care (e.g., no time, don't care, don't deserve it, no energy, sadness, embarrassment, guilt)
- ❏ Differentiate between self-care practices and those activities that feel obligatory
- ❏ Identify which self-care practices shifted into obligatory activities
- ❏ Identify various forms of life-enhancing movement that are relaxing to my body and mind
- ❏ Identify specific times/activities to spend with important people in my life
- ❏ Identify specific ways to self-soothe
- ❏ Engage in "beauty hunting" at least once daily
- ❏ Identify behaviors that are enjoyable in the moment but interfere with long-term self-care and positive body image (e.g., nicotine/substance use, impulsive behaviors)
- ❏ Notice the specific thoughts and emotions that occur when I feel depleted or exhausted
- ❏ Ask one person for help in accomplishing a task

Additional Resources

C. P. Cook-Cottone. *Embodiment and the Treatment of Eating Disorders: The Body as a Resource for Recovery.* New York: W.W. Norton & Company, 2020.

C. P. Cook-Cottone. *Mindfulness and Yoga for Self-Regulation: A Primer for Mental Health Professionals.* New York: Springer Publishing Company, LLC, 2015.

C. P. Cook-Cottone and R. K. Vuknovic. *Mindfulness for Anxious Kids: A Workbook to Help Children Cope with Anxiety, Stress, and Worry.* Oakland: Instant Help Books/ New Harbinger Publications, Inc., 2018.

J. Stanley. *Every Body Yoga.* New York: Workman Publishing Co., Inc., 2017.

M. C. Klein. *Yoga Rising: 30 Empowering Stories from Yoga Renegades for Every Body.* Woodbury: Llewellyn Publications, 2018.

C. P. Cook-Cottone. *Mindfulness and Yoga in Schools: A Guide for Teachers and Practitioners.* New York: Springer Publishing Company, LLC, 2017.

J. C. Norcross and J. D. Guy. *Leaving it at the Office: A Guide to Psychotherapist Self-Care.* New York: The Guilford Press, 2007.

Internet search for "progressive muscle relaxation, body scan"

Assessment 19.1: Mindful Self-Care Scale-Brief (MSCS-Brief)*

Circle the number that reflects the frequency of your behavior[1] (how much or how often) within the **past week (7 days)**.

Mindful Relaxation	Never (0 days)	Rarely (1 day)	Sometimes (2–3 days)	Often (4–5 days)	Regularly (6–7 days)
1. I did something creative to relax (drew, played an instrument, wrote creatively, sang, organized).	1	2	3	4	5
2. I listened to relax (to music, a podcast, radio show, rainforest sounds).	1	2	3	4	5
3. I sought out images to relax (art, film, window shopping, nature).	1	2	3	4	5
4. I sought out smells to relax (lotions, nature, candles/incense, smells of baking).	1	2	3	4	5
Total Mindful Relaxation score: add circled responses and divide by 4 =					

Physical Care	Never (0 days)	Rarely (1 day)	Sometimes (2–3 days)	Often (4–5 days)	Regularly (6–7 days)
1. I ate a variety of nutritious foods (vegetables, protein, fruits, grains).	1	2	3	4	5
2. I exercised for at least thirty minutes.	1	2	3	4	5
3. I took part in sports, dance or other scheduled physical activities (sports teams, dance classes).	1	2	3	4	5
4. I practiced yoga or another mind/body practice (Tae Kwon Do, Tai Chi).	1	2	3	4	5
Total Physical Care score: add circled responses and divide by 4 =					

Self-Compassion and Purpose	Never (0 days)	Rarely (1 day)	Sometimes (2–3 days)	Often (4–5 days)	Regularly (6–7 days)
1. I kindly acknowledged my own challenges and difficulties.	1	2	3	4	5
2. I engaged in supportive and comforting self-talk ("My effort is valuable and meaningful").	1	2	3	4	5
3. I gave myself permission to feel my feelings (allowed myself to cry).	1	2	3	4	5
4. I experienced meaning and/or a larger purpose in my life (for a cause).	1	2	3	4	5
Total Self-Compassion and Purpose score: add circled responses and divide by 4 =					

---

[1] These behaviors are simply guidelines that need to be individualized based on your own experiences and resources.

Supportive Relationships	Never (0 days)	Rarely (1 day)	Sometimes (2–3 days)	Often (4–5 days)	Regularly (6–7 days)
1. I spent time with people who are good to me (support, encourage, and believe in me).	1	2	3	4	5
2. I felt supported by people in my life.	1	2	3	4	5
3. I felt confident that people in my life would respect my choice if I said "no."	1	2	3	4	5
4. I felt that I had someone who would listen to me if I became upset (a friend, counselor, group).	1	2	3	4	5
Total Supportive Relationships score: add circled responses and divide by 4 =					

Supportive Structure	Never (0 days)	Rarely (1 day)	Sometimes (2–3 days)	Often (4–5 days)	Regularly (6–7 days)
1. I maintained a manageable schedule.	1	2	3	4	5
2. I kept my work/schoolwork area organized to support my work/school tasks.	1	2	3	4	5
3. I maintained balance between the demands of others and what is important to me.	1	2	3	4	5
4. I maintained a comforting and pleasing living environment.	1	2	3	4	5
Total Supportive Structure score: add circled responses and divide by 4 =					

Mindful Awareness	Never (0 days)	Rarely (1 day)	Sometimes (2–3 days)	Often (4–5 days)	Regularly (6–7 days)
1. I had a calm awareness of my thoughts.	1	2	3	4	5
2. I had a calm awareness of my feelings.	1	2	3	4	5
3. I had a calm awareness of my body.	1	2	3	4	5
Total Mindful Awareness score: add circled responses and divide by 3 =					

Total subscale scores between:
- **4–5** = high levels of mindful self-care
- **2.5–3.9** = moderate levels of mindful self-care
- **2.4 and below** = low levels of mindful self-care

Note. Reprinted with permission. Authors of the MSCS are Cook-Cottone and Guyker.* The use of the MSCS has been supported among community adults, as the MSCS is positively associated with body esteem and negatively associated with many aspects of eating disordered behavior among community adult samples. There are two other versions, MSCS-Clinical (eighty-four items), MSCS-Standard (thirty-three items). While the MSCS-Brief is presented above, the other two versions are available via www .catherinecookcottone.com/research-and-teaching/mindful-self-care-scale/ . Please contact the authors of this measure for permission to use the MSCS within research; there is no need to contact them to use it with clients or to complete it on your own.

*C. P. Cook-Cottone and W. M. Guyker. The development and validation of the Mindful Self-Care Scale (MSCS): An assessment of practices that support positive embodiment. *Mindfulness* 2018; **9**: 161–75.

Mindful Self-Care Scale-Brief Applications

- The MSCS-Brief allows you to understand your areas of strength and needed growth, as well as create action goals related to self-care.

  o What are your strengths? Your strengths are the circled items that are "4s" or "5s".

  o What are your growth areas? Growth areas are the circled items that are "3" or below.

- Based on your growth areas, identify three goals and an action plan for each.

  o For each goal, choose one task/activity to accomplish in the coming week. Put it on your calendar and create a reminder if needed. After you've accomplished the task, remember to give yourself credit for taking action in the direction of something that matters to you.

- Review your identified growth areas. What barriers exist in these areas, either inside yourself (internal) or in your life (external)? For example, feeling guilty or unworthy of self-care is an internal barrier. Not having money to engage in self-care is an external barrier.

  o What can you tell yourself to challenge internal barriers to mindful self-care?

  o If external barriers (such as limited financial resources) exist, what are some problem-solving steps you can take to make it more likely that you practice mindful self-care?

  o If you have already considered ways to use problem-solving, try using self-compassionate statements to remind yourself that the items on this assessment are guidelines to be individualized based on a person's unique life circumstances, experiences, resources, and more.

Assignment 19.1: Engaging in Flow

The idea of creative flow occurs when a person is engaged in a satisfying experience that includes enjoyment and total engagement with life. Mihaly Csikszentmihalyi, a psychologist and co-founder of positive psychology, indicated, "The best moments in our lives are not the passive, receptive, relaxing times . . . The best moments usually occur if a person's body or mind is stretched to its limits in a voluntary effort to accomplish something difficult and worthwhile" (1990). This quote describes the gifts of flow. Experiencing flow is similar to "being in the zone." Flow differs for each person based on personality, strengths, talents, and interests. Examples can include playing an instrument, participating in physical activity (dancing, playing a sport), writing, teaching, performing, and more.

Eight Qualities of Flow*

1. Concentrating on a task
2. Awareness of goals and rewards along with immediate feedback
3. Time feels different (e.g., appears to speed up, appears to slow down)
4. The experience itself is internally rewarding
5. Little strenuous effort, sense of ease
6. Sense of balance between the challenges of the task and our skills
7. Feeling a loss of self-awareness
8. Sense of control over the task

My experiences with flow include:

_____

_____

_____

_____

How often I engage in flow experiences at this time:

_____

_____

_____

_____

My goal for increasing engagement in flow activities:

_____

_____

_____

_____

How participating in flow experiences relates to self-care:

_____

_____

_____

_____

How participating in flow experiences relates to moving toward positive body image:

_____

_____

_____

_____

*From PositivePsychology.com

N. L. Wood-Barcalow, T. L. Tylka, and C. L. Judge. *Positive Body Image Workbook: A Clinical and Self-Improvement Guide.* Cambridge: Cambridge University Press, 2021.

Assignment 19.2: Comparison of Beauty Hunting and Appearance Hunting

Beauty hunting is the practice of looking for beauty with awareness in your immediate environment. We notice beauty in: large objects (cloud formations, waves on the sea, starlit sky), small objects (a ladybug on a flower, patterns on a leaf), joyful expressions (a puppy playing with a ball, child laughing), interactions among people (a couple sharing an ice cream cone, a smile toward a stranger), different forms of art (a mural on a city building, favorite song), and more. The idea behind beauty hunting is that beauty can be found all around, with the practice of focused intention and being present in the moment.

Now, consider how an emphasis on the physical attractiveness of people is a major component of society and individual experiences. Consider how this focus impacts your own body image and self-acceptance including seeking perfection for the body, engaging in routines to promote attractiveness, and prioritizing attractiveness in a partner. Imagine that the practice(s) of searching for attractive features within yourself and others could be referred to as *appearance hunting*.

For this journal assignment, consider your own experiences of "appearance hunting" versus "beauty hunting." Reflect on these questions: What specific attractiveness features am I focused on? How am I searching for attractiveness in others? How am I searching for attractiveness for myself? While looking for attractiveness in others, am I ignoring other aspects of beauty that go beyond appearance? While looking for attractiveness in myself, am I ignoring other aspects of beauty that go beyond my appearance? What would it mean to shift from "appearance hunting" to "beauty hunting?" What might I do differently? How might I see things differently? How does "beauty hunting" relate to moving toward a positive body image?

_____
_____
_____
_____
_____
_____
_____
_____
_____
_____
_____
_____
_____
_____
_____
_____
_____
_____

N. L. Wood-Barcalow, T. L. Tylka, and C. L. Judge. *Positive Body Image Workbook: A Clinical and Self-Improvement Guide.* Cambridge: Cambridge University Press, 2021.

Assignment 19.3: Balance

Having a sense of balance in life is an important aspect of self-care. Levels of balance can vary in different areas such as social life, emotional experiences, family life, profession/work/school life, spiritual and/or religious pursuits, physical health, emotional health, and psychological well-being. Take time to reflect on your current life experiences including how balanced you are in each of these domains by marking on the line. If unbalanced, create an action plan of how to move toward more balance. An example is included below.

Example: *Social Life*

I————————X——I

Unbalanced   Balanced

Action plan for change: *I will leave work at a reasonable time and meet a friend for dinner that I haven't seen for months.*

Social Life

I——I

Unbalanced   Balanced

Action plan for change:

Family Life

I——I

Unbalanced   Balanced

Action plan for change:

Professional/Work/School Life

I——I

Unbalanced   Balanced

Action plan for change:

Spiritual and/or Religious Pursuits

I——I

Unbalanced   Balanced

Action plan for change:

Physical Health

I——I

Unbalanced   Balanced

Action plan for change:

Psychological Well-Being

I——I

Unbalanced   Balanced

Action plan for change:

 N. L. Wood-Barcalow, T. L. Tylka, and C. L. Judge. *Positive Body Image Workbook: A Clinical and Self-Improvement Guide.* Cambridge: Cambridge University Press, 2021.

Emotional Health

I--I

Unbalanced   Balanced

Action plan for change:

Other

I--I

Unbalanced   Balanced

Action plan for change:

Other

I--I

Unbalanced   Balanced

Action plan for change:

Other

I--I

Unbalanced   Balanced

Action plan for change:

N. L. Wood-Barcalow, T. L. Tylka, and C. L. Judge. *Positive Body Image Workbook: A Clinical and Self-Improvement Guide.* Cambridge: Cambridge University Press, 2021.

Assignment 19.4: Fun and Pleasure

For this journal experience, reflect on the various experiences in life that you associate with fun and pleasure. Examples might be learning a new skill, dancing to a favorite song, playing an instrument, riding a bike, talking with a friend, going to or watching a sporting event, taking a hike, walking a puppy, advocating for a cause, making someone laugh, reading a book, spending time with a loved one, buying something, jogging, watching a sunset, and more. Consider the following questions: What types of experiences/activities might I like to try that seem like fun? What do I consider fun and/or pleasurable? Do I have enough pleasurable experiences in my life at this time? How have pleasurable experiences changed over time? How are pleasurable experiences related to self-care? How is fun and pleasure related to positive body image?

_____
_____
_____
_____
_____
_____
_____
_____
_____
_____
_____
_____
_____
_____
_____
_____
_____
_____
_____
_____
_____
_____
_____

N. L. Wood-Barcalow, T. L. Tylka, and C. L. Judge. *Positive Body Image Workbook: A Clinical and Self-Improvement Guide.* Cambridge: Cambridge University Press, 2021.

Assignment 19.5: Different Types of Self-Care I Commit To

Those with positive body image highlight the importance of continual self-care activities for good physical and mental health. Self-care is "the thing to do now to feel better later."*

Reflect on the following:

Examples of Different Types of Self-Care That I Enjoy:

- ❑ Physical (yoga, lifting weights, dancing):
- ❑ Emotional (watching a funny show, writing in a journal):
- ❑ Relational (spending time in-person with a loved one, texting a friend):
- ❑ Spiritual (prayer, attending a service, reading, meditating):
- ❑ Psychological (attending therapy, writing in a journal, addressing painful issues):
- ❑ Social (going to a community event):
- ❑ Other:
- ❑ Other:

Barriers to Incorporating Self-Care

- ❑ Thoughts: _____

  Examples: *I don't have time. I don't deserve it.*

- ❑ Emotions: _____

  Examples: *sadness, guilt, apathy, resignation*

- ❑ Behaviors: _____

  Examples: *prioritizing others before myself, no time in my schedule*

- ❑ Physical issues: _____

  Examples: *headaches, chronic pain, physical limitations*

- ❑ Financial issues: _____

  Examples: *not enough money, don't get paid for a few weeks*

- ❑ Other:
- ❑ Other:

Strategies to Overcome These Barriers

- ❑ Thoughts: _____

  Examples: *I need to make time for myself to improve my quality of life. I will remind myself that self-care behaviors have actually seemed to improve my motivation and effectiveness in the past.*

- ❑ Emotions: _____

  Examples: *Doing pleasurable things makes me feel good.*

- ❑ Behaviors: _____

  Examples: *I'm planning to do this once a week.*

- ❑ Physical issues: _____

  Examples: *I'll do this in the morning when I feel best.*

- ❑ Financial issues: _____

  Examples: *I can budget for activities that cost money. There are many activities that I can do that don't cost anything.*

- ❑ Other:
- ❑ Other:

N. L. Wood-Barcalow, T. L. Tylka, and C. L. Judge. *Positive Body Image Workbook: A Clinical and Self-Improvement Guide.* Cambridge: Cambridge University Press, 2021. **291**

How self-care relates to being effective in life:

_____
_____
_____
_____
_____

How self-care is associated with moving toward positive body image:

_____
_____
_____
_____
_____

*C. P. Cook-Cottone. *Embodiment and the Treatment of Eating Disorders: The Body as a Resource for Recovery.* New York: Norton, 2020.

N. L. Wood-Barcalow, T. L. Tylka, and C. L. Judge. *Positive Body Image Workbook: A Clinical and Self-Improvement Guide.* Cambridge: Cambridge University Press, 2021.

Assignment 19.6: Ways to Self-Soothe

The ability to self-soothe, or calm yourself when upset, is important for mental wellness and healthy relationships. There are different ways to self-soothe that are destructive (harmful, unhealthy, cause additional distress or problems), such as using substances, spending money that is not available, and engaging in impulsive behaviors (e.g., yelling, throwing things). There are ways to self-soothe that are constructive (helpful, healthy) such as deep breathing, getting rest or sleep, connecting with friends, listening to relaxing sounds, using positive self-talk, engaging in physical movement, talking with a trusted friend, laughing, focusing the mind, writing in a journal, participating in spiritual practice, allowing yourself to feel a range of emotions, doing something pleasurable, and more.

I get upset when:

_____
_____
_____
_____

When I'm upset, I:

_____
_____
_____
_____

I use these destructive methods to self-soothe:

_____
_____
_____
_____

I use these constructive methods to self-soothe:

_____
_____
_____
_____

When I'm upset in the future, I commit to the following constructive ways to self-soothe:

_____
_____
_____
_____

Using constructive ways to self-soothe moves me toward positive body image in these ways:

_____
_____
_____
_____

N. L. Wood-Barcalow, T. L. Tylka, and C. L. Judge. *Positive Body Image Workbook: A Clinical and Self-Improvement Guide.* Cambridge: Cambridge University Press, 2021.

Assignment 19.7: Recognizing and Preventing Exhaustion

Physical, emotional and social exhaustion are signs of being out of balance. There can be many reasons for exhaustion and burnout.

How I can tell when I'm physically exhausted:

_____

_____

_____

How I can tell when I'm emotionally exhausted:

_____

_____

_____

How I can tell when I'm socially exhausted:

_____

_____

_____

Exhaustion impacts my body image:

_____

_____

_____

Things I neglect when exhausted:

_____

_____

_____

Things I can do to buffer against exhaustion:

Daily:

_____

_____

_____

Weekly:

_____

_____

_____

Monthly:

_____

_____

_____

Yearly:

_____

_____

_____

N. L. Wood-Barcalow, T. L. Tylka, and C. L. Judge. *Positive Body Image Workbook: A Clinical and Self-Improvement Guide.* Cambridge: Cambridge University Press, 2021.

References

1. E. Brownn. Lifelong learner. Retrieved from www.eleanorbrownn.com [last accessed July 12, 2020].

2. C. P. Cook-Cottone. *Mindfulness and Yoga for Self-regulation: A Primer for Mental Health Professionals*. New York: Springer, 2015.

3. C. P. Cook-Cottone. *Mindfulness and Yoga in Schools: A Guide for Teachers and Practitioners*. New York: Springer, 2017.

4. C. P. Cook-Cottone. Mindful attunement. In: Tylka, T. L. and Piran, N. eds. *Handbook of Positive Body Image: Constructs, Protective Factors, and Interventions*. New York: Oxford University Press, 2019: 68–79.

5. C. P. Cook-Cottone. *Embodiment and the Treatment of Eating Disorders: The Body as a Resource for Recovery*. New York: Norton, 2020.

6. J. C. Norcross and J. D. Guy. *Leaving it at the Office: A Guide to Psychotherapist Self-Care*. New York: Guilford Press, 2007.

7. C. P. Cook-Cottone and W. M. Guyker. The development and validation of the Mindful Self-Care Scale (MSCS): An assessment of practices that support positive embodiment. *Mindfulness* 2018; **9**: 161–75.

8. R. Andrew, M. Tiggemann, and L. Clark. Positive body image and young women's health: Implications for sun protection, cancer screening, weight loss and alcohol consumption behaviors. *J Health Psychol* 2016; **21**: 28–39.

9. C. R. Figley. Compassion fatigue: Psychotherapists' chronic lack of self care. *J Clin Psychol* 2002; **58**: 1433–41.

10. S. L. Shapiro, K. W. Brown, and G. M. Biegel. Teaching self-care to caregivers: Effects of mindfulness-based stress reduction on the mental health of therapists in training. *Train Educ Prof Psychol* 2007; **1**: 105–15.

11. M. M. Linehan. *Cognitive-Behavioral Treatment of Borderline Personality Disorder*. New York: Guilford Press, 1993.

12. A. C. Kelly, D. C. Zuroff, and L. B. Shapira. Soothing oneself and resisting self-attacks: The treatment of two intrapersonal deficits in depression vulnerability. *Cogn Ther Res* 2009; **33**: 301–13.

13. R. N. Goldman and L. Greenberg. Working with identity and self-soothing in emotion-focused therapy for couples. *Family Process* 2013; **52**: 62–82.

14. C. P. Cook-Cottone, E. Tribole, and T. L. Tylka. *Healthy Eating in Schools: Evidence-Based Interventions to Help Kids Thrive*. Washington: American Psychological Association, 2013.

15. P. A. Jennings. *Mindfulness for Teachers: Simple Skills for Peace and Productivity in the Classroom*. New York: Norton, 2015.

16. M. Hart. The importance and elements of healthy nutrition. *Adv Eat Disord* 2016; **4**: 14–30.

17. D. Liska, E. Mah, T. Brisbois, et al. Narrative review of hydration and selected health outcomes in the general population. *Nutrients* 2019; **11**: 70.

18. J. Lim and D. F. Dinges. A meta-analysis of the impact of short-term sleep deprivation on cognitive variables. *Psychol Bull* 2010; **136**: 375–89.

19. F. J. Penedo and J. R. Dahn. Exercise and well-being: A review of mental and physical health benefits associated with physical activity. *Curr Opin Psychiatr* 2005; **18**: 189–93.

20. H. A. Hausenblas and E. A. Fallon. Exercise and body image: A meta-analysis. *Psychol Health* 2006; **21**: 33–47.

21. P. Z. Liu and R. Nusslock. Exercise-mediated neurogenesis in the hippocampus via BDNF. *Front Neurosci* 2018; **12**: 52. Retrieved from: www.frontiersin.org/articles/10.3389/fnins.2018.00052/full#B16 [last accessed July 12, 2020].

22. M. M. Wells. Office clutter or meaningful personal displays: The role of office personalization in employee and organizational well-being. *J Environ Psychol* 2000; **20**: 239–55.

23. M. Czikszentmihalyi. *Flow–The Psychology of Optimal Experience*. New York: Harper & Row, 1990.

24. A. N. Fabricatore, P. J. Handal, and L. M. Fenzel. Personal spirituality as a moderator of the relationship between stressors and subjective well-being. *J Psychol Theol* 2000; **28**: 221–8.

25. M. Tiggemann and K. Hage. Religion and spirituality: Pathways to positive body image. *Body Image* 2019; **28**: 135–41.

26. K. J. Homan. Attachment to God mitigates negative effect of media exposure on women's body image. *Psychol Relig Spiritual* 2012; **4**: 324–31.

27. K. J. Homan and B. N. Cavanaugh. Perceived relationship with God fosters positive body image in college women. *J Health Psychol* 2013; **18**: 1529–39.

Chapter 20

Fueling Our Bodies

Theory and Research Overview

I (Tracy) grew up alternating between being pressured to restrict food and to eat. My older sister seemed to always be on a "strict diet" and for a rather long period of time refused any food other than vegetables and yogurt. She was a role model for me, so at five years old, I followed her lead. I used her strategies, with the goal of losing weight. I even tried to convince people I didn't like chocolate so they wouldn't offer it to me. I learned it was acceptable to restrict (and wrong to enjoy) tasty food.

My mother sometimes allowed my brother to feed me when I was an infant, even after I had already eaten. With some persistence, my brother got me to eat more. My grandma, who lived through the Great Depression, would always ask me, "Do you want ice cream/cookies/pie?" and if I said "no," she would bring me the food anyway. If I left food on my plate, she would exclaim: "Eat! There are starving children everywhere!" She interpreted my refusal of food as a sign that I did not appreciate having food.

I understand that my family's behaviors were rooted in love. My sister loved hanging out with me and teaching me to value what she valued. My brother loved feeding me, and my mom loved seeing her children bond. My grandma loved being able to provide food for me and seeing me eat. I also see the normalcy within their behaviors. My story could be anyone's story, as dieting or restricting food intake is often promoted as desirable by society, and adults feel that they have to closely monitor what children eat [1]. Yet, I also see the problems within their behaviors. I was not permitted to feel hungry, eat, become comfortably full, and stop eating without shame, guilt, and pressure to eat differently. As a result, I was never able to notice how different foods impacted my body – I didn't know what foods I truly enjoyed, what foods gave me lasting energy, what foods made my body feel well, and what foods my body craved. In adolescence, I continued to diet, which prompted binge eating, emotional eating, and situational eating (eating because food is available, not because we are hungry for it), which are very common outcomes of dieting [2]. I grew up out of touch with my hunger cues, fullness cues, and appetite.

In graduate school, I began working with clients who had abnormal relationships with food (i.e., clients with eating disorders and other forms of disordered eating, such as chronic dieting). A therapy goal for one client was to have "a normal relationship with food." She exclaimed, "I want to change how I eat, but I don't know what 'a normal relationship with food' is like! What do I do to change?" I was at a loss. At that point, I had never had a normal relationship with food and could not describe it well. My supervisor recommended that I read the book, *Intuitive Eating: A Recovery Book for the Chronic Dieter* [3]. This book positively changed my life, my clients' lives, and the lives of many others.

Intuitive eating involves being connected to, trusting in, and responding to our bodies' internal hunger and fullness cues [3–6]. Intuitive eating is grounded in the belief that we are born with the wisdom for knowing what, when, and how much to eat. For instance, infants know when they are hungry, cry to let their caregivers know that it is time to eat, and turn their head away from the breast, bottle, or spoon when full [7]. Sometimes adults think they are benefitting children by teaching them to use external cues (e.g., portion control, calorie limits) to determine what, when, and how much to eat, when children's internal cues (e.g., appetite, whether they are hungry or full) could be used to guide their eating behavior. If adults pressure children to eat when they are not hungry and stop eating before they are full, these hunger and satiety cues can fade over time [7]. Thankfully, we can reconnect with these cues!

How can we become reconnected to our hunger and satiety cues? The ten principles of intuitive eating [3–4, 8] are helpful:

1. **Rejecting the diet mentality.** We catch ourselves when we think, "I'll be happier if I lose weight," and "I need to go on a diet." We then challenge these thoughts.

2. **Challenging the "food police."** We challenge the voices inside our head (or other people's voices) that tell us what we should eat, when we should eat, and how much we should eat (e.g., "You can't have ice cream," "You ate too much at breakfast and can't eat again until later").

3. **Making peace with food.** We do not categorize food as "good" or "bad," as categorizing food in this manner increases our preoccupation with it. Preoccupation with food may appear as being obsessed with only eating "good" or "clean" foods, and feelings of guilt after eating "bad foods." Food preoccupation is associated with binge eating, and making peace with food is linked to intuitive eating and well-being [9].

4. **Coping with emotions without using food.** It is common (and not harmful) to eat for emotional reasons at times. However, when emotional eating is frequent and prompts additional distress, it may become problematic for our well-being. A consistent pattern of emotional eating can raise guilt, shame, and anxiety in a culture that stigmatizes weight gain and higher-weight bodies. Furthermore,

repetitively using food to comfort or distract ourselves can keep us from uncovering and addressing what is underlying our negative emotions.

5. **Honoring hunger**. We don't avoid eating when we are hungry. Soon after we feel hunger in our bodies, we allow ourselves to eat. We consider **food as fuel** for our bodies.

6. **Feeling fullness**. Soon after we notice that our bodies are no longer hungry, or are comfortably full, we stop eating.

7. **Discovering the satisfaction factor**. We savor food and enjoy the eating experience, engaging our senses by noticing the taste, texture, smell, and appearance of food. This principle is similar to eating mindfully, or with awareness and attention.

8. **Respecting our bodies**. We listen to, appreciate, and take care of our bodies via mindful self-care (see Chapters 10 and 19).

9. **Exercising to feel the difference**. To the extent we are able, we engage our bodies in movement that works well with our bodies and feels pleasurable (see Chapter 21).

10. **Incorporating gentle nutrition.** We are mindful of our bodies' needs for energy and health and choose foods that help our bodies function well, all while eating in a flexible, rather than a restrictive, manner. This principle is implemented last. If the other principles are not in place before gentle nutrition is started, we run the risk of treating gentle nutrition like a diet or food rule (e.g., "I can never eat sugar because it sometimes makes me jittery") rather than a guiding principle (e.g., "I can eat sugar, but I may eat something else with it to offset blood sugar spikes which impair my concentration.").

Intuitive eating often uses a scale ranging from 1 (famished, undereating) to 10 (stuffed, binge eating), with 5 being "balanced," comfortable, and satisfied [4, 8]. This scale is meant to help us find a range that feels good for us (e.g., start eating around a "3", stop eating at a "5" or "6"). Throughout the process of rediscovering intuitive eating, it is important that we remain compassionate toward ourselves. For example, we don't judge ourselves when we fall outside of our "feel good" range (e.g., at parties, holidays). It is also important to practice assertiveness in response to others' pressures to eat or not to eat, in order to respect and care for our bodies.

The principles of intuitive eating can be clustered into four domains:

1. **Unconditional permission to eat.** This domain reflects our willingness to eat foods that we crave and to not judge foods using labels (e.g., "bad" or "good").

2. **Eating for physical rather than emotional reasons**. This domain reflects the primary reason we eat: do we eat because we are physically hungry or because we are experiencing emotions such as anxiety, loneliness, sadness, and boredom? Ideally, we most often eat because we are physically hungry and do not regularly use food as a coping mechanism for our emotions.

3. **Reliance on hunger and satiety (fullness) cues**. This domain reflects the extent to which we are aware of, trust in, and rely on our internal hunger and fullness cues to guide our eating behavior. In other words, are we aware (or unaware) of when we are hungry and full? Do we trust that our bodies know when we need food (or do we think our bodies send us signals to eat when we are not truly hungry)? Do we trust that our bodies know when to stop eating (or do we assume that our bodies try to sabotage us by wanting more food that is needed)? Do we eat when we feel hungry (or do we try to override hunger cues by ignoring or masking them, such as drinking water to feel full)? Do we stop eating when we feel comfortably full (or do we stop eating after a certain portion is eaten and/or eat beyond fullness)? If we answer "yes" to the first part of each question (and "no" to the second part), then we are trusting in and relying on our hunger and fullness cues. If not trusting in and/or following our hunger and fullness cues is a regular pattern, then it becomes problematic for our well-being.

4. **Body-Food Choice Congruence.** This domain reflects gentle nutrition, or our tendency to eat foods that satisfy our bodies and promote energy and stamina.

A clinical version of a scale assessing intuitive eating, the *Intuitive Eating Scale-2: Clinical Version* (IES-2C) [6], is provided in this chapter to determine your levels of overall intuitive eating and its four domains.

Research on intuitive eating shows that it is associated with, and helps promote, psychological well-being and health among various groups (adolescents, college students, adult community members) from many different countries. Specifically, intuitive eating is connected to higher self-compassion (see Chapter 8), mindfulness, emotional awareness, emotional regulation (our ability to calm ourselves when upset), distress tolerance (our ability to handle intense emotions effectively), life satisfaction, positive emotions (such as joy), self-esteem, optimism, and proactive coping and hardiness (viewing stress as a challenge and approaching it versus avoiding it) [5–6, 9–13]. In addition, intuitive eating is connected to lower depression and anxiety [9, 12–13, 15].

Intuitive eating is also strongly connected to higher body appreciation (see Chapter 10) and body image flexibility (see Chapter 8), and lower internalization of appearance ideals (see Chapter 4), body dissatisfaction, body shame, body surveillance (see Chapter 13), internalized weight stigma (see Chapter 5), and body comparison (see Chapter 15) [6, 9–11, 14–18].

Additionally, intuitive eating is linked to experiencing greater enjoyment and pleasure while eating, being relaxed and comfortable while eating, eating a wide variety of food, being mindful when eating, and choosing foods that are nutritious [19–20]. Intuitive eating may protect against the development of eating disorders [21], as it is linked to lower binge eating, bulimic symptoms, drive for thinness, situational eating, emotional eating, food preoccupation, and anxiety around food [6, 10, 15, 18–20, 22–23].

Intuitive eating is also associated with adaptive physical health indicators, such as lower triglycerides and higher high-density lipoprotein (HDL) cholesterol [24]. In a study including

31,955 women and 9,581 men, intuitive eating was associated with healthier dietary intakes [25]. In adolescents with type 1 diabetes mellitus, intuitive eating was linked to better glycemic control [26].

Understanding how intuitive eating is maintained or learned in a society that promotes dieting has been of interest to researchers and clinicians. The **acceptance model of intuitive eating** [16] has revealed that the foundation for intuitive eating is body acceptance, whereby others accept our bodies and we accept our bodies. When we perceive that others accept our bodies, we are more likely to appreciate our bodies, which in turn helps guide us to eat intuitively [16, 27–28]. While many studies have shown that intuitive eating is related to lower body mass index (BMI) [5–6, 11, 14–15, 17–19, 22–25, 29], we caution against interpreting this finding as "intuitive eating will lead to weight loss." It is equally likely that individuals who have lower body weights are more likely to be "left alone" – not pressured to diet – whereas those with higher weights are pressured to lose weight and diet. Attempts to control weight move individuals away from intuitive eating and toward disordered eating including symptoms such as binge eating [30].

Intuitive eating skills reach far beyond being *aware* of our internal hunger and satiety cues, although awareness is an important first step. Another essential ingredient to eating intuitively is valuing, trusting in, and responding to these cues; therefore, we need to trust our bodies to direct our eating. Trusting our bodies may prove to be hard when we are told to doubt our bodies' ability to guide our eating behaviors. In particular, we may fear that granting ourselves unconditional permission to eat will lead to overeating. However, there is no evidence to support this relationship. In fact, unconditional permission to eat is associated with lower emotional eating [5] and is *not linked at all* to uncontrolled eating [25]. Self-compassion is needed to trust our bodies. In fact, we eat more intuitively on days when we treat ourselves more self-compassionately than usual (see Chapter 8) [17].

Fortunately, intuitive eating skills can be taught, with positive outcomes. Women who completed an intuitive eating web-based program increased their intuitive eating and psychological well-being, as well as decreased their binge eating [31]. At a three-month follow-up, improvements in intuitive eating and psychological flexibility were maintained, and there were further improvements in binge eating and general mental health. Women who received a ten-week intuitive eating-specific intervention reported lower disordered eating and body dissatisfaction and higher body appreciation and mindfulness at a ten-week follow-up [32]. Intuitive eating can aid in the later stages of eating disorder recovery [33]. In an intervention at an eating disorder treatment center, patients developed intuitive eating skills, and their ability to eat intuitively was linked to positive treatment outcomes for each diagnostic category. The authors of this study discuss how to implement intuitive eating safely and effectively in inpatient and residential treatment programs. Also, interventions teaching intuitive eating skills have been shown to improve intuitive eating while decreasing disordered eating [22, 33–34]. Because intuitive eating interventions enhance psychological well-being and physical health, intuitive eating is extremely relevant for those who have a difficult time tuning into and trusting their bodies.

Treatment Planning Tools

Talking Points for Sessions

- Discuss the client's relationship with eating and food throughout life
- Address how feedback from others can impact the client's relationship with food and eating
- Discuss what it means to fuel the body
- Explore physiological and psychological responses to hunger and satiety cues
- Identify examples of "food policing" and impact on eating

Treatment Plan

Goals

- ❑ Recognize cues associated with hunger and satiety
- ❑ Recognize thoughts and emotions associated with maladaptive eating patterns
- ❑ Explore messages from important people in my life about eating
- ❑ Investigate the role of body trust in relation to food intake
- ❑ Examine the role of permission to experience hunger
- ❑ Examine the role of permission to experience fullness
- ❑ Explore whether my current eating patterns include a diet mentality
- ❑ Identify any personal patterns of food restriction followed by overeating
- ❑ Consider how I define a "normal relationship with food"
- ❑ Consider eating patterns that correspond with listening to my body's needs
- ❑ Identify themes of my inner "food police"
- ❑ Identify themes of external "food police" (e.g., family members, friends)
- ❑ Refrain from labeling foods (e.g., "good" or "bad")

Objectives

- ❑ Identify types of dysfunctional eating behaviors I have used
- ❑ Identify my food and eating rules
- ❑ Identify emotions and thoughts when I "break food rules"
- ❑ Identify foods I enjoy
- ❑ Recognize foods I do not enjoy
- ❑ Allow myself to eat and enjoy a particular food that I crave and use skills for any uncomfortable emotions (shame, guilt, anger, fear) or thoughts ("I shouldn't have eaten that")
- ❑ Identify my emotions, thoughts, and physical cues associated with hunger
- ❑ Identify my emotions, thoughts, and physical cues associated with fullness

❏ Reject the diet mentality this week by doing:
_____

❏ Notice the amount of time (minutes or percentage of the day) spent focused on food (e.g., what to eat, what not to eat, how long until eating again)

❏ Identify at least three effective coping skills that do not include food or eating

❏ Honor my hunger cues in the next week by doing the following: _____

❏ Remind myself that food is fuel when I label a food as "bad"

❏ Practice recognizing fullness by estimating the level (1 = very hungry to 10 = very full) after every few bites of food

❏ Remind myself that the brain alone uses about 20 percent of calories

❏ Identify examples of rigid eating patterns

❏ Identify examples of flexible eating patterns

❏ Recognize how negative comments from others can impact my food/eating choices and behaviors

❏ Identify the many reasons for eating

❏ Identify the various techniques I have used to override hunger cues

Additional Resources

E. Tribole and E. Resch. *Intuitive Eating, 4th Edition: A Revolutionary Anti-Diet Approach.* New York: St. Martin's Publishing Group, 2020.

E. Tribole and E. Resch. *The Intuitive Eating Workbook: Principles for Nourishing a Healthy Relationship with Food.* Oakland: New Harbinger Publications, Inc., 2017.

E. Resch. *The Intuitive Eating Workbook for Teens: A Non-Diet, Body Positive Approach to Building a Healthy Relationship with Food.* Oakland: Instant Help Books, 2019.

J. Hollenstein. *Eat to Love: A Mindful Guide to Transforming Your Relationship with Food, Body, and Life.* Somerville: Lionheart Press, a division of Padma Media, 2019.

N. Ellis-Ordway. *Thrive at Any Weight: Eating to Nourish Body, Soul, and Self-Esteem.* Santa Barbara: Praeger, 2019.

A. Pershing and C. Turner. *Binge Eating Disorder: The Journey to Recovery and Beyond.* New York: Routledge, 2018.

K.R. Koenig and P. O'Mahoney. *Helping Patients Outsmart Overeating: Psychological Strategies for Doctors and Health Care Providers.* Lanham: Rowman & Littlefield, 2017.

Assessment 20.1: Intuitive Eating Scale-2 (IES-2)

Please read each statement carefully before answering, and **circle** the number below the response that best characterizes your eating behaviors.

Unconditional Permission to Eat	Strongly Disagree	Disagree	Neutral	Agree	Strongly Agree
1. If I am craving a certain food* and it is available, I allow myself to have it.	1	2	3	4	5
2. When selecting food*, I allow myself to choose and eat what I desire.	1	2	3	4	5
3. I think of food* as neutral rather than categorizing it as good or bad, healthy or unhealthy.	1	2	3	4	5
4. I avoid certain foods* because they are high in fat, carbohydrates, and/or calories.	5	4	3	2	1
5. I have forbidden foods* that I try to avoid eating.	5	4	3	2	1
6. I get mad at myself when I eat certain foods.*	5	4	3	2	1
Total Unconditional Permission to Eat score: add items 1–6 and divide by 6 =					

*Only consider the foods that you have access to, can afford, and do NOT have a medical reason for avoiding, such as insulin resistance, food sensitivities, food intolerance, and allergies.

Eating for Physical Reasons	Strongly Disagree	Disagree	Neutral	Agree	Strongly Agree
7. I often eat when I'm feeling emotional (anxious, depressed, sad, lonely, angry, numb, empty, bored, etc.), even when I'm not physically hungry.	5	4	3	2	1
8. I often use food to help me soothe my negative or uncomfortable emotions.	5	4	3	2	1
9. I often eat when I am stressed out, even when I'm not physically hungry.	5	4	3	2	1
10. I often eat when I'm feeling positive (happy, excited, comfortable, etc.), even when I'm not physically hungry.	5	4	3	2	1
11. I am able to cope with my negative or uncomfortable emotions (anxiety, sadness, loneliness, etc.) without turning to food for comfort.	1	2	3	4	5
12. I find other ways to cope with stress and anxiety than by eating.	1	2	3	4	5
Total Eating for Physical Reasons score: add items 7–12 and divide by 6 =					

Reliance on Hunger and Fullness Cues	Strongly Disagree	Disagree	Neutral	Agree	Strongly Agree
13. I trust my body to tell me when to eat.	1	2	3	4	5
14. I trust my body to tell me when to stop eating.	1	2	3	4	5
15. I trust my body to tell me what to eat.	1	2	3	4	5
16. I trust my body to tell me how much to eat.	1	2	3	4	5
17. I rely on my hunger signals to tell me when to eat.	1	2	3	4	5
18. I rely on my fullness signals to tell me when to stop eating.	1	2	3	4	5
Total Reliance on Hunger and Fullness Cues score: add items 13–18 and divide by 6 =					

Body-Food Choice Congruence	Strongly Disagree	Disagree	Neutral	Agree	Strongly Agree
19. Most of the time, I desire to eat nutritious foods.	1	2	3	4	5
20. I mostly eat foods that make my body perform well.	1	2	3	4	5
21. I mostly eat foods that give my body energy and stamina.	1	2	3	4	5
22. Most of the time, I eat foods that help my body function well.	1	2	3	4	5
23. Most of the time, I don't eat foods that cause my body to have physical discomfort.	1	2	3	4	5
Total Body-Food Choice Congruence score: add items 19–23 and divide by 5 =					

You can also calculate a Total IES-2 score by adding up all circled numbers above and dividing by 23.

Total Intuitive Eating (or subscale) score between:

- **4–5** = high intuitive eating
- **3–3.9** = moderate intuitive eating
- **below 3** = low intuitive eating

Note. Authors of the IES-2 are Tylka and Kroon Van Diest.* The IES-2 has been translated into many different languages, with research upholding its relevance to adaptive eating behavior in many cultures [5]. Its structure and measurement properties (reliability, validity) have been supported in these various cultures. Please note that some items have been modified from the original IES-2 to better address the complexity of intuitive eating within clinical work. Please do not use this version in research without permission from Tracy Tylka; there is no need to contact her to use it with clients or to complete it on your own.

*T. L. Tylka and A. M. Kroon Van Diest. The Intuitive Eating Scale-2: Item refinement and psychometric evaluation with college women and men. *J Couns Psychol* 2013; **60**: 137–53.

Intuitive Eating Scale-2 Applications

- Look at your responses to the **Unconditional Permission to Eat** subscale.

  ○ For item 1 (*If I am craving a certain food and it is available, I allow myself to have it*), consider:

  - How often do food cravings occur? How often do you allow yourself to eat the foods that you crave? What impacts your decisions whether to eat the food?

  - How access to food (or lack of access) impacts your decisions related to eating. Are you more likely to eat certain foods that are immediately available versus having to go get them?

  ○ Item 3 (*I think of food as neutral rather than categorizing it as good or bad, healthy or unhealthy*) addresses the labels that are often used to describe food. If you responded "disagree" or "strongly disagree":

  - What are typical labels you use (e.g., good/bad, healthy/unhealthy)?

  - What emotions do you experience after eating foods that you label with a positive term? With a negative term?

  - Consider what it would be like to switch from using labels to viewing food in neutral terms.

  ○ Review your response to item 5 (*I have forbidden foods that I try to avoid eating*). Note that this does not include food allergies. For the foods that you forbid yourself to eat, do you ever eat them anyway?

  - If yes, under which circumstances do you "break this food rule?"

  - How do you feel when you eat them? How much do you consume?

  - What do you tell yourself about these experiences?

  - Pick a day/time and give yourself permission to eat this food and practice savoring every bite. Note how this experience is different.

  ○ Sometimes messages from others about food impacts our preferences (e.g., what we enjoy, what we don't enjoy). Think about the foods that you believe you enjoy and foods that you believe you do not enjoy. Choose a few of these foods and try them one by one, being especially mindful of the taste, texture, and smell of the food as you eat it. Now re-evaluate. You may notice that you do not enjoy some of the foods that you thought you enjoyed, and you may enjoy some of the foods that you thought you did not enjoy. If you wish, continue this experiment with other foods.

- Review your responses to the **Eating for Physical Reasons** subscale.

  ○ If you responded "agree" or "strongly agree" to the items regarding emotional eating:

  - What are the typical *uncomfortable* emotions you experience *before* engaging in emotional eating (anxious, depressed, sad, lonely, angry, bored)? What happens to the emotions after you're done eating? Do other emotions come up? If so, what are they?

  - What are the typical *comfortable* emotions you experience *before* engaging in emotional eating (happy, love, content, anticipatory, excited, jubilant)? What happens to the emotions after you're done eating? Do other emotions come up? If so, what are they?

○ Review your response to Item 8 (*I often use food to help me soothe my negative or uncomfortable emotions*) and consider if using food to soothe negative emotions is a pattern. Identify alternative soothing strategies to try next time you feel these emotions. Write a reminder card with these coping strategies, and keep it in a helpful location.

○ Item 12 (*I find other ways to cope with stress and anxiety than by eating*) addresses coping skills. What coping skills do you use to deal with stress and anxiety that do not include food or eating?

• Review your responses to the **Reliance on Hunger and Fullness Cues** subscale.

○ Consider the messages you have received over your life about relying on hunger and fullness cues. For example, have you felt pressure to "clean your plate" or "not waste food" despite feeling full? Perhaps cultural (e.g., military, food insecurity) considerations have been associated with overriding hunger and fullness cues.

○ To what degree do you currently feel permission to:

■ feel hunger?

■ eat?

■ become comfortably full?

■ stop eating without shame, guilt, and pressure to eat differently?

○ When you have a hard time eating when you are hungry and stopping when you are full, what self-compassionate statement can you say to encourage yourself towards positive body image?

• Review your responses to the **Body-Food Choice Congruence** subscale.

○ To what extent do the foods you eat provide lasting fuel for your body?

○ When choosing a food to eat, how often do you consider:

■ Whether it provides lasting fuel?

■ What nutrients it offers?

■ Whether it offers stamina to last until the next eating experience?

■ Whether it can cause physical discomfort?

○ As identified in item 22 (*Most of the time, I eat foods that help my body function well*), what are the foods that make your body function well? Function poorly?

○ Choose one food (or meal) at a time and evaluate how your body feels after you eat it (e.g., how long it keeps you full, how you perform after eating it, how your body feels the hours after eating it).

Assignment 20.1: Food Evaluations

Food and eating can be evaluated according to morality and character:

- **Morality**: saying or thinking things about food associated with morals or values such as "I was good today," "I only eat clean food," or "I gave in to temptation."
- **Character**: saying or thinking things about food that relate to sense of character such as "This is my cheat day," "I can't control myself," or "I failed with my diet," "I'm weak and can't handle my emotions."

Below, reflect on the various evaluative terms that you (have) use(d) for food items (e.g., carbohydrates are bad), related to eating, and/or your relationship with food. Consider the labels of food as "good or bad" or "healthy or unhealthy." Then consider what you meant when using that language. Last, identify alternate language about food or eating as a way to transform your relationship from food about morality or character to viewing food as just food.

Comment about Food, Eating, and/or Relationship with Food	Judgments in the Message	Alternate Language
I was bad today, because I was stressed and ate ice cream. I couldn't control myself!	*Morality* *Character*	*Eating ice cream doesn't make me a bad person who is completely out-of-control. I realize I was anxious and can use coping skills when feeling stressed in the future.*

304 N. L. Wood-Barcalow, T. L. Tylka, and C. L. Judge. *Positive Body Image Workbook: A Clinical and Self-Improvement Guide.* Cambridge: Cambridge University Press, 2021.

Assignment 20.2: Reasons for Eating

Listed below are reasons people engage in balanced eating, overeat (including binge eating), and undereat (e.g., limiting the amount or type of nutritional intake). Check reasons that apply to you and record any realizations. Then, identify actions or commitments as you move toward positive body image.

Reasons	Overeat	Eat	Undereat	Realizations	Commitment for Positive Change
Example: *Anger**	X		X	*I overeat when angry at my partner; I undereat when angry with myself.*	*I will identify my anger early and do one of these: workout, journal, talk to my friend, clean.*
Example: *To refuel my body*	X	X		*I tend to overeat when I need to refuel my body quickly.*	*I will eat more consistently to ensure that I fuel myself on a regular basis.*
Anger*					
It's pleasurable					
Boredom*					
To be social					
Loneliness*					
Afraid/fearful*					
Physically tired					
Emotionally tired					
Around others who enjoy eating					
Depleted energy					
Thirst					
Sadness*					
Anticipation*					
It's available					
Hard to say "no"					
Happiness/joy*					
Jealous of others*					
Pressure from others					
Sense of obligation					
Feel less than others					
Envious of others*					
To feel accomplished					
To refuel my body					

N. L. Wood-Barcalow, T. L. Tylka, and C. L. Judge. *Positive Body Image Workbook: A Clinical and Self-Improvement Guide.* Cambridge: Cambridge University Press, 2021.

Reasons	Overeat	Eat	Undereat	Realizations	Commitment for Positive Change
To feel better than others					
Disgust with myself*					
Disgust with others*					
My body tells me to					
Others are eating					
Guilt*					
It's part of the social experience					
It's necessary for existence					
Access to food					
Disappointment*					
Biological changes/needs (e.g., menstrual cycle)					
Remorse/regret*					
Keep my stomach full or empty					
Overwhelmed*					
To deal with physical pain					
To deal with emotional pain					
Love*					
Grief/bereavement*					
To deal with sense of failure					
To celebrate					
Shame*					
Negative body image					
Surprise*					
It's exciting					
Other:					
Other:					
Other:					

Notice the various reasons you have for overeating, balanced eating, and undereating, with recognition of how complex eating patterns can be. Items marked with an (*) represent emotional eating experience. Review your patterns of eating related to emotions. Consider completing Assignment 20.3; Emotional Eating as Coping.

N. L. Wood-Barcalow, T. L. Tylka, and C. L. Judge. *Positive Body Image Workbook: A Clinical and Self-Improvement Guide.* Cambridge: Cambridge University Press, 2021.

Assignment 20.3: Emotional Eating as Coping

Emotions such as love, joy, happiness, anger, sadness, fear, jealousy, envy, disgust, shame, guilt, surprise, and anticipation have existed throughout time for all humans across genders, nationalities, ethnicities, ages, social statuses, and financial resources. Emotions can tell us important information about ourselves, our surroundings, when to take action, when not to take action, how to keep safe, and more. Emotions can also be paired with others (e.g., shame and anger when someone criticizes you, love and sadness when saying goodbye to a friend who moves away). You have experienced each one of these emotions at any given time with varying degrees of intensity and duration. Additionally, you might judge some of these emotions (e.g., good or bad, helpful not helpful) based on your level of comfort with experiencing them.

It can be common to use eating as a way to cope or deal with emotions and overall life experiences. Relying on eating as the only or primary way to manage, deal with, or resolve emotions can have a negative impact in both the short-term and long-term.

For this assignment, consider your relationship with emotions and eating patterns over time while answering the following:

I eat when I experience these comfortable emotions:

_____
_____

I eat when I experience these uncomfortable emotions:

_____
_____

Eating when experiencing these emotions is effective:

_____
_____

Eating when experiencing these emotions is ineffective:

_____
_____

I eat as the only or primary way of coping when experiencing these emotions:

_____
_____

These are the short-term costs AND benefits of eating to deal with emotions:

_____
_____

These are the long-term costs AND benefits of eating to deal with emotions:

_____
_____

I would like to use these coping skills instead of eating:

_____
_____

These are the changes to emotional eating that I would like to make as I move toward positive body image:

_____
_____

N. L. Wood-Barcalow, T. L. Tylka, and C. L. Judge. *Positive Body Image Workbook: A Clinical and Self-Improvement Guide.* Cambridge: Cambridge University Press, 2021.

Assignment 20.4: Matching Emotions with Eating Patterns

Common emotions include love, joy, happiness, anger, sadness, fear, jealousy, envy, disgust, shame, guilt, boredom, frustration, surprise, and anticipation. You have experienced each one of these emotions at any given time. Additionally, you have likely related these emotions with eating patterns as this is a common experience.

Imagine eating patterns on a continuum with one end representing undereating and the other end representing binge eating, with various behaviors in between. The middle is considered balanced eating (e.g., not too much, not too little). Every person has likely engaged in some of these eating patterns in different circumstances: overeating at a holiday celebration, restricting when trying a diet, undereating when trying to change body shape or weight, binge eating after restricting for a lengthy amount of time, balanced eating when getting the amount of nutrients the body needs in the moment.

I--I--I

Undereating   Restricting   Balanced eating   Overeating   Binge eating

For this assignment, list the different types of emotions that you experience before, during and/or after the different types of eating. Record any realizations of how emotions correspond with your eating patterns.

Undereating:

_____
_____
_____

Restricting:

_____
_____
_____

Balanced eating:

_____
_____
_____

Overeating:

_____
_____
_____

Binge eating:

_____
_____
_____

N. L. Wood-Barcalow, T. L. Tylka, and C. L. Judge. *Positive Body Image Workbook: A Clinical and Self-Improvement Guide.* Cambridge: Cambridge University Press, 2021.

Reflections

These are the patterns I observe:

_____
_____
_____

These are the changes I would like to make as I move toward positive body image:

_____
_____
_____

N. L. Wood-Barcalow, T. L. Tylka, and C. L. Judge. *Positive Body Image Workbook: A Clinical and Self-Improvement Guide*. Cambridge: Cambridge University Press, 2021.

Assignment 20.5: Connecting with Internal Cues

The body offers internal cues to indicate hunger, fullness, and satisfaction for balanced eating. Examples of **hunger cues** can include stomach pains, growling stomach, headache, shakiness, irritability, and light-headedness. Examples of **fullness** can include bloating, pressure in stomach, sluggishness, and drowsiness. Examples of **satisfaction** are comfort and feeling "just right" – not hungry and not too full.

For various internal and external reasons, these cues can become disrupted, ignored, diminished, eliminated, and even confused with other signals which can have a significant impact on eating patterns. Check the factors that affect your internal eating cues then answer the questions below:

- ❏ Mood changes/emotions (sadness, anger, excitement, fear, embarrassment, shame)
- ❏ Psychological issues (low self-esteem, self-loathing)
- ❏ Distractions (work, school, pleasurable activities)
- ❏ Substance use (medications, caffeine, alcohol or other drugs, nicotine)
- ❏ Internal pressures that include beliefs about food, food rules, food anxieties
- ❏ External pressures from family, friends, partners, medical professionals, media messages ("you've eaten too much," "you need to clean your plate," "you shouldn't eat that")
- ❏ Categorizing food with labels (good/bad, healthy/unhealthy)
- ❏ Physical issues (e.g., impact of medication, pain, pregnancy, food allergies)
- ❏ Access to pleasurable/desired foods
- ❏ Cravings
- ❏ Lack of access to pleasurable/desired foods
- ❏ Time of day/circadian rhythm (e.g., working night shift)
- ❏ Amount of physical exertion
- ❏ Energy levels
- ❏ Senses (e.g., sight, scent, sound, touch, taste preferences)
- ❏ Memories or associations (e.g., comfort food)
- ❏ Events, parties, holidays, gatherings with loved ones
- ❏ Comparison with others (e.g., what or how much someone else eats)
- ❏ Consistent unbalanced eating habits such as restriction, restraint, deprivation, overindulgence, overeating, binge eating
- ❏ Cognitive issues (memory problems, attention issues, dementia)
- ❏ Trauma experiences/events
- ❏ Food used as a punishment
- ❏ Food used as a reward
- ❏ Other:
- ❏ Other:
- ❏ Other:

Factors that impact and/or could be misinterpreted as:

My hunger:

_____
_____
_____

My fullness:

_____
_____
_____

My satisfaction:

_____
_____
_____

N. L. Wood-Barcalow, T. L. Tylka, and C. L. Judge. *Positive Body Image Workbook: A Clinical and Self-Improvement Guide.* Cambridge: Cambridge University Press, 2021.

Awareness of internal cues:

How I know I'm hungry:

_____

_____

_____

How I know I'm full:

_____

_____

_____

How I know I'm satisfied:

_____

_____

_____

How I respond when internal cues might be conflicting with each other:

_____

_____

_____

Moving toward positive body image includes responding effectively and appropriately to internal cues. I commit to the following:

- ❑ Honor my hunger by eating
- ❑ Feel my fullness
- ❑ Give myself permission to eat desirable foods in moderation
- ❑ Practice mindfulness while eating
- ❑ Estimate my internal cues (hunger, fullness, satiety) on a continuum (1 = little/none to 10 = significant) before, during, and after eating
- ❑ Savor foods
- ❑ Use effective coping skills in response to emotions
- ❑ Reject the diet mentality
- ❑ Remind myself that "food is fuel"
- ❑ Other:
- ❑ Other:
- ❑ Other:

N. L. Wood-Barcalow, T. L. Tylka, and C. L. Judge. *Positive Body Image Workbook: A Clinical and Self-Improvement Guide.* Cambridge: Cambridge University Press, 2021.

Assignment 20.6: My Relationship with Food and Eating

For this journal assignment, write about your relationship with food and eating patterns throughout life. Consider the following: my current and former beliefs about food, using labels (e.g., "good versus bad," "healthy versus unhealthy"), how my eating habits have changed based on different needs, the short-term and long-term impact of comments and pressures from others about my eating/food choices, what it would be like to eliminate judgments and rules associated with foods, what it would be like to have unconditional permission to eat, what a "normal relationship" with food might look like, and more. Imagine how my relationship with food and eating might change as I move toward positive body image.

_____
_____
_____
_____
_____
_____
_____
_____
_____
_____
_____
_____

N. L. Wood-Barcalow, T. L. Tylka, and C. L. Judge. *Positive Body Image Workbook: A Clinical and Self-Improvement Guide.* Cambridge: Cambridge University Press, 2021.

Assignment 20.7: Unconditional Permission to Eat

Unconditional permission to eat is the willingness to eat foods that we crave while taking a neutral, judgment-free stance on food (i.e., believing that certain foods are neither "bad" nor "good"). Unconditional permission to eat also includes listening to the body's physical cues (e.g., hunger, fullness, satisfaction) as a way to guide oneself. It includes the recognition that food is fuel that can be experienced without rigid rules or anxieties. Respond to the following regarding **unconditional permission to eat:**

These are the emotions I associate with it:

_____
_____
_____

These are the thoughts I associate with it:

_____
_____
_____

These are potential barriers to practicing it:

_____
_____
_____

What would it mean for me to trust my body to know:
When to eat?

_____
_____

How much to eat?

_____
_____
_____

What to eat?

_____
_____
_____

Am I able to view food as fuel?

_____
_____
_____

If not, what do I need to do to change this perspective?

_____
_____
_____

I commit to practicing the following related to unconditional permission to eat:

_____
_____
_____

N. L. Wood-Barcalow, T. L. Tylka, and C. L. Judge. *Positive Body Image Workbook: A Clinical and Self-Improvement Guide.* Cambridge: Cambridge University Press, 2021.

Assignment 20.8: Breaking the Cycle of Food Anxieties, Rules, and Behaviors

Food anxieties are the fears (real and imagined) associated with eating. Examples include fears that eating will result in sickness or disease, that food is contaminated, how the food will be processed in the body, how food will taste, what the texture is like, that eating will result in immediate weight gain, and more. Over time, these food anxieties can turn into **food rules** (e.g., don't eat these types of foods, only eat between these times of day) as a way to manage anxiety. Food rules are individualized and can be learned from the environment such as reading an article that a certain food is "unhealthy" and should be avoided. Eventually, the food rules can turn into specific **food behaviors** (e.g., restriction, avoidance, fasting). A cycle can occur whereby any of these elements once activated can turn into the other.

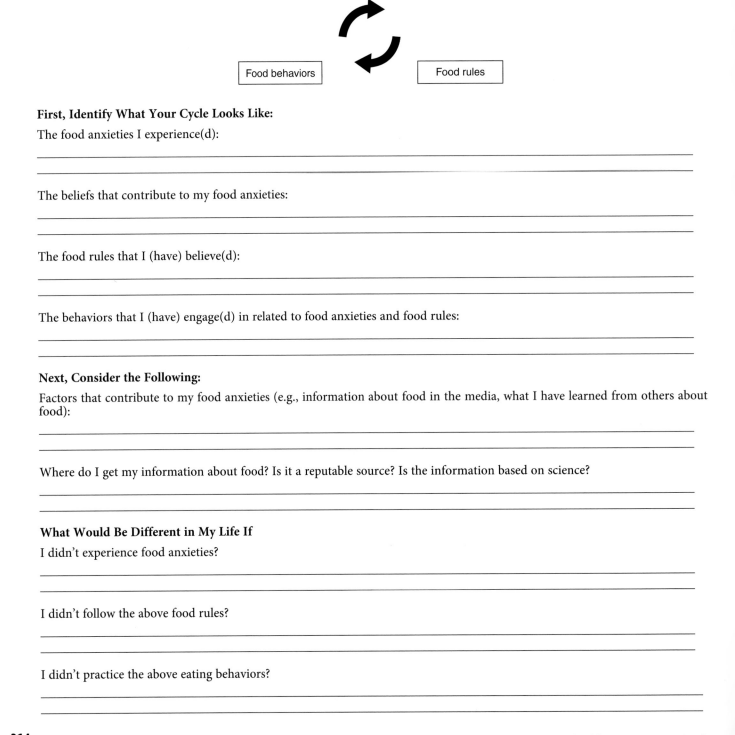

First, Identify What Your Cycle Looks Like:

The food anxieties I experience(d):

_____

_____

The beliefs that contribute to my food anxieties:

_____

_____

The food rules that I (have) believe(d):

_____

_____

The behaviors that I (have) engage(d) in related to food anxieties and food rules:

_____

_____

Next, Consider the Following:

Factors that contribute to my food anxieties (e.g., information about food in the media, what I have learned from others about food):

_____

_____

Where do I get my information about food? Is it a reputable source? Is the information based on science?

_____

_____

What Would Be Different in My Life If

I didn't experience food anxieties?

_____

_____

I didn't follow the above food rules?

_____

_____

I didn't practice the above eating behaviors?

_____

N. L. Wood-Barcalow, T. L. Tylka, and C. L. Judge. *Positive Body Image Workbook: A Clinical and Self-Improvement Guide.* Cambridge: Cambridge University Press, 2021.

What Undesirable Things Occur in This Cycle

Overeating/binge eating?

_____

_____

Mood changes?

_____

_____

Isolation/withdrawal?

_____

_____

Finally, Imagine Yourself Moving away from this Cycle and toward Positive Body Image

How I want to respond to food anxieties:

_____

_____

Food Rules that I Want to

Challenge:

_____

_____

Change:

_____

_____

Eliminate:

_____

_____

Eating Behaviors I Want to

Challenge:

_____

_____

Change:

_____

_____

Eliminate:

_____

_____

N. L. Wood-Barcalow, T. L. Tylka, and C. L. Judge. _Positive Body Image Workbook: A Clinical and Self-Improvement Guide._ Cambridge: Cambridge University Press, 2021.

Assignment 20.9: Purpose of Eating

There are numerous reasons for eating that go beyond that of internal hunger cues: psychological, relational, emotional, spiritual, behavioral, social, and more. Consider these various reasons for eating and how they impact your movement towards positive body image. Include your realizations below.

Examples:

Relational: I accept and eat the food provided by my in-laws even if I'm not hungry as I know that it's their way of showing me love.

_____
_____
_____

Emotional: I sometimes eat in response to my feelings. I like to eat comfort food when I'm sad and lonely.

_____
_____
_____

Spiritual: I fast during different holidays consistent with my spiritual beliefs.

_____
_____
_____

Social: I eat when gathering with friends as it is part of our connecting.

_____
_____
_____

Psychological:

_____
_____
_____

Relational:

_____
_____
_____

Emotional:

_____
_____
_____

Spiritual:

_____
_____
_____

Behavioral:

_____
_____
_____

N. L. Wood-Barcalow, T. L. Tylka, and C. L. Judge. _Positive Body Image Workbook: A Clinical and Self-Improvement Guide._ Cambridge: Cambridge University Press, 2021.

Social:

_____
_____
_____

Other:

_____
_____
_____

N. L. Wood-Barcalow, T. L. Tylka, and C. L. Judge. _Positive Body Image Workbook: A Clinical and Self-Improvement Guide._ Cambridge: Cambridge University Press, 2021.

References

1. L. L. Birch and J. O Fisher. Mothers' child-feeding practices influence daughters' eating and weight. *Am J Clin Nutr* 2000; **71**: 1054–61.

2. T. Mann, A. J. Tomiyama, E. Westling, et al. Medicare's search for effective obesity treatments: Diets are not the answer. *Am Psychol* 2007; **62**: 220–33.

3. E. Tribole and E. Resch. *Intuitive Eating: A Recovery Book for the Chronic Dieter.* New York: St. Martin's Press, 1995.

4. E. Resch and T. L. Tylka. Intuitive eating. In: Tylka, T. L. and Piran, N., eds. *Handbook of Positive Body Image and Embodiment: Constructs, Protective Factors, and Interventions.* New York: Oxford University Press, 2019: 68–79.

5. T. L. Tylka. Development and psychometric evaluation of a measure of intuitive eating. *J Couns Psychol* 2006; **53**: 226–40.

6. T. L. Tylka and A. M. Kroon Van Diest. The Intuitive Eating Scale-2: Item refinement and psychometric evaluation with college women and men. *J Couns Psychol* 2013; **60**: 137–53.

7. R. Li, K. S. Scanlon, A. May, et al. Bottle-feeding practices during early infancy and eating behaviors at 6 years of age. *Pediatr* 2014; **134**: S70–7.

8. E. Tribole and E. Resch. *Intuitive Eating: An Anti-Diet Revolutionary Approach,* 4th ed. New York: St. Martin's Press, 2020.

9. T. L. Tylka, R. M. Calogero, and S. Daníelsdóttir. Is intuitive eating the same as flexible dietary control? Their links to each other and well-being could provide an answer. *Appetite* 2015; **95**: 166–75.

10. A. C. Kelly and E. Stephen. A daily diary study of self-compassion, body image, and eating behavior in female college students. *Body Image* 2016; **17**: 152–60.

11. S. J. Schoenefeld and J. B. Webb. Self-compassion and intuitive eating in college women: Examining contributions of distress tolerance and body image acceptance and action. *Eat Behav* 2013; **14**: 493–6.

12. S. H Shouse and J. Nilsson. Self-silencing, emotional awareness, and eating behaviors in college women. *Psychol Women Q* 2011; **35**: 451–7.

13. T. L. Tylka and J. A. Wilcox. Are intuitive eating and eating disorder symptomatology opposite poles of the same construct? *J Couns Psychol* 2006; **53**: 474–84.

14. J. B. Webb and A. S. Hardin. An integrative affect regulation process model of internalized weight bias and intuitive eating in college women. *Appetite* 2016; **102**: 60–9.

15. C. Duarte, J. Pinto Gouveia, and A. Mendes. Psychometric properties of the Intuitive Eating Scale-2 and association with binge eating symptoms in a Portuguese community sample. *Int J Psychol Psychol Ther* 2016; **16**: 329–41.

16. L. C. Avalos and T. L. Tylka. Exploring a model of intuitive eating with college women. *J Couns Psychol* 2006; **53**: 486–97.

17. A. C. Kelly, K. E. Miller, and E. Stephen. The benefits of being self-compassionate on days when interactions with body-focused others are frequent. *Body Image* 2016; **19**: 195–203.

18. T. L. Tylka and N. L. Wood-Barcalow. The Body Appreciation Scale-2: Item refinement and psychometric evaluation. *Body Image* 2015; **12**: 53–67.

19. T. Smith and S. R. Hawks. Intuitive eating, diet composition, and the meaning of food in healthy weight promotion. *Am J Health Educ* 2006; **37**: 130–6.

20. T. L. Tylka, I. U. Eneli, A. M. Kroon VanDiest, et al. Which adaptive maternal eating behaviors predict child feeding practices? An examination with mothers of 2- to 5-year-old children. *Eat Behav* 2013; **14**: 57–63.

21. T. L. Tylka and A. M. Kroon Van Diest. Protective factors in the development of eating disorders. In: Smolak, L., and Levine, M. P., eds. *The Wiley-Blackwell Handbook of Eating Disorders* (Vol. 1). New York: Wiley, 2015: 430–44.

22. E. Carbonneau, N. Carbonneau, B. Lamarche, et al. Validation of a French-Canadian adaptation of the Intuitive Eating Scale-2 for the adult population. *Appetite* 2016; **105**: 37–45.

23. K. N. Denny, K. Loth, M. E. Eisenberg, et al. Intuitive eating in young adults. Who is doing it, and how is it related to disordered eating behaviors? *Appetite* 2013; **60**: 13–19.

24. S. Hawks, H. Madanat, J. Hawks, et al. The relationship between intuitive eating and health indicators among college women. *Am J Health Educ* 2005; **36**: 331–6.

25. G. M. Camilleri, C. Méjean, F. Bellisle, et al. Intuitive eating dimensions were differently associated with food intake in the general population-based NutriNet-Santé study. *J Nutr* 2016; **147**: 61–9.

26. B. J. Wheeler, J. Lawrence, M. Chae, et al. Intuitive eating is associated with glycaemic control in adolescents with Type 1 diabetes mellitus. *Appetite* 2016; **96**: 160–5.

27. C. L. Augustus-Horvath and T. L. Tylka. The acceptance model of intuitive eating: A comparison of women in emerging adulthood, early adulthood, and middle adulthood. *J Couns Psychol* 2011; **58**: 110–25.

28. R. Andrew, M. Tiggemann, and L. Clark. Predictors and health-related outcomes of positive body image in adolescent girls: A prospective study. *Dev Psychol* 2016; **52**: 463–74.

29. C. E. L. Madden, S. L. Leong, A. Gray, et al. Eating in response to hunger and satiety signals is related to BMI in a nationwide sample of 1,601 mid-age New Zealand women. *Public Health Nutr* 2012; **15**: 2272–9.

30. S. L Leong, A. Gray, J. Haszard, et al. Weight-control methods, 3-year weight change, and eating behaviors: A prospective nationwide study of middle-aged New Zealand women. *J Acad Nutr Diet* 2016; **116**: 1276–84.

31. S. Boucher, O. Edwards, A. Gray, et al. Teaching intuitive eating and acceptance and commitment therapy skills via a web-based intervention: A pilot single-arm intervention study. *JMIR Res Protoc* 2016; **5**: e180.

32. H. E. Bush, L. Rossy, L. B. Mintz, et al. Eat for Life: A work site feasibility study of a novel mindfulness-based intuitive eating intervention. *Am J of Health Promot* 2014; **28**: 380–8.

33. P. S. Richards, S. Crowton, M. E. Berrett, et al. Can patients with eating disorders learn to eat intuitively? A 2-year pilot study. *Eat Disord* 2017; **25**: 99–113.

34. J. L. Mensinger, R. M. Calogero, S. Stranges, et al. A weight-neutral versus weight-loss approach to health promotion in women with high BMI: A randomized-controlled trial. *Appetite* 2016; **105**: 364–74.

Life-Enhancing Movement

Chapter 21

Theory and Research Overview

What comes to mind when we hear the word "exercise?" The definition of exercise varies from person to person. Here are three examples. Colleen views exercise as a means to lose weight and shape her body. She only exercises when she is dieting, and then she pushes her body to its limit. She is sore from grueling workouts, cranky because she is not fueling her body sufficiently to give her energy, and often injured from the wear-and-tear on her body. To her, exercise is exhausting, taxing, and depleting. Roberto views exercise as a way to manage his appearance. He runs sixty miles a week, even when injured, and lifts weights for several hours every day, afraid that he will lose his lean body mass. Exercise has become compulsory for Roberto, something he feels he "has to do." If he doesn't maintain his routine, he thinks of himself as a "failure" and feels guilt and anxiety. Jasmine walks, hikes, dances, or engages in yoga nearly every day, and she determines which activity to do based on her interest. She views exercise as time to herself, or to connect with others in her walking group, and she feels empowered when she moves her body. If sick or injured, Jasmine takes a break from exercise to heal, but is excited to start back up again when her body recovers.

Perhaps we know people like Colleen, Roberto, and Jasmine, or we may see ourselves in them. I (Tracy) had a relationship with exercise similar to that of Jasmine during my childhood, Roberto during my early adolescence, and Colleen during my late adolescence and young adulthood. Thankfully, in my late twenties, I had a relationship with exercise similar to that of Jasmine once again, and I have been there ever since. Exercise can be very beneficial to our physical health and psychological well-being [1–2], but it can also be harmful if it becomes compulsive, obligatory, and/or driven by appearance-related concerns [3–5].

This chapter focuses on **life-enhancing movement**, or moving our bodies in ways that enhance our physical and psychological well-being throughout life, while honoring our ability levels, changes in physical ability with age, and pain levels. One component of life-enhancing movement is being attuned (or "in tune") with our bodies as we move [3, 6–7]. Being attuned in this manner involves engaging in physical activities that bring about joy, mindfulness, self-compassion, self-acceptance, body connection, and body trust as we move in ways that are pleasurable and healthful and avoid moving in ways that may harm or deplete our bodies [6–7]. We trust

in and rely on our bodies to help us determine when, what, where, why, and how to exercise.

Exercise may be one structured way to attain life-enhancing movement. Yet, exercise may be helpful or harmful, and therefore, it can be imagined along a continuum ranging from dysfunctional to life-enhancing. **Dysfunctional exercise** includes problematic exercise attitudes and behaviors [7–9], such as:

- Exercising despite being injured or in pain
- Exercising excessively
- Exercising in the absence of adequate hydration or nourishment (i.e., not drinking enough water or eating enough food to support exercise)
- Exercising to gain "permission" to eat
- Exercising to self-punish and/or self-harm
- Exercising for the outcome, such as weight control, rather than the process, such as experiencing joy from moving our bodies in the present
- Ignoring certain body signals, such as those telling us when to stop exercising and when to rest and recover
- Exercising becomes one of the most important parts of our identity
- Believing that there is one correct or perfect way to exercise
- Prioritizing exercise above everything else, such as time spent with loved ones
- Feeling shame, guilt, depressed, and anxious when a planned exercise is missed
- Comparing ourselves with others around exercise (e.g., how much we exercise in comparison to others, what types of exercises we do in comparison to others)
- Exercising for the primary purpose of losing weight (although exercise for weight loss is encouraged in our society, it can be characteristic of dysfunctional attitudes and beliefs toward exercise [8])

Exercise avoidance may also be problematic when negative thoughts and feelings about exercise and/or negative experiences are associated with it [10–11]. For example, if a child is made fun of for how they run, they may think that running is not for them, avoid running (including all sports and activities that include running), and hold negative attitudes toward running. If a person goes to the gym and feels self-conscious because their body is not similar to other gym members or they have negative body experiences at the gym (e.g., overhear negative comments made about their body, witness others staring at their body), they may avoid exercising for fear that others may judge them. Indeed, experiencing weight- and appearance-based judgments is associated with lower attuned exercise and higher dysfunctional exercise among women and men [6].

In contrast to dysfunctional exercise, **attuned exercise** includes adaptive attitudes and behaviors toward exercise [3, 6–7], such as:

- Exercising with mindful attention to how our bodies feel throughout the session
- Viewing exercise as a process (i.e., focusing on the enjoyment of moving our bodies in the moment) rather than an outcome (i.e., focusing on a desired result, such as weight control)
- Exercising with self-compassion and self-acceptance; that is, feeling and respecting our bodies' limits, such as stopping before exercise becomes painful or harmful
- Choosing the types and amount of exercise that bring joy
- Engaging in exercise that promotes becoming more connected and present within our bodies, such as attending to body signals (e.g., when to begin, when to stop, and when to rest)
- Ensuring that our bodies are adequately hydrated and nourished to provide "fuel" for exercise
- Viewing exercise as one part of our identity
- Exercising for enjoyment and to honor our bodies' functionality and health

The study of **attuned exercise** originated from Rachel Calogero and Kelly Pedrotty's work with women with eating disorders in residential treatment to address dysfunctional exercise attitudes and behaviors [3, 9, 12]. Calogero and Pedrotty developed and delivered an experience-based and educational exercise program that aimed to replace dysfunctional exercise with attuned exercise. This program consisted of weekly group-based sessions focused on creating positive associations with exercise through clients' awareness of and connection to their bodies. Exercise myths and misconceptions were challenged such as the belief that the primary purpose of exercise is to lose weight. Supervised and guided exercise activities (e.g., stretching, alignment and posture, yoga, strength training, balance, outdoor activities, recreational games) helped

clients focus on their moment-to-moment experience of their bodies during exercise. Then, clients shared their experiences with the group. Throughout, clients were encouraged to broaden what they consider exercise, discover physical activities that bring them joy and rejuvenation, and engage in these activities without compromising safety and self-care. Outcomes of the program revealed significant reductions in dysfunctional exercise attitudes and behaviors among clients, without negatively affecting their eating disorder treatment goals (e.g., weight restoration), relative to a control group of clients who received standard eating disorder treatment [12].

Three "**essential building blocks of attuned exercise**" were incorporated into the design of the program (see Figure 21.1). *Level 1* focuses on *safety* during exercise such as eating and hydrating our bodies appropriately to support physical activity, exercising in a safe place and in a safe manner, and reconnecting to our bodies and our experience during exercise. *Level 2* focuses on the *process* of exercise, or staying present in our bodies and self-compassionate during exercise, which helps minimize comparisons with others (e.g., how we look), negative self-judgments, and disconnecting from our bodies' experience. This level helps build trust in our bodies' signals to guide what types of activities we do, when to do them, and when to stop doing them. This level also helps promote balance, flexibility, and variety to support our bodies through physical activity. *Level 3* focuses on *joy or our experiences of pleasure* during physical activity. It includes activities that bring joy (instead of pain and dread) and that correspond with our unique strengths and interests. Level 3 helps identify activities that refresh our bodies and minds instead of exhausting and depleting them. Therefore, exercise is life-enhancing when there is a foundation of safety (health and well-being) on which we can focus on the process of becoming more aware, connected, and responsive to our bodies and come to experience joy through physical activity [6]. Of note, these levels are useful for when we hold dysfunctional attitudes and behaviors toward exercise, as well as for when we would like to get more out of our exercise experience [6–7].

Figure 21.1 The three building blocks of attuned exercise. Reproduced with permission.

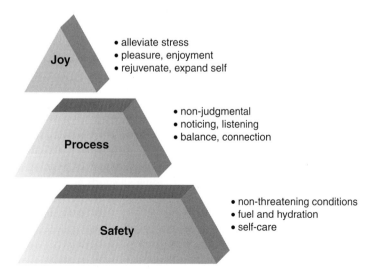

Yoga is a form of attuned exercise [13–14],[1] as it helps people fully experience the present moment and attend to body signals (e.g., what feels good, what does not feel good) throughout the practice [15–17]. Yoga is a mindfulness practice, and mindfulness practices have numerous health benefits including decreasing cortisol levels, which may help alter the neurophysiology of our bodies to facilitate healing, health, and well-being [17–20]. Additionally, those who practice yoga have been found to have greater body appreciation, body awareness, body responsiveness, and body satisfaction, as well as lower self-objectification compared to those who do not practice [21–25]. Along with yoga, other physical activities may foster attuned exercise attitudes and behaviors as well, such as dance, swimming, and more [6–7].

The *Attunement with Exercise Scale* (AWE Scale) measures the extent we engage in exercise that encourages self-care (versus self-harm), process (versus outcome), balance (versus imbalance), and rejuvenation (versus control) [6]. In this chapter, we include a clinical version of the AWE, which can help us understand where we fall on the continuum of exercise and how we may be able to strive toward attuned, life-enhancing movement in our relationship with exercise and our bodies.

Attuned exercise is connected to many of the other positive body image topics discussed in this workbook. Specifically, attuned exercise is related to higher levels of intuitive eating (see Chapter 20), body appreciation and responsiveness (see Chapter 10), self-compassion and mindfulness (see Chapter 8), and defining beauty broadly (see Chapter 7) [6]. Additionally, it is associated with lower levels of disordered eating, social comparison (see Chapter 15), body shame and guilt, body surveillance (see Chapter 13), compulsive exercise, exercise dependence, and exercising for the primary purposes of managing appearance and losing weight [6].

To conclude, life-enhancing movement honors our physical health and psychological well-being. It provides a pathway for us to remain attuned to our bodies during exercise; that is, we (a) move our bodies in ways that are safe for us, (b) are mindful of how our bodies feel during exercise, and (c) experience joy and pleasure as we move our bodies. It provides yet another way of caring for and nurturing our bodies and minds.

Treatment Planning Tools

Talking Points for Sessions

- Discuss the beliefs, emotions, and behaviors associated with the word "exercise" and different forms of physical activity
- Identify different types of organized, recreational, and leisure sports/activities enjoyed throughout life

- Address the differences between life-enhancing, mindful movement and that of excessive, obligatory or compulsive exercise

Treatment Plan

Goals

- ❏ Investigate my relationship with different types of physical activity over time
- ❏ Increase engagement in pleasurable and life-enhancing forms of movement
- ❏ Decrease involvement in types of physical activity that are uncomfortable, compulsive, or obligatory
- ❏ Engage in types of movement that enhance positive body image
- ❏ Identify specific food rules and behaviors that correspond with movement
- ❏ Refrain from physical activity when not physically feeling well (e.g., sickness, injury)
- ❏ Recognize what kinds of emotions prompt or "fuel" activity
- ❏ Explore the role of social connection with movement
- ❏ Identify the various goals and purposes of movement
- ❏ Participate in movement that is pleasurable and fun

Objectives

- ❏ Identify emotions and thoughts that occur when I'm unable to engage in physical activity
- ❏ Identify current and past forms of compulsive, obligatory movement
- ❏ Identify current and past forms of life-enhancing movement
- ❏ Consider what types of movement I participate in based on messages that I have received about my body, weight, or shape
- ❏ Identify the benefits associated with physical activity
- ❏ Identify the costs associated with excessive/compulsive/obligatory forms of activity
- ❏ Imagine how a person with positive body image responds to life-enhancing movement
- ❏ Identify specific reasons for avoiding physical activity
- ❏ Identify specific reasons for engaging in obligatory or compulsive activity
- ❏ Identify specific reasons for engaging in excessive activity
- ❏ Consider when participation in movement shifted from "choice" to that of "obligation"
- ❏ Identify types of movement "rules" that correspond with eating
- ❏ Record emotions and thoughts during and after life-enhancing forms of movement
- ❏ Focus on how my body feels in the moment when moving

---

[1] The type of yoga (e.g., Hatha), the focus of the yoga instructor (e.g., messages of body connection), and/or the setting where yoga takes place (e.g., absence of mirrors) may determine the extent a person remains attuned with their body throughout practice [13].

❏ Stop movement when I experience pain

❏ Say kind things to myself when engaging in movement

❏ Challenge the belief that I have to exercise in order to have permission to eat

❏ Challenge the belief that there is a "right" way to exercise

Additional Resources

Yoga with Adrienne (YouTube)

J. Stanley. *Every Body Yoga*. New York: Workman Publishing Co., Inc., 2017.

M. C. Klein. *Yoga Rising: 30 Empowering Stories from Yoga Renegades for Every Body*. Woodbury: Llewellyn Publications, 2018.

Assessment 21.1: Attunement with Exercise Scale-Clinical (AWE-C)

Please answer the following item stems by circling the response that is most consistent with your attitudes and behaviors toward exercise, which includes all physical activity. A response in the middle of the two endpoints indicates that you are *neutral*, which could mean that you agree with each endpoint at different times OR you do not identify with either endpoint. A "2" response indicates that your attitudes and behaviors are more consistent with the left endpoint than the right, and a "4" response indicates that your attitudes and behaviors are more consistent with the right endpoint than the left.

1. After I exercise, I feel . . .

Depleted 1	2	Neutral 3	4	Energized 5

2. Being an exerciser . . .

Organizes my entire life 1	2	Neutral 3	4	Is one small part of my identity 5

3. If I miss a day of exercise . . .

I feel guilty, anxious, and/or shameful 1	2	Neutral 3	4	I am all right; I don't feel badly about it or myself 5

4. During exercise . . .

I try to zone out and forget that I am working out 1	2	Neutral 3	4	I am mindful and aware of what my body is doing and how it feels 5

5. If I feel any pain during exercise . . .

I push forward until I am done with my workout 1	2	Neutral 3	4	I stop exercising 5

6. When exercising . . .

I often find myself wishing I looked like other people 1	2	Neutral 3	4	I rarely or never compare myself to others 5

7. After I engage in exercise . . .

No matter how much I've done, I feel like I should be doing more 1	2	Neutral 3	4	I am content and happy with how I moved my body 5

8. I am motivated to exercise more for . . .

My appearance (to lose weight, tone up, control weight, burn calories) 1	2	Neutral 3	4	Enjoyment and to improve how I feel 5

9. My typical exercise is that I . . .

Follow a specific exercise plan and don't deviate from it 1	2	Neutral 3	4	Allow myself to be physically active in whatever way I desire 5

I still push myself to try to get my workout done 1	2	Neutral 3	4	I stop exercising, rest, and focus on taking care of my body 5

11. My attitude towards exercise is that . . .

I dread it 1	2	Neutral 3	4	I enjoy it 5

12. When I exercise . . .

I do *not* make sure I have had enough to eat and drink to sustain my activity 1	2	Neutral 3	4	I make sure I have had enough to eat and drink to sustain my activity 5

13. I use exercise more . . .

To make up for eating or weighing too much 1	2	Neutral 3	4	To care for myself regardless of my weight or eating habits 5

14. If I am too tired on a day when I plan to exercise . . .

I push myself to exercise according to my plan 1	2	Neutral 3	4	I do *not* push myself to exercise or I find a gentler activity to do 5

15. When it comes to exercise . . .

I either avoid it or exercise until I am exhausted 1	2	Neutral 3	4	I exercise moderately on a fairly regular basis, but I give myself days for my body to recover 5

Total Attuned Exercise score: add items 1–15 and divide by 15 =

Total Attuned Exercise score between:

- **4–5** = high attuned exercise
- **3–3.9** = moderate attuned exercise
- **below 3** = low attuned exercise

Note. Reprinted with permission. Authors of the AWE-C are Calogero and Tylka.* For AWE-R (research version), contact Rachel Calogero at rcaloger@uwo.ca. Research supports the AWE-R's measurement properties (reliability, validity) and use in patient, young adult, and community samples [6]. Please contact the authors of the AWE-C for permission to use it within research; there is no need to contact them to use it with clients or to complete it on your own.

*R. M. Calogero and T. L. Tylka. The Attunement with Exercise Scale-Clinical (AWE-Clinical): A scale that can be used in therapy for improving embodiment and body image. Manuscript in preparation.

Attunement with Exercise Scale-Clinical Applications

- Consider your response to item 3 (*If I miss a day of exercise . . . I feel guilty, anxious, and/or shameful*).

  o What thoughts and emotions do you typically experience when you miss a day of exercise?

  o What types of unhelpful messages or rules about exercise have you been exposed to over your life, directly or indirectly? How do you respond if you "break" one of these rules?

  o If you experienced more positive body image, how might you respond to negative thoughts, feelings, and rules about exercise?

- For item 5 (*If I feel any pain during exercise . . .*), how can you tell in the moment when your body is in pain versus discomfort that is sometimes associated with challenging yourself physically? How do you typically respond to the pain? How would you like to respond to pain in the future?

- Item 8 (*I am motivated to exercise more for . . .*) addresses the motivations for exercise. Make a list of your motivations to exercise including changing the body (e.g., toning it, losing weight), enjoyment of the activity, an opportunity to be with others, and more. Review these motivations and reflect on how they relate to positive body image.

- For item 11 (*My attitude towards exercise is that . . .*), what are specific reasons for your attitude towards exercise (e.g., dreading it, enjoying it)?

  o How has your relationship with various types of physical activity changed over your life?

  o How can you make your current relationship with exercise more enjoyable, focused on the process, and overall life-enhancing?

- For item 14 (*If I am too tired on a day when I plan to exercise . . .*), what are signs you are too tired to exercise according to your plan?

  o What are some gentler alternate activities you can consider?

  o Can you offer yourself permission to not exercise?

  o What can you do to rest?

- Briefly check-in mentally and physically the next time you plan to exercise and ask yourself what type of life-enhancing movement does your body need in the moment? A walk with a friend or pet? A challenging work-out that involves mental concentration? Gentle stretching?

Assignment 21.1: Physical Activity throughout Life

Identify the different types of physical activity you have engaged in throughout your life such as organized sports (e.g., dance, football, track, rugby), recreational activities (e.g., biking, hiking), and general activities (e.g., walking places, playing games). Consider your favorite types of movement and the reasons they were/are pleasurable. Reflect on what former sports/activities you would like to resume or try at this time in your life. An example is offered.

	Childhood	Adolescence	Adulthood	Older Adulthood
Example: *General movement*	*Played tag with neighborhood friends, swam at community pool, rode my bike*	*Walked to and from school, went to dances, mowed the lawn for allowance, household chores, played basketball with friends*	*Gardening, household chores, walk the dog, go on hikes, moving at work, chased after kids*	*Yoga, Tai Chi*
Organized				
Recreational				
General movement				
Favorites				

Physical activity that I'd like to resume or try:

_____
_____
_____
_____

Physical activity that moves me closer toward positive body image:

_____
_____
_____
_____
_____

N. L. Wood-Barcalow, T. L. Tylka, and C. L. Judge. *Positive Body Image Workbook: A Clinical and Self-Improvement Guide.* Cambridge: Cambridge University Press, 2021.

Assignment 21.2: Dysfunctional versus Attuned Exercise

Sometimes it is easy to distinguish between dysfunctional and attuned exercise. Other times, it can be hard to know the difference based on various factors. Review the factors below, checking boxes as they apply to you, and answer the following questions:

❑ **Internal beliefs and rules:** "I have to exercise this much based on recommendations," "I can only eat this before or after exercise"

❑ **Emotions:** "I'll feel guilty if I don't do it," "I'm embarrassed to do that in front of others"

❑ **Body image disturbance:** "I need to exercise because I am fat," "I need to exercise to lose weight"

❑ **Self-imposed rules:** "I need to run this many miles a week"

❑ **Requirements for sports/military/job:** pressure to do a certain amount of push-ups and sit-ups, run a timed mile, need to pass fitness tests

❑ **Coaching from others:** being told what and how much to do, being told to ignore pain with exercise, being told to restrict appropriate amounts of water and/or nutrition

❑ **Form of punishment** (self or other imposed): need to exercise based on "bad behavior" and/or "for eating"

❑ **Focusing on numbers as most important:** exercising to reach a specific goal without care/consideration of how the exercise is impacting the body

❑ **Recommendations from professionals** (physician, trainer): being told to do certain types of activities for specific amounts of time

❑ **Comparison with others:** "I need to do this much based on what my friend does"

❑ **Seeking perfection:** constantly striving for a "personal best" (PB) record

❑ **Sole sense of identity:** unable to identify different components of self outside of exercise

❑ **Decreased interaction with others:** choosing to exercise rather than spending time with others

❑ **Other:**

❑ **Other:**

How I feel/felt when participating in dysfunctional exercise:

_____

_____

_____

How I feel/felt when participating in attuned exercise:

_____

_____

_____

Changes I would like to make with exercise as I move toward positive body image:

_____

_____

_____

N. L. Wood-Barcalow, T. L. Tylka, and C. L. Judge. *Positive Body Image Workbook: A Clinical and Self-Improvement Guide.* Cambridge: Cambridge University Press, 2021.

Assignment 21.3: Types of Life-Enhancing Movement

Types of life-enhancing movement that I currently do or would like to try:

	Not Interested In	Like To Do	Want To Try	Correspond with My Positive Body Image	Notes
Example: Hiking		X	X	X	*I always liked hiking during camp*
Example: *Jump rope*	X				
Yoga					
Pilates					
Weight lifting					
Bowling					
Bodyweight training (e.g., squats, push-ups, planks)					
Resistance band workouts					
Biking/cycling					
Rowing					
Spinning					
Hiking					
Surfing					
Tennis					
Basketball					
Baseball					
Football					
Soccer					
Rugby					
Boxing					
Lacrosse					
CrossFit training					
Tabata					
Swimming					
Interval training					

 N. L. Wood-Barcalow, T. L. Tylka, and C. L. Judge. *Positive Body Image Workbook: A Clinical and Self-Improvement Guide.* Cambridge: Cambridge University Press, 2021.

	Not Interested In	Like To Do	Want To Try	Correspond with My Positive Body Image	Notes
High Intensity Interval Training (HIIT)					
Dance					
Belly dancing					
Walking					
Jogging					
Calisthenics					
Skating					
Rollerblading					
Jump rope					
Playing tag					
Batting cage/playing catch					
Circuit training					
Aerobics					
Water aerobics					
Walking the dog					
Gardening					
Lawn care/yard work					
Washing the car					
Martial arts					
Tai chi/Qi gong					
Playing with kids					
Throwing darts					
Throwing axes					
Ultimate frisbee					
Golf					
Sailing					
Horseback riding					
Water polo					
Cricket					

	Not Interested In	Like To Do	Want To Try	Correspond with My Positive Body Image	Notes
Sexual intimacy					
Jumping on trampoline					
Doing chores					
Taking care of others					
Taking care of animals					
Other:					
Other:					

330 N. L. Wood-Barcalow, T. L. Tylka, and C. L. Judge. *Positive Body Image Workbook: A Clinical and Self-Improvement Guide.* Cambridge: Cambridge University Press, 2021.

Assignment 21.4: What Exercise Means to Me

For this journal assignment, consider the following: What thoughts do I associate with the term "exercise?" What emotions correspond with the term "exercise?" What types of movement do I consider exercise? What types of movement do I not consider exercise? How would I describe my current relationship with exercise? How has my relationship with exercise changed over time? What components of dysfunctional exercise have I experienced? I've experienced attuned exercise when doing which types of activities? How would I describe my ideal relationship with movement? What exercise moves me toward positive body image?

_____
_____
_____
_____
_____
_____
_____
_____
_____
_____
_____
_____

N. L. Wood-Barcalow, T. L. Tylka, and C. L. Judge. *Positive Body Image Workbook: A Clinical and Self-Improvement Guide.* Cambridge: Cambridge University Press, 2021.

Assignment 21.5: Responding to Body Cues Linked to Exercise

When we experience attunement with exercise, we trust in and rely on our bodies to determine when, what, where, why, and how to exercise. For various internal and external reasons, these cues can become disrupted, ignored, diminished, eliminated, and even confused with other signals which can have a significant impact on movement patterns. For this assignment, consider these factors when answering the questions below:

Factors that can impact awareness of and response to internal cues related to movement (check all that apply):

- ❏ Mood changes/emotions (sadness, anger, excitement, fear, embarrassment, shame)
- ❏ Psychological issues (low self-esteem, self-loathing)
- ❏ Goals or expectations (both realistic and unrealistic)
- ❏ Distractions (work, school, pleasurable activities)
- ❏ Substance use (medications, caffeine, alcohol or other drugs, nicotine)
- ❏ Internal pressures that include beliefs about exercise and exercise rules
- ❏ External pressures from family, friends, partners, medical professionals, media messages ("you need to exercise," "you exercise too much")
- ❏ Physical issues (e.g., pain, injury, limitations)
- ❏ Access to various forms of movement
- ❏ Lack of access to forms of movement
- ❏ Time of day/Circadian rhythm (e.g., working night shift)
- ❏ Intensity of physical exertion
- ❏ Comparison with others
- ❏ Energy levels
- ❏ Memories or associations with movement (e.g., pleasure or displeasure with sports)
- ❏ Cognitive issues (memory problems, attention issues, dementia)
- ❏ Trauma experiences/events:
- ❏ Movement used as a punishment
- ❏ Movement used as a reward
- ❏ Other:
- ❏ Other:
- ❏ Other:

Awareness of Internal Cues

How I know that my body wants to move:

_____
_____
_____

How I know that my body wants to stop moving:

_____
_____
_____

How I know when it is time to rest:

_____
_____
_____

How I know that my body needs time to recover:

_____
_____
_____

 N. L. Wood-Barcalow, T. L. Tylka, and C. L. Judge. *Positive Body Image Workbook: A Clinical and Self-Improvement Guide.* Cambridge: Cambridge University Press, 2021.

Moving toward Positive Body Image Includes Responding Effectively and Appropriately to Internal Cues Regarding Movement. I Commit to the Following

❏ Honoring my body's desire and need to move
❏ Offering permission and acceptance of rest days
❏ Practicing mindfulness while moving
❏ Refraining from movement when injured or exhausted
❏ Savoring the experience
❏ Rejecting unrealistic goals and expectations
❏ Engaging in movement that is fun and pleasurable
❏ Reminding myself that movement is an important part of physical and emotional health
❏ Other:
❏ Other:
❏ Other:

N. L. Wood-Barcalow, T. L. Tylka, and C. L. Judge. *Positive Body Image Workbook: A Clinical and Self-Improvement Guide.* Cambridge: Cambridge University Press, 2021.

Assignment 21.6: Breaking the Cycle of Exercise Rules and Behaviors

Exercise rules exist for a variety of reasons such as managing anxiety, responding to negative body image, feeling a sense of control, serving as motivation, providing structure, and more. Exercise rules are individualized and can come from the environment such as reading an article on the newest way to lose weight through movement. Eventually, the exercise rules can turn into specific **movement behaviors or routines**. A cycle can occur whereby any of these elements once activated can turn into the other:

Negative body image–> exercise rules–> movement behaviors

First, Identify What Your Cycle Looks Like

The negative body image thoughts and emotions I experience(d):

_____
_____
_____

The exercise rules that I (have) believe(d):

_____
_____
_____

The behaviors that I (have) engage(d) in related to these exercise rules:

_____
_____
_____

Next, Consider the Following

Factors that contribute to my negative body image (e.g., comments from others, body checking behaviors):

_____
_____
_____

Where do I get my information about exercise? Is it a reputable source? Is the information based on science?

_____
_____
_____

What Would be Different in My Life if

I didn't experience negative body image?

_____
_____
_____

I didn't follow the above exercise rules?

_____
_____
_____

I didn't practice the above movement behaviors?

_____
_____
_____

What undesirable things occur in this cycle:

❏ Exercise when injured
❏ Exercise when exhausted
❏ Don't allow rest days
❏ Refrain from pleasurable types of movement due to embarrassment
❏ Other:

N. L. Wood-Barcalow, T. L. Tylka, and C. L. Judge. *Positive Body Image Workbook: A Clinical and Self-Improvement Guide.* Cambridge: Cambridge University Press, 2021.

Finally, Imagine Yourself Moving Away from this Cycle and Toward Positive Body Image

How I want to respond to negative body image without using movement:

_____
_____
_____

Exercise Rules that I Want to

Challenge:

_____
_____
_____

Change:

_____
_____
_____

Eliminate:

_____
_____
_____

Movement Behaviors I Want to

Challenge:

_____
_____
_____

Change:

_____
_____
_____

Eliminate:

_____
_____
_____

N. L. Wood-Barcalow, T. L. Tylka, and C. L. Judge. *Positive Body Image Workbook: A Clinical and Self-Improvement Guide.* Cambridge: Cambridge University Press, 2021.

Assignment 21.7: Purpose of Movement

There are numerous reasons for engaging in movement, some of which are listed below. Consider these various reasons for movement and how they impact your positive body image. Check all that apply:

- ❏ Sense of obligation
- ❏ To gain muscle mass
- ❏ To lose weight
- ❏ To decrease fat
- ❏ To change shape
- ❏ To change size
- ❏ To reduce negative body image
- ❏ To punish myself
- ❏ To maintain health
- ❏ To increase strength
- ❏ To feel strong in my body
- ❏ To feel strong in my mind
- ❏ To increase flexibility
- ❏ To increase endurance
- ❏ To perform at optimal levels
- ❏ To do something that is effective
- ❏ To manage emotions
- ❏ To increase my mood
- ❏ To feel relaxed
- ❏ To feel refreshed
- ❏ To engage in introspection
- ❏ To feel exhausted
- ❏ To participate in spiritual pursuits
- ❏ To feel connected with a higher being
- ❏ To work on problems
- ❏ To get connected with my body
- ❏ To increase my heart rate
- ❏ To smile
- ❏ To sleep better
- ❏ To meet new people
- ❏ To enjoy the environment
- ❏ To maintain mental health
- ❏ To accomplish a personal goal
- ❏ To accomplish a team goal
- ❏ To have a sense of control
- ❏ To get positive feedback from others
- ❏ To get noticed
- ❏ To be envied by others
- ❏ To raise money for charities
- ❏ To help others accomplish their goals
- ❏ To have excitement in my life
- ❏ To interact and connect with others
- ❏ To challenge myself
- ❏ To eat what I like
- ❏ To eat the things that make my body feel good
- ❏ To increase sexual performance
- ❏ To enhance sexual pleasure
- ❏ To test what I can do
- ❏ To be proud of myself
- ❏ To demonstrate what I am capable of

N. L. Wood-Barcalow, T. L. Tylka, and C. L. Judge. *Positive Body Image Workbook: A Clinical and Self-Improvement Guide.* Cambridge: Cambridge University Press, 2021.

- ❏ To compete against others
- ❏ To feel a sense of mastery
- ❏ To prove myself
- ❏ To have fun
- ❏ To motivate myself
- ❏ To feel triumphant
- ❏ To get clarity on problems/issues in life
- ❏ To complete a task
- ❏ To motivate others
- ❏ To be a role model
- ❏ To work out tension
- ❏ To occupy time
- ❏ To be in the moment
- ❏ To promote "flow"
- ❏ To minimize pressures (e.g., appearance-focused)
- ❏ To have something to talk about with others
- ❏ To get somewhere
- ❏ To get a "high" or "rush"
- ❏ To do something daring
- ❏ To do what others cannot do
- ❏ To push myself to my limits
- ❏ To be alone with my thoughts
- ❏ To feel good during the activity
- ❏ To laugh during the activity
- ❏ To get my aggression out in healthy ways
- ❏ To channel my energy in positive ways
- ❏ To get respect
- ❏ To dominate over others
- ❏ To express my creativity
- ❏ To show off my physique
- ❏ To attract a mate/partner
- ❏ To be viewed as desirable or attractive
- ❏ To be viewed as strong
- ❏ To feel a sense of belonging
- ❏ To be around others with similar goals
- ❏ To spend time with or connect with an animal
- ❏ To boost confidence
- ❏ To inspire others
- ❏ To feel good after
- ❏ To acquire a new skill
- ❏ To perfect my form
- ❏ To manage pain
- ❏ To get rid of painful thoughts or emotions
- ❏ To decrease worries
- ❏ To redeem myself
- ❏ To promote longevity
- ❏ To be outside/in nature
- ❏ To perform with other athletes
- ❏ For self-care
- ❏ Other:
- ❏ Other:

N. L. Wood-Barcalow, T. L. Tylka, and C. L. Judge. *Positive Body Image Workbook: A Clinical and Self-Improvement Guide.* Cambridge: Cambridge University Press, 2021.

I would like to focus on the following purposes of movement that correspond with positive body image: _____

_____

_____

_____

N. L. Wood-Barcalow, T. L. Tylka, and C. L. Judge. *Positive Body Image Workbook: A Clinical and Self-Improvement Guide.* Cambridge: Cambridge University Press, 2021.

Assignment 21.8: My Body While Moving

While engaging in physical movement, I notice the many ways that my body functions effectively (e.g., how my heart beats faster in order to pump oxygen throughout my body). I will appreciate how my body responds and record realizations for one week.

_____
_____
_____
_____
_____
_____
_____
_____
_____
_____

Sunday:
_____
_____
_____

Monday:
_____
_____
_____

Tuesday:
_____
_____
_____

Wednesday:
_____
_____
_____

Thursday:
_____
_____
_____

Friday:
_____
_____
_____

Saturday:
_____
_____
_____

Assignment 21.9: Trying a New Activity

This is an activity that I'm interested in doing but have never tried or haven't done for a long time:

_____
_____

These are the reasons I haven't tried or done it:

_____
_____
_____
_____

These are the reasons I want to do this:

_____
_____
_____
_____

I commit to doing this activity by this day/time:

_____

To be Completed After Trying the Activity
I noticed these things while doing the activity:

_____
_____
_____
_____

I noticed these things after having done the activity:

_____
_____
_____
_____

I appreciate that I did this activity for the following reasons:

_____
_____
_____
_____

N. L. Wood-Barcalow, T. L. Tylka, and C. L. Judge. *Positive Body Image Workbook: A Clinical and Self-Improvement Guide.* Cambridge: Cambridge University Press, 2021.

References

1. F. J. Penedo and J. R. Dahn. Exercise and well-being: A review of mental and physical health benefits associated with physical activity. *Curr Opin Psychiatr* 2005; **18**: 189–93.

2. H. A. Hausenblas and E. A. Fallon. Exercise and body image: A meta-analysis. *Psychol Health* 2006; **21**: 33–47.

3. R. M. Calogero and K. N. Pedrotty-Stump. Incorporating exercise into the treatment and recovery of eating disorders: Cultivating a mindful approach. In: Maine, M., Bunnell, D., and McGilley, B. H. eds. *Treatment of Eating Disorders: Bridging the Research-Practice Gap.* New York: Elsevier, 2010: 425–41.

4. K. E. Elbourne and J. Chen. The continuum model of obligatory exercise: A preliminary investigation. *J Psychosom Res* 2007; **62**: 73–80.

5. M. B. Lichtenstein, C. J. Hinze, B. Emborg, et al. Compulsive exercise: Links, risks and challenges faced. *Psychol Res Behav Manag* 2017; **10**: 85–95.

6. R. M. Calogero, T. L. Tylka, B. Hartman McGilley, et al. Attunement with exercise. In Tylka, T. L., and Piran, N. eds. *Handbook of Positive Body Image and Embodiment: Constructs, Protective Factors, and Interventions.* New York: Oxford University Press, 2019: 81–90.

7. R. M. Calogero and K. N. Pedrotty. Daily practices for mindful exercise. In: L'Abate, L., Embry, D., and Baggett, M. eds. *Handbook of Low-Cost Preventative Interventions for Physical and Mental Health: Theory, Research, and Practice.* New York: Springer-Verlag, 2007: 141–60.

8. J. M. Mond and R. M. Calogero. Excessive exercise in eating disorder patients and in healthy women. *Aust N Z J Psychiatry* 2009; **43**: 227–34.

9. R. M. Calogero and K. N. Pedrotty. The practice and process of healthy exercise: An investigation of the treatment of exercise abuse in women with eating disorders. *Eating Disorders* 2004; **12**: 273–91.

10. L. R. Vartanian and J. G. Shaprow. Effects of weight stigma on exercise motivation and behavior: A preliminary investigation among college-aged females. *J Health Psychol* 2008; **13**: 131–8.

11. L. R. Vartanian and S. A. Novak. Internalized societal attitudes moderate the impact of weight stigma on avoidance of exercise. *Obesity* 2011; **19**: 757–62.

12. R. M. Calogero and K. N. Pedrotty. *The practice and process of healthy exercise: Identifying and treating exercise issues in women with eating disorders.* Orlando: International Conference on Eating Disorders, 2004.

13. C. P. Cook-Cottone and L. L. Douglass. Yoga communities and eating disorders: Creating safe spaces for positive embodiment. *Int J Yoga Ther* 2017; **27**: 87–93.

14. C. P. Cook-Cottone. *Mindfulness and Yoga for Self-Regulation: A Primer for Mental Health Professionals.* New York: Springer, 2015.

15. D. Neumark-Sztainer, R. F. MacLehose, A. W. Watts, et al. Yoga and body image: Findings from a large population-based study of young adults. *Body Image* 2018; **24**: 69–75.

16. D. Neumark-Sztainer, A. W. Watts, and S. Rydell. Yoga and body image: How do young adults practicing yoga describe its impact on their body image? *Body Image* 2018; **27**: 156–68.

17. P. Monnazzi, O. Leri, L. Guizzardi, et al. Antistress effect of yoga-type breathing: Modification of salivary cortisol, heart rate and blood pressure following a step-climbing exercise. *Stress Health* 2002; **18**: 195–200.

18. F. J. Schell, B. Allolio, and O. W. Schonecke. Physiological and psychological effects of Hatha-Yoga exercise in healthy women. *Int J Psychosom* 1994; **41**: 46–52.

19. J. West, C. Otte, K. Geher, et al. Effects of yoga and African dance on perceived stress, affect, and salivary cortisol. *Ann Behav Med* 2004; **28**: 114–18.

20. J. K. Kiecolt-Glaser, L. Christian, H. Preston, et al. Stress, inflammation, and yoga practice. *Psychosom Med* 2010; **72**: 113–21.

21. J. J. Daubenmier. The relationship of yoga, body awareness, and body responsiveness to self-objectification and disordered eating. *Psychol Women Q* 2005; **29**: 207–19.

22. L. Mahlo and M. Tiggemann. Yoga and positive body image: A test of the embodiment model. *Body Image* 2016; **18**: 135–42.

23. E. Halliwell, K. Dawson, and S. Burkey. A randomized experimental evaluation of a yoga-based body image intervention. *Body Image* 2019; **28**: 119–27.

24. A. E. Cox and A. K. McMahon. Exploring changes in mindfulness and body appreciation during yoga participation. *Body Image* 2019; **29**: 118–21.

25. A. E. Cox, S. Ullrich-French, T. L. Tylka, et al. The roles of self-compassion, body surveillance, and body appreciation in predicting intrinsic motivation for physical activity: Cross-sectional associations, and prospective changes within a yoga context. *Body Image* 2019; **29**: 110–17.

26. R. M. Calogero and T. L. Tylka. *The Attunement with Exercise Scale-Clinical (AWE-Clinical): A scale that can be used in therapy for improving embodiment and body image.* Manuscript in preparation.

Chapter 22 Adaptive Appearance Investment and Quality of Life

Theory and Research Overview

Appearance investment refers to the importance we place on our appearance and its significance to our identity, or who we are [1]. Our **appearance-related practices** (i.e., things we do to make ourselves look better) can reflect our appearance investment. Basing how we "should" look and which appearance-related practices we pursue on media appearance ideals can be quite harmful to our body image and well-being (see Chapter 4) [2–3]. Yet, certain appearance-related practices may not always be harmful. For example, I (Tracy) occasionally polish my toenails and enjoy trying new colors. I don't do it for anyone else – after all, I live in Ohio, and my feet are almost always covered with socks. I know that if all of the nail polish suddenly disappeared, I wouldn't be distressed or question my worth as a person. This perspective is characteristic of **adaptive appearance investment**, or regularly engaging in appearance-related self-care, such as grooming behaviors that reflect our unique style and personality [2, 4].

Maladaptive appearance investment also involves regularly engaging in appearance-related practices, but we do so because we are preoccupied with our appearance, believe that these practices define who we are, experience distress when these practices cannot be performed, and/or engage in harmful practices that interfere with self-care [2]. For example, when I was a teenager, I dieted and went to a tanning bed. I knew (but denied) that these practices were harmful when I was doing them, but taking care of my body wasn't a priority when I cared about my appearance more so than my health. Thankfully, in my late twenties, I started appreciating and caring for my body, engaging in safer appearance-related practices that enhanced or expressed my well-being.

Often maladaptive appearance investment emerges as **body checking**, or routinely examining the appearance of the body or body areas to determine its size, shape, or weight [5] (see Chapter 9). While we all check our appearance from time to time, when does it become concerning?

To help determine whether appearance investment is adaptive or maladaptive, we need to examine how much we engage in appearance-related practices and the meanings and importance we attribute to them [1, 6]. **Self-evaluative salience** is the level we measure our self-worth by our appearance [1]. Someone high on self-evaluative salience determines their self-worth based on their appearance (via body comparison) and places a heavy focus

on how others perceive their appearance. Self-evaluative salience is related to a more negative body image, poorer quality of life, lower self-esteem, and greater disordered eating attitudes and behaviors [7–8]. **Motivational salience** is how much we focus on our appearance and engage in appearance-related practices [1–2]. Someone high on motivational salience spends a great deal of time making themselves as physically attractive as possible and frequently checks their appearance in the mirror. Motivational salience is associated with internalizing appearance ideals (see Chapter 4) and disordered eating attitudes and behaviors [7]. Thus, focusing on and investing in our appearance to a large extent can be harmful to our well-being.

Holmqvist Gattario and Lunde [2] use **self-determination theory** as a framework to understand the difference between adaptive and maladaptive appearance investment. They propose that if we feel comfortable with who we are, then our appearance-related behaviors will (a) follow our own values, (b) be flexible and focus on health,[1] self-care, and expressing our personal style, and (c) won't take significant time and energy away from other important aspects of our lives (i.e., adaptive appearance investment). However, if we question who we are, we may (a) turn to media images for guidance for "who we should be and look like" and (b) engage in substantial and rigid appearance-related behaviors that are based on an obligation to "do whatever it takes" to achieve and maintain an "attractive" image, social status, and flawless appearance (maladaptive appearance investment).

We can further differentiate adaptive and maladaptive appearance investment by examining the motives behind appearance-related practices. Appearance-related practices can be divided into **beautification** (primary motive is to become more attractive) and **signification** (primary motive is another reason, such as a personal meaning or to mark the culture, class, religion, or other social group to which we belong) [9]. Table 22.1 illustrates some examples.

Beautification practices may be more aligned with maladaptive appearance investment, and signification practices may be more aligned with adaptive appearance investment [2, 9], but this may not always be the pattern. No matter how high we are on signification, realistically, beautification is likely the motivation behind some of our appearance-related practices. Also, some appearance-related practices may be motivated by both beautification *and* signification. Overall, maladaptive appearance investment increases the more

---

[1] It is important to be skeptical of appearance-related practices labeled as "healthy" by media sources, when their goal is to sell products and/or programs. For example, the diet industry labels weight-loss products as health promoting, when weight-loss products are linked to food preoccupation, binge eating, depression, and poor body image [10–11] (see also Chapter 4).

Table 22.1 Examples of Signification and Beautification in Appearance-Related Practices

Appearance-Related Practice	Reason for Appearance-Related Practice	
	Signification	Beautification
Tattoo	Nahla gets a tattoo to cover her mastectomy scar that she associates with strength, beauty, and resilience.	Nadja gets a tattoo because she thinks that it makes her look cool.
Dress	Jayniece wears beautiful regalia to honor her culture.	Mike chooses an expensive suit from a fashion designer in an attempt to make a good impression to others attending a wedding.
Manicure	Jessica paints her nails in a bright color that makes her happy to engage in self-care. She achieves "flow" while painting and feels good that she took time for herself.	Joanna feels compelled to keep her nails painted with a fresh coat at all times so they "look good." She won't go out in public with chipped nail polish.
Hot yoga	Jermaine attends hot yoga class to reinvigorate his tired muscles and to feel strong. He likes the mindfulness component of yoga and notices that his practice (balance, coordination, strength) is improving. He enjoys sweating during practice because it makes him aware of his body.	Randy attends hot yoga class because he is trying to lose weight. He chooses the most vigorous forms in the hottest studios. He is happy when he sweats due to the belief that he will weigh less.
Hair	Autumn loves to change her hair color frequently and experiment with colors. She chooses darker tints in the fall and winter and blonde with bright color highlights (pink, blue) in the spring and summer, which helps her feel connected to the seasons.	Lola is fearful that her gray hair will "show her age," so she makes sure she colors it regularly and yanks out gray hairs when they do appear.
Grooming	Jolene underwent laser therapy to remove facial hair to be more consistent with her gender identity.	Tanya sculpts her eyebrows to appear more attractive and to follow appearance-related trends.
Adornment	Max binds his chest to be more consistent with his gender identity.	Sarah wears a push up bra to be considered more attractive by others.

(a) beautification is the motivation behind our various appearance-related practices and (b) we have a strong investment in our appearance and others' reactions to our appearance.

Research supports these statements. Engaging in appearance-related practices to enhance identity, style, and self-care may contribute to a sense of personal uniqueness and well-being, which is connected to higher body appreciation [12–13] (see Chapter 10), whereas engaging in these practices primarily to change appearance is linked to higher negative body image [1]. Thus, when the primary motive for engaging in these behaviors is not appearance, but well-being, these practices may be beneficial. As an example, exercising regularly is positively associated with body appreciation, but only when our appearance-related motivations are low [14]. In other words, when we exercise primarily for its effect on our appearance (e.g., to lose weight, reshape our bodies), exercising loses its positive impact on our body image and well-being. Engaging in exercise for other reasons, such as enjoyment, health, and self-care, is positively connected to appreciating our bodies [15]. Therefore, it is important to explore the reasons (beautification and signification) behind our appearance-related practices. The activities within this chapter will help you achieve this goal.

That said, it is important to not criticize ourselves (or others) for choosing to engage in an appearance-related practice primarily for beautification. It is important to retain **body sovereignty**, or our right to determine what is best for our body, and others' right to determine what is best for their bodies. For example, someone who has had a mastectomy has the right to determine whether breast reconstruction is best for them. Someone who has a visible difference, whether biological or acquired, has the right to determine whether cosmetic surgery is best for them. Someone who is transgender has the right to determine their gender expression and how it relates to their appearance. Indeed, individuals who identify as transgender often feel a disconnect between their gender presentation and their gender identity. **Transgender congruence** is the degree to which those who are transgender feel genuine, authentic, and comfortable with their appearance as an expression of their gender identity [16]. For many, achieving transgender congruence means engaging in appearance investment practices and modifying appearance in various ways from nonsurgical to surgical interventions that are consistent with their gender identity, known as transitioning. Transgender congruence is associated with higher life satisfaction and meaning in life, as well as lower anxiety, depression, and body dissatisfaction, suggesting that altering appearance is important for their well-being and thus representative of adaptive appearance investment [16].

Appearance investment is connected to **body image quality of life**, which is the extent our body image positively, negatively, or neutrally impacts our general well-being in a variety of life domains [17]. The more maladaptive our body investment, the more maladaptive our quality of life. For example, when I had a negative body image, I focused on and invested in my appearance to a large extent. Yet, I felt inadequate. I had a negative body image quality of life, which then impaired my friendships (my friends grew sick of me complaining about my body), emotional well-being, and enjoyment in life. In contrast, when I made the choice to appreciate my body and move toward a positive body image (note that my size, shape, and weight didn't change, just my attitude), I became more confident and began to have deeper conversations with friends. My life satisfaction improved. Indeed, research indicates that *a more positive body image quality of life is related to higher self-esteem, optimism, and perceptions of social support as well as lower body dissatisfaction, self-evaluative salience, and disordered eating for women and men* [18].

In summary, focusing on and investing in our appearance to a large extent can be harmful to our well-being. Importantly, though, engaging in some appearance-related practices does not always negatively impact our well-being. Indeed, such practices can enhance our identity, style, and self-care to contribute to our positive body image quality of life. What separates the two (i.e., maladaptive from adaptive appearance investment) is the extent to which we engage in appearance-related practices, the importance we place on them, and our motives for engaging in them (e.g., beautification versus signification). This chapter includes scales that measure appearance investment (*Appearance Schemas Inventory-Revised* [17]) and body image quality of life (*Body Image Quality of Life Inventory* [17–18]), which can be used to understand our orientation towards our appearance and whether it benefits us or not. This chapter also includes the *Transgender Congruence Scale* for individuals who identify as transgender. Knowing our levels of appearance investment, body image quality of life, and transgender congruence (if applicable) as well as engaging in the activities in this chapter, can help us move towards attitudes and behaviors more aligned with positive body image.

Treatment Planning Tools

Talking Points for Sessions

- Identify different types of appearance-related practices that are used and the degree to which each practice is based on "choice" rather than "obligation"
- Identify frequency, importance, and motives of appearance-related practices
- Identify personal values and how they relate to appearance-related practices
- Differentiate between beautification and signification practices
- Discuss overall body image quality of life
- Discuss sense of comfort with gender identity

Treatment Plan

Goals

- ❏ Identify personal motives associated with my appearance-related activities
- ❏ Decrease my investment in looking toward others (e.g., media, friends) to determine how to look
- ❏ Decrease the amount of time that I engage in appearance-related practices viewed as obligatory
- ❏ Consider the importance of appearance in defining my self-worth
- ❏ Explore how much of my engagement in appearance-related practices is about trying to express my personal style versus changing my appearance to be more attractive to others
- ❏ Explore the importance of appearance at different points in my life
- ❏ Explore whether appearance is more important than other areas of my life
- ❏ Explore the role of self-evaluative salience within different systems (e.g., my family, community, culture)
- ❏ Consider how much my appearance-related practices focus on health and self-care
- ❏ Define what it means to have a positive body image quality of life
- ❏ Increase comfort in gender identity expression

Objectives

- ❏ Identify types of appearance-related practices that are beneficial
- ❏ Identify types of appearance-related practices that are harmful (e.g., lowers my sense of self-worth, interferes with my life)
- ❏ Identify appearance-related practices that are related to preoccupation
- ❏ Identify appearance-related practices that are associated with self-care
- ❏ Identify the amount of time (e.g., minutes, hours, percentage of time) I engage in appearance-related practices daily, weekly, or monthly
- ❏ Identify the amount of time I engage in grooming practices
- ❏ Identify the amount of time I engage in beautifying practices
- ❏ Record instances of specific body checking practices for one day
- ❏ Identify aspects of body sovereignty
- ❏ Identify individuals in my personal life and in media with whom I compare my appearance
- ❏ Create a specific plan to either reduce or eliminate one of my harmful appearance-related practices

❏ Create a specific plan to introduce one beneficial appearance-related practice that enhances my health and/or well-being

❏ Ask myself, "Is this harmful or beneficial?" before, during, and after engaging in appearance-related practices

❏ Identify the various ways I express my own personal style

❏ Make a list of all appearance-related practices and identify whether they are based on my own values and standards or the values/standards of others

❏ Identify examples of appearance-related practices that express a sense of "signification" for me

❏ Identify examples of appearance practices that express a sense of "beautification" for me

❏ Identify one action step to incorporate each week to get me closer to a positive body image quality of life

❏ Identify and implement specific steps to increase congruence with gender identity expression (e.g., clothing, hairstyle choice, pronoun choice)

Assessment 22.1: Appearance Schemas Inventory-R-Short Form (ASI-R)

The statements below are beliefs that people may or may not have about their physical appearance and its influence on life. Decide on the extent to which you personally disagree or agree with each statement and circle the number that represents your beliefs. There are no right or wrong answers.

Self-Evaluative Salience Subscale	Strongly Disagree	Mostly Disagree	Neither Agree Nor Disagree	Mostly Agree	Strongly Agree
1. When I see good-looking people, I wonder about how my own looks measure up.	1	2	3	4	5
2. I seldom compare my appearance to that of other people I see.	5	4	3	2	1
3. When something makes me feel good or bad about my looks, I tend to dwell on it.	1	2	3	4	5
4. If I like how I look on a given day, it's easy to feel happy about other things.	1	2	3	4	5
5. If somebody had a negative reaction to what I look like, it wouldn't bother me.	5	4	3	2	1
6. My physical appearance has had little influence on my life.	5	4	3	2	1
7. When I meet people for the first time, I wonder what they think about how I look.	1	2	3	4	5
8. In my everyday life, lots of things happen that make me think about what I look like.	1	2	3	4	5
9. If I dislike how I look on a given day, it's hard to feel happy about other things.	1	2	3	4	5
10. I fantasize about what it would be like to be better looking than I am.	1	2	3	4	5
11. By controlling my appearance, I can control many of the social and emotional events in my life.	1	2	3	4	5
12. My appearance is responsible for much of what's happened to me in my life.	1	2	3	4	5
Total Self-Evaluative Salience score: add items 1–12 and divide by 12 =					
Motivational Salience Subscale	Strongly Disagree	Mostly Disagree	Neither Agree Nor Disagree	Mostly Agree	Strongly Agree
13. I spend little time on my physical appearance.	5	4	3	2	1
14. I try to be as physically attractive as I can be.	1	2	3	4	5
15. I have never paid much attention to what I look like.	5	4	3	2	1

16. I often check my appearance in a mirror just to make sure I look okay.	1	2	3	4	5
17. When it comes to my physical appearance, I have high standards.	1	2	3	4	5
18. Dressing well is not a priority to me.	5	4	3	2	1
19. Before going out, I make sure that I look as good as I possibly can.	1	2	3	4	5
20. What I look like is an important part of who I am.	1	2	3	4	5
Total Motivational Salience score: add items 13–20 and divide by 8 =					

Total subscale scores between:

- **3.5–5** = high self-evaluative salience/high motivational salience
- **2.5–3.4** = moderate self-evaluative salience/moderate motivational salience
- **below 2.5** = low self-evaluative salience/low motivational salience

The authors of the ASI-R-Short Form are Cash, Melnyk, and Hrabosky.* Research supports the use of these measures with community and college samples.**

Note. Permission was granted by Thomas Cash to include the ASI-R-Short Form in this workbook. The ASI-R-Short Form cannot be used for research without a user's license (available at www.body-images.com).

*T. F. Cash, S. E. Melnyk, and J. I. Hrabosky. The assessment of body image investment: An extensive revision of the Appearance Schemas Inventory. *Int J Eat Disord* 2004; **35**: 305–16.
S. A. Rusticus, A. M. Hubley, and B. D. Zumbo. Measurement invariance of the Appearance Schemas Inventory-Revised and the Body Image Quality of Life Inventory across age and gender. *Assessment* 2008; **15: 60–71.

Appearance Schemas Inventory-R-Short Form Applications

- For item 3 (*When something makes me feel good or bad about my looks, I tend to dwell on it*), what behaviors (e.g., isolate, engage in appearance-related practices) do you typically do when you dwell on it?

  o How do those behaviors relate to preoccupation, self-worth, and your overall mood?

  o In order to move yourself in the direction of positive body image, how do you imagine responding the next time you notice the urge to dwell on your looks? Examples might include practice flexible thinking, mindfulness, valued action (pursuing activities that are personally meaningful), or participate in self-care.

- For item 6 (*My physical appearance has had little influence on my life*), reflect on the influence of appearance for you at various times throughout your life.

  o Consider a time when your physical appearance was not as important to you. How was your life different then? What other non-appearance-focused areas or activities (e.g., volunteering, artistic expression, social connection) were present and/or more important in your life?

  o After reflecting on these items, what action(s) might you take towards improved life balance and positive body image?

- Item 11 (*By controlling my appearance, I can control many of the social and emotional events in my life*) addresses the issue of control.

  o List the different types of behaviors you do with the intent to control your appearance. Consider whether any of these behaviors are maladaptive (e.g., feel uncomfortable when you can't perform them, the behaviors are associated with long-term harm). What would it be like to reduce or eliminate maladaptive behaviors?

  o Consider what things in life you can control related to yourself, others, and life events. What does this sense of control provide (e.g., safety, security, certainty, predictability)? What does this sense of control not provide (e.g., happiness, ease, comfort, peace)?

  o Consider what things in life you cannot control related to yourself, others, and life events. What do you notice about your emotions and thoughts with those things that cannot be controlled?

- Appearance standards are the focus of item 17 (*When it comes to my physical appearance, I have high standards*).

  o Consider what types of standards you have for your appearance. Where do they come from? How long have they been there? What happens if you don't meet one of those standards? What might happen if you tried to "lower" or change these standards?

- For item 20 (*What I look like is an important part of who I am*), reflect on what is important in your life.

  o List all the different areas of your life that are important such as appearance, family, friends, work/school, physical health, mental well-being, spiritual pursuits, and more. Consider the relative importance of each aspect of your life. Is appearance the most important part of you? Are other aspects more important? Does the level of importance correspond with your values? Are there any changes that you would like to make related to what is important?

Assessment 22.2: The Body Image Quality of Life Inventory

People differ in terms of how their body image experiences affect other aspects of their lives. Body image may have positive effects, negative effects, or no effect at all. Listed below are various ways that your own body image may or may not influence your life. For each item, circle how and how much your feelings about your appearance affect that aspect of your life. Before answering each item, think carefully about the answer that most accurately reflects how your body image usually affects you.

−3	−2	−1	0	+1	+2	+3
Very Negative Effect	Moderate Negative Effect	Slight Negative Effect	No Effect	Slight Positive Effect	Moderate Positive Effect	Very Positive Effect

	−3	−2	−1	0	+1	+2	+3
1. My basic feelings about myself – feelings of personal adequacy and self-worth.	−3	−2	−1	0	+1	+2	+3
2. My feelings about my adequacy as a person of my gender – feelings of masculinity or femininity.	−3	−2	−1	0	+1	+2	+3
3. My interactions with people of my own gender.	−3	−2	−1	0	+1	+2	+3
4. My interactions with people of another gender.	−3	−2	−1	0	+1	+2	+3
5. My experiences when I meet new people.	−3	−2	−1	0	+1	+2	+3
6. My experiences at work or at school.	−3	−2	−1	0	+1	+2	+3
7. My relationships with friends.	−3	−2	−1	0	+1	+2	+3
8. My relationships with family members.	−3	−2	−1	0	+1	+2	+3
9. My day-to-day emotions.	−3	−2	−1	0	+1	+2	+3
10. My satisfaction with my life in general.	−3	−2	−1	0	+1	+2	+3
11. My feelings of acceptability as a sexual partner.	−3	−2	−1	0	+1	+2	+3
12. My enjoyment of my sex life.	−3	−2	−1	0	+1	+2	+3
13. My ability to listen to my body to determine what and how much I eat.	−3	−2	−1	0	+1	+2	+3
14. My activities for physical exercise.	−3	−2	−1	0	+1	+2	+3
15. My willingness to do things that might call attention to my appearance.	−3	−2	−1	0	+1	+2	+3
16. My daily "grooming" activities (getting dressed and physically ready for the day).	−3	−2	−1	0	+1	+2	+3
17. How confident I feel in my daily life.	−3	−2	−1	0	+1	+2	+3
18. How happy I feel in my everyday life.	−3	−2	−1	0	+1	+2	+3
Total Body Image Quality of Life score: add items 1–18 and divide by 18 =							

Total Body Image Quality of Life score between:

- **-2.01 to -3** = strong negative effect of body image on quality of life
- **-1.01 to -2** = moderate negative effect of body image on quality of life
- **-1 and +1** = little to no effect of body image on your quality of life
- **+1.01 to +2** = moderate positive effect of body image on quality of life
- **+2.01 to +3** = strong positive effect of body image on quality of life

The authors of the BIQLI Inventory are Cash, Jakatdar, and Williams.* Research supports the use of these measures with community and college samples.

**Note. Reprinted with permission. Permission also was granted by Thomas Cash to include the BIQLI Inventory in this workbook. The BIQLI Inventory cannot be used for research without a user's license (available at www.body-images.com).

*T. F. Cash, T. A. Jakatdar, and E. F. Williams. The Body Image Quality of Life Inventory: Further validation with college men and women. *Body Image* 2004; **1**: 279–87.

T. F. Cash and E. C. Fleming. The impact of body image experiences: Development of the Body Image Quality of Life Inventory. *Int J Eat Disord* 2002; **31: 455–60.

Body Image Quality of Life Inventory Applications

- For item 1 (*My basic feelings about myself – feelings of personal adequacy and self-worth*), consider the following:

  - Where do you get your sense of self-worth?

  - In what instances or experiences (not related to appearance) do you experience a sense of personal adequacy?

- Consider your response to item 10 (*My satisfaction with my life in general*):

  - How much of your life satisfaction is focused on your body image? What is that experience like?

  - What would it be like to shift the focus from body image to other aspects? What other aspects of life could contribute to overall life satisfaction? How might this shift impact your thoughts, emotions, and behaviors?

  - Imagine that your appearance were to change drastically in a short period of time due to a life event (e.g., illness, accident, surgery). How might drastic changes to your appearance impact your satisfaction with life?

- Consider the ways that you treat your body and how much of it is impacted by your body image experiences as addressed in items 13 (how much to eat), 14 (physical exercise), 15 (willingness to do certain activities that draw attention to the body), and 16 (grooming activities). Imagine how you might treat your body differently in these areas upon experiencing positive body image.

- Reflect on your response to item 16 (*My daily "grooming" activities . . .*).

  - First, create a list of grooming activities that you consider beneficial which are based on self-care and health.

  - Then, create a list of grooming activities you consider harmful which interfere with your life and sense of self-worth.

  - Note any realizations and reflections.

- Imagine you felt more competent, connected, and comfortable with your identity based on non-appearance values. How would your responses to this Inventory be different? How would your daily life be different?

351

Assessment 22.3: Transgender Congruence Scale (TCS)

Transgender congruence is the degree to which individuals who identify as transgender feel genuine, authentic, and comfortable with their external appearance and presence (i.e., **appearance congruence**) and accept their genuine gender identity (**gender identity congruence**) rather than the gender assigned to them at birth.

For the following items, please indicate the response that best describes your experience *over the past two weeks*. **Gender identity** is defined as the gender(s) that you experience yourself as; it is not necessarily related to your assigned gender at birth.

	Strongly Disagree	Somewhat Disagree	Neither Agree Nor Disagree	Somewhat Agree	Strongly Agree
1. My outward appearance represents my gender identity.	1	2	3	4	5
2. I experience a sense of unity between my gender identity and my body.	1	2	3	4	5
3. My physical appearance adequately expresses my gender identity.	1	2	3	4	5
4. I am generally comfortable with how others perceive my gender identity when they look at me.	1	2	3	4	5
5. My physical body represents my gender identity.	1	2	3	4	5
6. The way my body currently looks does <u>not</u> represent my gender identity.	5	4	3	2	1
7. I am happy with the way my appearance expresses my gender identity.	1	2	3	4	5
8. I do <u>not</u> feel that my appearance reflects my gender identity.	5	4	3	2	1
9. I feel that my mind and body are consistent with one another.	1	2	3	4	5
Total Appearance Congruence score: add items 1–9 and divide by 9 =					
10. I am <u>not</u> proud of my gender identity.	5	4	3	2	1
11. I am happy that I have the gender identity that I do.	1	2	3	4	5
12. I have accepted my gender identity.	1	2	3	4	5
Total Gender Identity Acceptance score: add items 10–12 and divide by 3 =					
Total Transgender Congruence score: add items 1–12 and divide by 12 =					

Total subscale and scale scores between:

- **3.5–5** = high transgender congruence
- **2.8–3.4** = moderate transgender congruence
- **below 2.8** = low transgender congruence

Note. Reprinted with permission. The authors of the Transgender Congruence Scale are Kozee, Tylka, and Bauerband.* Research supports the use of these measures with community samples of individuals who identify as transgender. Please contact the authors of the TCS for permission to use it within research; there is no need to contact them to use it with clients or to complete on your own.

*H. B. Kozee, T. L. Tylka, and L. A. Bauerband. Measuring transgender individuals' comfort with gender identity and appearance: Development and validation of the Transgender Congruence Scale. *Psychol Women Q* 2012; **36**: 179–96.

Transgender Congruence Scale Applications

• Journal about:

   ○ The parts of your identity that are not reflected in your appearance

   ○ The parts of your identity that are reflected in your appearance

• For item 2 (*I experience a sense of unity between my gender identity and my body*), reflect and journal on the following:

   ○ Experiences of unity between your identity and current body

   ○ Experiences of a lack of unity between your identity and current body

• Item 4 (*I am generally comfortable with how others perceive my gender identity when they look at me*) addresses the social context of appearance and gender identity. Review your response to this item, and consider in what ways you are:

   ○ Comfortable when others perceive you in these particular ways:

   ○ Uncomfortable when others perceive you in these particular ways:

• Consider your response to item 7 (*I am happy with the way my appearance expresses my gender identity*). How does your answer to this item relate to your overall life satisfaction? To your overall body image?

• Identify the factors that impact your sense of gender identity pride as noted within item 10 (*I am not proud of my gender identity*) such as physical comfort with body (e.g., secondary sex characteristics), psychological comfort, support/acceptance from others, experiences with criticism/rejection, and spiritual/religious beliefs. How has your sense of gender identity pride impacted how you care for yourself (physically, emotionally, relationally, etc.)?

• How does transgender congruence relate to the various positive body image topics presented in this workbook (see Chapters 4–22)?

   ○ If you are low on transgender congruence, do you believe it is possible to work toward positive body image?

      ■ If yes, how so? Which topics could you work toward?

      ■ If no, for what reasons? Which topics would be difficult to work toward?

Assignment 22.1: Motives for Appearance-Related Practices

It is common for people to engage in appearance-related practices such as wearing a certain style of clothing, styling hair in a particular way, participating in movement to have an impact on the body and more. There are various motives that correspond with appearance-related practices.*

For this assignment, identify a specific appearance-related practice that you engage in on a regular basis and write on the line below. Then consider how relevant each of the motives (in bold) are by circling a number on a scale from 0 (not at all) to 10 (extremely). Journal about your realizations at the end of this assignment. Note: you can make copies of this assignment in order to reflect on the motives for various appearance-related practices.

Appearance Related Practice: _____

Beautification: to feel increased or enhanced attractiveness

0   1   2   3   4   5   6   7   8   9   10
Not at all   Extremely

Signification: to experience a sense of purpose

0   1   2   3   4   5   6   7   8   9   10
Not at all   Extremely

Enjoyment: to feel pleasure or joy

0   1   2   3   4   5   6   7   8   9   10
Not at all   Extremely

Satisfaction: to feel a sense of accomplishment or pride

0   1   2   3   4   5   6   7   8   9   10
Not at all   Extremely

Uniqueness: to demonstrate a sense of personal style

0   1   2   3   4   5   6   7   8   9   10
Not at all   Extremely

Emphasize assets: to highlight strengths

0   1   2   3   4   5   6   7   8   9   10
Not at all   Extremely

Self-care: to participate in rejuvenating and/or rewarding behaviors focused on myself

0   1   2   3   4   5   6   7   8   9   10
Not at all   Extremely

Identity: to project aspects of my preferred identity(ies)

0   1   2   3   4   5   6   7   8   9   10
Not at all   Extremely

Positive feedback: to receive positive feedback from myself or from others

0   1   2   3   4   5   6   7   8   9   10
Not at all   Extremely

Pressure: to relieve a sense of pressure or obligation to conform to certain standards

0   1   2   3   4   5   6   7   8   9   10
Not at all   Extremely

Preoccupation: to get rid of negative thoughts

0   1   2   3   4   5   6   7   8   9   10
Not at all   Extremely

N. L. Wood-Barcalow, T. L. Tylka, and C. L. Judge. *Positive Body Image Workbook: A Clinical and Self-Improvement Guide.* Cambridge: Cambridge University Press, 2021.

Other:

0	1	2	3	4	5	6	7	8	9	10

Not at all   Extremely

Realizations:

_____

_____

_____

_____

_____

*K. Holmqvist Gattario and C. Lunde. Appearance-related practices: Can they be part of a positive body image? In: Daniels, E. A., Gillen, M. M., and Markey, C. H. eds. *Body Positive: Understanding and Improving Body Image in Science and Practice*. New York: Cambridge University Press, 2018: 111–34.

N. L. Wood-Barcalow, T. L. Tylka, and C. L. Judge. *Positive Body Image Workbook: A Clinical and Self-Improvement Guide*. Cambridge: Cambridge University Press, 2021.

Assignment 22.2: Commitments to Reduce Harmful Appearance-Focused Activities

For this assignment, consider all of your appearance-focused practices. Examples might be working out, wearing make-up, altering your hair (e.g., dying, coloring, straightening), removing body hair, altering your skin color (e.g., tanning, lightening creams), getting your nails done, and more. Of the practices that you have identified, reflect on which ones are uncomfortable or harmful to you (physically, emotionally, and psychologically) and/or prevent your progress towards a positive body image. Finally, identify commitments of what you can do to reduce or eliminate appearance-focused activities that are harmful. An example is provided.

My Appearance-Focused Activities

Example: *Straightening my hair.*

_____
_____
_____
_____

These Activities Are Uncomfortable and/or Harmful

Example: *I realize that the purpose of straightening my hair is to fit the majority culture standard. Doing so is not only time consuming and damaging to the health of my hair, but it also reinforces the belief that I have to make this change in order to accept myself.*

_____
_____
_____

Commitments to Reduce or Eliminate These Activities

Example: *I will decrease the amount of times I straighten my hair, and rather focus on embracing natural hair texture as part of ethnic pride.*

_____
_____
_____
_____

N. L. Wood-Barcalow, T. L. Tylka, and C. L. Judge. *Positive Body Image Workbook: A Clinical and Self-Improvement Guide.* Cambridge: Cambridge University Press, 2021.

Assignment 22.3: Body Checking

Body checking is the practice of assessing how the body meets or does not meet some expectation or standard. Checking includes a range of behaviors from looking in reflective objects, measuring parts of the body, weighing, pinching/poking, and more. The purpose of checking (e.g., reassure, serve as motivation, reduce uncomfortable emotions) can differ from the actual outcomes (e.g., increased insecurity, embarrassment, fear) which can lead to more checking behaviors. Ultimately these body checking behaviors can turn into **maladaptive appearance investment practices** which results in moving away from positive body image.

Identify the types of body checking practices that you engage in. Reflect on the intended purpose and the actual outcome of the behavior. Record your realizations. An example is provided.

Body Checking Practice	Purpose/ Intention	Actual Outcome	Realizations
Example: *Weighing*	*To see if there has been any change in my weight*	*Upset and frustrated that my weight has increased*	*I'm preoccupied with my weight. My day is ruined when the number goes up. I feel worse about myself than better.*
Looking in the mirror or another reflective surface (e.g., store window)			
Pinching			
Weighing			
Checking muscles			
Checking fat			
Measuring body parts			
Sitting/standing in certain positions			
Other:			
Other:			
Other:			

N. L. Wood-Barcalow, T. L. Tylka, and C. L. Judge. *Positive Body Image Workbook: A Clinical and Self-Improvement Guide.* Cambridge: Cambridge University Press, 2021.

Assignment 22.4: Appearance Investment Journal

For this journal assignment, consider the importance of appearance in your life and how it affects your overall quality of life. Reflect on the following: When did my appearance become important to me? How has the importance of my appearance changed over time? Is appearance more important than other areas of life? What do I neglect in order to focus on my appearance? How do my core values correspond with investment in my appearance? What beliefs do I have about my appearance? Do I believe that my quality of life would change if my appearance could change? What efforts have I engaged in to change my appearance? Have I ever been satisfied with my appearance? What would satisfaction look like? Can I move toward positive body image without changing my appearance?

_____
_____
_____
_____
_____
_____
_____
_____
_____
_____
_____

N. L. Wood-Barcalow, T. L. Tylka, and C. L. Judge. *Positive Body Image Workbook: A Clinical and Self-Improvement Guide.* Cambridge: Cambridge University Press, 2021.

Assignment 22.5: Gender Identity and Appearance Investment Journal

For this journal assignment,* consider your gender identity in relation to appearance investment. Reflect on the following: How do I describe my gender identity? What has shaped my gender identity over the years? Does my identity currently match that of my external appearance or anatomy? To what extent do I experience distress related to the sex assigned at my birth versus that with which I identify? In what ways do I feel disconnected from my physical body related to assigned gender features? In what ways am I dissatisfied with my appearance?

How much time do I spend focusing on my appearance (e.g., daily, weekly, monthly)? What appearance investment practices do I engage in: in order to "pass," to feel congruent, to not draw attention to myself, to become more attractive, and to demonstrate body sovereignty? What appearance practices do I consider maladaptive? Adaptive? Necessary? What changes, if any, would I like to make to appearance investment practices? How do these practices change depending on environment?

How does my gender identity correspond with my body acceptance? What, if any, gender affirming treatments and procedures would I like to pursue with the goal to experience greater congruence between my identity and appearance? What positive outcomes do I anticipate with body alterations? What, if any, gender transitions would promote positive body image?

_____
_____
_____
_____
_____
_____
_____
_____
_____
_____
_____
_____

*This assignment was inspired by the work from J. K. McGuire, J. L. Doty, J. M. Catalpa, et al. Body image in transgender young people: Findings from a qualitative community-based study. *Body Image* 2016; **18**: 96–107.

N. L. Wood-Barcalow, T. L. Tylka, and C. L. Judge. *Positive Body Image Workbook: A Clinical and Self-Improvement Guide.* Cambridge: Cambridge University Press, 2021.

References

1. T. F. Cash, S. E. Melnyk, and J. I. Hrabosky. The assessment of body image investment: An extensive revision of the Appearance Schemas Inventory. *Int J Eat Disord* 2004; **35**: 305–16.

2. K. Holmqvist Gattario and C. Lunde. Appearance-related practices: Can they be part of a positive body image? In: Daniels, E. A., Gillen, M. M., and Markey, C. H. eds. *Body Positive: Understanding and Improving Body Image in Science and Practice*. New York: Cambridge University Press, 2018: 111–34.

3. H. Dittmar. *Consumer Culture, Identity, and Well-being: The Search for the "Good Life" and the "Body Perfect."* New York: Taylor & Francis, 2008.

4. T. L. Tylka and N. L. Wood-Barcalow. What is and what is not positive body image? Conceptual foundations and construct definition. *Body Image* 2015; **14**: 118–29.

5. D. C. Walker, D. A. Anderson, and T. Hildebrandt. Body checking behaviors in men. *Body Image* 2009; **6**: 164–70.

6. T. F. Cash and A. S. Labarge. Development of the Appearance Schemas Inventory: A new cognitive body-image assessment. *Cognitive Ther Res* 1996; **20**: 37–50.

7. S. E. Melnyk, T. F. Cash, and L. H. Janda. Body image ups and downs: Prediction of intra-individual level and variability of women's daily body image experiences. *Body Image* 2004; **1**: 225–35.

8. S. A. Rusticus, A. M. Hubley, and B. D. Zumbo. Measurement invariance of the Appearance Schemas Inventory-Revised and the Body Image Quality of Life Inventory across age and gender. *Assessment* 2008; **15**: 60–71.

9. R. Russell. Cosmetics use: Psychological perspectives. In: Cash, T. F. ed. *Encyclopedia of Body Image and Human Appearance* 2012. London: Academic Press, 2012: 366–71.

10. T. L. Tylka, R. M. Calogero, and S. Danielsdottir. Is intuitive eating the same as flexible dietary control? Their links to each other and well-being could provide an answer. *Appetite* 2015; **95**: 166–75.

11. T. Mann, A. J. Tomiyama, E. Westling, et al. Medicare's search for effective obesity treatments: Diets are not the answer. *Am Psychol* 2007; **62**: 220–33.

12. M. M. Gillen and J. Dunaev. Body appreciation, interest in cosmetic enhancements, and need for uniqueness among US college students. *Body Image* 2017; **22**: 136–43.

13. S. Parker, M. Nichter, M. Nichter, et al. Body image and weight concerns among African American and White adolescent females: Differences that make a difference. *Hum Organ* 1995; **54**: 103–14.

14. K. J. Homan and T. L. Tylka. Appearance-based exercise motivation moderates the relationship between exercise frequency and positive body image. *Body Image* 2014; **11**: 101–8.

15. T. L. Tylka and K. J. Homan. Exercise motives and positive body image in physically active college women and men: Exploring an expanded acceptance model of intuitive eating. *Body Image* 2015; **15**: 90–7.

16. H. B. Kozee, T. L. Tylka, and L. A. Bauerband. Measuring transgender individuals' comfort with gender identity and appearance: Development and validation of the Transgender Congruence Scale. *Psychol Women Q* 2012; **36**: 179–96.

17. T. F. Cash, T. A. Jakatdar, and E. F. Williams. The Body Image Quality of Life Inventory: Further validation with college men and women. *Body Image* 2004; **1**: 279–87.

18. T. F. Cash and E. C. Fleming. The impact of body image experiences: Development of the Body Image Quality of Life Inventory. *Int J Eat Disord* 2002; **31**: 455–60.

Chapter

23

Next Steps in the Journey

Now that we are nearing the end of the workbook, it's time to reflect on your positive body image journey. You have likely faced challenges and experienced changes along the way. One way to guide the reflective process is to review your "take-home" realizations from each chapter (see Assignment 2.14). Another possibility is to think back to how you thought and felt about, and behaved toward, your body when you started this process. Compare it to how you think, feel, and behave now (see Assignment 23.1 for a guide).

While you likely have many positive changes to reflect on, your journey is not over. The truth is, for as long as we have bodies, our body image journeys continue. Our purpose for this chapter is to help you maintain and even strengthen the positive changes in your body attitudes, thoughts, and behaviors you have made well into the future. We hope our workbook is a source that you can refer back to when needed.

Dr. Sonya Lyubomirsky, a researcher that studies the science of happiness, found that we need to engage in **intentional activities** (e.g., counting our blessings, doing random acts of kindness, scheduling planned acts of kindness) to increase our happiness, and we need to keep doing these activities in order to maintain our increased happiness [1]. In other words, we have to invest in maintaining our newfound happiness. This investment is important because of the **hedonic treadmill** [2], which is our tendency to return to our previous levels of happiness when we are not engaged in efforts to maintain the gains. The hedonic treadmill can happen with positive body image as well. Therefore, to offset the hedonic treadmill, we need to engage in intentional activities to help us maintain and sustain our positive body image.

Below are examples of intentional activities that you can engage in to continually invest in yourself and your improved positive body image. These activities were adapted from Lyubomirsky's list of intentional activities for increasing and sustaining happiness [1, 3], which are supported by research [4–5], and can also be applied to increasing and sustaining positive body image. While some examples are mentioned in certain chapters, it is useful to have them presented together in this closing chapter for ease of reference.

You may find these activities to be especially useful when situations emerge that have the potential to disrupt your progress (e.g., there is a new diet that you feel pressured to try, you go through a stressful time and self-care falters, you find yourself comparing your body to others). In fact, we all encounter situations that can disrupt our progress from time to time. Yet, it is also important to invest in these activities even when things are going well. For instance, when practiced regularly, they can strengthen your protective filter (see Chapter 17). Keep in mind that these activities are only suggestions, and others may work better for you.

- **Savor sensory experiences**, or be attentive and appreciative of them. Notice things that are beautiful about you and around you (e.g., engage in "beauty hunting"). Notice how the touch of a partner or a massage makes you feel good about your body. Savor your body as you engage in life-enhancing movement. Savor foods that you enjoy.

- **Nurture positive relationships** that help your body relieve stress through laughter and connection. Notice who unconditionally accepts your body and interact with these people. Connect with social groups that are body positive (e.g., Health At Every Size™ and intuitive eating support groups on social media). Mentor others to love and appreciate their bodies. Deepen your relationship with a higher power and/or engage with nature.

- **Notice and regularly express gratitude** toward your body for what it does for you on a daily basis. Reflect on what you are grateful for – from the mundane (e.g., your fingers allow you to type) to the magnificent (e.g., your body created another person, your body fought cancer). Express your gratitude to your body through a letter, talking while looking into a mirror, a journal entry, or pausing and reflecting internally. Express gratitude toward your culture for its traditions, features, and connections.

- You have likely made and achieved several goals on your positive body image journey. **Continue to set goals** that are internally motivated, authentic, behavioral, and flexible. For instance, set mindful self-care goals, which will nourish your body, health, and well-being.

- Body-related threats can be met by **engaging in positive coping**, such as thinking about your body in a flexible (versus rigid) way, reframing negatives into positives, and engaging in actions that are consistent with your values. When the problem is concrete and specific, perhaps concentrate on what needs to be done, focusing on one step at a time (e.g., if you see a picture of yourself you don't like, focus on steps to approach your body with compassion). When facing an overwhelming or uncontrollable situation (e.g., an injury or illness), seek support from those who accept and encourage you, your spirituality, and connection with nature.

- **Commit to both spontaneous and planned acts of kindness** and compassion toward your body. Spontaneous acts may include taking a nap or nature walk to energize your body, choosing to filter body-related information in a positive way, removing something relatively unimportant from a busy to-do list, and talking to someone with body dissatisfaction about the benefits of working towards a positive body image. Planned acts may include attending a yoga class every week, meditating for five minutes daily, and scheduling a massage once a month.

- **Engage in flow**, as flow brings about energized focus, full involvement, and enjoyment in the moment-to-moment process of an activity. Appreciate the functionality of your body and mind (and how the body and mind interact) as you are engaged in a flow activity. Flow is yet another way your body connects you to the various joys in life.

- **Cultivate optimism**, which creates hope for the future and pathways toward achievement. Think about where you were when you started your positive body image journey, where you are now, and where you may be a few months and even years from now. Imagine that everything has gone as well as it possibly could – you have worked hard and succeeded in feeling, thinking, and behaving positively about your body. Write about this experience and describe the steps you need to take to get to this future.

- **Be connected to something greater than yourself.** Identify how you can use your body to improve the world around you in ways that you value. Search for the sacred in your body. Acknowledge the unique characteristics of your body and treat your body "as a temple" – with love, respect, and care.

- Continue to regularly **engage in self-care** for your mind and body (sample activities are described in Chapters 19–21). Practice these activities and investigate new ways to relieve stress and honor your physical health and psychological well-being.

- **Learn to forgive yourself** for past attitudes and behaviors, such as disliking your body, not appreciating and noticing the unique characteristics and functionality of your body, and engaging rigid thinking and eating behaviors to try to modify your body. Ironically, being upset at ourselves for past negative body-related attitudes and behaviors can interfere with our body's future health and well-being. Also, **forgive others** for not offering unconditional acceptance for your body – if they are still in your life, forgive them (however, to protect yourself, it may be helpful to set a boundary and only interact with them if they are willing to offer unconditional acceptance now). According to Buddha, "Forgiveness doesn't excuse their behavior. Forgiveness prevents their behavior from destroying your heart."

- **Avoid overthinking and social comparison.** Stop focusing on your appearance-related thoughts and refrain from comparing your appearance to others (see Chapter 15). Rather, turn to activities that instead generate positive emotions (e.g., happiness, peacefulness, amusement, and pride) within your body. For instance, take a restorative yoga or Tai Chi class. Cuddle a pet. Hug a friend or partner.

While you continue on your body image journey, you may become distracted from your positive body image goals. During these times, it is important to give yourself plenty of self-compassion, refocus, and reinvest in your journey. Instead of "practice makes perfect," focus on "practice makes permanence." In other words, the more you engage in intentional activities, such as the ones above and the many assignments throughout this workbook, the more positive body image thoughts, feelings, and behaviors will become part of your everyday life. If you are finding it difficult to refocus and reinvest, it may be helpful to reassess your original goals, seek professional help, and/or seek alternative approaches such as spiritual guidance or complementary alternatives to Westernized approaches.

We now have reached the end of the workbook, but our journey continues. Mihaly Csikszentmihalyi [8] described flow as "The best moments in our lives are not the passive, receptive, relaxing times . . . The best moments usually occur if a person's body or mind is stretched to its limits in a voluntary effort to accomplish something difficult and worthwhile." Writing this workbook has been a source of flow and positivity for us – challenging ourselves, dedicating a significant amount of time, and believing that positive change is possible. We appreciate your own investment in and dedication to this workbook and allowing us to be part of your journey toward positive body image. Remember to engage in your own flow and encourage others to do the same.

Assignment 23.1: Reflections on My Journey

Beginning of Body Image Work

• What I thought about my body:

_____
_____

• How I felt about my body:

_____
_____

• How I treated my body:

_____
_____

• How others influenced my body image then:

_____
_____

• What my focus was when I began this process:

_____
_____

Where I Am Currently in My Journey:

• What I have learned about my body along the way:

_____
_____

• What I have learned about myself:

_____
_____

• What I think about my body:

_____
_____

• What I feel about my body:

_____
_____

• How I treat my body:

_____
_____

• How others influence my body image now:

_____
_____

• My focus now:

_____
_____

• My overall commitments to myself:

_____
_____

N. L. Wood-Barcalow, T. L. Tylka, and C. L. Judge. *Positive Body Image Workbook: A Clinical and Self-Improvement Guide.* Cambridge: Cambridge University Press, 2021.

References

1. S. Lyubomirsky. *The How of Happiness: A New Approach to Getting the Life You Want.* New York: Penguin Press, 2008.

2. E. Diener, R. E. Lucas, and C. Napa Scollon. Beyond the hedonic treadmill: Revising the adaptation theory of well-being. *Amer Psychol* 2009; **61**: 305–14.

3. S. Lyubormirsky, K. M. Sheldon, and D. Schkade. Pursuing happiness: The architecture of sustainable change. *Rev Gen Psychol* 2005; **9**: 111–31.

3. The Flourishing Center. *12 Intentional Activities for Increasing Life Satisfaction.* New York: The Flourishing Center, 2014.

4. K. M. Sheldon and S. Lyubormirsky. Achieving sustainable gains in happiness: Change your actions, not your circumstances. *J Happiness Stud* 2006; 7: 55–86.

5. N. L. Sin and S. Lyubormirsky. Enhancing well-being and alleviating depressive symptoms with positive psychology interventions: A practice-friendly meta-analysis. *J Clin Psychol* 2009; **65**: 467–87.

6. M. Csikszentmihalyi. *Flow: The Psychology of Optimal Experience.* New York: Harper & Row, 1990.

Index